PERCEIVING GOD

OTHER WORKS OF WILLIAM P. ALSTON

Divine Nature and Human Language: Essays in Philosophical Theology

Epistemic Justification: Essays in the Theory of Knowledge

Philosophy of Language

The Problems of Philosophy: Introductory Readings (coeditor with Richard B. Brandt)

Readings in Twentieth-Century Philosophy (coeditor with George Nakhnikian)

The Reliability of Sense Perception

Religious Belief and Philosophical Thought: Readings in the Philosophy of Religion (editor)

PERCEIVING GOD

The Epistemology of Religious Experience

William P. Alston

Cornell University Press

Ithaca and London

First published 1991 by Cornell University Press.
Second printing 1993.
First printing, Cornell Paperbacks, 1993.

International Standard Book Number 0-8014-2597-2 (cloth)
International Standard Book Number 0-8014-8155-4 (paper)
Library of Congress Catalog Card Number 91-55068
Printed in the United States of America
Librarians: Library of Congress cataloging information appears on the last page of the book.

♾ The paper in this book meets the minimum requirements of the American National Standard for Information Sciences—Permanence of Paper for Printed Library Materials, ANSI Z39.48-1984.

FOR VALERIE

Contents

Acknowledgments

I have been thinking about the topic of this book for at least fifty years. This on-and-off consideration developed into a major preoccupation in the late 1970s. That led to a series of articles on various aspects of the subject (Alston 1981, 1982, 1983, 1986a, 1986b, 1986c, 1988a, and 1988b). Work on the project was further advanced by a one-week workshop I held on the subject at Syracuse University in 1985, by presentations at the NEH Summer Institute in Philosophy of Religion at Western Washington University in 1986, and by a Wheaton College (Illinois) Summer Philosophy Seminar in 1988, which was devoted to the topic. Versions of the published papers were presented and discussed at various institutions, and parts of the material were treated in graduate seminars at Syracuse University. Finally, I was awarded an NEH Fellowship for University Teachers in 1988–89 to write the present book. Thus whatever defects the book exhibits cannot be traced to a lack of long and careful consideration or to the absence of ample feedback.

I am grateful to many people for their contributions to my thinking on the topic and to the writing of this book in particular. The earliest sustained attempts to work through my ideas on our experience of God were strongly influenced by John Hick's treatment in *Faith and Knowledge* (2d ed., 1966) and to a lesser extent by various other works, including Baillie (1939). My views have developed in the context of close interaction with Alvin Plantinga, Nicholas Wolterstorff, and George Mavrodes, the most sustained period of which was 1979–80, during which I had the privilege of participating with these people in a number of sessions at the Calvin College Center for Christian Studies. Among the many other people from whose writings and conversation I have profited I think especially of Robert and Marilyn Adams, Robert Audi, Jonathan Bennett, Stephen T. Davis, Paul Draper, Hugh Fleetwood, William Hasker, James Keller, Norman Kretzmann, Terence Penelhum, Nelson Pike, Joseph Runzo, Axel Steuer, Eleonore Stump, Peter van Inwagen, William Wainwright, and Keith Yandell. I owe a special debt of gratitude to Robert Audi, Nelson Pike, and Alvin Plantinga for their extensive comments on a penultimate draft of this book. Other people to whom I am indebted for comments on the manuscript include Robert Adams, Jonathan Bennett, M. Jamie Ferreira, Richard Gale, Daniel Howard-Snyder, Norman Kretzmann, and William Wainwright. Last but not least, the final product has been immeasurably enriched by the feedback I received from participants in the workshops, institute, and seminars mentioned earlier as well as from a seminar on the manuscript given by Norman Kretzmann at Cornell University. Special thanks go to students in my seminars at Syracuse University, who saved me from many grievous errors and contributed in other ways as well.

Various parts of the book are foreshadowed in the published essays mentioned in the first paragraph. However, the only publication substantial portions of which are incorporated into the present work is "Religious Diversity and the Perceptual Knowledge of God," *Faith and Philosophy*, 5, no. 4 (October, 1988), pp. 433–48. I am grateful to the editor of *Faith and Philosophy* for permission to reproduce large stretches of this article in Chapter 7 of this book.

I would like to express my appreciation for the help and support afforded me in this and other endeavors by John G. Ackerman, director of Cornell University Press, who is everything an author could ask for in an editor. Thanks go to the secretarial staff in the Department of Philosophy at Syracuse University for untiring efforts in reproducing and collating various drafts of the manuscript, especially Mary Ellen O'Connell for her herculean efforts at the Xerox machine. Finally, my love and gratitude go to my wife, Valerie, for her unflagging love and support in the most trying of times, and to her this book is dedicated.

WILLIAM P. ALSTON

Syracuse, New York

PERCEIVING GOD

Introduction

i. Character of the Book

The central thesis of this book is that experiential awareness of God, or as I shall be saying, the *perception* of God, makes an important contribution to the grounds of religious belief. More specifically, a person can become justified in holding certain kinds of beliefs about God by virtue of perceiving God as being or doing so-and-so. The kinds of beliefs that can be so justified I shall call "M-beliefs" ('M' for *manifestation*). M-beliefs are beliefs to the effect that God is doing something currently vis-à-vis the subject—comforting, strengthening, guiding, communicating a message, sustaining the subject in being—or to the effect that God has some (allegedly) perceivable property—goodness, power, lovingness. The intuitive idea is that by virtue of my being aware of God as sustaining me in being I can justifiably believe that God *is* sustaining me in being. This initial formulation will undergo much refinement in the course of the book.

One qualification should be anticipated right away. The above formulation of my central thesis seems to be referring to God and thus to presuppose that God exists. Moreover, in using the "success" terms, 'the awareness of God' and 'the perception of God', it seems to presuppose that people are sometimes genuinely aware of God and do genuinely perceive God. Since the book is designed for a general audience that includes those who do not antecedently accept those presuppositions, this is undesirable. We can avoid these presuppositions by the familiar device of specifying the experiences in question as those that are *taken by the subject* to be an awareness of God (or would be so taken if the question arose). One can agree that there are experiences that satisfy this description even if one does not believe that God exists or that people ever genuinely perceive Him.

This is basically a work in epistemology, the epistemology of religious perceptual beliefs. I will go into descriptive questions concerning the experience of God, but only so far as is required for the epistemological project. I will set the treatment of our central problem in the context of a general epistemology, though, naturally, we will not be able to give a full presentation of the latter. The reader is warned, however, that fairly heavy doses of abstract epistemological discussion can be expected, especially in Chapters 3 and 4. For those whose interests lie elsewhere, Chapter 3, after section ii, could safely be skimmed or omitted.

At the outset I should make it explicit that though I will be concerned with the epistemic value of the perception of God, I by no means suppose that to be its only, or even its most important, value. From a religious point of view, or more specifically from a Christian point of view, the chief value of the experience of God is that it enables us to enter into personal relationships with God; most importantly, it makes it possible for us to enjoy the relation of loving communion with God for which we were created. But my topic in this book will be the function of the experience of God in providing information about God and our relations to Him.

I have been speaking in terms of epistemic *justification*, rather than in terms of *knowledge*, and the focus will be on the former rather than on the latter. This is partly because I can't *know* that God is loving unless it is *true* that God is loving, and the latter in turn implies that God exists, something I will not be arguing for in this book, except by way of arguing that some beliefs about God are justified. It is also partly because of difficult and controverted questions as to just what is required for knowledge. I will make a few remarks on the knowledge of God in section vii of Chapter 7, but no proper treatment will be attempted.[1]

How wide a net am I casting with my notion of (putative) perception of God? This depends on the concept of God by reference to which we determine whether a given person takes a given experience to be a perception of God. We might be using the term to cover any supposed object of religious worship or anything taken as metaphysically ultimate. However, I will be concentrating more narrowly on the concept of God as it has developed in the major theistic religions—Judaism, Christianity, and Islam. This means that our examples of (putative) perception of God will be taken from those traditions and will be cases in which the subject takes him/herself to be aware of a being that exhibits the features deemed crucial in those traditions for the status of divinity. Moreover, since, as I will be arguing, we cannot look on M-belief formation as a single unified doxastic (belief-forming) practice, we will be forced to think in terms of the form such a practice takes within one or another religious tradition. For this purpose I choose the Christian tradition, the one I know best and, to some extent, from the inside. Although the main lines of the epistemological discussion are intended to have general application, it will be more effective to discuss a particular practice as an exemplar, rather than to say everything in maximally general terms. Other traditions will come

[1]For an approach to the topic in terms of reliability theory see Alston 1991b.

into the picture not only as other cases of the general phenomenon, but also as giving rise to incompatible bodies of belief and thus posing problems for the epistemic claims made for Christian perceptual beliefs about God. This side of the matter will be addressed in Chapter 7.

I want to make explicit at the outset that my project here is to be distinguished from anything properly called an "argument from religious experience" for the existence of God.[2] The thesis defended here is not that the existence of God provides the best explanation for facts about religious experience or that it is possible to *argue* in any way from the latter to the former. It is rather that people sometimes do perceive God and thereby acquire justified beliefs about God. In the same way, if one is a direct realist about sense perception, as I am, one will be inclined to hold not that internal facts about sense experience provide one with premises for an effective argument to the existence of external physical objects, but rather that in enjoying sense experience one thereby perceives external physical objects and comes to have various justified beliefs about them, without the necessity of exhibiting those beliefs (or their propositional contents) as the conclusion of any sort of argument.

Am I suggesting that the belief in the *existence* of God is susceptible of a perceptual justification? Well, yes and no. Typically those who take themselves to perceive God are already firmly convinced of the reality of God, and so they don't suppose that to be (part of) what they learn from the experience. In the same way I was already firmly convinced of the existence of the furniture in my house before I cast my eyes on it this morning. What one typically takes oneself to learn from a particular perception is that, e.g., God is communicating a message to me now or that the furniture is in the same arrangement today as yesterday. Nevertheless, there are exceptions. I sometimes see some item of furniture for the first time, and thereby perceptually learn of its existence as well as of some of its properties. And more than one person has passed from unbelief to belief through (putatively) experientially encountering God. Moreover, there is the point nicely made by Alvin Plantinga (1983, p. 81) that even if 'God exists' is not the propositional content of typical theistic perceptual beliefs,[3] those propositional contents self-evidently entail it. 'God is good' or 'God gave me courage to meet that situation' self-evidently entail

[2]Most discussions of the place of "religious experience" in the epistemology of religious belief are carried on in terms of such an argument. See, e.g., Mackie 1982, chap. 10, and O'Hear 1984, chap. 2. Swinburne 1979, chap. 13, casts his discussion in terms of such an argument, even though what he defends is more like what I am defending in this book. (See Chapter 5, section ii, for a comparison of my enterprise with Swinburne's.) Even those who unambiguously think of the matter as I do sometimes fall into thinking of the problem as one of whether "religious experience" furnishes sufficient "evidence" for the existence of God. See, e.g., Gutting 1982, pp. 147–49. The discussion of this whole area would be greatly improved by one's keeping in mind the distinction between holding that certain experiences constitute veridical perceptions of God, and holding that certain experiences can be used as premises in an argument (explanatory or otherwise) to the existence of God.

[3]'Perceptual belief' is my term, not Plantinga's. He speaks of "properly basic beliefs". See Chapter 5, section ii, on the relation of my views to Plantinga's.

'God exists', just as 'That tree is bare' or 'That tree is tall' self-evidently entail 'That tree exists'. Hence if the former beliefs can be perceptually justified, they can serve in turn, by one short and unproblematic step, to justify the belief in God's existence.

I have been speaking of the perception of God as serving to justify beliefs with a restricted range of propositional contents—M-beliefs. That implies that if the complete belief system of a religion is to be justified, there will have to be other grounds as well. The only alternative would be that the whole system can be built up on the basis of M-beliefs by acceptable modes of derivation; and that seems unlikely, especially for a historical religion like Christianity, to which claims about God's action in history are essential. Thus even if the claims of this book for the perceptual justification of M-beliefs are made out, there is the further problem of how this fits into the total basis for a religious belief system. That issue will be broached in the final chapter, though a full treatment lies outside the bounds of this book.

In the present intellectual climate it would be well to make it explicit that this discussion is conducted from a full-bloodedly realist perspective, according to which in religion as elsewhere we mean what we assert to be true of realities that are what they are regardless of what we or other human beings believe of them, and regardless of the "conceptual scheme" we apply to them (except, of course, when what we are talking about is our thought, belief, or concepts). I take this to be a fundamental feature of human thought and talk. Thus, in epistemically evaluating the practice of forming M-beliefs I am interested in whether that practice yields beliefs that are (often) true in this robustly realist sense—not, or not just, in whether it yields beliefs that conform to the rules of the relevant language-game, or beliefs that carry out some useful social function. I must confess that I cannot provide an external proof that this practice, or any other doxastic practice, achieves that result, as I shall make fully explicit in Chapters 3 and 4. Such support as I muster for that conclusion will be of a different sort. Nevertheless, what I am interested in determining, so far as in me lies, is whether the practice succeeds in accurately depicting a reality that is what it is however we think of it.

Even if our age were firmly realist in its predilections, my central thesis would still be in stark contradiction to assumptions that are well nigh universally shared in intellectual circles.[4] It is often taken for granted by the wise of this world, believers and unbelievers alike, that "religious experience" is a purely subjective phenomenon. Although it may have various psychosocial functions to play, any claims to its cognitive value can be safely dismissed without a hearing. It is the purpose of this book to challenge that assumption and to marshal the resources that are needed to support its rejection.

Although it is no part of my aim here to explain why people hold religious beliefs, I will mention one possible bearing of the book on a question of that

[4]Though not in the population at large. See p. 36 for some sociological data on this.

sort. Contemporary American nonbelieving academics, in philosophy and elsewhere, often find it curious that some of their intelligent and highly respected colleagues are believers even though they do not claim to possess any conclusive arguments for their religious beliefs. I believe that what is revealed in this book concerning the role of the experience of God in providing grounds, both psychological and epistemic, for religious belief can help to explain this phenomenon.[5]

ii. Preview of Chapters

Here is a preview of coming attractions. In Chapter 1, I explain how I am thinking of the (putative) experience of God that, I will be claiming, provides justification for M-beliefs; I also provide numerous reports thereof. The focus will be on what are taken to be *direct, non-sensory* experiences of God. In calling them "experiences" I am thinking of them as involving a *presentation, givenness*, or *appearance* of something to the subject, identified by the subject as God. It is this *presentational* character of the experiences that leads me to range them under a generic concept of perception. I present, and say a few words in favor of, the Theory of Appearing as an account of perception. According to this theory, what perception *is* is the awareness of something's appearing to one *as such-and-such*, where this is a basic, unanalyzable relationship, not reducible to conceptualizing an object as such-and-such, or to judging or believing the object to be such-and-such. If this is right, it follows without more ado that direct experiential awareness of God is a mode of perception (though if it is to be veridical, God must exist and be properly related to the subject). One plausible requirement for veridical perception of God is that God must be among the causes of that experience; it is argued that we have no reason to rule out that possibility. It is suggested that the construal of experience of God as *perception* can be defended on the basis of other theories of perception as well. The claim that people sometimes do perceive God is also defended against various other objections. I do not aspire to *prove* the genuineness of perception of God; that would require that we prove the existence of God and His causal role in producing the experiences in question. The aim is rather to rebut objections to the conviction of the subjects that they are directly aware of God, and to point out that if their conviction is correct they are also properly taken to be *perceiving* God. The terms 'mystical experience' and 'mystical perception' are introduced for the modes of experience and perception in question.

Chapter 2 lays out the general account of epistemic justification, and of the justification of perceptual beliefs, that I will be employing. There is an extensive discussion of the extent to which, in both sensory and mystical percep-

[5]I throw this out as a suggestion. I have no relevant statistical surveys in my pocket.

tion, beliefs about what is perceived are based on experience alone, and the extent to which they are partially based on "background beliefs". It is concluded that purely experientially based perceptual beliefs cover more territory than is often supposed, though by no means the whole territory. Hence I will think of our customary perceptual belief forming practices as including both sorts of cases. The unifying common feature is that for all perceptual beliefs the basis consists, in whole or in part, of perceptual experience. Attention is also given to the question of how one identifies the subject of a perceptual belief, particularly when the subject is identified as God.

As the issues are laid out in Chapter 2, our main problem is whether the ways in which people typically form M-beliefs on the basis of their experience (plus, perhaps, background beliefs) yield prima facie justified beliefs. And since we are working with a reliability constraint on justification (a mode of forming beliefs is justificatory only if it is reliable), we are faced with the question of whether this mode of forming M-beliefs is sufficiently reliable. Since the epistemology of sense perception has been much more extensively studied, the idea suggests itself of determining whether our typical ways of forming sense-perceptual beliefs can be shown to be reliable. Chapter 3 is devoted to a survey of attempts to establish the reliability of sense perception without running into "epistemic circularity" (using sense perception itself as a source of premises). The conclusion is that none of these attempts succeeds. Either they are infected with epistemic circularity in spite of themselves, or they are ineffective for other reasons. Thus, even if the same is true of mystical perception, it can't be judged epistemically inferior to sense perception on those grounds.

But, then, do we have any sufficient basis for taking sense perception and other familiar sources of belief to be reliable and to confer justification? Chapter 4 tackles that question. Building on work by Thomas Reid and Ludwig Wittgenstein, it develops the notion of a "doxastic practice", a way of forming beliefs and epistemically evaluating them. Examples of such practices (or families of such practices, depending on your taste in individuation) would be those involving reliance on sense perception, introspection, memory, rational intuition, various kinds of reasoning, and mystical experience. I argue that it is rational to engage in any socially established doxastic practice that we do not have sufficient reasons for regarding as *unreliable*. The defense of this principle is, in part, practical: given that there are no noncircular ways of distinguishing between reliable and unreliable basic doxastic practices, it would be foolish to abstain from established practices, even if we could. The claims of a doxastic practice can also be strengthened by "significant self-support", exemplified by the way in which reliance on sense perception and reasoning therefrom puts us in a position to predict and control the course of events. This is *self*-support because we can't determine that our prediction and control is successful except by relying on sense perception.

In Chapter 5 we return to our central concern, the justification of M-beliefs.

Applying the doctrine of Chapter 4, we look at the possibility of treating *M-belief formation on the basis of mystical perception (plus, in some cases, background beliefs)* as a socially established doxastic practice. Although it is found to exhibit all the defining characteristics thereof, in one respect it is too rich. When we consider the background system of concepts and beliefs that furnish potential "overriders" for prima facie justified M-beliefs, we find markedly different systems in different religions. That forces us to distinguish different mystical, perceptual belief-forming practices for the different major religious traditions. Hence the most effective way to proceed is to consider one such practice as typical. I choose the Christian practice (CMP, for 'Christian mystical practice') for this purpose. In the remainder of the chapter I consider reasons for denying the CMP is a full-fledged perceptual doxastic practice. The most important of these are (1) the partial distribution of mystical perception, (2) the extent to which there is a shared system of checks and tests for particular perceptual beliefs, and (3) the differences between the system of checks we have here and the one we have for sense perception. I conclude that none of this disqualifies CMP from the rights and privileges due a socially established doxastic practice.

Even if CMP is rightly regarded as prima facie rationally acceptable, this status could be overthrown by sufficient reasons for considering it to be unreliable. In Chapter 6, I consider candidates for such reasons, most notably (1) naturalistic explanations of mystical experience, (2) contradictions in the output of CMP, and (3) alleged conflicts with the outputs of secular practices, particularly the sciences and their extrapolation into a naturalistic metaphysics. Again, I conclude that none of this is disqualifying. The chapter ends with a consideration of the significant self-support that is provided by CMP.

The severest difficulty for my position stems from the way in which we are forced to "Balkanize" the sphere of mystical perception. Since there is a plurality of mystical, perceptual doxastic practices with mutually contradictory output and/or background belief systems, how can it be rational to accept one of these rather than any of the others (or none at all) without having sufficient *external* reason for regarding it as sufficiently reliable? In Chapter 7, I address this problem on a worst-case scenario, according to which we have no such external reason. On the basis of various analogies I conclude that, though this is not epistemically the best of all possible worlds, it is rational in this situation for one to continue to participate in the (undefeated) practice in which s/he is involved, hoping that the inter-practice contradictions will be sorted out in due time. There is also a discussion of the relation between the epistemic status of first hand perceptual beliefs and the epistemic status of beliefs based on reports of the former.

As indicated earlier, the support given to M-beliefs by mystical experience is only one part of the total basis of religious belief, in Christianity and elsewhere. What are these other possible grounds, and how does mystical experience interact with them in the larger picture? That is the topic of Chapter 8. I distinguish between various kinds of experiential grounds, various sorts of "revelation", and natural theology. I reduce this diversity to two main headings: perceptual presentation and inference to the best explanation. It is then suggested that the different grounds interact not only by adding up to a total case that is greater than any of its components, but also in more intimate ways—for example, by one source contributing to the background system presupposed by another source, or by one source helping to remove doubts about another.

CHAPTER I

The Experience of God: A Perceptual Model

i. Preliminaries

The chief aim of this book is to defend the view that putative direct awareness of God can provide justification for certain kinds of beliefs about God. In this chapter I will set the stage for that defense by explaining how I am thinking of (putative) direct awareness of God, what its crucial features are, what territory it covers, over what important differences it ranges, and on which stretches of the territory we will be concentrating. I shall illustrate all this by a sample of reports of such experiences, drawn both from "professional" contemplative mystics, and from humble laypersons. All examples will be drawn from the Christian tradition, with which I am most familiar, but the phenomenon is by no means confined to Christianity. I will suggest and defend a "perceptual model" for the experiences under consideration. That is, I shall argue that if we think of perception in the most general way, in which it is paradigmatically exemplified by but not confined to sense perception, putative awareness of God exhibits this generic character. Thus it is properly termed (putative) perception of God. Any such argument will have to employ some particular account of sense perception, and this is a notoriously controversial topic. I shall be advocating my own view of the matter, the Theory of Appearing, but I shall also indicate how the experiential awareness of God could be construed as a mode of perception on other theories.

I will also undertake to answer various objections to the claim that it is *possible* for human beings to perceive God. That is, if God does really exist, there is in principle no bar to this. I will not argue in this chapter that the possibility is realized, that some human beings do genuinely perceive God. For one thing, 'perceive' is a "success" term, entailing the existence of its object, and I will not argue that God exists. Such argument for this as will be found in the book is indirect; if beliefs "about God", entailing or presupposing that God exists, are justified by being based on putative experiential awareness of God, then so is the belief that God exists. Nor will I try to show in this chapter that, even assuming that God does exist, anyone is ever in the right relation to Him to be perceiving Him. If we are working *within* an established doxastic (belief-forming) practice of forming perceptual beliefs, we can make use of standard ways of determining whether a particular subject, S, is genuinely perceiving a given object, X, at a certain time. But in working within that practice we are *assuming* that such perceptions do actually occur; that is a fundamental presupposition of the practice. From within the practice of forming perceptual beliefs on the basis of sense perception we have ways of determining whether S saw a bird. But these ways have been built up by taking a number of perceptions as genuine and accepting the beliefs about the environment based on those perceptions.

And so it is with a practice of forming beliefs about God on the basis of experience. This book does not start by assuming that such a practice is what it purports to be; on the contrary, the book argues for that thesis. I don't want to assume that people really perceive God and that (some of the) beliefs based on those perceptions are true. I want to address people who antecedently reject those assumptions as well as those who accept them. Thus I am conducting the discussion from a standpoint outside any practice of forming beliefs on the basis of those alleged perceptions. And so far as I can see, the only way of arguing, from that standpoint, that people do genuinely perceive God is to argue for the epistemological position that beliefs formed on the basis of such (putative) perceptions are (prima facie) justified. If that is the case, we have a good reason for regarding many of the putative perceptions as genuine; for if the subject were not often really perceiving X why should the experience involved provide justification for beliefs about X? This reverses the usual order of procedure in which we first seek to show that S really did perceive X and then go on to consider what beliefs about X, if any, are justified by being based on that perception. But we can proceed in that order only if we are working from within a perceptual belief-forming practice. The question of the genuineness of the alleged perception can be tackled from the outside only by defending the *epistemological* assumptions embedded in the practice in question.[1] Thus the case for the reality of perception of God will emerge from the book as a whole, most of which (Chaps. 2–7) is one long argument for the thesis that certain kinds of beliefs about God can be justified by being based on putative perception of God. This chapter will be a *phenomenological* examination of awareness of God. We will be seeking to display its phenomenological structure, how it "comes to" the subject, as well as considering its varieties and its extent, and asking whether it is *possible* that it should satisfy other requirements for being a genuine perception of God.

The qualifications in the above should make it clear that I have no intention

[1]In Chapter 8 we will recognize other grounds for beliefs about God, and it is conceivable that the genuineness of perception of God could be established on those other grounds. In saying what I do here, I am assuming that this is not the case. In Chapter 8 there will be some discussion of what can be expected from different grounds of religious belief.

of claiming that every time someone supposes himself to perceive God he is actually doing so. I take it to be tolerably obvious that not every such supposition is correct, any more than that every supposed sense perception of, for example, a lake is the genuine article. (Sometimes the supposed lake is a mirage.) The most I will be seeking to support (indirectly) is that sometimes people who suppose themselves to be perceiving God are actually doing so.

Here are some terminological stipulations. As is implicit in the above, 'awareness of X' and 'perception of X' are "success" terms. Whatever my state of consciousness, so far as that is wholly within my head, I can't be truly said to be *aware* of an external object, X, or to have *perceived* X, unless X exists and unless I stand in whatever relation to X is required for this. Since I didn't want to assume at the outset that these conditions obtain for the experiential awareness of God I have been appending the qualifier 'putative' to 'awareness of God' and 'perception of God'. But from now on, in order to avoid intolerable circumlocutions, I hereby cancel the "success" character of 'awareness' and 'perception' until further notice. From now on 'awareness (perception) of God' is to be understood as 'what the subject takes (or would take if the question arose) to be an awareness (perception) of God'. When I want the success implication I will say something like '*genuine* perception of God'. Second, in order to have a term parallel to sense perception, one that is more compact than 'perception (awareness) of God', I will, with some trepidation, speak of *mystical perception*; 'mystical experience' will be used for the mode of experience involved in that sort of perception (just as sense experience is the mode of experience involved in sense perception). The trepidation is due to the fact that, as will be made explicit later, the range of our category by no means coincides with that of "mystical experience" on any of the most common understandings of that term.

I have just been trading on the obvious point that not all putative direct awareness (perception) of God need be the genuine article. But we must recognize a discrepancy in the other direction as well. There can be genuine awarenesses of God that the subject does not take as such. First, no such taking may occur because the subject is not attending to the matter, though she would so construe the experience if the question arose.[2] A second possibility is that one may actually be experiencing God without even being disposed to identify the object of the experience as God if the question arose, just as one can see a cyclotron without realizing that what one sees is a cyclotron.[3] I may be aware of God's sustaining me in being, while I suppose that I am merely feeling particularly fit and chipper at the moment; or I may

[2]This may not seem to be a live possibility since experiences of God are typically so overwhelming that they could hardly go unnoticed, nor could one fail to consider what it is that one is experiencing. However, this reaction stems from an exclusive concentration on the "mountaintop" brand of mystical perceptions and ignores the low intensity, background experiences of God's constant presence that figure importantly in the lives of many devout persons.

[3]For a powerful presentation of the position that all (or most) of us are experientially aware of God all (or most) of the time, see Baillie 1939.

be "hearing" God speak to me (not with audible words), while I take this to be just thoughts floating through my mind. Perception of God can be genuine without being putative as well as vice versa. Our direct concern here is with the putative perceptions, and that for two reasons. First, our only access to the subject matter is through the reports of persons who take themselves to be experientially aware of God. Second, we are centrally concerned with the epistemological question of whether certain kinds of beliefs about God can be based on experience in such a way as to be justified by being so based. And where one bases a belief about God on an experience (in the most direct fashion), one is obviously taking that experience to be an awareness of God. And, on the other side, a belief that X is present can be justified by an experience even if that experience is not a veridical experience of X. I might be justified by my visual experience in supposing that there is a lake in the distance, even though it is only a mirage. Hence, the category we need for our epistemological purposes is that of those experiences that seem to the subject to be direct awarenesses of God. Nevertheless, we are concerned with this category only because of the possibility that some of its members are genuine perceptions of God.

Although in this book I am centrally concerned with the epistemological value of mystical perception, I certainly don't want to suggest either that this is its only theoretical interest, or that this is its main importance for the religious life. I certainly don't think that God presents Himself to our experience primarily to render certain beliefs justified. On the contrary, according to the Christian tradition the main significance of mystical perception is that it is an integral part of that personal relationship with God that is the fundamental aim and consummation of human life. Without God and me being aware of each other in a way that, on my side, is properly called 'perception', there could be no intimate relationship of love, devotion, and dialogue that, according to Christianity, constitutes our highest good.

ii. Some Initial Examples

Let's begin with what I take to be paradigm cases of experiential awareness of God, some "professional" and some lay.

> (1) . . . all at once I . . . felt the presence of God—I tell of the thing just as I was conscious of it—as if his goodness and his power were penetrating me altogether. . . . I thanked God that in the course of my life he had taught me to know him, that he sustained my life and took pity both on the insignificant creature and on the sinner that I was. I begged him ardently that my life might be consecrated to the doing of his will. I felt his reply, which was that I should do his will from day to day, in humility and poverty, leaving him, The Almighty God, to judge of whether I should some time be called to bear witness more conspicuously. Then, slowly, the ecstasy left my heart; that is, I felt that God had withdrawn the

communion which he had granted. . . . I asked myself if it were possible that Moses on Sinai could have had a more intimate communication with God. I think it well to add that in this ecstasy of mine God had neither form, color, odor, nor taste; moreover, that the feeling of his presence was accompanied by no determinate localization. . . . But the more I seek words to express this intimate intercourse, the more I feel the impossibility of describing the thing by any of our usual images. At bottom the expression most apt to render what I felt is this: God was present, though invisible; he fell under no one of my senses, yet my consciousness perceived him. (Anonymous report in James 1902, pp. 67–68)

(2) One day when I was at prayer . . . I saw Christ at my side—or, to put it better, I was conscious of Him, for I saw nothing with the eyes of the body or the eyes of the soul [the imagination]. He seemed quite close to me and I saw that it was He. As I thought, He was speaking to me. Being completely ignorant that such visions were possible, I was very much afraid at first, and could do nothing but weep, though as soon as He spoke His first word of assurance to me, I regained my usual calm, and became cheerful and free from fear. All the time Jesus Christ seemed to be at my side, but as this was not an imaginary vision I could not see in what form. But I most clearly felt that He was all the time on my right, and was a witness of everything that I was doing . . . if I say that I do not see Him with eyes of the body or the eyes of the soul, because this is no imaginary vision, how then can I know and affirm that he is beside me with greater certainty that if I saw Him? If one says that one is like a person in the dark who cannot see someone though he is beside him, or that one is like somebody who is blind, it is not right. There is some similarity here, but not much, because a person in the dark can perceive with the other senses, or hear his neighbor speak or move, or can touch him. Here this is not so, nor is there any feeling of darkness. On the contrary, He appears to the soul by a knowledge brighter than the sun. I do not mean that any sun is seen, or any brightness, but there is a light which, though unseen, illumines the understanding. (St. Teresa 1957, chap. 27, pp. 187–89)

(3) At times God comes into the soul without being called; and He instills into her fire, love, and sometimes sweetness; and the soul believes this comes from God, and delights therein. But she does not yet know, or see, that He dwells in her; she perceives His grace, in which she delights. And again God comes to the soul, and speaks to her words full of sweetness, in which she has much joy, and she feels Him. This feeling of God givers her the greatest delight; but even here a certain doubt remains; for the soul has not the certitude that God is in her. . . . And beyond this the soul receives the gift of seeing God. God says to her, 'Behold Me!' and the soul sees Him dwelling within her. She sees Him more clearly than one man sees another. For the eyes of the soul behold a plentitude of which I cannot speak: a plenitude which is not bodily but spiritual, of which I can say nothing. And the soul rejoices in that sight with an ineffable joy; and this is the manifest and certain sign that God indeed dwells in her. (Angela of Foligno, "Livre de l'Expérience des Vrais Fidèles", pp. 170, seq. Quoted in Underhill 1955, p. 282)

(4) That which the Servitor saw had no form neither any manner of being; yet he had of it a joy such as he might have known in the seeing of the shapes and substances of all joyful things. His heart was hungry, yet satisfied, his soul was full of contentment and joy: his prayers and hopes were all fulfilled. And the Friar could do naught but contemplate this Shining Brightness; and he altogether forgot himself and all other things. Was it day or night? He knew not. It was, as it were, a manifestation of the sweetness of Eternal Life in the sensations of silence and of rest. Then he said, 'If that which I see and feel be not the Kingdom of Heaven, I know not what it can be: for it is very sure that the endurance of all possible pains were but a poor price to pay for the eternal possession of so great a joy. (Henry Suso, *Life*, chap. 3, quoted in Underhill 1955, p. 187)

(5) But as I turned and was about to take a seat by the fire, I received a mighty baptism of the Holy Ghost. Without any expectation of it, without ever having the thought in my mind that there was any such thing for me, without any recollection that I had ever heard the thing mentioned by any person in the world, the Holy Spirit descended upon me in a manner that seemed to go through me, body and soul. I could feel the impression, like a wave of electricity, going through and through me. Indeed, it seemed to come in waves and waves of liquid love; for I could not express it in any other way. (Anonymous report in James 1902, p. 250)

(6) I attended service at a church in Uppsala. . . . During both the Confession of Sin and the Prayer of Thanksgiving which followed Communion, I had a strong consciousness of the Holy Spirit as a person, and an equally strong consciousness of the existence of God, that God was present, that the Holy Spirit was in all those who took part in the service. . . . The only thing of importance was God, and my realization that He looked upon me and let His mercy flood over me, forgiving me for my mistakes and giving me the strength to live a better life. (Anonymous report in Unger 1976, p. 114)

Let's note some salient features of these accounts. (A) They report an *experiential* awareness of God. (B) The awareness is *direct*. (C) The awareness is reported to be *of God*.

iii. Experiential Presentations of God—Sensory and Non-Sensory

(A) The awareness is *experiential* in the way it contrasts with thinking about God, calling up mental images, entertaining propositions, reasoning, engaging in overt or covert conversation, remembering. Our sources take it that something, namely, God, has been *presented* or *given* to their consciousness, in generically the same way as that in which objects in the environment are (apparently) *presented* to one's consciousness in sense perception. The most fundamental fact about sense perception, at least as far as its intrinsic character is concerned, is the way in which seeing my house differs from thinking about it, remembering it, forming mental images of it, reasoning about it, and so on. It is the difference between *presence* (to consciousness) and absence. If I stand before my house with my eyes shut and then open them, I am suddenly *presented* with the object itself; it occupies part of my visual field; it appears to me as blue and steep roofed. People who report being experientially aware of God take this to contrast with thinking about God in just the same way. This is sufficiently clear from our initial examples. "God was present . . . my consciousness perceived him" (1). "He appears to the soul by a knowledge brighter than the sun" (2). In (3) "seeing God" (this is clearly not seeing in a way that involves visual qualia, for the "eyes of the soul behold . . . a plentitude which is not bodily but spiritual") is contrasted with experiencing love and sweetness that she *believes* comes from God, in which case He is not directly presented to her consciousness. Here are some other reports in which the contrast is spelled out.

> (7) There was one thing that I was ignorant of at the beginning. I did not really know that God is present in all things; and when He seemed to me so near, I thought that it was impossible. Yet I could not cease believing that He was there, since I seemed almost certainly to have been conscious of His very presence. Unlearned persons told me that He was there only in His grace. But I could not believe this, because, as I have said, He seemed to be really present. (St. Teresa 1957, p. 127)

This is just the contrast drawn by Angela in (3) between the presence of God and the presence of His effects (including the effects of His "grace").

> (8) Now it fares in like manner with the soul who is in rest and quiet before God: for she sucks in a manner insensibly the delights of *His presence*, without any discourse. . . . She sees her spouse *present* with so sweet a view that reasonings would be to her unprofitable and superfluous. . . . Nor does the soul in this repose stand in need of the *memory*, for she has her lover *present*. Nor has she need of the imagination, for why should we represent in an exterior or interior image Him whose *presence* we are possessed of? (St. Francis of Sales, *Treatise on the Love of God*, Bk. VI, chap. ix. Quoted in Poulain 1950, pp. 75–76)

In the Catholic mystical tradition there is a major divide between ordinary or "acquired" prayer, and "infused contemplation".[4] In the former the person uses her mental and linguistic powers to speak to God, form subjects for

[4]"Without giving a definition here of extraordinary contemplation, which it belongs to mysticism to do, we will point out the two characteristic notes which distinguish it from contemplation or ordinary prayer: (1) an inner perception . . . of a very special presence of God . . . ; (2) a suspension, complete or only partial, of acts of the intellect, the memory, the imagination, and the exterior senses which might prevent the will from possessing this ineffable divine presence in perfect peace. All prayer or contemplation which is not accompanied by these two characteristic notes, no matter how great its perfection and whatever its effects, does not go beyond ordinary or acquired prayer." Fr. Duplancy in Vacant's *Dictionnaire de Théologie*, Fol. 1, col. 2041. Quoted in Poulain 1950, p. 80.

meditation, dwell on them, and react to them affectively. But in "infused contemplation" the subject is passive; no effort of will is needed; no powers of attention or reasoning, no activities of formulating propositions are involved. Instead God is *presented* to their awareness in a way that does not depend in any way on their own efforts. Mystics often report how struck they are by this difference when they first cross the divide and how difficult it is to understand what is happening.

(9) When, after a long cultivation of purity of heart, God would enter into a soul and *manifest Himself to it openly by the gift of His holy presence . . . the soul finds itself so delighted with its new state, that it feels as if it had never known or loved God before*. (Fr. Lallemant, *Spiritual Doctrine*, quoted in Poulain 1950, p. 77)

In pointing out that mystical experience is a matter of something's *presenting* itself to one's experience, we are dissenting from the numerous theorists who construe experiences of the sort we are discussing as purely subjective feelings or sensations to which is superadded an *explanation* according to which they are due to God, the Holy Spirit, or some other agent recognized by the theology of the subject's tradition. An excellent recent example of this approach is found in *Religious Experience* by Wayne Proudfoot (1985). Proudfoot goes so far as to identify the "noetic" quality that James and many others have noted in mystical experience with the supposition by the subject that the experience must be given a theological rather than a naturalistic explanation.[5] It seems clear to me, on the other hand, that our sources are reporting a distinct sense of something's (taken by them to be God) *presenting* itself to their awareness in generically the same way as that in which physical objects present themselves to our awareness in sense perception. Perhaps Proudfoot and his ilk think that is a mistaken way to do the phenomenology of sense perception as well. Perhaps they think that here too we have essentially subjective experiences together with a certain kind of causal explanation. If so, I suggest that they are flying in the face of the unambiguous testimony of experience.

But though mystical perception is like sense perception in the fact of *presentation*, it is frequently utterly unlike it in content, at least in those numerous cases in which no awareness of sensory qualia is involved, no colors, shapes,

[5]Pp. 136–39, 236. The treatment of "religious experience" as essentially consisting of "feelings" or other affective states is very common. Thus in Schleiermacher, the fountainhead of concentration on religious experience in the study of religion, we find the basic experiential element of religion treated as a "feeling of absolute dependence". Rudolf Otto and William James also concentrate on feelings. It must be confessed that in all these cases the theorists also characterize religious experience as cognitive of objective realities in ways that seem incompatible with the classification as *affective*. I doubt very much that any consistent account of religious experience can be found in the works of any of these people. Nevertheless, it remains true that their concentration on affect has frequently been taken out of context and as such has powerfully influenced succeeding generations.

sounds, smells, and the like. This is stressed by several of the above cases, particularly (1), (2), and (3). Here is further testimony in reports sent to the Religious Experience Research Unit in Manchester College, Oxford, in response to a newspaper advertisement asking for such reports. They are taken from Timothy Beardsworth, *A Sense of Presence* (1977).

(10) Then, in a very gentle and gradual way, not with a shock at all, it began to dawn on me that I was not alone in the room. Someone else was there, located fairly precisely about two yards to my right front. Yet there was no sort of sensory hallucination. I neither saw him nor heard him in any sense of the word 'see' and 'hear', but there he was; I had no doubt about it. He seemed to be very good and very wise, full of sympathetic understanding, and most kindly disposed towards me. (P. 122)

(11) There was no sensible vision, but the room was filled by a Presence which in a strange way was both about me and within me. I was overwhelmingly possessed by Someone who was not myself, and yet I felt I was more myself than I had ever been before. (P. 122)[6]

Many people find it incredible, unintelligible, or incoherent to suppose that there could be something that counts as *presentation*, that contrasts with abstract thought in the way sense perception does, but is devoid of sensory content. So far as I can see, this simply evinces a lack of speculative imagination. Why suppose that the possibilities of experiential givenness, for human beings or otherwise, are exhausted by the powers of *our* five senses? To begin with the most obvious point, it is certainly possible that other creatures should be sensitive to physical stimuli other than those to which our five senses are responsive. For that matter, our bodily sensation involves modes of presentation that do not seem to exhibit any of the familiar qualia from the external senses. Then, to push the matter a bit further, why can't we also envisage presentations that do not stem from the activity of any physical sense organs, as is apparently the case with mystical perception. To be sure, if mystical perception is as analogous to sense perception as I take it to be, it must involve distinctive phenomenal content. We will attend to that in due course. But for now the point is that there is no reason to doubt that phenomenal content may be very different from any that is produced by our external senses and may not result from the stimulation of any physical sense organ. It is this possibility that our subjects suppose themselves to have realized.

However, not all mystical perception is devoid of sensory content. Here are some samples from Beardsworth 1977:

[6]In these reports the object is not explicitly identified as God. They could be covered by our criterion if it were changed to something like "an experience that the subject interprets as a direct awareness of a being that appears to him/her as God might be expected to appear".

(12) During the night of September 9th 1954, I awoke and looking out of my window saw what I took to be a luminous star which gradually came nearer, and appeared as a soft slightly blurred white light. I was seized with violent trembling, but had no fear. I knew that what I felt was great awe. This was followed by a sense of overwhelming love coming to me, and going out from me, then of great compassion from the Outer Presence. After that I had a sense of overpowering peace, and indescribable happiness. (P. 30)

(13) *In a state of intense inner wretchedness*, of such intensity that my mind seemed on the point of breaking, I got up at 4 a.m. and began wandering aimlessly on the wooded hillside. This went on for some time until, unexpectedly, the words of the 130th psalm sounded clearly in my mind: 'And plenteous redemption is ever found in Him; and, from all its iniquities, He Israel shall redeem.' With these words a light seemed to envelop me, and there flowed into my desolate heart such a flood of Love and Compassion that I was overwhelmed and overpowered by the weight of it. I was stricken by such wonder and amazement that I burst into tears of joy; it seemed to flow through my whole being with a cleansing and healing virtue. From that moment I knew that Love is the nature of reality. (Pp. 30-31)

(14) All at once I *felt someone near me*, a Presence entered this little room of which I became immediately conscious. . . . Dazed I knelt by the nearest chair and here is the physical phenomenon that has recurred many times since. Into my heart there came a great *warmth*. The only way I can describe it is in the words of disciples on their way to Emmaus 'our hearts burned within us'. My hand raised in prayer also glowed from tips to wrist with a blessed warmth, never before experienced. (Pp. 113–14)

Sometimes more complex visual imagery is involved.

(15) It happened one morning that the Servitor [Suso] saw in a vision that he was surrounded by a troop of heavenly spirits. He therefore asked one of the most radiant amongst these Principals of the Sky to show him how God dwelt in his soul. The angel said to him, "Do but fix your eyes joyously upon yourself, and watch how God plays the game of love within your loving soul." And he looked quickly, and saw that his body in the region of his heart was pure and transparent like crystal: and he saw the Divine Wisdom peacefully enthroned in the midst of his heart, and she was fair to look upon. And by her side was the soul of the Servitor, full of heavenly desires; resting lovingly upon the bosom of God, Who had embraced it, and pressed it to His Heart. And it remained altogether absorbed and inebriated with love in the arms of God its well-beloved. (Henry Suso, chap. vi, in Underhill 1955, P. 286)

Auditions are, of course, quite common, with or without accompanying visions. Again from Beardsworth 1977:

(16) At one time I reached utter despair and wept and prayed God for mercy instinctively and without faith in reply. That night I stood with other patients in the grounds waiting to be let in to our ward. . . . Suddenly someone stood beside

me in a dusty brown robe and a voice said 'Mad or sane, you are one of My sheep'. I never spoke to anyone of this but every since, twenty years, it has been the pivot of my life. (P. 91)

(17) When I was middle-aged and the 2nd World War upon us, there came a night when I was in deepest distress of mind. I was alone in my bedroom, pacing the floor. . . . Suddenly, I heard a voice firmly say 'Be still and know that I am God!' It changed my life. I got into bed, calm and confident. (P. 92)

In cases involving sensory content we may distinguish between *hallucinations*—that is, apparent sense perception of externally located physical objects where no such objects physically exist—and *mental imagery*, in which the item bearing sensory content is presented as imaginary rather than as located in the external environment. Thus in auditions it may be as if the sound of a voice is coming from outside, or it may be that the subject is aware of auditory imagery (an inner voice). The same distinction can be made for the other sense modalities. Reports are often not explicit on this point, but sometimes clear indications are provided. In (12) the "luminous star" was seen as outside the window, and in (16) the spoken message came from an external figure in a dusty brown robe. In (13), by contrast, the experience was of an "inner voice".

To be sure, not all "religious experiences" with sensory content are taken to be perceptions of God. Visions of saints, of the heavenly city, of the Virgin Mary, of doves, are not.[7] Indeed, it may be doubted that any experience with sensory content could be a presentation of God. Since God is purely immaterial how could He appear to one as looking or sounding (literally)[8] a certain way? Well, the above quotations make it clear that many have taken sensory presentations to be an awareness of God. Anyone to whom this seems fundamentally wrongheaded is invited to consider the following. It is a familiar point from sense perception that the way an object phenomenally appears may not correspond exactly to the way it is. Details may be discrepant: a square tower may look round from a distance; a white object may look red under certain lighting; and so on. More fundamentally, there is a long tradition that holds that secondary qualities like colors do not really characterize physical substances. Thus it is not inconceivable that God should appear to us as looking bright or sounding a certain way, even though He does not, in His own nature, possess any sensory qualities. Nor would it necessarily be unfitting or unworthy for Him to do so. It may be that, given our powers and proclivities, this would be the best way for Him to get a certain message across; just as,

[7]Visions of Jesus Christ represent a special case, since, according to Christian doctrine, to see Christ is to see God.

[8]Later we shall go into the point that in the Christian mystical tradition there is talk of "spiritual sensations" construed on the analogy of sensations from the five external senses. But these are *not* thought of as involving (literal) sensory qualia.

even if physical substances are not really colored, the system of color appearances enables us to make many useful distinctions between them.

Nevertheless, I am going to concentrate in this book on non-sensory mystical perception. It seems clear that a non-sensory appearance of a purely spiritual deity has a greater chance of presenting Him as He is than any sensory presentation. If God appears to one, non-sensorily, as loving, powerful, or good, the appearance, so far as it goes, could correspond fairly closely with the way God is Himself.[9] While if we experience God as looking or sounding a certain way, that can't be the way He is, not even approximately.[10]

To be sure, this issue is complicated in Christianity by the fact that according to Christian doctrine Jesus of Nazareth is both man and God; so that to see him, even in human form, is to see God. This means that the doctrine that God is a purely spiritual being is qualified in Christianity. Nevertheless, even here the fact remains that God in His essential nature is purely spiritual. In the case of Christ there is a distinction between the divine and the human nature, and only the latter is physical and directly sensorily perceived. Hence it remains true that a non-sensory experience gives us a better chance of grasping what God is like in Himself than does any sensory experience.

iv. Direct and Indirect Awareness of God

Now for (B) *directness*. What concept of directness is this and with what is it being contrasted? After all, we might take any experiential *presentation* to be ipso facto direct. What distinguishes perception from abstract thought is that

[9]Possibly only "fairly closely" because it may be that our grasp of these properties deviates to a greater or lesser degree from the form they take in the nature of God.

[10]It is worthy of note that the great mystics generally hold sensory appearances in slight regard. Here is a statement of the fourteenth-century mystic Walter Hilton. "Should you see any light or brightness, whether outwardly or in your imagination, which is not visible to other people, treat it with caution. And should you hear any sweet melody or suddenly taste a sweet but unaccountable savour in your mouth, or a fiery heat in your breast, or any other kind of pleasurable sensation elsewhere in your body, be on your guard. Even if a spirit such as an angel appears to you in bodily form to comfort and guide you, or if you have some experience that is not attributable to any bodily creature, treat it with reserve both then and afterwards, and test the reactions of your soul. If the pleasure that you feel leads you to abandon the thought and contemplation of Jesus Christ, and your spiritual exercises and prayer, so that you neglect self-examination and cease to long for virtue and the spiritual knowledge and love of God, then beware. And take care lest you allow the inmost desire of your heart, your pleasure, and your peace of mind to depend principally on these experiences, regarding them as part of the joy of Heaven and the happiness of the angels, so that you do not wish to pray or think of anything else. For if your sole desire is to preserve and enjoy such experiences, beware of these feelings, for they come from the devil. Therefore, however pleasing and attractive they may appear, reject them and do not yield to them." (Hilton, 1957, p. 11) Here Hilton is downgrading sensory experiences because of the danger of their distracting attention from more important matters and of being sought for their own sakes. But they are also unfavorably evaluated by mystics from a cognitive point of view, since, so they suppose, they are so much more easily produced by the Devil. "It is the same with another of God's methods of instructing the soul, that by which He speaks to it without words. . . . He introduces into the innermost parts of the soul what He wants it to understand, presenting it not in pictures or in the form of words. . . . This, I think, is the state with which the devil can least interfere" (St. Teresa 1957, chap. 27, pp. 189–90).

the object is *directly presented* or *immediately present* to the subject so that 'indirect presentation' would be a contradiction in terms. To tease out a concept of directness that has an opposite within the category of presentation, let's go back to sense perception, where we can find our way around more easily. We can distinguish *directly* seeing someone from seeing her in a mirror or on television. We have *presentation* on both sides of this distinction. Even when I see someone in a mirror or on television, the person appears to me as such-and-such, as smiling, tall, or smartly dressed. That person can be identified with an item in my visual field. This contrasts with the case in which I take something as a sign or indication of X but do not see X itself (X does not appear anywhere within my visual field), as when I take a vapor trail across the sky as an indication that a jet plane has flown by. Here I don't see the plane at all; nothing in my visual field looks like a plane. Let's call this latter kind of case *indirect perceptual recognition*, and the former kind (seeing someone on television) *indirect perception*. We can then say that indirect is distinguished from direct perception of X by the fact that in the former, but not in the latter, we perceive X by virtue of perceiving something else, Y. In the indirect cases I see the person, T, by virtue of seeing the mirror or the television screen or whatever. On the other hand, when I see T face to face there is nothing else I perceive by virtue of perceiving which I see T. No doubt there is a chain of causal intermediaries between T and my visual experience. Light reflected from T strikes my retina, the disturbances from which are transmitted. . . . But I don't perceive any of this. I don't see X through *seeing* or otherwise perceiving anything else.

To be sure, there is a sense in which I perceive T through having a visual experience, and that point puts us in a position to recognize a still more direct mode of awareness. Consider one's awareness of one's own conscious states: one's feeling, sensations, thoughts, and imaginings. Here there is no state of consciousness distinct from the object of awareness through which one is aware of that object. When I am aware of feeling excited, there is not a conscious state of being aware of my feeling that is distinguishable from the feeling—the way there is a conscious visual experience of the computer which is distinguishable from the computer.[11] Here we have a form of presentation that is even more direct that directly seeing the computer. Our own states of consciousness are *given* to us with maximum immediacy, not given to us *through* anything. Whereas in direct perception of external objects, though the object is not presented through the *perception* of anything else, it is presented through a state of consciousness that is distinct from the object of experience and of which we can become explicitly aware in the more direct way. Let's summarize this by distinguishing three grades of immediacy.

(A) Absolute immediacy. One is aware of X but not through anything else, even a state of consciousness.

[11]This account will not be universally accepted. But if it is only so much as plausible, that will suffice to explain my concept of a maximally direct awareness.

(B) Mediated immediacy (direct perception). One is aware of X through a state of consciousness that is distinguishable from X, and can be made an object of absolutely immediate awareness, but is not perceived.

(C) Mediate perception. One is aware of X through the awareness of another object of perception.

When I say that the state of consciousness through which one directly perceives X is not itself *perceived*, I am thinking of perception as involving at least as much mediation as we have in B. So we get a sort of nesting relationship. The next grade beyond absolute immediacy (A) is (B) an awareness of X through a (possible) object of (A), and the next grade (C) is an awareness of X through an actual object of (B). It is not of the first importance just how the term 'perception' is integrated into this system, but I take the above to be a natural way of doing it.

To get back to our examples, they all seem to be cases of (B). Our subjects are quite able to distinguish their states of consciousness from that which they take themselves to be perceiving, namely, God. Thus in (1) we are told that the way he "was conscious of it" involved its being "as if his goodness and his power were penetrating me altogether". Example (2) speaks of a "light which, though unseen, illumines the understanding", (4) of "the sensations of silence and of rest". "I could feel the impression, like a wave of electricity, going through and through me. Indeed, it seemed to come in waves and waves of liquid love (5)". In (8) it is said that God is seen with "so sweet a view"; in (12) we hear of "a sense of overwhelming love coming to me, and going out from me." Here is another example, an anonymous report cited by James.

> (18) I remember the night, and almost the very spot on the hilltop, where my soul opened out, as it were, into the Infinite, and there was a rushing together of the two worlds, the inner and the outer. It was deep calling unto deep—the deep that my own struggle had opened up within being answered by the unfathomable deep without, reaching beyond the stars. I stood alone with Him who had made me, and all the beauty of the world, and love, and sorrow, and even temptation. I did not seek Him, but felt the perfect unison of my spirit with His. *The ordinary sense of things around me faded. For the moment nothing but an ineffable joy and exultation remained. It is impossible fully to describe the experience. It was like the effect of some great orchestra when all the separate notes have melted into one swelling harmony that leaves the listener conscious of nothing save that his soul is being wafted upwards, and almost bursting with its own emotion. The perfect stillness of the night was thrilled by a more solemn silence.* The darkness held a presence that was all the more felt because it was not seen. I could not any more have doubted that *He* was there than that I was. Indeed, I felt myself to be, if possible the less real of the two. My highest faith in God and truest idea of him were then born in me. . . . Then, if ever, I believe, I stood face to face with God, and was born anew of his spirit. . . . Having once felt the presence of God's spirit, I have never lost it again for long. My most assuring evidence of his

existence is deeply rooted in that hour of vision, in the memory of that supreme experience, and in the conviction, gained from reading and reflection, that something of the same has come to all who have found God. (James 1902, pp. 66–67)

I have italicized the description of the experience to distinguish it from the specification of its object, "Him who had made me".

In making this point I have been concentrating on the non-sensory cases; with sensory perceptions it is obvious that, just as in ordinary sense perception of the physical environment, there is an experience with a distinctive phenomenal character that can be distinguished from the object perceived. Note that our subjects characterize the mode of consciousness, in distinction from the object, in two ways. First, and most fundamentally, it is characterized by what the object is appearing *as*—as good and powerful, loving,[12] or whatever. Second, there are more subjective features of the experience: that there is an "ineffable joy and exultation", it involves a "calm, a repose, and an interior sweetness", and so on. In both characterizations there is a specifiable mode of consciousness through which God is perceived.

This shows that our cases are distinct from what we have called Absolute Immediacy, but we must also point out their distinction from Mediate Perception. We rarely find an explicit pronouncement on this point in our sources, for they are rarely concerned to distinguish their experience from perceiving God in nature or society, though occasionally we find a statement like the following.

(19) . . . in the mystic union, which is a *direct apprehension* of God, God acts immediately upon the soul in order to communicate Himself to her; and it is God, *not an image of God*, not the illusion of God, that the soul perceives and attains to. (Fr. Roure, in *Les Études*, Aug. 5, 1908, p. 371. Quoted in Poulain 1950, p. 83)

For the most part, however, the basis for taking our sources to be reporting cases of Mediated Immediacy rather than Mediate Perception is that, while speaking of a direct awareness or presentation of God, they do not mention any other presented or perceived object, in or through which they are aware of God. In the nature of the case this argumentum ad silentium is all that we can expect.

Extreme mystical experience in which all distinctions are transcended in an undifferentiated unity is properly thought of as absolute immediacy. If no distinctions can be made within the seamless unity, then there is no possibility of distinguishing the experience involved from the object of awareness. Indeed, the immediacy here is more absolute than in one's awareness of one's own conscious states. There we at least have the distinction between subject

[12]Later in the chapter we will have more to say about what God appears to our subjects *as*.

and object, but even that drops out in the kind of mystical experience reported in the following.

(20) As pure water poured into pure water remains the same, thus, O Gautama, is the Self of a thinker who knows. Water in water, fire in fire, ether in ether, no one can distinguish them: likewise a man whose mind has entered into the Self. (*The Upanishads*, tr. Max Müller 1884, Vol. II, p. 334)

(21) What he sees . . . is not seen, not distinguished, not represented as a thing apart. The man who obtains the vision becomes, as it were, another being. He ceases to be himself, retains nothing of himself. Absorbed in the beyond he is one with it, like a center coincident with another center. (Plotinus, *Enneads*, VI, 9. Tr. in O'Brien 1964, p. 23)

(22) Every man whose heart is no longer shaken by any doubt, knows with certainty that there is no being save only One. . . . In his divine majesty the *me*, and *we*, the *thou*, are not found, for in the One there can be no distinction. Every being who is annulled and entirely separated from himself, hears resound outside of him this voice and this echo: *I am God*. He has an eternal way of existing, and is no longer subject to death. (Gulshan-Raz, quoted in James 1902, p. 411)

But for the same reason, if we take the disclaimer of any distinctions literally, these experiences fall outside our category, since there is no distinguishable *object* of awareness that can be taken to be God. When a theistic mystic who supposes God to be an objective reality reports an experience of an undifferentiated unity, she is best construed not as denying the existence of any real distinctions, for example, between herself and God, but as simply reporting that she is aware of no such distinctions, or of any other, at that time.[13]

This is the best point at which to make explicit the divergence between our use of 'mystical experience' (and 'mystical perception') and the most common acceptation of the term among scholars of the subject. The latter is tailor-made for what I have just called 'extreme mystical experience' in which all distinctions are transcended, even the distinction of subject and object. For example, W. T. Stace in his influential work *Mysticism and Philosophy* (1960) lists common characteristics of the two types of mystical experience he recognizes, extrovertive and introvertive. They coincide in the following features.

(3) Sense of objectivity or reality.
(4) Blessedness, peace, and so on.
(5) Feeling of the holy, sacred, or divine.
(6) Paradoxicality.
(7) Alleged by mystics to be ineffable.

They differ in the first two features. For extrovertive we have

[13]Nelson Pike makes this point well in *Mystic Union: An Essay in the Phenomenology of Mysticism* (Ithaca, N.Y.: Cornell University Press, forthcoming).

(1E) The Unifying Vision—all things are One.

(2E) The more concrete apprehension of the One as an inner subjectivity, or life, in all things.

Whereas for introvertive we have

(1I) The Unitary Consciousness; the One, the Void; pure consciousness.

(2I) Nonspatial, nontemporal. (Pp. 131–32)

William Wainwright in his *Mysticism* (1981) characterizes mystical experience more simply.

> While modern English speakers use 'mystical experience' to refer to a wide variety of preternatural experiences, scholars have tended to restrict the term to
> (1) 'unitary' states which are
> (2) noetic, but
> (3) Lack *specific* empirical content. (P. 1)

Thus our category of mystical experience and "mystical experience" (more commonly so called) fail to coincide at several points. For one thing, putative experiences of God need not be paradoxical, nor need they be lacking in specific empirical content. However, the most important distinction concerns the absolute unity that is central to the more common use of the term. As I have just been pointing out, experiences taken by their subjects to be direct awareness of God do not typically exhibit, even phenomenologically, any such absolute unity; and even where they do, this can be seen as an extreme case of a *union* with God that more usually allows a consciousness of the interpersonal relationship. 'Mystical experience' and 'mystical perception', as we use those terms, do not imply absolute undifferentiated unity.

Turning now to indirect perception of God, that is a popular topic in contemporary philosophical and theological literature. There is much talk of experiencing God in the beauties of nature, of hearing God's voice in the Bible or in sermons or in the dictates of conscience, of being aware of God's providential activity in the events of our lives, of seeing God's hand at work in salvation history, and so on. Here are some samples.

> (23) There was a mysterious presence in nature and sometimes met within the communion and in praying by oneself, which was my greatest delight, especially when as happened from time to time, *nature became lit up from inside* with something that came from beyond itself (or seemed to do so to me). (Beardsworth 1977, p. 19)

> (24) I feel him [God] in the sunshine or rain; and awe mingled with a delicious restfulness most nearly describes my feelings. (James 1902, p. 70)

> (25) The eyes of my soul were opened, and I beheld the plenitude of God, wherein I did comprehend the whole world, both here and beyond the sea, and the abyss and ocean and all things. In all these things I beheld naught save the

> divine power, in a manner assuredly indescribable; so that through excess of marvelling the soul cried with a loud voice, saying 'The whole world is full of God'. (Angela of Foligno. Quoted in Underhill 1955, p. 252)

Here are some theoretical statements of the importance of indirect perception of God.

> To judge from the history of religions, God has been known for the most part in connection with other objects; not so much separately, if ever separately, as in relation to things and events which have served as media or as *mediators* for the divine presence. We find the early knowers of God worshipping him under the guise of sun, moon, and stars; of earth and heaven; of spirits and ancestors; of totems, of heroes, or priest-kings; and of the prophets themselves. Speaking broadly, there are two distinct phases of experience wherein God is apt to appear in the experience of Nature and in social experience. Not everywhere in Nature, but at special points, well-known and numerous enough, the awareness of God seems, as it were, to have broken through, or to have *supervened upon* our ordinary physical experience of those objects. . . . So of social experience: it is not everywhere, but at special junctures and crises, that the awareness of God has come to men; at the events of death and birth, or war and wedlock, of dream and disease and apparition. (Hocking 1912, pp. 230–31)

In his Gifford Lectures, *The Sense of the Presence of God* (1962), John Baillie insists that faith is a "primary mode of awareness. Faith does not deduce from other realities that *are* present the existence of God who is *not* present but absent; rather it is an awareness of the divine Presence itself, however hidden behind the veils of sense" (pp. 88–89). So we genuinely perceive God Himself; this is not merely a perceptual identification of the absent. Nevertheless, our perception of God is always through nature, history, and society. ". . .where I find myself in most assured contact with reality is in the relation with God that is mediated to me through my relation with my fellows, and in the relation with my fellows that is mediated to me through my relation with God" (p. 39). "I have no *right* to ignore the claims made upon me by the presence of my neighbour. . . . But to say that I am not permitted is to talk the language, not of any merely prudential or humanist morality, but of religious faith. It is to acknowledge that through the need of my neighbour a claim is being made upon me by unconditioned being, which is to say by God . . . it is in the world that I encounter my neighbour, and God through my neighbour, and my neighbour through God" (pp. 85–86).[14]

The concentration on indirect perception of God may stem from a sense that there is something suspicious or worse—incoherent or impossible—in the notion of a direct awareness of God. This may be owing to some of the

[14]See also I. M. Crombie, "Theology and Falsification", in Flew & MacIntyre 1955, pp. 111–15; Rahner 1987, pp. 52ff.

reasons we shall be discussing later in this chapter. But it may also be because of the view that all perception of objects has an indirect or mediated character. We can see this latter conviction at work in John Hick's *Faith and Knowledge* (1966), in which the chief cognitive relationship to God is said to consist in "an interpretation of the world as a whole as mediating a divine presence and purpose". "Behind the world—to use an almost inevitable spatial metaphor—there is apprehended to be an omnipotent, personal Will whose purpose toward mankind guarantees men's highest good and blessedness. The believer finds that he is at all times in the presence of this holy Will. Again and again he realizes, either at the time or in retrospect, that in his dealings with the circumstances of his own life he is also having to do with a transcendent Creator who is the determiner of his destiny and the source of all good" (p. 115). This account of the *interpretation* of the world and the events of one's life as manifesting a divine presence and purpose sounds like what I termed "indirect perceptual recognition" rather than indirect perception. Isn't this analogous to taking a vapor trail as a sign of the recent presence of a jet plane, but without actually seeing the plane? But Hick, after saying, "We become conscious of the existence of other objects in the universe . . . either by experiencing them for ourselves or by inferring their existence from evidence within our experience", insists: "The awareness of God reported by the ordinary religious believer is of the former kind. He professes, not to have inferred that there is a God, but that God as a living being has entered into his own experience" (p. 95). How can he claim that what he calls "interpretation" belongs with the latter rather than with the former? He does so by claiming that all experience of the world involves interpretation and the resultant consciousness of "significance". Even the paradigm sensory cases of things being presented to, and present to, one's consciousness, as contrasted with inferring them from something else, themselves involve interpretation, being aware of something *as such-and-such, taking* it to be such-and-such (pp. 98–113).

Now I do not agree with Hick that all experience of objects involves interpretation, taking the object to be such-and-such. No doubt normal, adult sense perception, and spiritual perception as well, is heavily conceptualized; in being perceptually aware of the environment, we are typically simultaneously aware of what various things are, what they look like and are like, and what their practical significance is for us. Normal perceptual experience is shot through with "interpretation". Nevertheless, what makes this a matter of perceiving the house, rather than just thinking about it or remembering it, is the fact of *presentation, givenness*, the fact that something is presented to consciousness, is something of which I am *directly aware*. And this is something that is distinguishable from any elements of conceptualization, judgment, belief, or other forms of "interpretation", however rarely the former may be found without the latter in adult experience.[15] Thus I cannot agree that to

[15]For a powerful defense of this position see Dretske 1969, chap. 2.

perceive a house *is* to interpret our experience as manifesting a house, or to take what is experienced as being a house. To perceive a house is for a house to be directly presented to one's experience, to *look* a certain way to one if it is visual perception. And any sort of interpretation is something over and above that.

But although I don't share Hick's reasons for supposing all forms of human experience of God to be indirect, the fact remains that the distinction between direct and indirect perception is quite clear in the sphere of sense perception, as was brought out earlier. If the same distinction can be found within spiritual perception, both sorts will have to be dealt with. Until very recently, when I discussed a draft of this chapter in a seminar, I was not convinced that indirect *mystical* perception actually occurs. I thought I was unable to distinguish cases ordinarily so classified, like those cited in (23)–(25) above, from what I call "indirect perceptual recognition", taking something to manifest, indicate, or be the effect of, the divine presence or activity. In visual sense perception the distinction is clear. In indirect perception, as seeing Reagan on television, something is *presented* to my experience that looks like Reagan, whereas when I take a vapor trail as an indication that a jet plane has passed by recently, nothing presented to my awareness looks like a jet plane. But when people say that they experience God in the beauties of nature or in the words of a sermon, is anything presenting itself to their experience that "looks" like God? Since I took it not to be clear that this question was to be answered affirmatively, I correspondingly took it to be unclear that there is any indirect *perception* here. Indeed, I suspected that in all cases advertised as such, what we really have is a taking X to be an indication of God, where this is so rapid and spontaneous as to be confused with a genuine experiential presentation of God.

However, the students in my seminar brought me to realize that I had been ignoring an obvious possibility. If, as I am deeply committed to hold, we can understand what it is for God to be directly presented to one's awareness, *why shouldn't something that is phenomenologically just like that happen by way of one's direct awareness of something in creation*? If God can appear to me as loving or powerful or glorious when I am not sensorily aware of a field of oats or the words of the Bible, why shouldn't He also appear to me as loving or powerful or glorious when that comes *through* my sense perception of the field of oats or whatever? I now find that I have nothing to say against this possibility, and hence no reason to discredit those who report their cognition of God in these terms rather than in terms of indirect perceptual recognition.

Nevertheless, I will still be focusing on direct perception of God in this book. The main rationale for this is that it is the simpler phenomenon (involving only one object of perception) and hence it should be thoroughly investigated before we pass on to the more complex two-object version. Direct perception will keep us fully occupied.

v. The Experience Is of *God*

(C) Remember that our working criterion for mystical perception is that the experience is, or would be, taken by the subject to be an awareness of God. Just how is this identification to be thought of? What must the subject say, think, or be disposed to say or think, in order to satisfy it? If she uses the name 'God' or its correlate in some other language to identify what is perceived, that would do it, provided we lack reason to suppose that her use of the name is markedly idiosyncratic. But of course the name isn't the heart of the matter. An experience would still count provided the subject took the object to be of a certain sort. But what sort? To answer this question would be to specify a set of necessary conditions for X's being God, or do something looser along the same line, such as providing a list of "God-making characteristics". I don't want to go into that here; our purposes will be satisfied by the following. We can just refer to the characteristics deemed to be most central to God in the leading theistic religions—Judaism, Christianity, and Islam—and say that so long as the subject is thinking of the perceived object in some such terms, she is identifying that object as God. No doubt, there is much controversy both within each religion and between these religions on various points concerning the divine nature. Nevertheless, we can identify a (loosely demarcated and open-ended) set of characteristics on which there is a massive consensus, provided we don't insist on too much precision in the specification of each. These would include *being the source of existence of all other than itself, goodness, justice, moral lawgiver, having a purpose for the creation, and offering salvation to mankind.*[16] So long as S is thinking of the perceived object as being (roughly) within this (roughly demarcated) territory, she is identifying the object as God.

It will strike some readers as exceedingly odd that I limit mystical perception to cases in which subjects identify (or would identify) what is experienced as God, construed theistically. How about devotees of nontheistic religions, like Buddhism and some forms of Hinduism? And how about people with no religious commitment at all? Can't they have mystical experiences? The first stage of an answer is once again to point out the technical and stipulative character of my terms 'mystical perception' and 'mystical experience'. I by no means wish to rule out by terminological fiat the possibility that a monistic Hindu may be directly aware of an ultimate, impersonal undifferentiated unity, still less that he may have a "mystical experience", more ordinarily so called. My reason for separating out a category of "theistically interpreted mystical experiences" stems from my central epistemological con-

[16]One does not have to be using these terms univocally with their use in application to human beings in order to satisfy our condition.

cerns. In Chapter 5 I will show that when we think about the practice of forming beliefs about the Ultimate on the basis of putative perceptions thereof, we must distinguish at least as many such practices as there are distinct religions. At that point I will further narrow my focus to Christian mystical perception. But this is basically a bookeeping matter, a matter of how best to set things up for the central epistemological argument. Experiences of other religions—theistic and nontheistic—will not be ignored, dismissed, or discriminated against. Their claims to equal treatment will be given a full hearing in Chapter 7.

To be sure, it is not strictly accurate to say that I limit mystical experiences to those that are theistically interpreted. I have already alluded to the point that our criterion will not pick out all members of the category of direct perception of God, since one may in fact be perceiving God without realizing that it is God one is perceiving or even, perhaps, that one is perceiving anything at all. But, of course, the monistic Hindu would claim that he is neither perceiving a theistic God nor supposing himself to do so. And as just pointed out, that case will receive a hearing. However, this discussion suggests one interesting possible subtype of unwitting perception of God. Suppose that a personal deity is the being that is perceived in certain forms of experience not only in theistic religions but also in nontheistic religions. In that case devotees the latter religions would be directly aware of God, even though they wouldn't be thinking of the perceived object in theistic terms as a personal agent.

Many writers object to thinking of God as a particular "object" of experience. Here is one of the more discriminating expositions of this idea from Paul Tillich's *Systematic Theology* (1953).

> In the cognitive realm everything toward which the cognitive act is directed is considered an object, be it God or a stone, be it one's self or a mathematical definition. In the logical sense everything about which a predication is made is, by this very fact, an object. The theologian cannot escape making God an object in the logical sense of the word, just as the lover cannot escape making the beloved an object of knowledge and action. The danger of logical objectification is that it never is merely logical. It carries ontological presuppositions and implications. If God is brought into the subject-object structure of being, he ceases to be the ground of being and becomes one being among others (first of all, a being beside the subject who looks at him as an object). He ceases to be the God who is really God. . . . If there is a knowledge of God, it is God who knows himself through man. God remains the subject, even if he becomes a logical object. . . . But there is a third sense in which the objectifying scheme is used. Making an object can mean depriving it of its subjective elements, making it into something which is an object and *nothing* but an object. Such an object is a "thing", in German a *Ding*, something which is altogether *bedingt* ("conditioned"). The word "thing" does not necessarily have this connotation; it can stand for everything that is. But it is counter to our linguistic feeling to call human beings "things". They

are more than things and more than mere objects. They are selves and therefore bearers of subjectivity.[17] (Pp. 191–92)

Using Tillich's terminology, I am thinking of God as an *object* of perception only in the "logical" sense. A term like 'object' may have connotations that are inappropriate in this context, but these connotations do not constitute any part of its meaning. In thinking of God as an "object" of experience, I am not suggesting that God is simply "one being alongside others" (He is quite a special being), much less that He is a lifeless, inanimate *thing* that passively allows Himself to be scrutinized. On the contrary, He is a supreme personal being with Whom we are in personal interaction and Who is eminently active in our lives. Nor does speaking of God as an object of experience (or even as an "item" in the phenomenal field) imply that He is there *alongside* others. ("in the knowledge of God a posteriority does not mean that we look out into the world with a neutral faculty of knowledge and then think that we can discover God there directly or indirectly among the realities that present themselves to us objectively" Rahner 1978, p. 53.) That may or may not be the case. He could be an object of experience in the basic sense in question even if He is the only thing of which we are aware when we are aware of Him. In short, to say that God is the *object* of some experience implies no more than that some people sometimes experience God, are experientially aware of him, that sometimes God presents Himself to our experience.

People who decry thinking God as an "object" tend to be rather slippery, but it may be that there is a hidden agenda in some or all cases. That is, it may be that their aversion to thinking of God as an object of experience rests on a reluctance or refusal to recognize that there *is* such a being as God Who objectively exists as such, and with whom it behooves us to come to terms whether we like it or not, and whether this is provided for in our "conceptual scheme" or not.[18] If that is what is behind the objection to object-talk, then there is a real issue, and a crucial issue, between us. My talk of God as an object of experience does definitely presuppose that God exists as an objective reality, indeed that He is maximally real. And on this point I am in agreement with the people on whose experiential reports I am relying.

Readers may be surprised that we have not included *ineffability* among the central features of mystical experience. One cannot but be struck, in our examples as well as elsewhere, by the constantly reiterated insistence that the experience is *indescribable*. For example, "a plentitude of which I cannot speak: a plenitude which is not bodily but spiritual, of which I can say nothing (3)." Again,

[17]This last point is especially associated with the work of Martin Buber, particularly his *I and Thou*, trans. Ronald Gregor Smith (Edinburgh: T. & T. Clark, 1937).

[18]I will not try to decide whether this characterization fits Tillich. In this connection see his denial that God is a "a being", even the highest being, and his denial that we can speak of God as existing (1953, chap. 10, esp. pp. 261–63).

> (26) . . . although God seems at that moment very far from the soul, He sometimes reveals His grandeur to it in the strangest way imaginable. This way is indescribable; and I do not think that anyone could believe or understand it who has not already experienced it. (St. Teresa 1957, chap. 20, p. 139)

Citations could be multiplied ad libitum. These repeated asseverations have led James to include ineffability among his four distinguishing marks of mysticism. Nevertheless, I feel that this is blown out of all proportion. Despite statements like those just quoted, our subjects manage to say quite a lot about their experiences and about what they take themselves to be experiencing. This is well illustrated in our examples. In sections ix and x we will be surveying the variety of features and activities of God which people take themselves to be experientially aware of, and the variety of subjective features of the experiences that are reported. In the face of all this one can hardly take literally the claim that the experiences are *ineffable*. I believe that such claims are best taken as denials that the experience can be specified literally in terms taken from common experience, so that recourse must be had to metaphor, analogy, symbols, and so on, if one is to give a detailed account.[19] But that is a situation in which we not uncommonly find ourselves when dealing with matters that fall outside the range of common experience, whether in science, religion, or philosophy. It is by no means peculiar to mystical experience.

vi. Some Differences in Mystical Perceptions

Let's look for a moment at some of the important differences over which our basic category ranges. We have already considered one, the sensory–nonsensory contrast. Another is the distinction between focal and background experiences. The former get the big press: these are cases in which the awareness of God occupies one's attention to the exclusion of all else. It is natural that we should be preoccupied with the more extreme forms of the phenomenon, since they present the salient features in sharp relief. But it would be a methodological artifact to suppose that mystical perception is confined to such cases. There are many testimonies to a sense of the presence of God that is of much lower intensity and persists for long periods of time as a constant background for the flux of everyday experience.

> (27) God surrounds me like the physical atmosphere. He is closer to me than my own breath. In him literally I live and move and have my being. (James 1902, p. 71)

[19]Indeed, some of our subjects are more discriminating in their disclaimers. Thus in (1) we find "I feel the impossibility of describing the thing by any of our usual images"; in (5), "Indeed, it seemed to come in waves and waves of liquid love; for I could not express it in any other way". That is, not in any way other than metaphorically.

(28) *This experience of the reality of God in Christ*, precisely at a point of doubt, when belief in Christ was being taken from me, has become a strong inspiration for the future. The words of the Bible and prayers have subsequently become the internal contact with God that I now continually possess, even when in difficulties. (Unger 1976, p. 115)

(29) This divine Saviour said to me: that He would endow me with a new grace, still greater than all those that He had hitherto bestowed on me, which was that I should never lose sight of Him, *having Him always intimately present*: a favour which I regard as the crown of all those that I have hitherto received of His infinite mercy, as since that time I have had this divine Saviour *intimately present* without any interruption. (St. Margaret Mary, quoted in Poulain 1950, pp. 85–86)

Just as one can sensorily perceive the same physical object with different degrees of attention, and just as a sensorily perceived object can be more or less within the focus of attention, so it would seem to be with the perception of God. I see no reason to think that these long-lasting background awarenesses of God are a radically different sort of phenomenon from the overwhelming momentary awareness that blots out all else. Since the subject identifies the object as the same, and since some of what that object presents itself as being is the same, it would seem to be the part of reason to suppose that the background awareness is simply a lower level variant of the same sort of phenomenon we have in the big, splashy Cecil B. de Mille experiences. Hence I feel justified in taking what we can learn from the latter as a key to the nature and status of the former.

There is also the difference between experiences that come spontaneously, without prior preparation, and those that occur in the context of a systematic discipline that is, at least in part, aimed at the cultivation and development of experienced communion with God. As I've already made explicit, I am drawing on both groups for my examples. I see no reason to suppose that any of the epistemological and ontological issues with which we are concerned will be significantly affected by this difference. I won't try to argue for that here. Such support as I give for it will consist in the success with which I deal with the issues without taking this distinction into account.

Since I am not specially concerned with systematically cultivated mystical perception, I will not be dealing with many interesting features of mystical traditions in monastic communities. In the context of the Catholic mystical tradition, this means that I will not be using distinctions between different stages of the mystic life, distinctions between "the prayer of quiet", "simple union", "ecstatic union", and so on.[20] All these stages exhibit the generic features I take to be definitive of my category.[21]

[20]For systematic treatments of these stages see Underhill 1955, Poulain 1950.

[21]For support for this judgment, see Farges 1926 and Poulain 1950.

vii. "Religious Experience"

A word is in order concerning the relation of my category to "religious experience". I often find the use of this term to be obfuscating, and I try to avoid it wherever possible. In the widest sense, 'religious experience' ranges over any experiences one has in connection with one's religious life, including any joys, fears, or longings one has in a religious context. Indeed, the term is not restricted to particular states of consciousness. There is also the use of 'experience' that it has in such phrases as 'He has had a lot of experience in this job'. When 'experience' is so used in 'religious experience' it can cover the whole extent of one's religious life—one's thoughts, reasoning, doubts, and insights about God and one's relations thereto, one's striving to lead the Christian life, one's successes and failures in this enterprise, and so on. My category is much narrower; it embraces only those experiences in which it seems that God "appears" or "presents Himself" to one as so-and-so. This is sufficient reason for my avoidance of 'religious experience', but there are others. The term has come to be used recently in certain circles for a "dimension" or "aspect" of all experience, an understanding that can be traced back to the influence of Schleiermacher.

> The knowledge of God is, nevertheless, a *transcendental* knowledge because man's basic and original orientation toward absolute mystery, which constitutes his fundamental experience of God, is a permanent existential of man as a spiritual subject. This means that the explicit, conceptual and thematic knowledge, which we usually think of when we speak of the knowledge of God . . . is a reflection upon man's transcendental orientation towards mystery. . . . It is not, however, the original and foundational mode of the transcendental experience of this mystery. It belongs necessarily to the very nature of human knowledge that thought is self-reflexive, that we think of a concrete object *within* the *infinite* and apparently empty horizon of thinking itself.
>
> We are oriented towards God. This original experience is always present. . . . This unthematic and ever-present experience, this knowledge of God which we always have even when we are thinking of and concerned with anything but God, is the permanent ground from out of which that thematic knowledge of God emerges which we have in explicitly religious activity and in philosophical reflection. (Rahner 1978, pp. 52–53)[22]

This again is markedly different from the subject matter of this book. I do not deny that there is a dimension of all experience that has the status and function claimed by the likes of Rahner, though I am not completely sold on it either. However, the present point is that my concerns in this book lie elsewhere.

Let me further say, as yet another reason for steering clear of 'religious experience' talk, that I find it a particularly unfortunate feature of much con-

[22]See also the treatment of "limit experiences" in Tracy 1978, chap. 5, and the references there to Lonergan. Another good source is Edwards 1983.

temporary literature that the term is used as if it had a single clear and well-demarcated meaning. People will, without any antecedent tying down of the concept, ask with respect to a given experience whether it really is (counts as) a *religious experience*. Long discussions will be conducted on whether religious experience is cognitive, is essentially a matter of feeling, is confined to certain special "peak experiences", plays a central role in religion, provides evidence for religious beliefs, and so on.

Our concentration on putative direct awareness of God should not be taken in any way as a derogation of other forms of religious experience, including other forms that possess, or claim to possess, a cognitive significance. In particular, it is worth stressing that the general experience of the presence and activity of God in one's life, the more or less constant and pervasive sense that God's providence is shaping the pattern of one's life, that God is guiding, sustaining, and directing one, can be of enormous religious importance, and may well contribute something to the grounds of one's religious beliefs—even if none of this ever erupts into anything that clearly presents itself as a direct *presentation* of God to one's consciousness, even of a low-level, peripheral sort. Moreover, one's experience of the changes in one's life that follow a conversion, or one's experience of the gradual improvement of one's character in the course of sincere attempts to open oneself up to the influence of the Holy Spirit, can be of cognitive significance, in addition to other forms of significance, as presenting explananda that are naturally explained theologically.[23] I am concentrating in this book on clear cases of (putative) direct awareness of God, since I have some definite epistemological points to make about it. But I hope that I am not guilty of supposing that importance resides only with topics I am capable of handling.

viii. Does Mystical Perception Involve a Genuine Presentation?

To sum up the discussion to date, we are using the term 'mystical perception' for putative direct experiential awareness of God. Despite the fact that my category only partially overlaps mystical experience usually so-called, the term is being employed *faute de mieux*, since, for reasons just given, I am especially anxious to avoid the term 'religious experience' for my category, and I feel the need for something more streamlined than 'awareness (perception) of God', even with the 'putative' tacitly understood. Mystical perception is direct in the same way as (face-to-face) sense perception of objects; the object is not perceived through the perception of some other object, but there is a distinction between the conscious experience involved and the object perceived. Thus it is less direct than our awareness of our own conscious states and less direct than the awareness of the One in "classical" mystical experi-

[23]These other modes of experience will be brought into the picture in Chapter 8.

ence. Although mystical perception may or may not involve sensory content, I will be focusing on the non-sensory variety, since, in my judgment, it has a better claim to be a genuine direct perception of God.

In the remainder of this chapter I want to consider more carefully and more critically whether what I call 'mystical perception' does indeed deserve the title 'perception'. Since we have developed the concept of perception from our familiarity with sense perception, any attempt to extend it to non-sensory modes will involve arguing that there is a basic commonality across this divide. That is, we will have to show that non-sensory direct awareness can be properly construed as another species of the same genus to which vision, audition, and the other modes of sense perception belong. This will require giving an analysis of the generic concept of perception and showing that the conditions of its application are or can be satisfied by "mystical perception".

In carrying this out I will give separate treatment to the intrinsic (internal) and the extrinsic (external) features of perception. I will first consider the nature of perception as a mode of consciousness, its phenomenological character, what the subject seems to herself to be consciously undergoing when perceiving something. Then I will consider what further conceptual requirements there might be. As for the intrinsic requirements I will argue that mystical perception does in fact satisfy them. But since the external features have to do with the "success" features of the term 'perceive', including the existence of the object and its being in the right relation to the perceiver, and since I have already disavowed any intention to show in this chapter that those requirements are satisfied by mystical perception, I will confine myself to arguing that it is *possible* for "mystical perception" to satisfy them.

At the outset let me acknowledge the many salient differences between sense perception and mystical perception, over and above the fact that the latter may not involve sensory content. Sense perception is insistently and unavoidably present in all our waking hours, and the experiential awareness of God is a rare phenomenon except for a very few souls. Sense perception, especially vision, is vivid and richly detailed, bursting with information, whereas the experience of God is dim, meager, and obscure. Sense perception is shared by all human beings, whereas the experience of God, though more widely dispersed than is often supposed,[24] is still by no means universal. But despite these differences I want to claim a generic identity of structure.

As intimated earlier, what I take to be definitive of perceptual consciousness is that something (or so it seems to the subject) *presents* itself to the subject's awareness as so-and-so—as red, round, loving, or whatever. When I stand before my desk with my eyes closed and then open them, the most striking difference in my consciousness is that items that I was previously

[24]In Stark and Glock 1968 there is a report of a survey of a wide range of Christian denominations that indicates that 75 percent of Christians take themselves to have been at some time aware of the presence of God.

merely thinking about or remembering, if conscious of them in any way, are now *present* to me; they occupy space in my visual field. They are *given* to my awareness in a way that sharply contrasts with anything I can do by my own devices to conjure them up in imagination, memory, or abstract thought. I can't expect everyone to agree with this claim; the philosophy of perception is at least as controversial as other areas of philosophy. But it seems clear to me that this is what most centrally differentiates perceptual consciousness from other modes of consciousness, both from nonexperiential cognition of the types just mentioned and also from other modes of experience, like feeling depressed, that do not involve the presentation of objects. The agreement on my claim will be maximized if all parties are clear as to its purely phenomenological character. I am not saying at this point, as I will be when I present the Theory of Appearing, in section xi, that this mode of consciousness is what perception *is*, that it is both necessary and sufficient for perceiving X that X be given to one's awareness in this way. No, at this point I am making the less ambitious claim that this phenomenon of apparent presentation of an object is what differentiates perceptual consciousness from other modes of consciousness. This can be accepted even by those who hold that this impression of object givenness is only superficial and that it masks much more complex structures that are necessary for genuine perception.

Let me say a bit more about this relationship that from the side of the subject is called *direct awareness* and from the side of the object is called *presentation, givenness*, or *appearance*. It is a mode of cognition that is essentially independent of any conceptualization, belief, judgment, or any other application of general concepts to the object, though it typically exists in close connection with the latter. It is what Russell (1910–11) called "acquaintance" and Moore (1953, chap. 2) called "direct apprehension", though I don't wish to be saddled with all the philosophical views attached to this notion by these philosophers and others.[25] As I see it, for something to *look* red to me is not the same as for me to *take* it to be red, *construe* or *conceptualize* it as red, even though its looking red typically evokes those reactions if the subject has the conceptual equipment so to react. Moreover, appearance is a nonintentional relationship by any of the usual tests. X can't appear to me unless it exists; and if X appears to me and X = Y, it follows that Y appears to me.

This concept of the direct awareness of objects (particulars), though it has had a long and illustrious history, has been subjected to severe criticism by the nineteenth-century idealists and their pragmatist epigoni[26], all of whom were convinced that there could be no form of cognition that is not mediated

[25]These associated views include the view that physical objects cannot be presented, that beliefs about what is presented are infallible, incorrigible, and indubitable, and that all empirical knowledge is built up on the sole basis of presentations.

[26]See Bosanquet 1911, Bk. 2, chap. 9; Bradley 1914, chap. 8, and 1922, Terminal Essay II; Blanshard 1939, chaps. 25–28; Peirce, "Questions Concerning Certain Faculties Claimed for Man", in 1934, Vol. 5; Dewey 1938, chap. 8.

by general concepts and judgment, a view that seems to me a baseless prejudice. Hence they took it that something's looking red to me just *is* my taking it to be red or thinking of it as red. The roots of that view are Kantian, and by now it has attained the status of a dogma in the philosophy and psychology of perception.[27] I suspect that an important source of the view is a confusion between direct awareness of an object, X, and awareness of X *as* possessing some property, P (or the knowledge, or justified belief, *that* the object has P). The latter, obviously, involves conceptualization and judgment, but it does not follow that the mere awareness of the object does so. More recently the concept has fallen victim to the equally arbitrary prejudice of analytical philosophers against unanalyzable concepts. In opposition to all this it seems clear that sensory experience essentially involves a *presentation* of objects to consciousness in a way that does not *necessarily* involve the application of general concepts to those objects or taking them to such-and-such, and that it is this feature of perception that clearly distinguishes it from just thinking about an object, remembering it, or fantasizing about it. No doubt, in normal perception this direct awareness of X is intimately entangled with conceptualization and judgment, but in unusual cases it can exist alone, and even when it doesn't it is recognizable as that element of the complex that makes it *perceptual* consciousness rather than abstract thought. After all, conceptualization and judgment are common to normal perception and abstract thought. Therefore, they can't be what distinguishes perception from the latter.[28] I shall take it, then, that it is both necessary and sufficient for a state of consciousness to be a state of perceptual consciousness that it (seem to the subject to) involve something's presenting itself to the subject, S, as so-and-so, as purple, zigzagged, acrid, loud, or whatever. A case of perceptual consciousness is a case of something's looking, smelling . . . so-and-so to S. And so the question of whether mystical perception satisfies the internal requirements for being perception is just the question of whether it is, phenomenologically, a case of God's experientially appearing to the subject *as* such-and-such.

In taking this position on perceptual consciousness, I am *not* denying that a person's conceptual scheme and beliefs can affect the way in which an object presents itself to him. Things do look and sound differently to us after we are familiar with them. My house presents an appearance to me now that is different from the first time I walked into it. Whereas Stravinski's *The Rite of Spring* sounded like a formless cacophony the first time I heard it, it now presents itself to me as a complex interweaving of themes. In saying this I am not going back on my assertion that X's presenting itself to one's awareness as P is not the same as S's *taking* S to be P. But I am acknowledging that X's looking (sounding . . .) P to one *can be influenced* by S's knowledge, beliefs,

[27]Good recent presentations are found in Runzo 1977, 1982.

[28]See the earlier discussion of Hick's view that all perception involves "perceiving as", and the reference to Dretske's attack on this view in fn. 15.

and conceptualizations, even though X's looking a certain way to S does not consist in S knowing or believing something about it or conceptualizing it in a certain way.[29]

All this puts us in a position to consider the question of whether mystical experience exhibits this perception-making feature, whether it involves an (apparent) presentation of something (God) to the subject as being or doing so-and-so. This consideration can be succinct. In section i the first salient feature we found in our paradigm cases of mystical experience was that (as it seems to the subject) "something, viz., God, has been *presented* or *given* to their consciousness, in generically the same way as that in which objects in the environment are (apparently) *presented* to one's consciousness in sense perception". This is richly exhibited in our sample of reports. To be sure, our sources do not couch their reports in my technical terminology. Nor do normal reports of sense perception. Nevertheless, it seems clear that the experiences reported are naturally construed in terms of *presentation* and *direct awareness*. This is particularly explicit in cases (2)–(7), but it is sufficiently clear in the rest as well. Thus we may take it that mystical experience satisfies the phenomenological requirement for being a mode of perception.

I don't know what could be said against this except to claim that these people are all confused about the phenomenological character of their experience. Let's consider the following charge.

> These people were all having strongly affective experiences that, because of their theological assumptions and preoccupations, they confused with a direct experience of God. Thus (1) was in a unusual state of exaltation that he *interpreted* as the power and goodness of God penetrating him. In (4) Suso experienced, as he says "a manifestation of the sweetness of Eternal Life in the sensations of silence and of rest", all of which can be

[29]This means that I need not take sides in the debate currently raging among scholars of mysticism over whether there is a culturally neutral, common experiential core that underlies the "interpretation" given this in terms of particular theologies. For common experiential core partisans see Stace 1960, Zaehner 1961, and Smart 1965. On the other side we have the claim that the theology and other aspects of the interpretative framework of the subject influence the intrinsic experiential character of the experience, so that there is no mode of experience that is common to, say, Christian and Buddhist mystics. See especially Katz 1978 and other essays in the same volume. Since I recognize that belief systems *can* affect the phenomenal character of experience, but also recognize that it does not do so in every case, I can let this dispute be settled as it will and continue to maintain the views put forth here.

Although I recognize the subject's conceptual scheme and belief tendencies can affect the *way* something appears to her, I do *not* acknowledge that it can affect *what it is* that appears to her. When I look at my living room, the same objects present themselves to my visual awareness as on the first occasion I saw it (with that furniture in place), even though they look differently to me on the two occasions. It is essential not to confuse what object(s) is appearing to my experience, and what it appears as. This distinction has also succumbed to the current obsession with the omnipotence of conceptualization. It is frequently maintained that our conceptualization and judgments determine *what* we are aware of (perceive), as well as how it appears to us. This seems to me to fly in the face of facts. Contrary to Runzo 1982, it is the same thing, the same piece of equipment that the nuclear physicist and the primitive tribesman sees in the laboratory, even though what they take it to be (and, no doubt, how it looks to them) varies widely.

enjoyed without God Himself appearing to his experience in any way. Person (5) was experiencing some unusual bodily sensations that he described metaphorically, first as like a wave of electricity going through him and then as "waves and waves of liquid love". Another possibility is that the person is suddenly seized with an extremely strong conviction of the presence of God, together with sensations and feelings that seem to confirm it. Thus Teresa in (2) says that she "had a most distinct feeling the He was always on my right hand, a witness of all I did".

It is conceivable that one should suppose that a purely affective experience or a strongly held conviction should involve the experiential presentation of God when it doesn't, especially if there is a strong need or longing for such a direct awareness. But even if an individual's account of the phenomenology of his or her own experience is not infallible, it must certainly be taken seriously. Who is in a better position to determine whether S is having an experience as if of something's presenting itself to S as φ than S? We would need strong reasons to override the subject's confident report of the character of her experience. And where could we find such reasons? I suspect that most people who put forward these alternative diagnoses do so because they have general philosophical reasons for supposing either that God does not exist or that no human being could perceive Him, and they fail to recognize the difference between a phenomenological account of object presentation and the fact that a certain object, *as the subject conceives it to be*, presents itself to the subject's awareness. In any event, once we get straight about all this, I cannot see any reason for doubting the subjects' account of the character of their experience, whatever reasons there may be for doubting that God Himself does appear to them.

In Proudfoot 1985 we find some interesting confusions that undoubtedly contribute to the failure to recognize the essentially nonconceptual, nonjudgmental character of *appearance* or *presentation*, both in SP and MP, and contribute to the supposition that these putative experiential presentations really involve an *interpretation* of an essentially subjective experience. In particular there is a confusion between what is involved in identifying an experience as of a certain sort and what the experience *is* or consists of. Thus Proudfoot repeatedly argues that since concepts are involved in identifying an experience as *religious*, as *mystical*, as *noetic*, the experience itself is not "independent of concepts".

> Schleiermacher offers distinguishing marks to enable one to identify the appropriate feeling. Though he argues that the experience is prior to concepts and beliefs . . . the religious moment cannot be specified without reference to God, the infinite, or the whole. Reference to such concepts is required for the description or identification of the experience. Beyond that, Schleiermacher even says that a criterion of the religious experience is that one believes it to be produced by God or the universe. Reference to a belief about the cause of the experience is built into the rules for identifying the experience. (Pp. 13–14)

> To summarize, the account of piety as an affective state, which Schleiermacher offers in *On Religion*, contains two components. First, he contends that ideas and principles are foreign to religion and that piety is a matter of feeling, sense, or taste distinct from and prior to concepts and beliefs. Second, he identifies piety as a sense and taste for the infinite, an identification that requires . . . a judgment that this feeling is the result of divine operation. Both components are required by Schleiermacher's program, and they are incompatible. (P. 15)

> In *The Christian Faith* as in *On Religion*, Schleiermacher defends the incoherent thesis that the religious consciousness is both independent of thought and can be identified only by reference to concepts and beliefs. (P. 18)

> The attempts of scholars as diverse as Eliade and Phillips to preclude issues of explanation from entering into accounts of religious experience and belief are undercut by the recognition that explanatory commitments are assumed in the identification of an experience as religious. (Pp. 217–18)

Proudfoot presumably would apply this same argument to me and contend that since I am picking out what I call 'mystical experience' by reference to how the subject does or would regard it, I am inconsistent in supposing such experiences to be basically nonconceptual and nonjudgmental in nature. But this line of argument is either a confusion or a gross nonsequitur. From the fact that we use concepts to identify something as of a certain type (How else?!), it does *not* follow that *what* we are identifying "involves" concepts and judgments. If it did, we would be unable to classify anything but cognitive psychological states. From the fact that we use a concept to pick out cabbages as vegetables, it does not follow that cabbages are, have, or use concepts or judgments. Closer to home, pick your favorite case of a conscious state that does not involve concepts and judgments in its own nature—a pain or a throb. But to identify a state as a pain I must employ a concept, the concept of pain, naturally. But then, we see that we were mistaken in supposing that pains are nonconceptual!! I can't see that this argument is any better than the one about cabbages, and the same applies to Proudfoot's assault on Schleiermacher. To be sure, it may well be that Schleiermacher cannot, consistently with his other key views, maintain that "piety" or the "sense of the infinite" or the "feeling of absolute dependence" is free of concepts, for it may be that he does so characterize these states that they do involve one or more *beliefs*, for example, that everything depends on God for its existence. But if so, this will be because of his *characterization* of the states, not because he uses concepts to classify them in a certain way.

Not all theorists who dissent from our reading of the character of mystical experience are unbelievers or skeptics, nor do they all denigrate the importance of mystical experience. Some of the leading Catholic mystical theologians oppose the idea that mystical experience involves a direct awareness of (what seems to be) God. Thus Saudreau, *The Mystic State* (1924), holds that "in the mystical state . . . there is this double element: a superior knowledge of God, which, although general and confused, gives a very high idea of his incomprehensible greatness; secondly, an unreasoning but very precious love which God himself communicates, and to which the soul, in spite of all its efforts, could never raise itself" (65). That is, Saudreau holds that mystical experience involves a certain kind of supernaturally communicated *knowledge* of God that is very convincing to the subject, along with strong affective reactions of love. But this does not amount to perception. On the contrary, what the mystic apprehends is propositional, "the truths known by faith: the greatness, perfections, amiability, incomprehensibility of God" (57). He interprets talk of God's presence within or to the person as expressing an inference from the effects God works on the soul to the agent of those effects (77).[30] Saudreau is anxious to insist that the Catholic mystics base themselves on the faith of the church and do not make any claims to be cutting themselves loose from that, going by their own experiences alone. Moreover, he is emphasizing the "obscure" character of the awareness of God in mystical experience, stressed by many mystics, and he is anxious to distinguish the kind of awareness of God found in the mystics from the blinding clarity of the beatific vision. But his view flies in the face of the strong and consistent testimony contained in our sources, and in many more like them, to the effect that it is possible, and actual, that human beings are sometimes aware of something appearing to them, something that they take to be God.

An additional reason for accepting our subjects' account of the phenomenology of their experiences is that the more sophisticated of them explicitly consider alternative construals and reject them in favor of the view that God Himself is present to their experience. Thus in (7) Teresa considers the possibility that "He was present only by his grace", that is, that her experience was produced by God for sanctifying purposes but that she was not directly aware of God Himself. But she rejects this as a false reading of her experience. "I could not believe that, because, as I am saying, He seemed to me to be present Himself". Again Angela of Foligno in (3) contrasts the direct perception of God as "plentitude" with God's instilling into the soul "fire, love, and sometimes sweetness; and the soul believes this comes from God, and delights therein. But she does not yet know, or see, that He dwells in her; she perceives His grace, in which she delights". Here Angela is not dealing with alternative construals of the same experience but rather with experiences of different sorts enjoyed at different times. But again the point is that she clearly distinguishes the types and, at certain times, identifies her state as one

[30]For an excellent discussion of this view, along with an allied view in Browne 1925, see Wainwright 1981, pp. 161–65. I am taking Saudreau to be contesting my account of the *phenomenology* of mystical experience, but that may be a mistake. He may just be contesting the ontology of it, holding that, however it seems to the subject, she cannot be directly perceiving God Himself. That would put his contentions in the same category as those of, e.g., Garrigou-Lagrange, discussed on pp. 61–63.

of directly "seeing" God, rather than as enjoying effects of God's activity. The fact that these people can make these distinctions and are confident in characterizing their experience now in one way and now in another, adds to the credibility of their reports.[31]

ix. Modes of Divine Appearance

However we are not yet out of the woods, vis-à-vis the internal requirement for perception. Remember that our account of sense-perceptual consciousness was that (so it seems) something is presenting itself to one's experience *as* having a certain color, shape, sound, odor, or whatever. Now in order for this generic concept to be applicable to mystical perception, the object doesn't have to be displaying sensory qualia to the subject, any more than something heard has to be displaying visual qualia. We have already defended the proposition that the generic notion of perception is not conceptually tied to any particular selection of phenomenal qualities. But it is tied to the notion of something's presenting itself as phenomenally qualified in some way or other. And is that the case with "mystical perception"?

There is no doubt that our subjects take God to have appeared to them *as* so-and-so. Thus (1) supposes God to have presented Himself to his experience as *goodness* and *power*, and as *communicating* certain messages. Angela in (3) takes God to have presented Himself to her as a *plentitude*, and Suso in (4) as *Shining Brightness*. The author of (5) took the Holy Spirit to present itself to him as "*waves and waves of liquid love*". All these people report ways in which God appeared to their experience, what God was presented to their experience as being or doing.

Let us make a list of some of the "modes of appearance of God" cited in our sources, together with the numbers of quotations in which they are mentioned. It will be useful to divide these into what God is experienced as *being*, and what God is experienced as *doing*.

(A) What God is experienced as *being*.

1. Good. 1, 10
2. Powerful. 1, 25
3. Plentitude. 3, 25
4. Loving. 5, 12, 13
5. Compassionate. 12, 13
6. Wise. 10
7. Glorious. 24

[31]It is clear that Teresa and Angela are not just making a purely phenomenological claim, but are expressing their certainty that God Himself, creator of Heaven and Earth, was what they were directly aware of on these occasions. Nevertheless, this claim carries with it the weaker phenomenological claim, and that is what we are concerned with in this context.

(B) What God is experienced as *doing*.

1. Speaking. 1, 2, 3, 16
2. Forgiving. 6
3. Strengthening. 6
4. Sympathizing. 10

But there is still a problem. Most of the items on this list do not give us what we need for our perceptual model. In sense perception the perceived object presents itself as bearing certain phenomenal qualities—color, shape, pitch, smells, tastes, and "feels". But most of the modes of appearance specified by our sources cannot possibly be regarded as consisting of phenomenal qualities.[32] Consider putative features of God like power, goodness, love, and plenitude, and putative actions like forgiving and strengthening. Power and goodness are complex dispositional properties or bases thereof, dispositions to act in various ways in various situations. And to forgive or to strengthen someone is to successfully engage in certain actions with a certain intention. How can something present itself to one's experience as good or powerful, or as strengthening or forgiving one, in the same sense as that in which it can be experienced as red, round, acrid, or bitter? It looks as if the subject was expecting to be aware of God and hence took herself to be aware of a being that is powerful, supremely good, and infinitely loving. That is not something that could be read off the phenomenal surface of experience.

To come to grips with this objection we must be more explicit than heretofore about the notion of phenomenal qualities and their difference from what we may call "objective" qualities. Let's make the distinction in terms of concepts rather than qualities, since I don't want to assume that the same quality can't be grasped both as phenomenal and as objective.

(1) A *phenomenal* concept is a concept of the intrinsic qualitative distinctiveness of a way of appearing. When I use 'red' in a phenomenal sense in saying that something looks red, I am simply recording the qualitative distinctiveness of the way it visually appears to me, and that's all. I am saying nothing about its continuing powers and proclivities, its entanglements with other things, its intrinsic nature, or anything else that goes beyond the visually sensible character of its look. When, on the other hand, I use 'red' in a *objective* physical-property sense, I am saying something about the disposition of the object to look one or another way under one or another set of circumstances, and/or its physical structure, powers, or capacities. Most of our concepts fall into the "objective" category. There is a rather limited number of qualitatively distinctive ways in which things can present themselves to our experience.[33] And even with respect to these, the terms that express the

[32]I am indebted to Tom Downing for first calling this problem to my attention.

[33]At least, there is a very limited number of basic or atomic ways, and as I shall soon be pointing out, we are not much given to working with phenomenal concepts of complex modes of appearing.

phenomenal concepts thereof will also be used for associated objective concepts, as the example of 'red' shows.

Next, let's note that we frequently report how something looks, or otherwise appears, not by recording a phenomenal distinctiveness of the appearance, but by conceptualizing it in some other way. The other sorts of "appears as . . ." concepts can be classified as follows.

(2) *Comparative*. This is to say what sort of object can be expected to appear, in these circumstances or in normal circumstances, as this object is appearing. Thus to say 'This tie looks red (to me now)' could be to say 'This tie looks to me now as a red tie would be expected to look under normal conditions'. Here we are not using a phenomenal concept of red or any other phenomenal concept. Rather, we are using objective concepts of red tie, normal conditions, and so on, and characterizing this look by comparing it with other looks characterized in these objective terms.

(3) *Doxastic*. This is to say something about the belief to which this appearance could be expected to give rise. To use the doxastic concept of looking red in saying 'The tie looks red' is to say 'The tie looks so as to normally lead one to believe that it is red'. Here, again, none of the concepts employed are phenomenal, even the concept of 'red', for the belief that the tie is red, to which the look is being said to normally give rise, is the belief that the tie has a certain physical property.

(4) *Epistemic*. This is like (3), except that the look is characterized in terms of what beliefs it can justify or provide an adequate basis for rather than in terms of what beliefs it can be expected to engender. Here 'The tie looks red' means 'If one formed the belief that the tie was red on the basis of the way it looks, that belief would be justified'.

Please note that we are not distinguishing different ways or modes of appearing (looking) but rather different ways of conceptualizing, specifying, or identifying appearances. One and the same look of the tie to one and the same person at a certain time could be reported correctly in each of these four ways.

It is important to note that a phenomenal concept is, so to say, always in the background even when not explicitly employed. If I make a true report by using a comparative concept in saying 'X looks red', I am presupposing that there is some qualitative distinctiveness to the appearance that could be captured by a phenomenal concept, even though I am using no such concept at the moment. For I am supposing that there is some way in which an X like this looks under normal conditions, and this way would have its intrinsic nature captured by a phenomenal concept. The same comment is to be made for the doxastic and epistemic concepts. In other words, when we report appearances by the use of comparative, doxastic, or epistemic appear–concepts, we are conceptualizing appearances by some of their relational features. But something can enter into relations only if it has an intrinsic nature to constitute what enters into those relations; this intrinsic nature is what is captured by a phenomenal concept.

Now for the bearing of all this on our problem. Our critic was pointing out that such concepts as power, goodness, and love are not phenomenal concepts. And so they are not. However, that does not show that our sources could not be accurately reporting how God appears to their experience by using such concepts. We have just noted various alternatives to the use of phenomenal concepts in specifying how something looks or otherwise appears. In particular, there are comparative concepts. To further illustrate this with sense perception, I could correctly report that X looked like a house or a Porsche or a bald eagle or tasted like a white Burgundy or sounded like Handel, or, to switch to the particular, that something looked like Susie's house or Jason's Porsche, thereby giving you an idea of how it looked, tasted, or sounded. Yet I am using objective, nonphenomenal concepts in doing so. No doubt, in each case some complex pattern of visual, gustatory, or auditory qualia is being presented by virtue of the awareness of which I can tell that the object looks like a house, Jason's Porsche, or whatever.[34] And no doubt, it is in principle possible to form and use a phenomenal concept of just that phenomenal pattern. But we rarely make use of any such concepts, and for good reasons. The diversity of such patterns is enormous; we could hardly put a concept of each such distinctive pattern in our repertoire, even if we restricted ourselves to those we actually encounter. Nor do there seem to be any intuitively natural principles for classifying such patterns into types on the basis of intrinsic features.[35] Hence what we do instead is to group such patterns, such complex "looks", into types on the basis of extrinsic features, most usually on the basis of how a certain sort of objective thing (event, state of affairs) will look under certain frequently recurring types of conditions. Thus we group the phenomenally heterogeneous looks of houses, under not unusual conditions of observation, into a general concept of 'looks like a house'.[36] Moreover, and this is the point I have been leading up to, we typically report all but the most elementary ways of perceptual appearing in these comparative terms. Except for basic sensory qualities like color, shape, size, loudness, softness and bitterness, we report how a thing looks, sounds, tastes, feels, and so on, by specifying some objective kind that could be expected to look, sound, and so on, in that way. It looks like a cow, it sounds like a

[34]To be sure, people don't always recognize perceived objects solely on the basis of their phenomenal appearance; background knowledge sometimes figures in as well. There will be various Porsches that look, from this distance and angle and in this light, just like Jason's. But I happen to know that Jason's Porsche is parked in this vicinity. See Chapter 2, section ivC, for more on this. However, we can safely suppose that the phenomenal appearance is always at least part of what I go on in recognizing perceived objects; so there will always be some pattern of sensory qualia that plays an essential role in the proceedings.

[35]It is also worth mentioning that we are incapable of analyzing such complex looks into their constituent, basic sensory qualities and spelling out how they are combined into the totality. However, this in itself would be no bar to a liberal use of concepts of complex phenomenal patterns, provided it were feasible to attach a concept to each such pattern, grasped holistically.

[36]These concepts are quite vague; there is no sharp boundary between 'looks like a house' and 'doesn't look like a house'. But this doesn't prevent the concepts from being useful.

gong, it smells like a pineapple. Nor is this due to laziness or an excessive interest in the objective as opposed to the subjective. As we have seen, we are left with no real alternative. Being in no position to classify complex appearances on the basis of their intrinsic features, we are driven to classify them in terms of what objective sorts typically appear in that way. Even where we set out to explain what it is about the look of something that leads us to classify it as, for example, a tree, we rarely have recourse to phenomenal concepts. I am likely to reply that it has a trunk, branches, and leaves—or that it has the look of something with a trunk, branches, and leaves. But these part-looks are being reported in comparative terms just as much as the whole-look that is being explained.

And so it is here. Our sources too are using comparative concepts to specify how they are being appeared to. They are saying something like: I was aware of God as presenting the kind of appearance it would be reasonable to expect a supremely powerful (good, loving) being to present. And so from the premise that they are not using phenomenal concepts, it does not follow that they fail to report how God appears to their experience.

One may doubt that there could be a distinctive way in which a good, powerful, compassionate being, or one who is speaking, forgiving, or comforting, appears to one's experience. But what would be the grounds for such a doubt? That one is unfamiliar with any such modes of appearance from sense perception? But that would flagrantly beg the question. More generally, we should not suppose that we can identify a priori any limits on what objective features can manifest themselves in patterns of phenomenal qualia. Apart from (sense) experience we would not have been able to anticipate that trees are, generally, recognizable by their look, while physicists are not. In mystical perception, too, one can learn only from experience what features and activities of God can be recognizable by the way God presents Himself to one's experience. And as we have seen from our sample, the testimony of experience is that the features we have listed are so identifiable.

To be sure, in using a comparative concept of *looks like a P* to characterize an experience, S is assuming that he knows what a P looks like (in normal conditions or whatever), and this assumption may be challenged. How does (1) know how a supremely good or powerful being would present itself to his experience? How does Angela know how "plentitude" would manifest itself experientally? How does (5) know how a supremely loving being would manifest love to one's experience? The obvious answer is that it is the person's experience with more humble exemplifications of these features that puts him/her in this position. If one has been involved in loving relationships with other human beings, one knows what it is like to be aware of another person's expressing his love for one. One's experience with more or less good human beings has presumably given (1) some idea as to what it is like, experientially, to be interacting with a good person manifesting his goodness, as contrasted with what it is like experientially to be interacting with an evil person manifesting that quality. And so on. This enables the subject to use these comparative terms to conceptualize a certain mode of divine appearance.

Some mystical perceptual judgments do not yield to the above solution. I am thinking particularly of claims by mystics to have learned from experience such things as how God is three persons in one nature.[37] Here we would be hard pressed to find extramystical perceptions on the basis of which one could have learned how a trinity of three persons in one substance manifests itself in experience. Here I will plead modesty of aspiration level. I will be satisfied if I can defend the epistemic status of somewhat more modest perceptual reports about God, such as those illustrated in the passages with which we are working.

To be sure, there is a difficult problem about all this, a problem that affects sense perception as well as mystical perception. Our discussion has reflected the fact that in both areas of perception we typically attribute to external objects, on the basis of perceptual experience, objective properties that go beyond anything that is displayed in that experience, for example, being a dog or being very powerful. In both areas we are, at least tacitly, assuming that the phenomenal complex in question is a reliable indication of the presence of the objective property being attributed. What justification can there be for such assumptions? In the above I cited the subject's experience of such matters. But for that to work, at least on the usual assumptions about nondeductive empirical reasoning, at some stage we must have learned by experience that X looked a certain way and was, for example, a dog. But how did we learn the latter conjunct by experience? If *any* perceptual attribution of objective features rests on an assumption of a reliable-indication connection between a phenomenal appearance and the possession of that feature, how can we get started on building up an empirical basis for such an assumption? Any putative bit of empirical evidence is something we are entitled to only if we are *already* justified in making that kind of assumption in that case. This seems to lead to the unpalatable conclusion that we can never empirically justify such assumptions and hence that either they must remain unjustified or they receive some a priori justification.

This is substantially equivalent to the problem we will be wrestling with in Chapters 2–4, as to how we can justify our reliance on our customary ways of going from experiential presentations to beliefs about objective reality. My treatment of the problem will emerge from those chapters.

x. Phenomenal Qualia of Mystical Perception

So far so good. It can hardly be doubted that we have made progress in framing an intelligible conception of an experience in which one takes God to

[37]See St. Teresa 1957, chap. 34, pp. 304–5.

be appearing to one as so-and-so. But we have not answered our question as to the basic phenomenal qualities of this modality. We have spoken unspecifically of the way(s) in which a loving being might characteristically appear to one. But we have not specified any basic phenomenal qualities for mystical perception, analogous to color and shape for the visual modality and temperature and texture for the tactile. Where does that leave our project?

It must be confessed that we are quite incapable of enumerating the basic phenomenal qualities of which "divine phenomena" are configurations. That's the bad news. But the good news is that we can understand why this should be the case. To see this let's reflect on why it is that we are able to carry off this job for sense perception. The basic point is this. We know quite a bit about the ways in which sensory experience depends in a regular way on its physical, physiological, and psychological conditions. We have discovered quite a bit about the stimulus conditions of various sensory qualities, and we have been able to subject the experience of those qualities to a considerable degree of stimulus control. The more rudimentary forms of these accomplishments predate recorded history; this is why we have had an intersubjectively shared language for sensory qualities since time immemorial. Our knowledge has been greatly extended in the last 150 years by physiological psychology, and as a result we have been able to dimensionalize and study various sensory qualia and gain much more understanding of them and their role in perception. But nothing like this has happened with respect to the perception of God, nor is it at all likely to. We know nothing of the mechanisms of such perception, if indeed it is proper to talk of mechanisms here; nor can we grasp any useful regularities in the conditions under which God will appear in one or another qualitatively distinctive way to one's experience. Perhaps such conditions have to do with God's purposes and intentions, and if so that gives us absolutely no handle on prediction and control. Thus we lack the most elementary prerequisites for analyzing divine appearances into the phenomenal elements, cataloging them, associating them intersubjectively with names, dimensionalizing them, and so on. The reason this is good news is that it explains why we would be in a position of almost complete ignorance here even if there are basic phenomenal qualities that make up the intrinsic character of divine appearances. Thus our deficiencies in this regard give us no reason to doubt that divine appearances do have distinctive phenomenal features.

One nagging worry is the possibility that the phenomenal content of mystical perception wholly consists of affective qualities, various ways the subject is feeling in reaction to what the subject takes to be the presence of God.[38] No doubt such experiences are strongly affectively toned; my sample is entirely typical in this respect. The subjects speak of ecstasy, sweetness, love, delight,

[38] I am grateful to Linda Zagzebski for forcing me to remove my head from the sand and face this issue.

joy, contentment, peace, repose, bliss, awe, and wonder. Our inability to specify any other sorts of non-sensory phenomenal qualities leads naturally to the suspicion that the experience is confined to affective reactions to a believed presence, leaving room for no experiential presentation of God or any other objective reality.

But does this last conclusion follow? How damaging would it be to our subjects' construal of their experiences if these suspicions were well founded? Does the restriction of phenomenal content to affect rule out the possibility of an objective reality's appearing to the subject therein? Well, why should it? After all, my experience of other human beings as friendly, hostile, demanding, open, and warm features prominently my own affective reactions to their demeanor and behavior. But in these cases, it will be said, there is the sensory presentation of the other person on which this is built. Could the affective content carry the whole load?

To come to grips with this question we have to consider the status of sensory phenomenal qualities. What is *their* ontological status? Since the seventeenth century it has been widely held that the "secondary" phenomenal qualities do not really characterize material substances as they are in themselves. Phenomenal colors, sounds, and tastes are purely subjective; they are either ways in which we are conscious (adverbial view) or they are, or qualify, special "mental" objects that have no being over and above their role in furnishing phenomenal content to experience. Berkeley and others have argued that we cannot pick and choose among sensory qualities in this way; if some are purely subjective, they all are. And the view that they are all subjective is one that has not infrequently been taken. The point of this excursus on the status of sensory qualities is that even if, as seems possible, sensory phenomenal qualities are as subjective as affective qualities, that does not prevent them from serving as a phenomenal vehicle of the perception of objective external realities. Of course some who have gone so far as to take all sensory qualities to be subjective have denied or doubted that they can so serve, at least on a realist construal of the objects perceived. But that is by no means an inevitable consequence of the subjectivity of sensory qualities. We are encouraged by these considerations to take seriously the possibility that veridical perception of objective realities could be mediated by phenomenal content that is purely subjective. Thus even if the whole phenomenal content of the experience of God were affective, I would not take that to rule out the possibility of veridical perception of God.

According to certain Catholic theologians and philosophers, the affective reactions in mystical experience, in particular supernaturally infused love, performs just this function. Here is a twentieth-century exposition of this from Jacques Maritain (1938).

> We say that under the special inspiration of the Holy Ghost love thus passes to the side of the object and takes on an objective condition, not so as to be a known

> object but rather a means of knowledge or *objectum quo* (that *through which* the object is known, an analogue to sensory experience in sense perception). . . . What we are calling here the *objectum quo* is . . . the passions which the soul actually undergoes, actual effects that serve as a real medium of knowledge under the illumination of the Holy Ghost. . . . In short, the objective intermediary in this case is neither an infused idea not a principle of inference; it is, rather, an actual infused love that arises under the illumination of the Holy Ghost through an *objectum quo* in which and by which an experienced contact occurs between God and the soul. . . . This is not an absolutely immediate knowledge (only the beatific vision is immediate in this case), but it is a knowledge of God that is truly immediate, even though imperfectly so, without passing from a created *quod* (that which is known), that would be first known, to a divine *quod*. Thus, God is not only attained without reasoning . . . but He is Himself touched and experienced in an obscure manner. (P. 261)

There could hardly be a clearer exposition of the point that the mystical perception is what we have called "mediated immediacy", a genuine experiential awareness of God that does not involve some other object of knowledge or perception (another *quod*) but that also is not an absolute immediacy excluding anything through which (*quo*) one is aware of God. And that through which one is aware of God is, according to this view, the love that is infused in the soul by the action of the Holy Spirit.

But although I do not see that it is impossible that a direct perception of God should be effected through affective qualities, I can't see that the supposition that this is so is any more than a suspicion, based on our lack of an intersubjective language for mystical nonaffective qualia. Since we have already pointed out that the conditions for developing such a list are not satisfied in mystical perception, we cannot expect to have a language for such qualia even if they exist. In this connection note that one does not have to be able to isolate and identify basic phenomenal qualities in order to experience them and use them as vehicles of perception. Children learn to recognize people, buildings, and toys without having any conception of the way in which the sensory appearances of things are built up from elementary phenomenal qualities. Fortunately we have the capacity to learn to respond to complex phenomenal totalities without analyzing them into their ultimate constituents. Fortunately, because otherwise only a consummate introspective psychologist could find his way home from the office.

To further shore up the supposition that mystical perception involves distinctive, nonaffective phenomenal qualia, we can advert to the doctrine of "spiritual sensations" that was developed in the Catholic mystical tradition, beginning as far back as Origen in the third century[39] and continuing to our own day. The idea is that mystical perception involves a variety of phenomenal qualia the similarities and differences among which parallel to an impor-

[39]*Commentary on the Song of Songs*, I, 4 (1957).

tant extent the similarities and differences among sensory qualia. Some cases of mystical perception differ from other cases in a way analagous to the way seeing differs from touch. Touch, unlike seeing, involves a direct contact with the object; seeing reveals much more detail concerning the object and provides a much more convincing view of its nature and identity. And some mystical perceptions involve a more intimate contact with God, while others reveal Him more fully. Here are some passages in which these ideas are set forth. There is an excellent presentation of this subject in Poulain 1950 (Chap. 6), from which the following quotations are taken.[40]

(30) As the body has its five exterior senses, with which it perceives the visible and delectable things of this life, and makes experience of them, so the spirit, with its faculties of understanding and will, has five interior acts corresponding to these senses, which we call seeing, hearing, smelling, tasting, and touching spiritually, with which it perceives the invisible and delectable things of Almighty God, and makes *experience* of them. (The Ven. Louis du Pont, *Meditations, Introduction*, XI; Poulain 1950, p. 101)

Touch

(31) Often in this state God descends from heaven; often He visits the soul that is lying in darkness and the shadow of death . . . but he *so makes His presence to be felt that He does not* reveal his Face. He sheds His sweetness inwardly, but He does not make His beauty manifest. He sheds His sweetness, but He does not display His brightness. His sweetness therefore is felt, but His beauty is not seen. He is still surrounded with clouds and darkness; his throne is still the pillar of a cloud. Truly, what is felt is exceeding sweet and *full of caresses*; but what is seen is all in darkness, for He does not yet appear in the light. And although He appears in the fire, it is a fire that warms rather than illumines. . . . The soul, then, can verily *feel her Beloved* in this state, but, as has been said, *it is not permitted to her to see Him* (Richard of St. Victor, *De Gradibus Violentae Charitatis*. Poulain 1950, p. 100)

(32) It is not only in the state of glory that God is known experimentally, but also in our earthly state. God is known here, obscurely and by faith, it is true; but He can be known by a certain *experimental touch without being seen*. In the same way, we do not see our soul, but we feel her as an object that is present having experimental knowledge of the fact that she animates the body, that she gives life to it . . . God makes Himself really present, in a special manner. (De Vallegornera, no. 868. Poulain 1950, p. 106)[41]

[40]I am indebted to Nelson Pike for calling this subject to my attention.

[41]The mystics often compare the non-sensory direct awareness of God with our awareness of our mental operations. The term 'experimental' that often occurs in these writings is used in a sense that is becoming obsolete, a sense more naturally expressed today by 'experiential', rather than in the sense of having to do with *experiments*.

Taste

(33) She knows what He is, indeed she even tastes Him by the divine *contact*, of which the mystics speak, and which is a *supernatural* knowledge whereby the soul knows what God is; not from having seen Him, but from having *touched Him*. For of the spiritual senses, tact is the most delicate, although of the corporeal senses it is the most gross. This *experience* of God gives a perception of Him which is more exquisite and which approaches to Him more nearly than any other thing can do. (Fr. Surin, *Traité de l'amour de Dieu*, Vol. I, Bk. III, chap. vi. Poulain 1950, p. 106)

Smell

(34) The soul perceives a *certain fragrance* as we may call it, as if within its inmost depths were a brazier sprinkled with sweet perfumes. Although the spirit neither sees the flame nor knows *where it is*, yet it is *penetrated by the warmth and scented fumes* which are even sometimes felt by the body. Understand me, the soul does not feel any real heat or scent, but something far more delicious, which I use this metaphor to explain. (St. Teresa, *Interior Castle*, Fourth Mansion, chap. ii, 6. Poulain 1950, p. 112)

As for sight, there is a tendency in this tradition to consider the spiritual analogue of bodily sight to be reserved to the blessed in heaven. Note how in several of the above passages the writer indicates that we can be aware of the presence of God by touching Him though we cannot presume to see Him. Nevertheless, there are passages, such as (2) and (3) above, in which a spiritual analogue of sight is claimed. As for hearing, there are so many passages in which people speak of hearing God speak to them, though not in a way that involves the ears or an auditory imagery, it is hardly necessary to cite any. For example.

(35) I was walking along a long, lonely country road by myself; worried sick and in near despair. Then came the experience. It lasted about 20 minutes—I sensed a presence, on my right keeping level with me as I went along. A mental message was conveyed in my mind; the sense of it being: 'Don't worry; it will all turn out all right.' (Beardsworth 1977, pp. 121–22)

Note how in the above passages we have both straight analogies between a particular bodily sense and a particular mystical perception, as in the passage from St. Teresa, and a more complex analogy between the difference between kinds of bodily sensation and the difference between kinds of mystical experience. Thus in (2) the relation between spiritual touch and spiritual sight is analogized to the difference between seeing a friend in broad daylight and touching him in the dark. There are even some hints as to the qualia involved in the several modes of spiritual perception. Thus Richard of St. Victor in (31) speaks of the divine *sweetness and the caresses* that are felt. There is much erotic imagery in mystical literature, and some of it gives further analogical suggestions as to the phenomenal character of spiritual touch.

> (36) God, who was formerly in the soul of the just *as a hidden treasure*, by way of sanctifying grace, now presents Himself to her as *a Treasure that is found*. He enlightens her, He *touches* her, He *embraces* her, He *penetrates* her, He flows into her faculties, He *gives Himself to her*, He *fills her* with the fullness of His Being. The soul, in return, ravished by His charms and by the spectacle of His beauty, *holds Him, embraces Him, clasps Him* closely, and, all on fire with love, she flows, she plunges, she buries and loses herself deliciously in God with sentiments of inconceivable joy. Thence comes the great diversity of names that are given to the mystical union, such as *kiss, perfume*, celestial rain, unction, Divine inflowing, transformation, love in fruition, deifying love, and several other similar expressions, that denote the different impressions of the unitive love of which we are now speaking. (Fr. Nouet, *Conduite de l'homme d'Oraison*, Bk. VI, chap. xiv. Poulain 1950, p. 111)

If one still feels dissatisfied with the fact that none of these people come right out and tell us what are the basic phenomenal qualia of mystical perception, I can only recur to the point made above that the lack of any effective stimulus control over these qualia make it impossible for us to attach terms to them directly in such a way to establish a publicly shared vocabulary for them. Our only recourse is to analogies with experienced qualia for which that treatment is possible. And that is what our informants are doing. Our sources clearly suppose that there is distinctive phenomenal content to their perceptions of God, that God is present to them in ways that impart a distinctive character to their experience. And their inability to enumerate these qualia no more prevents them from perceiving God through being aware of the qualia than the inability of one of us to analyze a rural scene into its constituent basic visual qualia prevents us from perceiving that scene.

xi. External Conditions of Perception

So much for the internal requirement, that the mode of consciousness be distinctively perceptual. Now for the question of whether mystical experience could satisfy further requirements for being perception. I have already made it explicit that I shall not be concerned in this chapter to argue that such conditions are in fact satisfied, especially since they involve the existence of the object.[42] I will be concerned only to argue that if God exists it is a real possibility that experiences like the ones under consideration constitute genuine perceptions of Him.

We are seeking further conditions for S's perceiving X, where this is a

[42]Actually mystical experience could still be perceptual even if God does not exist; it could be perception of something(s) else. I shall ignore this possibility.

generic sense of 'perceive' that is not necessarily confined to sense perception. However, sense perception is our paradigm, the example from which we derive the generic concept, the case that has been studied the most thoroughly and about which we know the most. Hence the proper procedure is to consider what additional conditions are necessary for S's sensorily perceiving X, abstracting from a requirement of *sensory* qualia and any others that differentiate sense perception from other varieties; and then consider whether it is possible that those requirements should be satisfied by a nonsensory experiential awareness of God.

But this procedure is not completely straightforward. Sense perception is as controversial as anything else in philosophy and psychology. Different theories give different accounts of what is necessary and sufficient for S's perceiving X. Since I cannot take the space in this book for a full-dress defense of my favored theory, I will have to consider the question on each of several theories, or rather broad types of theory. I shall have to be sketchy, but I believe that I can say enough to accomplish the purpose at hand.

First let me say that I am thinking of these theories as accounts of the *concept* of perception, of what we mean by 'perceive' and our various more specific perceptual terms, rather than as accounts of the nature of perception, as a kind of psychological state or process.

The simplest story is given by my favored theory, The Theory of Appearing, but before we can fully appreciate it a little more background is needed. Let's return to the notion of something's *appearing* or being *presented* or *given* to one's experience as so-and-so. I have been insisting that this is what perceptual experience seems to the subject to involve. And I believe that we can get considerable verbal agreement that this is what the concept of object perception amounts to. To see X is for X to look a certain way to one; to hear X is for X to sound a certain way to one. And so on. But this agreement conceals fundamental differences. The most radical one is this. According to the Theory of Appearing the notion of X's appearing to S as so-and-so is fundamental and unanalyzable. And since this relationship, being unanalyzable, is not analyzable in terms of conceptualizations, beliefs, takings, or anything else of the sort, it really does have the non- or pre-conceptual character we saw earlier that perceptual appearing seems phenomenologically to have. Because of all this the analysis of the concept of object perception given by the Theory of Appearing is of breathtaking simplicity. For S to perceive X is simply for X to appear to S as so-and-so. That is all there is to it. At least that is all there is to the *concept* of perception. Thus the Theory of Appearing is a form of "direct" realism, even "naive" realism, in that it endorses our spontaneous, naive way of taking sense experience as involving the direct awareness of an object that is presented to consciousness, usually an external physical object. It differs from the most naive conceivable form of realism only in recognizing that what an external object presents itself as may diverge from what that object actually is.

Other theories of perception, on the other hand, take the fact of appearing to be complex and analyzable. We can get the best fix on this contrast by noting the following difference between the Theory of Appearing and all its rivals. The former takes the relation of appearing to be constitutive both of sensory experience and the sense perception of objects. That is, it holds that any case of sensory experience, whether veridical or not, has an "act-object" structure. Sensory experience is essentially a matter of something's "appearing" or "presenting itself" to a subject, S, as bearing certain phenomenal qualities. This saddles it with the question of what it is that is presented to sense experience in cases of complete hallucination when nothing of the sort that seems to be presented is really there. (Remember that this relation of appearing is nonintentional, so that X appears to S only if X actually exists. My dog can't appear to you unless he's there any more than he can bite you unless he's there.) This question can be satisfactorily answered by saying that in these cases it is a vivid mental image that presents itself to the subject's experience, but I will not be able to go into this issue.[43] My present point is that the Theory of Appearing construes both sense experience itself and the perception of external objects in terms of the same kind of act-object structure. Hence if we ask the question "What must be added to a certain visual experience in order for it to be true that S sees a certain tree?", the answer given by the Theory of Appearing is "Nothing, provided that tree is what is appearing to S in that experience". And if it is not that tree that is appearing, no set of additional conditions would make it the case that S sees that tree. Again, this is because the Theory of Appearing, so to say, brings the external object into the most fundamental description of the state of consciousness in question, since it takes sensory consciousness to have a relational, act-object structure, one relatum of which is usually an external physical object.

But on other theories of perception something has to be added to the sense experience in order that the subject actually perceives an external object. For on all other theories the account of the nature of sensory consciousness is explicitly designed to avoid any mention of a cognitive relationship to an object, and it is so designed in order to accommodate the alleged point that sensory consciousness can be exactly the same whether or not there is an external perceived object.[44] Hence on these views, some extra condition(s) is needed to make it the case that an external object, X, is being perceived. (Call these views "externalist" theories of perception.)[45] On the Sense Datum Theory, sensory awareness is, as in the Theory of Appearing, taken to have an

[43]If the theory held that a mental image is what presents itself to the subject's awareness in all perception, it would be substantially equivalent to the sense-datum theory. But as I construe the theory, it takes a mental image to be what is directly presented to consciousness only in those cases in which no external physical object or state of affairs is available for this role.

[44]The Theory of Appearing is committed to denying this apparently obvious point. It holds that introspective indistinguishability is not a safe guide to identity of ontological constitution.

[45]See Alston 1990.

act-object structure, but the objects are restricted to nonphysical entities that have the sole function of being the bearers of phenomenal qualia. And on the Adverbial Theory sense experience is thought of as a certain *way* or *manner* of being conscious, not an awareness *of* an object. (There are other views as to the nature of sense experience, for example, that it is a certain mode of "mental representation", but we shall have to confine ourselves in this brief treatment to the two just mentioned.)[46] Now it is obviously conceptually possible for me to be aware of a certain sense datum or to be sensing in a particular way without actually perceiving a given tree or any other external object. Hence one or more additional conditions are required over and above S's undergoing a sensory experience of a certain sort. They will involve some relationship of the external object, X, to the experience in question. What sort of relation will do the trick? Two have been stressed in the history of the subject: causal and doxastic. Let's take a brief look at each.

It is abundantly obvious that in visual and other sense perception the perceiver is in causal interaction with the object perceived. The object figures importantly in the causal chain leading to the sensory consciousness involved. This encourages us to suppose that it is by virtue of being causally related to X that a sensory consciousness is involved in, or counts as, a perception of X. But, unfortunately for this approach, it is equally obvious that even if this is necessary for perceiving X it is, without further qualification, not at all sufficient. By no means everything that figures importantly in the causal chain leading to a certain visual experience is thereby seen. The chain in question contains neurophysiological processes in the brain and elsewhere; but they are not seen. This means that in order for me to see X, by virtue of having a certain sensory experience, E, X must figure in the production of E *in a certain way*. Just what way is that? We can give an informative answer to that question for each sense modality. In vision, for example, the object (directly) seen is the one reflected light from which strikes the retina, without being reflected from something else in the meantime, thereby setting up a chain of excitation through the nervous system to the brain that eventuates in the experience in question. But what can we specify by way of a causal condition for S's perceiving X, whatever the particular modality, a condition that differentiates the object perceived from other causal influences? No one has suggested any such thing in the literature, and I doubt very much that it can be done. About all we can say here is that, on externalist theories, in order that S perceive X by virtue of undergoing sensory experience, E, there must be some "suitable" way in which X figures in the causation of E.

As for a doxastic condition, the basic idea is that what is seen by virtue of

[46]I am inclined to think that "representational" theories, as well as "doxastic" theories like those of D. M. Armstrong and G. Pitcher, which characterize sensory experience simply in terms of the process of forming beliefs or belief tendencies by the action of the senses, fail to take seriously enough the crucial role of sense experience in perception.

undergoing a particular experience is what this experience generates beliefs about. This obviously has to be qualified, since one can see X without beliefs about X being generated; perhaps one already believed everything about X that one could come to believe on the basis of experience, or perhaps one has reasons to the contrary that inhibit the formation of the beliefs that would otherwise eventuate from that perception. Various qualifications can be introduced to handle these difficulties. For example, it could be said that it is the generation of belief *tendencies* that is crucial here, where it is possible to have a tendency to a belief that p, even though various factors prevent such a belief from actually arising. Again, a sensory experience can obviously generate beliefs about things other than what is perceived; just to take the most obvious point it can generate beliefs about itself. Moreover, by trains of association it can generate beliefs about an indefinitely large variety of items. Again, something will have to be done to narrow the field. Leaving the fine print for another occasion, let's just note that perception obviously is a source of belief (knowledge) about the objects perceived, and that so fundamental a fact about perception might well be exploited in attempting to spell out what it is to perceive X.

To sum up, on the Theory of Appearing, for S to perceive X is just for X to be the entity that is appearing to S as so-and-so; and on externalist theories, to perceive X, in undergoing experience, E, is for X to figure in a certain way in the causal chain leading up to E, and/or for E to lead to beliefs, or tendencies to beliefs, about X. Hence in considering whether it is possible for Angela of Foligno to be genuinely perceiving God in having the experience reported in (3), we shall ask the following questions. (These are all to be understood as arising after it has been assumed that God exists.) (1) Is it possible that God should be what is appearing to her in that experience? (2) Is it possible that God should figure in the causation of that experience in such a way as to count as what is perceived? (3) Is it possible that that experience should give rise to beliefs about God?

A further word about the relation of these questions to the different analyses of the concept of object perception. It looks as if each question is designed to determine the possibility of perceiving God, given a certain account of object perception. But that is only approximately true. The difference between (2) and (3) corresponds to different suggestions as to how an object has to be related to an experience in order to be what is perceived in that experience, but (2) and (3) are by no means mutually exclusive. A theory can embrace both, as Armstrong's does.[47] Or it can involve more complicated constructions based on both, as Alvin Goldman's does.[48] Moreover, a complete externalist theory will include not only a specification of how the object must be related to the experience but also how sensory experience is to be

[47]See Armstrong 1961.
[48]See Goldman 1977, pp. 257–84.

construed; differences on this latter point do not line up neatly with differences on the former. As for the Theory of Appearing, even though it takes X's appearing to S as necessary and sufficient for S's perceiving X, it is open to the possibility that even though the former is unanalysable it still might be that some kind of causal relation of X to S's experience might be a necessary condition of X's being what is appearing to S in that experience (though this necessity cannot be based on a complete analysis of the concept). And certainly the Theory of Appearing can recognize that appearances of X typically give rise to beliefs about X. Hence a consideration of (2) and (3) are not without interest even from the standpoint of the Theory of Appearing.

xii. Is It Possible for God to Be Presented to One's Experience?

Let's turn to question (1). My attitude toward that issue is as follows. I don't see any general a priori constraints on what can appear to our experience. We have to learn from experience what we can be experientially aware of. What a priori considerations could have led us to anticipate that stars but not electromagnetic fields can occupy a place in a visual field? Therefore, if it is a question of whether it is possible that an entity of certain type can present itself to our experience, we have to say that apart from empirical considerations, including our ascertaining by experience that this possibility is realized, we have nothing to go on and so no reason to deem it impossible. In the mystical case it is tolerably obvious that there are no empirical considerations that count against the possibility.[49] The only empirical data we have that are relevant to the issue at all, namely, the claim by many people to have directly experienced God, obviously count in favor of supposition. Therefore, I would say that the possibility in question is prima facie credible; to deny it we would need strong negative arguments. Let's see whether we can find any.

(1) "We don't have a clue as to *how* one could be directly aware of some concrete entity except through sensory input. What is the mechanism of this mode of cognition? Just how does God make His presence or His activity "felt"? What does He do to "impress" Himself on us? How is "information" about Him picked up and processed? Until we have at least the beginnings of an answer to these questions, we can safely ignore the possibility of a non-sensory experiential awareness of God."

It must be admitted that we have no idea as to the "mechanism" of this mode of awareness, if, indeed, there is any such thing. Perhaps God doesn't work through natural, much less physical, means to make Himself perceptible by us. Perhaps He supernaturally brings about the requisite experience, as

[49]I am inclined to think that what we know about sense perception provides a strong empirical argument against the possibility of God's directly appearing to *sensory* experience. But I can't see that any empirical considerations count against the supposition that God presents Himself to our experience in a non-sensory fashion.

Catholic mystical theology has always held. If God exists, an assumption on which this discussion is being conducted, this is a possibility that cannot be ignored. But the main point here is that the credentials of this alleged mode of perception do not depend on our understanding of how it is effected. After all, people were amply justified in supposing themselves to see physical objects in their environment long before anyone had any adequate idea of the mechanisms involved. No doubt, people at least realized that that one sees with one's eyes and hears with one's ears long before the dawn of recorded history; but it is easy to imagine unusual cases in which even this realization is absent and one still knows that one sees trees and the like. Just manipulate a subject from birth so that the usual cues to the role of the eyes in seeing are cut off or distorted, but allow visual experience to be otherwise produced normally. In any event, the main point is that knowledge that one is perceiving certain objects is compatible with a great deal of ignorance as to how this is brought about. And it is arbitrary to select a certain portion of this "know-how" and declare it to be a necessary condition for crediting even the possibility of X's appearing to one.

(2) "God is too "big", to put it crudely. How can the infinite, unlimited, omnipotent source of all being and Lord of all creation be contained within the paltry confines of my experience? How can I hope to have a direct awareness of so transcendently vast an "object"? To answer this we will have to get misleading pictorial associations out of the way. The perceived object doesn't literally have to take up residence within my head, mind, or experience in order for me to perceive it. Appearance is best thought of as a relational fact; the object is related to me in a certain way. And relative size has nothing to do with that; objects of any differences of magnitude can be variously related to each other. It is also salutary to remind ourselves that, in sense perception and elsewhere, I don't have to perceive the whole of X in order to perceive it. I rarely, if ever, perceive the whole of any physical object I see; but if I see enough of X under the right conditions, I am properly credited with seeing X.

(3) There are theological objections to the possibility of perceiving God. It is no part of my purpose in this book to deal with Christian theology, or any other theology, but I will point out briefly that such objections do not seem to me to tell against the perception of God as I understand it. First, there are various biblical statements to the effect that no man has ever "seen" God.

> Though God has never been seen by any man, God himself dwells in us if we love one another. (I John 4:12)[50]

> My face you cannot see, for no mortal man may see me and live. (Exodus 33:20)

One could devote a lot of space to the exegesis of the biblical texts just quoted, and others to the same effect, but let me just say that it is not at all

[50]All biblical quotations are from *The New English Bible with Apocrypha*, 1976.

clear to me that they are to be construed as denying the possibility of a non-sensory presentation of God of the sorts reported by our sources. Perhaps John was denying *visual* presentation of God. Or perhaps the writers were denying that we can have the kind of clear, unmistakable, chock-full-of-information sort of awareness of God that we have of physical objects when we see them with our eyes. That is all undoubtedly true, but it has no tendency to show that we don't have any kind of perception of God. After all, feeling and smell don't give us such a clear, sharp, and loaded-with-information cognition of an object as vision does, but nonetheless they are modes of perception.[51]

A powerful strain of Catholic mystical theology emphasizes the point that even at the heights of mystical experience one has, at best, an "obscure knowledge" of God, that being aware of the divine essence or seeing God "face to face" is reserved for the blessed in heaven and is not for us in this life. On these grounds it is denied that anyone can really be directly perceiving God in this life. Garrigou-Lagrange writes as follows in *Christian Perfection and Contemplation*, (1937):

> . . . infused contemplation does not require an immediate perception of God, which would make us know Him as He is. This immediate perception of God does not exist, in fact, in the great anxieties of the passive nights of the senses and of the soul, which are, nevertheless, mystical states and are accompanied by infused contemplation. Does this perception exist in the other phases of the mystical ascent? Nothing permits such an affirmation; on the contrary, everything leads us to think that it is impossible . . . St. Thomas states explicitly and proves that no vision inferior to the beatific vision can make us know God as He is in Himself; no created, infused idea can manifest just as He is, Him who is being itself, who is eternally subsistent intellection itself. . . . All mystics tell us that they perceive, not God himself, as He is, but the effect of His action on their souls, especially in the sweetness of love which He causes them to experience. . . . This is the way that we know God, not immediately as He is, but by the effects which He produces in us. (Pp.266–71)[52]

As for the statement that this is what "all mystics tell us", I believe that the passages we have quoted in this chapter are sufficient to refute it. If they are using words in anything like their established senses, they are telling us that God Himself appeared to their experience, not that they were only aware of His effects. Indeed, we have noted them making this very contrast and com-

[51]It is also worth noting that several biblical passages seem to take an opposed line. "Jacob called the place Peniel, 'because', he said, 'I have seen God face to face and my life is spared'" (Genesis 32:30). "But my servant Moses is not such a prophet; he alone is faithful of all my household. With him I speak face to face, openly and not in riddles. He shall see the very form of the Lord" (Numbers 12:7–8). "I knew of thee then only by report but now I see thee with my own eyes" (Job 42:5)

[52]This is clearly along the same lines as the views of Saudreau briefly noted in section viii. As pointed out there in a footnote, it may be that Saudreau should be taken as denying, with Garrigou-Lagrange, that the mystics really do directly perceive God, rather than that this is the way their experience seems to them to be.

ing down on the side of direct perception. But more to the immediate point is Garrigou-Lagrange's argument. He is obviously assuming that the only alternative to a direct awareness of the essence of God is an awareness of divine effects. But why suppose this? Why shouldn't I directly perceive God without perceiving His essence? In sense perception we constantly perceive things without perceiving their essences. Even with vision, our preeminent sense, objects present themselves not as *having a certain essential nature*, but rather as having certain superficial features: colors, shapes, relative position in space, and what is firmly connected with features such as these. People perceived water for many millennia without having any idea that its chemical constitution is H_2O. And so it is with those who take themselves to be directly aware of God in mystical experience. They take themselves to be aware of God as displaying certain features—goodness, power, plenitude, lovingness—or as doing certain things—speaking, strengthening, forgiving—not as being aware of the divine essence.[53] To directly perceive X is for X to present itself to one's experience as so-and-so, where the so-and-so is typically not essential. Indeed, it is not even necessary for direct perception of X that X actually have the features it presents itself as having. I can directly perceive a book that looks blue, even though the book is really grey and only looks blue because of the lighting. Our failure to grasp the divine essence does not prevent us from directly perceiving God.[54]

Garrigou-Lagrange, in the section from which I quoted, argues that because of the simplicity of God one cannot directly perceive God in a partial fashion.

> God, however, being incapable of division, cannot show Himself partially in such a way that He would make Himself seen as He is. The divine attributes exist in Him *formaliter eminenter*, and they are only virtually distinct, because they are really identical in the eminence of the Deity. Consequently nobody can see one of them as it is, without seeing the others and without seeing the Deity itself. (P. 266)

In response, I would say that if the doctrine of divine simplicity really does render impossible a direct perception of God that does not involve an awareness of the divine essence, that is a good argument against that doctrine. However, I don't believe that the doctrine has the consequences claimed here. Aquinas and other advocates of the doctrine are clear that, despite the identity of all the divine attributes with the divine essence, and, indeed, with the

[53]Look back at our list on pp. 43–44.

[54]Farges (1926) in his defense of the view that God is directly perceived in mystical experience suggests that it is by virtue of the mystic's consciousness of the action of God in his soul that the mystic is able to perceive God Himself. This action produces a certain effect that functions as an "impressed *species* (likeness)" *through* which or *by* which (*quo*) the mystic is able to be aware of God. Thus this "impressed species" functions as the phenomenal consciousness through which God is perceived. God can thus be truly perceived Himself even though one is not aware of His essence. See especially pp. 275–78.

divine existence, we can truly attribute many predicates to God that are not synonymous with each other. Because of the way our intellects work, we have to, so to say, break up the divine simplicity into components and treat them separately.[55] God, as it were, accommodates Himself to our limited mode of intellection so that we may gain such knowledge of Him as is possible for us, even though it does not succeed in representing Him as He is. That being the case, why should not the same thing be true of human perception of God? Why should it not be possible that God should appear to S's experience as good, powerful, or loving without simultaneously displaying to that experience the full riches of His essence, in a way analogous to our conceptual grasp of His nature? That means, no doubt, that we grasp Him in an imperfect manner suited to our limitations, rather than that He is "seen as He is". But that should be the reverse of surprising.[56]

Before leaving theological considerations, let me point out the strong theological considerations within Christianity that support the idea that it is possible for human beings to perceive God. For there is a strong emphasis in Christian doctrine and Christian thought on the point that God has created us for loving communion with Himself. To be sure, this thesis by itself is compatible with the idea that such communion is reserved for life after death, but there is much in the Bible and in Christian thought that points in the opposite direction. For example: "Jesus replied, 'Anyone who loves me will heed what I say; then my Father will love him, and we will come to him and make our dwelling with him'" (John 14:23). And if loving communion between God and man is possible, then each side must be able to perceive the other. Otherwise it hardly deserves the title of "loving communion".

I conclude that, apart from the possible relevance of the doxastic and causal conditions to be considered next, there is no bar in principle to God's being what is presented to one's awareness, as that presentation is construed by the Theory of Appearing.

xiii. Causal and Doxastic Conditions of Perception

Now we turn to questions (2) and (3). I will begin with (3), since it need not delay us long. It is clear that putative perception of God normally, if not invariably, gives rise to beliefs about God. To be sure, those who perceive God as loving, powerful, and so on, typically believed that God is so characterized long before they had that experience. But the same is true of sense perception, where my 50,000th look at my house doesn't generate any new beliefs. Partisans of a doxastic condition typically handle this by saying that in these cases tendencies to beliefs or reinforcements to belief are engendered

[55]See, e.g., *Summa Theologiae*, I, Q. 13, art. 4 (1945).
[56]Cf. Farges 1926, pp. 288–92.

even if no new beliefs result. The same move can be made here. However, it is also true that in both modes of perception new beliefs will virtually always be engendered. Even if I don't see anything new about my house on that umpteenth look, I at least learn that it is blue and high *today*. When what we perceive is an *agent*, the new beliefs tend to be more interesting. On my 50,000th look at my wife I not only learn that she is still beautiful, but I learn what she is doing now. And similarly with God. One who perceives God will thereby come to learn that God is strengthening her or comforting her *then*, or telling her so-and-so *then*.[57] The doxastic condition presents no problem.

The causal condition calls for more discussion. First, there is no reason to think it impossible that God, if He exists, does causally contribute to the occurrence of mystical experiences. Quite the contrary. If God exists and things are as supposed by classical theism, God causally contributes to every occurrence. That follows just from the fact that nothing would exist without the creative and sustaining activity of God. And with respect to many things, including experiences of all sorts, God's causality presumably extends farther than that, though the precise story will vary from one theology to another. To fix our thoughts, let us say that at least some of these experiences[58] occur only because God intentionally presents Himself to the subject's awareness as so-and-so.

It may well be pointed out, as I did earlier, that not every causal contributor to an experience is perceived via that experience. When I see a house, light waves and goings on in my nervous system form parts of the causal chain leading to the visual experience, but I don't thereby perceive them. Thus it is not enough that God figure somehow or other in the causes of the experience; He would have to make the right kind of causal contribution. But what is the right kind? There's the rub. This question has no general answer applicable to all perceptual modalities. The causal contribution a seen object makes to the production of visual experience (roughly, transmitting light directly to the retina) is different from the causal contribution a felt object makes to the tactile experience, different from the causal contribution a heard object makes to the aural experience, and so on. And how do we tell what the crucial causal contribution is for each modality? We have no a priori insight into this. We cannot abstract from everything we have learned from perception and still

[57]This may seem to presuppose that God has a temporal mode of existence, lives through a temporal succession of moments, rather than existing in "an eternal now"; but it need not carry that presupposition. The temporal location of an action of God can be given by the temporal location of its worldly effect, leaving the divine will side of the transaction free to enjoy an atemporal mode of being. For more on this see Stump and Kretzmann 1981 and my "Divine-Human Dialogue and the Nature of God" in Alston 1989b.

[58]Let me remind the reader that I am by no means concerned to argue that every putative perception of God is a genuine perception of God. See Chapter 2, section iii, and Chapter 5 for the epistemological correlate of this, that in some (many) cases the prima facie justification provided by a putative perception of God for beliefs about God is overriden by contrary considerations.

ascertain how an object must be causally related to a visual experience in order to be what is seen in that experience. Quite the contrary. We learn this by first determining in many cases *what* is seen, felt, heard, and so on, in those cases, and then looking for some causal contribution that is distinctive of the object perceived. That is, we first have to determine what is seen; then on the basis of that we can determine how an entity has to be causally related to the visual experience to be seen therein. We have no resources for doing it the other way around, first determining the specific causal requirement and then picking out objects seen on the basis of what satisfies that requirement.

The application of all this to the topic of divine perception is as follows. We will have a chance of determining how God has to be causally related to an experience in order to be perceived therein only if we can first determine in a number of cases that God is being perceived. And since that is so, we can't rule out the possibility (actuality) of perceiving God on the grounds that God can't be (isn't) related to the relevant experience in the right way. For unless we do perceive God we are unable to determine what the right way is. Hence, so long as God does make some causal contribution to the relevant experiences, we can't rule out God's being perceived in those experiences on the grounds that He isn't causally related to them in the right way. To be sure, by the same token we cannot show that we do (can) perceive God by showing that God is (can be) causally related to the appropriate experiences in the right kind of way. But showing this is no part of our purpose here. It will be sufficient to show that, so far as we can see, there is no reason to doubt that it is possible that God should satisfy an appropriate causal requirement for being perceived in at least some of the cases in which people take themselves to be directly aware of Him.

Several paragraphs back I was assuming that God's causal contribution to a mystical experience by virtue of which He can be an object of that experience would have to be something over and above the way in which His creative and conservative activity is a necessary condition for the existence of everything in creation. I said that I would assume that "at least some of these experiences occur only because God intentionally presents Himself to the subject's awareness as so-and-so". And I do think it is quite possible that this "intentional presentation" of Himself involves some divine activity over and above that which is directed to everything else in creation. But the reverse is possible also. It may be that God satisfies the causal condition for being *perceivable* in a certain experience just by keeping that experience in existence. But then why don't we perceive God in every experience? Perhaps we do without realizing it.[59] Another possibility is this. Although God satisfies all the conditions on His side for being perceivable in every experience, there are various obstacles on our side that, most of the time, inhibit that perception. On this alternative the situation is like that in which a tree is doing its part to

[59]This position is defended at length in John Baillie 1939.

consummate my visual perception of it (it is reflecting light in my direction, and it is not too far away), but there is an opaque object between us, and the light in question never reaches me. Or, more interiorly, the neural stimulation from that light gets sidetracked in the nervous system and never reaches the brain. Or, still more interiorly, my attention is wholly taken up with something else, and I am not consciously aware of the tree. It is not difficult to think of analogues to these barriers and inhibitors in mystical perception, even where God is doing His part.

xiv. Conclusion

I take all this to be substantial support for the claim that mystical experience can be construed as *perception* in the same generic sense of the term as sense perception. What is the significance of this result? I take the main significance to be its bearing on the cognitive significance of mystical perception. If mystical experience is a mode of experience that is perceptual, so far as its phenomenological character is concerned, and if it is in principle possible that the other requirements should be satisfied for mystical experience to be the experiential side of a genuine perception of God, then the question of whether mystical experience does count as genuine perception of God is just a question of whether it is what it seems to its subject to be. And this question arises for mystical perception in just the same way as for sense perception, making possible a uniform treatment of the epistemology of the two modes of experience. Whereas if we adopt the most common alternative to the perceptual construal—that mystical experience is a purely subjective mode of consciousness that the subject typically interprets as being due to a transcendent cause[60] —the epistemological question will be whether this *hypothesis* of a transcendent cause can be supported. This means that the subject must have sufficient *reasons* for this supposition if it is to be justified, whereas on the perceptual contrual there is at least the possibility of a direct knowledge of God, not based on reasons, provided a direct realist understanding of perception is in general possible.

To take mystical experience as a form of perception is not to beg the question as to the upshot of the inquiry. It still could be true that sense perception is genuine perception of its putative objects, whereas mystical perception is not, and that sense perception provides justified belief and knowledge about its objects—whereas mystical perception yields no such results for any beliefs about anything. The point is only that the problems, both as to the nature of the perception and as to the epistemic status of the perceptual beliefs stemming therefrom, arise in the same form for both. Whereas on the widespread view that mystical experience is to be construed as purely subjective feelings, sensations, and the like, to which supernaturalistic causal hypotheses are added, the issues concerning the two modes of experience will look very

[60]See p. 16.

different (unless one is misguided enough to treat sense perception in the same fashion). For on this subjectivist construal, the subject is faced with the task of justifying a causal hypothesis before he can warrantedly claim to be perceiving God; whereas if the experience is given a perceptual construal from the start, we will at least have to take seriously the view that a claim to be perceiving God is prima facie acceptable just on its own merits, pending any sufficient reasons to the contrary. In this book I will be arguing for a view of just that sort.

In this chapter I have, from time to time, been inveighing against the view that mystical experience consists simply in subjective feelings or sensations, which are typically believed by their subjects to have a supernatural explanation. But I should not give the impression that all my predecessors on this topic have been so benighted. On the contrary, a long tradition sees mystical experience as distinctively perceptual. A notable figure here is Jonathan Edwards.[61] We have already had occasion to note that various figures in the tradition of Catholic mystical theology take mystical experience to be a form of perception. Chapters 8 and 9 of Farges 1926 not only espouse, but attribute to St. Thomas the view that a direct perception of God is possible in this life, and actual in the mystics. This interpretation of St. Thomas has drawn fire from Saudreau and from Garrigou-Lagrange, but however that exegetical controversy is resolved, there is clearly a distinct strand in the Catholic tradition that is favorable to a perceptual model for mystical experience. Finally, a contemporary work, Unger (1976) forthrightly defends treating experiential awareness of God as a mode of perception, albeit on the basis of a very different theory of perception from the one I favor. Against the background of these predecessors, I take my main contributions to consist in developing an analysis of mystical perception on the basis of a general theory of perception that takes as central the notion of perceptual *presentation*, and in answering objections to this construal from various quarters.

Let me summarize the results of this chapter. We have isolated a class of experiences in which the subject takes him/herself to be directly aware of God, with particular emphasis on that subclass in which the experience is non-sensory. A scrutiny of the reports of such experiences reveals that the mode of consciousness involved is distinctively perceptual; it seems to the subject that something (identified by the subject as God) is directly presenting itself to his/her awareness as so-and-so. We looked at other conditions that are taken by one or another account of perception to be necessary for such an experience to constitute a genuine perception of God, and we concluded that if God exists it is possible for at least some of these experiences to have that status. On the basis of these results we are now ready to embark on the central issue of this book: whether such experiences provide justification for certain kinds of beliefs about God.

[61]See Edwards 1959 and Wainwright 1990.

CHAPTER 2

Epistemic Justification: Perceptual and Otherwise

i. Preview

What I take the previous chapter to have shown is that the perception of God is a real possibility. There are no principled objections to supposing that many cases in which a person takes herself to be directly aware of God constitute a genuine experiential cognition of God that has the same basic structure as sense perception of the physical environment. I did not attempt to show that this possibility is ever actually realized. Moreover, the analysis of the perception of God given in Chapter 1 is only a prolegomenon to the main aim of the book—to show that putative perception of God can provide justification for certain beliefs about God and thereby contribute to a basis for religious belief. In carrying out this latter task we will at the same time be supporting the claim that the possibility of perceiving God is realized. For if putative perception of God can serve to justify beliefs about God's perceivable qualities and activities, that tends to show that this putative perception is the genuine article. If what seems to me to be a direct experiential awareness of X puts me in a position to form justified beliefs about X's perceptible features, that warrants me in supposing that X itself is indeed presenting itself to my awareness; otherwise how could the experience justify my beliefs about X? We have to stop short of the claim that the perceptual justification of perceptual beliefs *entails* that the experience is genuine perception. I may be perceptually justified in believing that there is a lake in front of me even if I am a victim of a mirage and no lake is being perceived. But this is just an isolated incident that occurs against the background of innumerable cases in which perceptual justification involves authentic perception of the object. It strains credulity to suppose that an entire sphere of putatively perceptual experience could be a source of justification for perceptual beliefs, while there is no, or virtually no, genuine perception of the objects involved. Therefore, if putative experience of God provides justification for beliefs about God, that provides very strong support for supposing that such experiences are, at least frequently, genuine perceptions of God.[1]

To be sure, this all depends on the sense of justification in which it is shown (or rendered reasonable to suppose) that putative perception of God can provide justification for beliefs about God. In particular, it depends on whether the concept of justification involved exhibits "truth conducivity", that is, on whether my being justified in believing that p entails that it is at least likely that it is true that p. Those who use a non-truth-conducivity conception of justification will, naturally enough, deny that the fact that sense experience provides justification for beliefs about physical objects is a good reason for supposing that putative sense perception of physical objects is often the real thing. For if beliefs about physical objects could be justified by being based on sense experience, even if that did not render them probably true, why should we suppose that this justificatory relation has any tendency to show that the experience in question is genuine perception of those objects? But if, on the other hand, our conception of justification does exhibit truth conducivity, as mine will, the argument does go through. If being based on putative perceptions of X renders beliefs about X likely to be true, it must be that, in general, such experiences are in the kind of effective contact with facts about X that render them genuine perceptions of X.

My main task here will be to block out the general epistemological concepts and assumptions I will be using in arguing that mystical perception is a source of justification for M-beliefs (beliefs about perceivable attributes and activities of God that are based on putative perception of God[2]). First we need to make explicit the concept of epistemic justification we will be using. Then we will have to focus on the justification of perceptual beliefs. Here we will attend to the respective role of perceptual experience and of background beliefs in the formation and the justification of perceptual beliefs.[3] We can then

[1]The argument as just presented ignores the point, to be made in this chapter, that part of the basis, and part of the justification, of perceptual beliefs is often to be found in other beliefs that the subject brings to the perceptual situation. Therefore we can't suppose it generally true, as would be suggested by the above, that justified perceptual beliefs always, or even generally, owe their justification solely to the perceptual experience involved. Nevertheless, even when that qualification is duly noted, it remains true that the justification is always sufficiently dependent on the experience that when the belief is justified, that provides a strong reason for supposing that the putative perception is genuine.

[2]This qualification ("based on a putative perception of God") is needed for our purpose, for we are concerned with the epistemic status of such beliefs *when based on perceptual experience*, not when based, e.g., on authority.

[3]I have been oscillating between speaking of experience (sensory or mystical) and of putative perceptions (sensory or mystical) as a source of justification. I should explain what is going on. I have been thinking of sensory (mystical) experience as the conscious element in sense (mystical) perception, and taking it that further conditions must be satisfied beyond being in a certain state of consciousness if one is to genuinely perceive X in undergoing that conscious state. (This is true even on the Theory of Appearing, so long as "being in a certain state of sensory consciousness" is construed phenomenologically. For it could seem to me that X is appearing to me, and

turn, in Chapters 3 and 4, to a consideration of what basis we have to suppose that perceptual beliefs, both sense perceptual and mystical perceptual, when formed in standard ways, are justified. That will put us in a position to carry out the central aim of the book, to argue for the thesis that M-beliefs are (often) justified, to respond to objections to that thesis, and to draw implications for the epistemology of religious belief generally.

ii. General Epistemological Background

Epistemology is concerned both with the justification of belief and with knowledge. The nature of each, as well as their relationship, has always been a matter of controversy. Here is a relatively uncontroversial entrée to the territory. To know that p, for example, that it is raining here now, is to be in an effective cognitive contact with the fact that it is raining here now; it is to be so disposed that one's cognitive state "registers" its raining here now, effectively discriminates the presence or absence of rain. Being epistemically justified in believing that it is raining here now is more difficult to characterize neutrally, even in that rough a fashion. As a first approximation, it has to do with my having something to go on that strongly indicates rain; the indications available to me are of the sort one could expect to have if there is rain. From my perspective on the world there seems to be rain here and now.

Anything beyond this (and perhaps up to this) and we are mired in controversy. There are disputes over whether justified belief is required for knowledge, whether belief is required for knowledge or is even compatible with knowledge, whether knowledge requires the impossibility of error, whether justification requires only that one *have* sufficient indications of the truth of the belief or also requires that the belief be based on (held because of) those indications, and so on. Obviously, we cannot go into all that in this book. After briefly indicating some of the most important issues, I will present my theory of justification and offer a brief defense.

I will ignore views of knowledge according to which it is incompatible with

---

hence that I am perceiving X, when in fact it is not X that is doing the appearing.) In terms of this distinction, what should we consider to provide the justification for a justified perceptual belief? Should we say that my belief that the gate is open is justified by arising from a perception of the open gate, e.g., seeing it, or by arising from a certain sensory experience? In a normal case of veridical perception either locution would seem to be acceptable. However, we need to range over abnormal and unveridical cases as well. Sometimes when I think I see an open gate, and so form the belief that the gate is open, but do not in fact satisfy all the conditions for seeing an open gate, we will still wish to hold that my belief is "perceptually" justified. In that case the sensory experience is the only viable candidate; there is no perception of the open gate to contend with it for the honor. Hence if we want a single unified account, we will speak of the perceptual belief's being justified by arising from the experience that is involved in the (putative) perception in question. That will be my canonical account of the matter. However, where it does no harm I shall sometimes for stylistic reasons relapse into speaking of the perception as providing the justification. That can always be translated back into the standard formulation.

belief, and assume that to know that p is to have a true belief that p that satisfies certain further requirements. I can make this assumption with a clear conscience since the focus in the book will be on justification rather than on knowledge. This is mainly because of the truth condition for knowledge. I can't argue that some people know that God is loving without arguing that it is true that God is loving, and it is no part of my aim in this book to establish theological propositions.

To turn to justification, the first point is that I will be working with the concept of a subject S's *being justified in believing that p*, rather than with the concept of S's *justifying* a belief. That is, I will be concerned with the *state* or *condition* of being justified in holding a certain belief, rather than with the *activity* of justifying a belief. It is amazing how often these concepts are conflated in the literature. The crucial difference between them is that while to justify a belief is to marshall considerations in its support, in order for me to *be* justified in believing that p it is not necessary that I have *done* anything by way of an argument for p or for my epistemic situation vis-à-vis p. Unless I *am* justified in many beliefs without arguing for them, there is precious little I justifiably believe.

There is an important distinction between *mediate* or *indirect* justification and *immediate* or *direct* justification. To be mediately justified in believing that p is for that belief to be justified by *reasons*, that is, by other things one knows or justifiably believes. Here the justification comes via appropriate inferential or grounding relations between the target belief and the beliefs that constitute one's reasons for it. Thus if I am justified in believing that it rained last night by seeing puddles of water on the street, my belief that it rained last night is justified by virtue of the fact that it is based on the belief that there are puddles of water. To be immediately justified in believing that p is for that belief to be justified by something other than reasons. This is a wastebasket category; it includes any justification by something other than justified beliefs on the subject. Prominent candidates for immediate justifiers are (a) experience of what the belief is about, (b) the self-evidence of the proposition believed, and (c) the propositions believed being of a certain category, for example, a proposition about one's current conscious experience. According to many direct realists, I can be justified in believing that the book is red just by virtue of basing that belief on the book's looking red to me, and not, even in part, on anything else I know or justifiably believe. We should not suppose that justification is always either purely mediate or purely immediate. A given belief may draw some of its justification from experience and some from other justified beliefs. And it may be that the contribution from both sources is needed to bring its justification up to what is required for rational acceptability. As we shall see, perceptual beliefs not infrequently exhibit this mixed status.

The connection between these two sets of distinctions is this. If one conflates being justified with the activity of justification, one will be led to think that all justification is mediate. For one *justifies* a belief only by adducing supporting reasons, that is, pointing out what will provide mediate justification. This leads to an unwarranted denial of the possibility of immediate justification.[4]

A final preliminary distinction is that between *prima facie* and *unqualified* justification. To be prima facie justified in believing that p by virtue of the satisfaction of conditions, C, is to be so situated that one will be unqualifiedly justified in that belief provided there are no sufficient "overriders", that is, no sufficient considerations to the contrary. These considerations might be reasons for believing that not-p ("rebutters"), or they might be reasons for supposing that C fails to provide adequate justification in this case ("underminers"). Unqualified justification is simply justification without any such qualifications attached: justification no matter what else.

Before getting to my favored construal of epistemic justification, let me make what I hope are two uncontroversial points.

(1) Justification is an evaluative status; to be justified is to be in an evaluatively favorable position. For one to be *epistemically* justified in holding a belief,[5] as opposed to *prudentially* or morally justified, is for it to be a good thing, *from the epistemic point of view*, for one to believe that p (then, under those conditions). We may think of the epistemic point of view as defined by the aim at maximizing the number of one's true beliefs and minimizing the number of one's false beliefs.[6]

(2) Justification is a matter of degree. If I am justified in believing that Sam is guilty because of the evidence I have for this, I can be more or less justified depending on the amount and strength of the evidence.

It should not be supposed that all those who speak of epistemic justification are expressing the same concept; quite the contrary.[7] In "Concepts of Epistemic Justification" (in Alston 1989b), I have explored some of the differences. The major divergence is over whether being justified in believing that p consists in some sort of "deontological" status, for example, being free of blame for believing that p or having satisfied one's intellectual obligations in

[4]See, e.g., Lehrer 1974, pp. 187–88; John Pollock, "A Plethora of Epistemological Theories", in Pappas 1979, p. 106.

[5]In this book I shall not be distinguishing between 'S's belief that p is justified', 'S is justified in believing that p', and 'S justifiably believes that p'. They will be taken as alternative ways of saying the same thing. In this they differ from a locutions like 'S has a justification for believing that p' and 'S would be justified in believing that p'. Locutions in the former group, but not in the latter, imply that S does believe that p and they constitute an evaluation of that state.

[6]More is required for an adequate characterization of this point of view. How about the relative weight to be given the two parts of this aim? And what about other desiderata such as the need for true beliefs on important rather than trivial matters? We will not be able to go into all that in this brief treatment.

[7]The differences I speak of here are not differences in the conditions required for the justification of one or another type of belief. Obviously there are many disagreements over this. I speak rather of differences over what justification *is*, differences as to what it is for which the alleged conditions are said to be conditions.

doing so. The nondeontologists will generally take justification to be some other sort of evaluative status, for example, believing in a way that is favorable from the standpoint of the aim at truth and the avoidance of falsity. In the article just mentioned and in "The Deontological Conception of Epistemic Justification" (Alston 1989b), I reject all versions of a deontological concept on the grounds that they either make unrealistic assumptions of the voluntary control of belief or they radically fail to provide what we expect of a concept of justification. Hence I will be thinking in terms of some nondeontological, or as I will say, "evaluative" conception in a more distinctive sense of 'evaluative', in which it has to do with the good rather than the right, with *value* rather than with the likes of duty, obligation, blame, and responsibility.

On a nondeontological conception, to be justified in believing that p is to be in a *strong position* for realizing the epistemic aim of getting the truth. In order to go further into the sort of strong position conception I advocate, I will have to raise some further issues on which theorists are divided. I will begin by making the plausible assumption that to be in an epistemically strong position in believing that p is to have an adequate ground or basis for believing that p. Where the justification is mediate this ground will consist in other things one knows or justifiably believes. Where it is immediate it will consist typically of some experience, including under that heading one's awareness of the self-evidence of a proposition. There are problems about this assumption taken as unrestrictedly general. It is not obvious, for example, what to identify as the ground of a justified memory belief. But that need not bother us in this book, where we will be concerned with perceptual beliefs for which there is an obvious experiential ground, perhaps together with other beliefs.

I should also point out that in this book I am setting coherentism aside without a hearing. Talk of a ground or basis of a belief can be given a "linear" or a "holistic" reading. On the latter, the ground of any belief is the total set of the subject's beliefs, and justification depends on how the particular belief fits into that system, as well as on internal features of that system (its "coherence"), whereas on the linear reading, the ground of a particular belief is much more restricted, for example, a particular experience or a very few of the subject's other beliefs or some combination thereof. I believe that coherentism, and any other form of a holistic theory of justification, is subject to crippling disabilities, particularly the point that there is an indefinitely large number of mutually incompatible systems that satisfy equally well any plausible standards of coherence; but I will not have time to go into that. I feel the more comfortable in this summary dismissal of coherence in that, so far as I can see, religious belief does about as well on a coherentist epistemology as anything else; and so I am subjecting M-beliefs to a much more stringent test in using a linear epistemology.

Now for our first issue. Is it enough for justification that I *have* an adequate ground in my possession? Or is it also necessary that my belief is *based on* that ground, that I hold the belief because of that ground. Suppose that I *have* an adequate ground for believing that Tim is trying to get me fired, in the form of various things I know about Tim's activities and (presumable) intentions. And I do believe that he is trying to get me fired. But I believe this not because of the excellent evidence I have for this but because of my paranoia, which would lead me to that belief whether I had such evidence or not. In fact the evidence plays no role at all in my coming to, and continuing in, the belief. In this case should we say that I am *justified* in believing that Tim is trying to get me fired? Well, there certainly is something epistemically desirable about my situation. The evidence I have does put me in a favorable position to get the truth in believing this. One might say that I "have a justification" for the belief, and if one were assessing my situation prior to my forming any belief on the matter one way or the other, one might say that it is a justifiable thing for me to believe. Nevertheless, if we are assessing the belief I actually have, and that is our focus in this book, there is definitely something amiss. Since I hold the belief on a markedly disreputable basis, we can hardly give unqualified epistemic approval to my doxastic state. Hence I will opt for the "source relevant" option, and take the position that in order for me to justifiably believe that p it is necessary not only that I *have* an adequate ground but that my belief be based on that ground, be held because of it.[8]

I have said that justification requires an adequate ground. But what is it for a ground to be adequate, adequate for the justification of the belief for which it is a ground? Remember the point that justifiably believing is believing in a way that is valuable vis-à-vis the aim at maximizing true belief and minimizing false belief. That suggests that the ground of a belief will suffice to justify it only if it is sufficiently indicative of the truth of the belief. If the ground is to be adequate to the task, it must be the case that the belief is very probably true, given that it was formed on that basis.[9] Unless the belief's basis served to render it probably true, then forming a belief on that basis would not be desirable from the epistemic point of view.

This severely objective conception of adequacy introduces an "externalist" component. The controversy between *externalism* and *internalism* looms large in contemporary epistemology. These terms are subject to more than one con-

[8]I mean this requirement to hold both of the initial acquisition of the belief and of its continued possession. In both cases the requirement is that the belief be "supported" by the ground in question, that the ground furnish the explanation of the fact that the belief is held. This is often spoken of as a *causal* requirement, but I don't want to get into the question of whether it is appropriate to impute a causal relation here. Here I will often be specifically concerned with belief acquisition, and I will usually omit mention of the basis of belief retention—but the wider bearing of the requirement should always be kept in mind.

[9]Here I presuppose some suitable *objective* conception of probability, according to which the probability of a certain state of affairs on another state of affairs is determined by the lawful structure of the world. That is, I assume that there is some viable form of a "propensity" theory of probability on which it is an objective fact about the way the world is that the probability of there being a tree in front of me is some determinate function of the fact that I am having a certain kind of visual experience, plus further facts about my situation.

strual.[10] Here we will understand *internalism* to be the view that the justificational status of a belief is, at least typically, open to the reflective grasp of the subject. A subject can, normally, determine what the justificational status of a particular belief is just by raising the question. And *externalism* is simply the denial of this constraint; it holds that justificational status need not be directly accessible to the subject. Internalism is obviously attractive for several reasons: it promises a secure basis for the development of epistemological theories, it offers a secure refuge from scepticism by guaranteeing a direct knowledge at least of justification, and it conforms to the intuition that whether I am *justified* in a belief is a matter of the credentials of the belief from my perspective on the world. But if wishes were horses, beggars would ride. However nice it would be if internalism were true, that just doesn't seem to be the way things are. There are strong reasons for denying that the justificational status of our beliefs is typically as open to reflective scrutiny as internalism demands.[11] Moreover, internalist justification would not seem to have the implications for (the probability of) truth that is required of justification by the epistemic point of view. Whatever it is that I know when I allegedly know just by reflection on the matter that my belief that p is justified, it does not seem to be something that implies that p is likely to be true. How could I determine, just by asking myself whether my belief that nothing can travel faster than the speed of light is justified, that this belief is likely to be true?[12] Finally, if internalism requires for the justification of S's belief that p that S be *justified* in supposing that the ground of that belief is adequate, a nasty infinite regress looms.[13] For all these reasons I do not look favorably on an internalist perspective on the adequacy of grounds, according to which what is required for justification is that the grounds be adequate, *so far as the subject can tell*. I adopt instead the view broached above, that justification requires that the ground be adequate in the objective sense that the ground be such as to render it objectively likely that the belief be true. This is an externalist conception, since there is no reason to suppose that these objective probability relations are ascertainable just on reflection. They have to do with the lawful structure of the world, and I can't expect to discern that just by looking within my breast.

In "An Internalist Externalism" I balanced my externalist perspective on the *adequacy* of grounds with an internalist perspective on the *existence* of grounds, requiring of a "justifying ground" that it be the sort of thing that is typically recognizable by the subject just on reflection. This paradigmatically includes beliefs and experiences. To simplify the discussion in this book I am going to omit this internalist constraint. I believe that as a matter of fact

[10]For an exploration of this conceptual terrain see my "Internalism and Externalism in Epistemology" (in Alston 1989b).

[11]For an exposition of these reasons see "Internalism and Externalism in Epistemology".

[12]This point is generally conceded by internalists.

[13]See my "An Internalist Externalism" (in Alston 1989b).

almost everything our beliefs are based on is a sort of thing that is typically reflectively accessible to its subject; if our beliefs are based almost entirely on other beliefs and on experiences, that thesis will be secured.[14] But I will not build that conviction into my account of justification. I will take the justification of belief to be a function of the adequacy of whatever the belief is based on, whether reflectively accessible or not. However, this distinction is of little importance for our central concern in this book, where the beliefs in question (M-beliefs) are based (at least in part) on experiences of which the subjects are oviously directly aware.

I am going to use the above account of justification in my examination of the justificational status of M-beliefs. In one way, this limits the scope of my results. Those who prefer some other conception of justification will, quite properly, not take me to have shown that such beliefs are justified in their understanding of 'justified'. But this does not disturb me, for two reasons. First, I feel that the requirements for justification are more stringent on my conception than on that of its most prominent competitors. As we shall see in the next chapter, it is impossible to show directly, without epistemic circularity, that even familiar sense-perceptual beliefs are formed in such a way as to pass this test. Hence if I can successfully defend the position that (some) M-beliefs are justified on my conception, I will have shown that they can pass one of the most difficult tests in the field. It is much easier, for example, to pass coherentist requirements by being part of a coherent system (assuming that we can figure out what coherence is). And as for the form of internalism concerning the adequacy of grounds rejected above, one who holds M-beliefs on the basis of experience can easily convince himself that he has about as much direct intuition of the justified status of these beliefs as he has concerning the justified status of sense perceptual or memory beliefs. Second, if you prefer to use some other conception of justification, forget the term 'justified' and simply take this book as a discussion of the question of whether M-beliefs are (sometimes) based on a ground that is in fact adequate. That is obviously a question of enormous import, however we decide to use the term 'justified'.

To avoid any imputation of false advertising I will give a bit more of a sneak preview of my results. The defense of the justification of M-beliefs, in the above sense of 'justified', will be considerably weaker than one might wish, though no weaker, in its general outlines, than a defense of the justificatory status of more uncontroversial beliefs, such as sense-perceptual beliefs. At that juncture I will point out that instead of a weak defense of justification in a strong sense, we could settle for a strong defense of justification

[14]Notice that this does not imply that one is typically conscious of the basis of a belief, and of its functioning as such, in the heat of belief formation. One undoubtedly is often conscious of this, but it is by no means the rule. Perceptual beliefs in particular are often generated at too fast and furious a rate for this to be possible.

in a weaker sense, one that might plausibly be taken as the one we should be centrally concerned with. All this will come out in Chapters 4 and 5.

iii. The Justification of Perceptual Beliefs

Our central concern is with the epistemic justification of M-beliefs. Remember that M-beliefs are a particular species of perceptual beliefs; they are beliefs, based on mystical perception, to the effect that God has some perceivable property or is engaging in some perceivable activity. To set this topic in a wider context I shall, for the remainder of this chapter, look generally at the justification of perceptual beliefs, concentrating on sense perception concerning which there is an extensive literature, but keeping an eye on the possible applications to mystical perception. At this point I had better be more explicit as to just how I am using the term 'perceptual belief'.

(1) A perceptual belief is a belief about a perceived object, about an object that perceptually presents itself to the subject. Thus the term does not extend to beliefs *that the subject is perceiving something or other*. It covers, for example, the belief that the window is open, when I suppose myself to be seeing that window, but not the belief that I am *seeing* the window or that I *see* the window to be open. I am not suggesting that beliefs of the latter sort are uninteresting or unimportant, or that they do not deserve to be called "perceptual beliefs". The reason for my focus is that beliefs about what is perceived are more elementary and basic than beliefs about perception. We learned to form beliefs about the perceived environment before we learned to form beliefs about our perception of the environment. In addition, my concern with the justificatory efficacy of mystical perception concerns the possibility that it provides a basis for beliefs about God, rather than beliefs about the subject's perceptual achievements.

(2) A perceptual belief is *based on* the subject's perceptual experience of the object, at least in part. It is based on how the object looks, sounds, smells, or whatever. It can also be based partly on other beliefs, though not all perceptual beliefs are. But even where other beliefs figure in the basis they do so by filling out the experiential basis, not by providing a basis independent of that. Let me explain.

Sometimes a perceptual belief is based solely on how the perceived object looks, sounds, feels. . . . Thus it seems plausible to suppose that when I believe of a flower I see that it is purple, this belief would typically be based just on the way the flower looks to me. It *may* be that if I lacked certain other beliefs about physical objects and their properties—for example, the belief that objects about me are colored and that purple is one of those colors—I would not be able so much as to form that belief. But that is not to say that, for example, the belief that objects are colored forms part of my basis for believing that this flower is purple, and hence that I must be justified in holding the former in order that the latter be *justified*. A necessary condition of my having the belief at all (whatever its epistemic status) is not a necessary condition of the belief's being justified rather than unjustified.[15]

But sometimes other beliefs are involved in this basis. I look at a house I am passing and form the belief that it is your house. My belief is partly based on the look of the house. It looks like your house, and if it didn't I wouldn't take it to be your house. Nevertheless, there are a number of houses around the country that look indistinguishable from yours to a casual glance. But since I know that I am on the block on which you live, I am thereby enabled to go from that look to the belief that it is your house. Here the independent information—that you live on this block—is not an independent basis for the belief that this is your house. Rather it serves to fill out my experiential basis for the belief—the visual presentation, the way the house looks.

(3) A perceptual belief is based on perceptual experience *directly*, rather than through being based on other beliefs. To illustrate the latter side of the contrast, consider a case in which I form a perceptual belief and infer from it another belief about the same object. I see a man on a ladder leaning against the house next door, and I form the perceptual belief that this is the case. I then suppose that the best explanation of his being in that position is that he is painting the house (although I do not see him doing so). Again, I form the perceptual belief that a tall thin man is entering the house across the street, and since I know that the owner of the local hardware store lives there I infer that the man in question is the owner of the local hardware store (although I could not recognize him as such). In each of these cases the second belief does not count as a perceptual belief, though the first does. In both cases the second belief was based solely on another belief; perceptual experience played no part as a proximate ground for that belief, though an experience did figure in its remote ancestry. To be a perceptual belief in the sense in which I am using the term, the belief must stem directly from a perceptual presentation, though, as we have seen, other beliefs may facilitate this derivation.

The distinction between perceptual beliefs with a purely experiential basis and those partly based on other beliefs will be paralleled by a distinction, among justified perceptual beliefs, between those that are purely immediately justified and those that are partly mediately justified. The theory of justification I am using takes justification to be a function of the adequacy of what the belief is based on. If it is based purely on experience, and that basis is adequate, it will be purely immediately justified. It it is based partly on experience and partly on other beliefs, its justification will be partly immediate and partly mediate. Thus, of the above cases (assuming they involve justified

[15]There are those who hold that even in these maximally simple cases of the attribution of simple sensible properties, the belief cannot be purely immediately justified but requires support from other beliefs. I will be considering this issue shortly.

belief), the belief that a man is on a ladder next door was represented as purely immediately justified, whereas the belief that that is your house was a mixed case, involving both mediate and immediate justification. Since nothing counts as a perceptual belief unless it is directly based, at least in part, on experience, no perceptual belief can be purely mediately justified.

The immediate justification component for a perceptual belief can be given quite a simple general formulation.

(1) When a belief of mine that X is ϕ is based, at least in part, on an experience in which X appears to my experience as ϕ (or so it seems to me), that experience contributes to the justification of that belief.[16]

This account applies to both purely immediately justified and partly mediately justified perceptual beliefs, the difference being that for the former this contribution is sufficient by itself to render the belief prima facie justified. But, unfortunately, the mediate justification component cannot be so concisely set out. There is no analogously unified way of saying what there is, in all cases, about the relation between the supporting beliefs and the perceptual belief thereby supported that enables the former to contribute to the justification of the latter. There is a wide variety of supporting beliefs, related variously to the perceptual belief supported. Shortly we will be sampling this diversity.

Any ordinary justification of perceptual beliefs is prima facie only. I will first make this point for purely immediate justification. Any support that an experience gives to a belief about what is putatively experienced is subject to being overriden either by sufficient reasons to think the belief false (a *rebutter*), or by sufficient reasons to think that in this instance the ground of the belief does not wield its usual justificatory force (an *underminer*). The flower looks purple to me; but if I have overwhelmingly strong evidence that there are no purple flowers in this garden, or if I know that there is something about the lighting that makes white flowers look purple, I am not, overall, justified in believing the flower to be purple just on the basis of that experience. The purple look is sufficient to render me prima facie justified in believing the flower to be purple, but in this case that prima facie status (initial credibility) is overriden by other things I know or justifiably believe. I won't always make this qualification explicit, but from now on all reference to the immediate justification of perceptual beliefs is to be understood as prima facie. And this means that any claims to such justification presuppose a "background system" of beliefs against which a particular perceptually supported belief can be checked for possible overriders—an "overrider system" as I will often call it.

[16]This formulation is in terms of the Theory of Appearing. Analogues can be constructed for other theories of perception by suitable replacements for the description of the sensory experience involved. Thus by substituting for "an experience in which X appears to my experience as ϕ (or so it seems to me)" something like "my sensing X-is-ϕ-ishly" or "my sensing in an X-is-ϕ manner", we convert (1) into an Adverbial Theory version (provided it makes sense to talk this way, something of which I am very dubious).

Note that this claim goes against the well-advertised view that experience of God is "self-authenticating". "Of such a Presence it must be true that to those who have never been confronted with it argument is useless, while to those who have it is superfluous".[17] I have termed the view "widely advertised" rather than "widely held", since, like solipsism, "naive" realism, and other popular straw men, I find the view much more widely criticized than espoused. I can report that on scrutinizing seven or eight attacks on self-authentication, most of them cited no formulations by defenders of the view, and of those who did, none of the sources cited unambiguously sets forth a self-authentication claim. My own search for forthright espousals has also borne little fruit. Nevertheless, the view is discussed sufficiently often to deserve notice.[18] One philosopher who is at least quite friendly to the idea is Robert Oakes.[19] He provides the following formulation of the claim (1985).

> The experiences in question are of such a nature that I do not *require* any criterion to be certain that they are veridical. Rather, I have *non*-criterial certainty that such is the case. Alternatively, that my relevant experiences constitute veridical apprehensions of God's presence is *immediately* apparent to me since the experiences in question have the very special epistemic status of being *self-authenticating*, i.e., of *guaranteeing their own veridicality* to their epistemic subjects. Accordingly, every such experience provides me with *infallible justification* for believing that it constitutes a veridical awareness of God's presence. (Pp.217–18)

This is an excellent formulation of the self-authentication claim. It is not just the claim that the subjects of the experiences are completely *convinced* of their authenticity. It is the more objective claim that the experiences carry with them an adequate *sign* or *mark* of their authenticity, so that, as Oakes says, the experience itself provides a *justification* for believing that it is an awareness of God's presence.

Along with most other contemporary philosophers, I see no reason to accept such a strong claim. And, as we will see in Chapter 5, I am at one with the main trend of the Christian mystical tradition in this. Delusory experiences can be phenomenally indistinguishable from veridical ones, in the mystical realm as well as the sensory. Nothing in the experience itself suffices to distinguish one from the other. But, and this is a crucial point, this fact does not prevent beliefs formed by "reading off" what is presented in the experience from being prima facie justified just by that fact. The fact that it is for all the world as if X is given to my experience as ϕ at least creates a strong presumption that X is ϕ, even though the experience itself does not guarantee that this is so.

[17]Baillie 1939, p. 132. See also Farmer 1943, p. 40.

[18]For attacks see Martin 1959, chap. 5; John Mackie 1982, chap. 10; Penelhum 1971, pp. 172–76. Flew (1966, chap. 6) seems to take it that virtually the whole issue concerning "religious experience" is whether it is self-authenticating.

[19]See his 1979 and 1985.

Though I have indicated a level of aspiration for the immediate justification of perceptual beliefs that is below *justification all things considered*, the level could be lowered still further. But first a terminological note. Although justification is a degree concept, when I speak of justification tout court that is to be understood as a degree of justification sufficient for rational acceptance. Hence in suggesting that a belief may be prima facie justified solely by experience, I am suggesting that this mode of justification can suffice for rational acceptance, in the absence of sufficient overriders. But one might hold that the most a belief can get from experience alone is some lesser degree of justification. On this view, experience can *contribute* to the justification of a perceptual belief, but the belief will need additional support from other beliefs to be rationally acceptable. A choice between these positions is not crucial for this book. As will be made explicit shortly, my basic thesis is that M-beliefs, when formed in the *usual* or *standard* way, are often justified. This standard way includes, I believe, both cases in which the basis is purely experiential and cases where it also includes background beliefs that the subject brings to the experience. But even I am mistaken about this, and it is restricted to the latter possibility, the defense I will provide for the basic thesis will remain intact.

Where other beliefs are included in the basis of a perceptual belief, it is not so clear that the justification will always be merely prima facie. What if the basis was sufficiently rich to rule out any possibility of overriders? Well, in that case, of course, the justification is unqualified. But that's not the way perceptual belief formation goes. Where background beliefs form part of the basis, they never contribute anything that strong. Rather, they shore up the experiential support by supplying relevant information about the local situation, as in the painting example given above, or about the relation of the experience to what is believed.[20] Thus, for all practical purposes, we can take partly mediately justified perceptual beliefs to be only prima facie justified as well.

iv. Doxastic Grounds of Perceptual Beliefs

I have expressed the opinion that perceptual beliefs are sometimes based solely on an experiential presentation, and are sometimes prima facie justified thereby. Many epistemologists deny that any perceptual beliefs (at least any that go beyond the bare minimum of believing of an object that it appears to S as so-and-so) are purely immediately justified. In terms of our theory of epistemic justification, they hold that other beliefs always form part of the basis for a perceptual belief—so that if the latter is justified it must be, at

[20]Shortly we will be exploring the variety of beliefs that can figure in the basis of perceptual beliefs.

least in part, because the other beliefs in its basis are themselves justified. I will examine this view. Even if so extreme a position has to be rejected, as I will try to show, it is important for this book to consider how far purely immediate justification of perceptual beliefs extends. I will first discuss this in reference to sense perception. Sections v and vi of this chapter apply the results to mystical perception.

I have already acknowledged that perceptual beliefs are sometimes based partly on other beliefs; that is not at issue. The only question is whether they are ever based solely on experience, and if so how often. I will proceed by discussing various kinds of alleged doxastic bases of perceptual beliefs. I shall argue that even though background beliefs of each kind (except for the second) sometimes form part of the basis, they need not do so even where they are relevant to the epistemic status of the perceptual belief. The result of the discussion will be to leave some room for purely experiential justification of perceptual beliefs, though it by no means covers the whole territory.

A. Beliefs about Perceptual Experience

Far and away the most common argument for the impossibility of purely immediately justified perceptual beliefs is that perceptual beliefs about objects in the physical environment are always based on beliefs about the subject's perceptual experience. When I hear the telephone ringing and form the belief that it is, that belief, so it is said, is based on my belief that I am having a certain kind of experience (in terms of the theory of appearing, that I am presented with a ringing sound). When I form the perceptual belief that an apple is before me, that belief is based on the belief that I am having a visual presentation of a certain sort. On this view, the only empirical beliefs that can be purely immediately justified are beliefs about one's own experience.

Along with other direct realists, I consider it to be a decisive refutation of this view that we rarely form beliefs about the character of our perceptual experience. I by no means deny that we can do so, and sometimes do. But I most emphatically deny that we always or even frequently do so. It is the exception rather than the rule. Typically our attention is focused on what we are perceiving in the environment. It is only under relatively rare conditions that our attention is directed inward to our own experience—when it is hard to believe that what we seem to be seeing is really there, or when we are engaged in epistemological reflection. Of course, it can be claimed that though we are not normally conscious of forming beliefs about our experience, we do so unconsciously, and unconsciously base beliefs about the external world on them. That is conceivable, but I see no reason to suppose that it is the case. In terms of cognitive processes, it would seem that the experiential presentations themselves are quite enough to elicit the belief about the perceived object, without having to go through the phrase of first eliciting beliefs about the experience itself and then inferring something about the perceived object from that.

The position I am attacking has been nourished by various confusions. I think particularly of confusions between what a belief is based on, on the one hand, and what it would take to defend (justify, establish) the belief, on the other hand. If a perceptual belief of mine is challenged, I might well advert to my experience, supporting the former by referring to how the object in question looks, sounds, or feels to me. But this has no implications for what my belief is based on. I should also acknowledge that if someone is working with a conception of justification different from mine, the fact that perceptual beliefs are not typically based on beliefs about experience may have no tendency to show that the former are not justified by the latter. Thus if justification is made to hang on whether the subject could adequately respond to challenges, or on what the subject *has* in the way of possible supports, then my claims about bases of perceptual belief, even if accepted, would cut no ice. But for the moment I am only concerned to argue that on my chosen account of justification, perceptual beliefs are not typically justified by beliefs about the subject's perceptual experience.

B. Perceptual Cues

Let's consider the attribution of simple "sensible qualities" like color, shape, and size. Here the topic of perceptual "cues" is relevant. It is a truism of the psychology of perception that the way something appears to us, looks, sounds, and so on, is dependent on a number of factors; it seems plausible to suppose that the psyche in some way takes account of those factors in constructing the sensory appearance, though subjects normally have absolutely no awareness of doing so, or indeed any awareness whatsoever of these cues. For example, it has repeatedly been shown experimentally that the apparent distance of an object varies with such factors as size of retinal image, apparent brightness, shading, texture density, retinal disparity, and binocular convergence. Some psychologists take it that beliefs about these factors, or some other mode of cognition thereof, is functioning as a basis for the appearance. To be sure, our present interest is in possible doxastic bases for beliefs, not for sensory appearances, whatever it would be to have a "basis" for the latter. But it has also been held on the basis of experimental evidence, that perceptual beliefs (judgments) of distance are based on cognitions of factors of the sort just mentioned.

It is a matter of intense controversy in both philosophy and psychology just how to think about this matter. On one extreme is the view that *inference* is involved, that the subject performs an unconscious inference from premises concerning the cues to a conclusion concerning the way X looks. At the other extreme is the view that the processes that yield sensory experience involve nothing like beliefs or inference at all, that it is all a matter of "purely causal" transactions, with no sort of intentionality or "taking account of" of any sort being involved. Intermediate positions hold that some kind of "subdoxastic" taking account of is involved; these are less complex than full-blooded beliefs but nevertheless involve a rudimentary sort of cognition of the relevant factors.

I won't try to settle this issue here. If beliefs about binocular convergence and the like are functioning as grounds for distance beliefs, they are doing so in a maximally hidden way, and it is difficult to find sufficient reasons for supposing they are so functioning, given the availability of simpler hypotheses of the sort just mentioned. It is more to the present purpose to consider doxastic grounds that are clearly sometimes operative, the only question being how often.

C. Adequacy Assumptions

Let's turn to beliefs attributing nonsimple sensory predicates to external objects. As we saw in Chapter 1, when we make such attributions on the basis of sense experience, we are assuming, at least in practice, that a certain complex pattern of sensory qualities, which we would typically not be able to describe as such in any detail, is a reliable indication that the predicate in question applies. Call such assumptions "adequacy assumptions (beliefs)". When I take it that X is a house, or your house, or a chair, or the chair we just bought, or a copy of *Process and Reality*, or a wave, or Coit Tower, or my wife, or a primrose, I am, in effect, supposing that the particular pattern of sensory qualia X is presenting to me at that moment is, at least in those circumstances, a reliable indication of X's being a house, or your house, or a chair. That being the case, am I not basing my belief not just on the sensory appearance of X but also on my belief that a sensory appearance of that sort is a reliable indication that what is appearing is a house . . . ? Isn't every case of nonsimple sensory-predicate attribution subject to evaluation, at least in part, in terms of mediate justification?[21]

How we settle this question depends, obviously, on what it is for a belief to be based on another belief. Thus far I have been working with an intuitive conception of this relationship. I can't go into the matter deeply here, but I will say this. Our paradigm for such basing is the case in which we make a conscious inference from one or more believed propositions to another one. But we have to recognize cases of beliefs being based on others where no such conscious inference is involved. Thus if I believe that Susie has left town because you told me so, my belief that Susie left town is based on my belief that you asserted this, even if I do not consciously infer the latter from the former. To generalize to such cases we need to form a wider concept of "what I was taking account of" or "what I was going on" in coming to believe that p, where a conscious inference from the former to the latter is a specially transparent case of this wider phenomenon.

In assessing the idea that perceptual beliefs are based on adequacy assump-

[21]See Bonjour 1985, 2.3, for an argument along these lines.

tions, let's confine ourselves initially to cases in which facts about the circumstances play no role, cases in which S is, at least tacitly, supposing that the sensory appearance is sufficient for identification in any circumstances (in which S might find himself). This is the kind of case one could express by saying "I could recognize her anywhere". One thing is clear. Perceivers are not usually aware of any such assumption as part of the basis of the perceptual belief. Nor is it the sort of thing they could become aware of by resolutely turning their attention to the matter. Indeed, I dare say most perceivers have never been aware of any such propositions in any connection. If you were to ask the typical perceiver, even a reasonably sophisticated one, on what basis she takes the object before her to be a house, she would most likely say something about the way it looks (minimally that it looks like a house), but would not add that what looks like that is (usually) a house. This is not an absolutely decisive reason for denying that the adequacy belief is part of the basis, for it is conceivable that it functions as such without the subject's being aware of this; but the lack of reflective access at least carries a strong negative presumption.

To be sure, a sufficiently reflective person can easily come to realize that her perceptual identification of Coit Tower is to be credited only if the sensory array with which she was presented is an adequate indication of the presence of Coit Tower. But that is not the same thing as coming to realize that the identification was *based on* an assumption of adequacy. The first sentence of the paragraph does imply that an adequate *defense* of a claim that *one's perceptual belief was justified* would involve a defense of the thesis that the sensory array was an adequate indication of Coit Tower. But none of this implies either that the perceptual belief was based on that thesis or that holding the perceptual belief justifiably requires that one be justified in holding the adequacy thesis. The former is obvious on the face of it, since frequently something is required to defend a belief even though it played no role in the subject's coming to have the belief. If this were not the case our beliefs would be more invariably defensible than is the case. The latter implication can be readily seen to fail also once we are free from the level confusion between being justified in believing that p (That is Coit Tower), and being justified in the higher level belief that *one is justified in believing that p*. Being justified in the adequacy assumption is required for the latter but not for the former.[22]

[22]Note that the argument depends on the fact that my theory of justification takes the justification to hang on what grounds that belief is based on, its actual psychological source. If one holds, as many epistemologists do, that justification depends on what (accessible) grounds a person *has* for a belief, or on what grounds a person would cite if the belief were challenged, then it would be a different ball game. I could not argue, as I have just done, that assumptions of the adequacy of the appearance to support what is believed often do not play a justificatory role *because* they are not actual *grounds* of the belief. So long as the person would cite such assumptions in defending the belief, or so long as the person *has* that adequacy belief, it could still figure in justification. That is to say, the sphere of purely immediate justification of perceptual beliefs is smaller on some other theories of justification. Indeed, on the theory that takes justifiers to be

But surely the degree of adequacy of the sensory indication plays some role in the epistemic status of the perceptual belief. How can we understand this if we deny that the perceptual belief is based on a belief in adequacy? Very simply. The adequacy of the sensory basis can figure as a requirement for the justificatory efficacy of that basis. That is, rather than being part of the basis on which the belief is formed, it can figure as the thesis that the basis is sufficient for the job at hand. If that is the case, then in order for the target belief to be justified it is not necessary that the subject be *justified in believing* this assumption; it is only necessary that the assumption be *true*. Whatever the basis of a belief, that basis can serve to justify the belief only if it is adequate to the task, only if it is *true* that that basis constitutes a sufficient indication of the truth of the target belief. If the basis of the Coit Tower identification were to include not only a certain visual experience but also the belief that that experience is a reliable indication of the presence of Coit Tower, then that expanded basis would serve to justify only if *it* as a whole is sufficiently indicative of the truth of the perceptual belief. Once we look at the matter in this way, we can see a familiar fallacy in insisting that an assumption of the adequacy of the sensory basis *must* figure in the ground of a perceptual belief. It is the fallacy of supposing that what it takes for a condition, C, to be sufficient for P (call this "what it takes" 'A') must itself be part of any sufficient condition for P. The fallacy is immediately evident once we see that if A is satisfied, then, by the very terms of the example, C is sufficient for P by itself, and A need not be added to it to get sufficiency. A historically famous discussion of this fallacy, or a close relative thereof, is exposed in Lewis Carroll's essay "What Achilles Said to the Tortoise" (1895), in which the author brings out the catastrophic consequences of insisting that the rule of inference that licenses a certain argument must itself be added to the premises if the argument is to be valid. Supposing that the adequacy of my justifying grounds must itself be one of those justifying grounds confuses the role of what justifies and that by virtue of which it does so, just as surely as confusing the premises of a valid argument and that by virtue of which they suffice to entail the conclusion.[23]

confined to what the subject would cite in defense of the belief, there can be no immediate justification at all. On this view the reasons cited in defense of a belief are what provide the justification.

[23]Some versions of the fallacy are too obviously unwarranted to exercise much attraction. Consider the claim that the causal law that is satisfied by a certain causal transaction must itself be reckoned among the causes of the effect. Reflection on such obviously fallacious claims can help us to appreciate the same fallacy when it occurs in less obviously unacceptable guise. There are interesting connections between the above discussion and the psychology of perceptual belief formation. If we think of the adequacy assumption as part of the basis, we think of an explicitly formed belief in adequacy as part of the input taken account of by the belief-forming mechanism. That may be typical of early stages of perceptual learning. Whatever the innate components of our perceptual recognitional capacities, many of these capacities are obviously learned. We have to learn what sensory arrays are typically presented by trees, office buildings, computers, and

Thus we can readily understand the role of adequacy assumptions in epistemic justification without supposing that they must figure in justifying grounds. I am not claiming that such assumptions cannot figure as grounds or that they never do so. I am merely contesting the claim that they must do so, and hence that the justification of the kinds of perceptual beliefs currently under consideration can never be purely immediate.

The above discussion, like the discussion of comparative concepts in Chapter 1[24], gives rise to questions as to what sort of basis one can have for adequacy assumptions. How can I know, or become justified in believing, that a certain phenomenal array is a reliable indication of a certain individual or a certain objective property, either in general or in certain kinds of contexts? If I am to have good inductive reasons for accepting the principle that what looks like *that* is your house, then I must have learned on a number of occasions that what looked that way was your house. But it seems that I can ascertain this in a particular case only if I already have the appropriate adequacy principle to work with. And so it seems that we can never get started. This kind of puzzle pops up at various points when we try to understand empirical knowledge. As another example, consider how we can have inductive evidence for the general principle that a certain facial expression reliably indicates depression. Again, to pile up the evidence we have to ascertain that the facial expression coexists with depression in a number of particular cases. But, it seems, we can't determine this in a particular case unless we already have an adequacy principle for attributions of depression to work with.

The answer to this particular puzzle involves the point that, on my theory of epistemic justification, there are no "higher-level" requirements for justified belief. In order for me to be justified in taking X to be your house on the (sole) basis of a certain look (perhaps in circumstances of a certain kind), it is not necessary that I be justified in the general belief that the look in question is a reliable indication of your house; it is necessary only that it *be* a reliable indication, and that I take the perceived object to be your house on the basis of that look, in the right circumstances. It is only if we fall into a level confusion that we suppose that my being justified in the adequacy principle, which is required for my being justified in the higher level belief that *I am*

---

pencils. When we are first assimilating this, it may be that more or less conscious beliefs to the effect that pencils typically look like *this* are operative in the formation of judgments that what I am now seeing is a pencil, rather than an apple or a comb. But as in many other sorts of learning, the process becomes compressed with the passage of time, and intervening stages are omitted. Just as the practiced driver no longer needs to think to himself "First I push in the clutch and then shift the gears", so the practiced perceiver no longer needs to say to himself "When something looks like this it is most likely a pencil". He has simply internalized the tendency to go from sensory appearances like this to a belief that what he is seeing is a pencil. The supposition that adequacy beliefs typically form part of the basis of belief is, in effect, a false supposition that all of us are mostly in an early stage of perceptual learning.

[24]Section ix.

justified in taking X to be your house, is also required for the lower level belief that X is your house. Once we recognize this, we see that it is possible to assemble inductive evidence for the adequacy principle without already having been justified in accepting the principle.[25]

D. Contextual Beliefs

Let us now turn to the role of beliefs about the context of perception. Here there is a stronger case for a mediate justification component. First, the *setting* (the *situation*) in which the perception takes place is relevant. The look of X by itself does not always serve to identify it. Many houses look very much alike, especially in these latter days of tract houses; so my identification of a certain house as your house may be partly based on my awareness of where I am. If I know that I am in Syracuse, or on Sedgwick Avenue, a casual glance at X may suffice to identify it as your house, since I can take it that no other house in that area looks like that. But if I have been kidnapped and kept blindfolded for many days and then am released without any indication of where I am, a glance at a house may well not suffice to assure me that it is yours. People, alas, change their appearance with age. I can recognize you from the way you look if the looking is in 1988; but if I supposed the year to be 1938, I wouldn't take a person who looked like that to be you. And so it goes.

Second, various factors other than the perceived object affect its appearance, such as distance from the observer, angle of view, and the state of the medium. I will take the position of the observer vis-à-vis the object as representative of this group, and refer to them generally as *positional* factors. To be sure, it is an old story in the psychology of perception that "constancy mechanisms" drastically reduce the change in appearance that would be predicted (for vision) from the retinal image alone. As we approach or withdraw from an object, the proportion of the visual field it occupies can change very considerably without its looking smaller or larger.[26] Nevertheless, there are limits. From 35,000 feet in the air a house definitely does look smaller than it does from close up. Under drastic enough changes of lighting, things will appear to be colored differently. Things look different in a fog than they do in clear air. If a scene looked to me up close the way a town looks to me from an airplane flying at 35,000 feet, I would take it to be a tiny model town rather than the real thing. Thus it seems that I am taking account of my

[25]In this matter as elsewhere we are not, of course, confined to passively receiving bits of empirical data. We can also act on the assumption that what we see is a house, and note whether the results bear out that assumption. And, needless to say, it is not necessary for each person to base adequacy principles on his/her own experience alone. Here as elsewhere instruction and testimony are employed to share what has been learned with the community at large.

[26]There are controversies here over what is to be credited to the look and what to our beliefs, interpretations, or conceptualizations. But even when everything has been credited to the latter that reasonably could be, it remains that constancy mechanisms do make a difference to how things look.

distance from the object in judging, from the airplane, that what I am looking at is a real town with real houses. And so for the other cases. And if that is so, doesn't that mean that when I am at a more normal distance from a block of houses, I am taking account of that, too, in judging them to be real houses? Considerations like this make it plausible to suppose that information about one's *position* vis-à-vis the perceived object(s) is always, or usually, taken into account in forming perceptual beliefs. And that again makes it plausible to suppose that when perceptual beliefs are justified that is, in part, because they are based on justified beliefs about the context of the perception.

Finally, consider some more deeply hidden factors. If I supposed myself to be confronted with laser images or a 3–D movie or a movie set, that would certainly affect the perceptual judgments I make on the basis of a certain kind of sensory input. Does that imply that on more usual occasions an assumption that I am not involved in anything that unusual is part of my basis for my perceptual beliefs? Again, if I supposed that people, trees, dogs, and tables were constantly being annihilated and instantaneously replaced with exact replicas I would form somewhat different beliefs from a certain sensory array than I normally do. Does that imply that an assumption of relative constancy and permanence of physical substances is part of the basis for my normal perceptual beliefs? Let's call these "*normality* assumptions".

With respect to all these kinds of "contextual beliefs" we can look into the possibilities that they form part of the bases of perceptual beliefs by considering whether subjects are typically aware of their perceptual beliefs having bases of these sorts. The case is weakest for the normality assumptions in my third category. I may become convinced, and rightly convinced, that my usual modes of perceptual belief formation are reliable only if certain metaphysical principles are true, and only if conditions are normal in certain respects. But, as we saw in discussing adequacy assumptions, this does not amount to these assumptions figuring in the basis on which the perceptual beliefs are adopted. It only implies that, whatever that basis is, it will be adequate only if these assumptions are true. And, so far as we can tell, such assumptions do not normally figure in the basis. Nothing could be further from my mind than normality of conditions or the metaphysics of the physical world when I come to believe that the house I am looking at has bay windows. Similar points hold for our second category, the position of the perceiver vis-à-vis the object. Perhaps such matters figure in the processing of sensory information in a nondoxastic fashion; but, so far as I can tell, it is ordinarily no part of my basis for my believing that *what I am looking at is a house* that I am not 35,000 feet above the ground or even that I am fairly close to the object. Sometimes we do consciously take account of such conditions when making a perceptual judgment. And sometimes when we do not make any full dress conscious appeal to such factors we can become aware on reflection that they were figuring in our basis for taking the object to be so-and-so. But this would seen to be the exception rather than the rule.

There is a stronger case for including situational conditions (where S is, what time it is) in the basis. Sometimes I even consciously take into account where I am in forming a perceptual belief. Since I am in California, that large body of water stretching from the surf out into the far distance must be the Pacific, not the Atlantic. Since I am in New York City, those two tallest buildings must be the World Trade Center. But again it seems unlikely that this is the normal case. Even if just after forming the belief, I reflect that if I hadn't known I was in New York City I wouldn't have judged those buildings to be the World Trade Center, it doesn't follow that being in New York City was part of my basis for the belief. There are other possibilities. The livest of these is that the reflection in question uncovers what I take to be required for the adequacy of the basis rather than part of the basis itself. It would seem that usually I just go by how something looks, sounds, . . . in perceptually recognizing it. However, I am less certain of this judgment here than with the positional and normality conditions. Typically we do have a lot of information about where we are located at a given moment, and that does often affect our perceptual judgments. But my purpose here is not to show that mediate justification plays no significant role in perceptual belief, but only to point out that this role is less than might appear at first sight.

Here, just as with the adequacy assumptions treated earlier, we are faced with the task of explaining what kind of relevance contextual beliefs have where they are not functioning as part of the basis. With the adequacy assumptions the tack was obvious; clearly they have to do with the justificatory adequacy of the basis. Can we make the same move here? I have already pointed out this possibility for situational beliefs, and "positional" factors can have the same significance. But there is a difference. Here the adequacy assumption is not that the sensory pattern, A, is *generally* indicative of the presence of a ϕ. It is rather that, given an underlying supposition that A is an adequate basis for an attribution of ϕ only in certain circumstances rather than others, the belief in question is that the present circumstances are of the former sort. That gives the belief a greater claim to be considered part of the basis, for it does indicate something distinctive about this situation rather than just amounting to a blanket approval of the phenomenal-objective connection. But, by the same token, it offers us a different kind of alternative to holding that it must form part of the basis. Remember the point that the justification of perceptual beliefs is always prima facie, subject to being overriden by sufficient indications to the contrary. This gives us another way in which a belief can be relevant to the justification of another belief. It can be *negatively* relevant by constituting an (actual or possible) overrider or by ruling out such. Consider a case in which the belief that conditions are normal is definitely not functioning as part of the basis for belief B, but where if conditions were abnormal the sensory basis for B would not be an adequate one. Here the assumption of normality is relevant just because if one were justified in denying it the sensory justification would be canceled. That can explain the nagging sense that the assumption does have an important bearing on the justificatory status of the belief, even where it is not functioning as part of the basis. Situational and positional beliefs can, of course, have this significance also. Pointing out that you are in the wrong situation to judge that something that looks like that is my house, or that from your perspective of observation that's not the way the Empire State Building would look, can override the prima facie justification provided by your experience.

Here is a point that is implicit in the above discussion of adequacy assumptions and contextual beliefs. What makes it possible for such background information not to figure as a partial basis for a perceptual belief is that the information has been internalized in the form of perceptual skills, skills of perceptual recognition, and no longer needs to figure as propositional contents of beliefs. Having thoroughly learned what you look like, I no longer have to retrieve a belief that you look that way in order to recognize you. As in other cases of overlearning, I have developed the tendency to go directly from the look to a belief that you are before me, rather than following the more laborious route of applying a belief about your appearance to my visual presentation to obtain the belief that the person before me is you. It is analogous to familiar examples of motor skills like driving a car. When we are first learning to drive a car we have to go through propositionally structured instructions to get the job done. But after the skill is thoroughly learned, all that is short-circuited. We "automatically" react to a variety of situations in the right way to get the job done. And so it is with perceptual skill learning. The more thorough the learning, the less we have to make use of propositionally coded beliefs to go from the perceptual presentation to the belief about what is presented.

E. The Perceptual Identification of Individuals

Our discussion of the role of background beliefs has dealt with the justification of both the subject and the predicate components of perceptual beliefs. We have considered the role of background beliefs both in identifying the perceived object and in judging that it has certain properties. In both cases we have argued that the justification might be either purely immediate or partly mediate. As for the former, we have suggested that I might both be able to justifiably take the perceived object to be your house and be able to justifiably believe of it that is shingled, just on the basis of the way it looks. In both cases background beliefs would normally be playing some role, even if they are not part of the basis. But it may be felt that object identification poses greater difficulties for immediate justification than does property attribution, and hence that it should receive special treatment.

At the most general level subject identification presents exactly the same problems for the justification of perceptual beliefs as property identification, thinking of the former in terms of recognizing the subject as the one that bears certain properties.[27] In both cases there are questions as to whether the perceptual appearance is a reliable indication, perhaps in certain circumstances, of the possession of certain properties by the perceived objects, whether assumptions about this must appear in the basis of the belief in order that it be justified, and how such assumptions themselves can be justified. And so all the considerations addressed in this section apply to both subject and predicate components of perceptual belief. This can be seen from the fact that any property that can figure in subject identification can also figure as predicate. Instead of forming the belief that your house needs painting, I could form the belief that *that* is your house, or that that building that needs painting is your house. Instead of forming the belief that that copy of the *Critique of Pure Reason* is ragged, I could form the belief that that book is a copy of the *Critique of Pure Reason*. Hence subject and predicate identification pose no radically different problems for the mode of justification of perceptual beliefs.

However, there might well be an important difference of degree in the possibility of purely immediate justification for subject identification and for predicate attribution. Although it is sometimes possible for me to recognize a particular individual—Susie, your house, or the Empire State Building—just by the way it looks (perhaps in a certain kind of situation), we are more likely to have reasons for the identification of an individual than for the attribution of a property (in a perceptual belief), though these reasons will often consist in other perceptual beliefs. An indefinitely large plurality of unique individuals is out there to be recognized, whereas there are comparatively few properties we have any real need to distinguish. Hence it is more feasible for us to store relatively fixed ways of recognizing properties by their appearance than to build up comparably direct ways of recognizing individuals. In the latter case we typically proceed, rather, by storing ways of perceptually recognizing distinguishing properties of individuals and then using those capacities to recognize the individuals. Thus we recognize buildings by noting their shapes, colors, materials, and arrangements of doors and windows, and we recognize people by their size, facial configuration, hair color, and so on.[28] I am not

[27]Let me set aside two reasons for not thinking of the perceptual recognition of individuals in this way. First, we can employ *de re* locutions for reporting perceptual beliefs, locutions like 'S believes *of x* that it is ϕ' rather than 'S believes that x is ϕ'. In the de re version I, the reporter, take responsibility for picking out the object about which S believes that it is ϕ; I do not address myself to how S picks it out. But that is just to evade the problem; it doesn't make it go away. It remains true that S picked out x (as that to which he was attributing ϕ), and we are trying to understand what is involved in that. Second, we might follow Kripke 1972 in holding that I can pick out a particular individual by using a proper name just by virtue of the causal antecedents of my use of that name. That view, on a rigorous construal, would imply that I need not be thinking of a perceived object as possessing certain properties when I use a proper name to identify that object. But even though in "Referring to God" (Alston 1989a), I argued for an application of this view to talk about God, still, in religion and elsewhere, people normally do identify what they perceive, talk about, and have beliefs about as something that possesses certain properties; we are concerned with what is required for that.

[28]To be sure, I could recognize a building by its shape and configuration of windows even if

suggesting that this is anything more than a difference of degree. We can and do identify individuals directly from their sensory appearance; and we can and do spot properties on the basis of other properties (I was able to tell that it was hot by the fact that steam was coming out). Nevertheless, it would seem that property attribution more often figures in the basis for object identification than in the basis for the attribution of other properties.

Note that a kind of doxastic basis of perceptual beliefs has just surfaced that differs from the kinds discussed in section v. The beliefs that seem to figure most often in the basis of object identification are beliefs that the perceived object has certain properties. When such beliefs do not figure in the basis, can they still be relevant in some other way? Yes. Suppose I identify John Newton just by the way he looks? Can my knowledge that he is tall and silver haired with a craggy face play any role in the identification? Yes, it can. It may be that the look by which I identified him sufficed for the purpose only because that very look was also sufficient for attributing the properties of being tall, silver haired, and craggy faced to the perceived object, even though I made no such attribution. Again, these properties can be relevant by virtue of the fact that any reasons for denying that the person I am looking at is tall, silver haired or craggy faced will override my purely experiential basis for my identification.

F. Conclusion

The upshot of the discussion in this section is as follows. Background beliefs not infrequently figure in the total basis of perceptual beliefs, and in these cases the justification of the latter depends in part on the justification of the former. Nevertheless this is less common than it seems on first sight, and we can often explain the justificatory relevance of background beliefs without supposing them to be part of the basis, and so part of the prima facie justification. Thus there is considerable scope for purely immediately justified perceptual beliefs, even though partly mediately justified beliefs must also be taken into account.

v. Application to Mystical Perception

I now want to bring out how the points I have been making about sense perceptual beliefs apply to M-beliefs as well. First there is the general point

---

nothing other than the sensory presentation figures in the basis; it is just that it is those aspects of the presentation that lead me to identify the building as Old Main. But what I mean to be saying in the text is that it is common to *note* that the perceived object has these features (in other words, form the perceptual belief that it has those features) and use that belief as part of the basis for the identification of the building.

that the belief must be based, at least in part, on an (at least apparent) experiential presentation of what the belief is about in order to count as an M-belief, as a perceptual belief about God. Hence if the belief is justified, at least part of that justification will accrue to it by virtue of its relation to that experience. This will be in accordance with principle (I) on p. 79. If God appears to me as ϕ (or at least so it seems to me), then that will contribute to justifying a belief that God is ϕ; if the belief is purely immediately justified, that will be the whole story. If one is aware of what one takes to be God as loving or almighty, then, if no partly doxastic basis is involved or required for justification, a belief that God is loving or almighty formed on that basis is thereby prima facie justified. If one is aware of what one takes to be God as comforting one or saying that P to one, then, with similar restrictions, a belief that God is comforting one or saying that P to one is thereby prima facie justified.

The points made earlier about the role of background beliefs in sense perceptual judgments also apply here to some extent. All the reasons canvassed there for supposing there to be no or few purely immediately justified beliefs apply to mystical perception. (1) Typically, as we saw in Chapter 1, the predicates applied to God in M-beliefs possess a content that goes beyond what is explicitly displayed in the experience. And so it might appear that a typical M-belief is partly based on the belief that what is displayed in experience is a reliable indication of the applicability of the predicate involved. (2) As for contextual factors, "situational" and "positional" considerations have little or no application, since God is not spatially located vis-à-vis the perceiver, and the situation of the perceiver has doubtful relevance to the justificatory force of a mystical experience.[29] But normality assumptions are clearly relevant. Any reasons for suspecting the experiences to be artificially induced, or the work of the Devil, or due to nervous or mental imbalance, would, arguably, reduce or cancel their justificatory force. And, on the other hand, various consequences of one's experience are, properly I will argue at a later stage, taken to certify its justificatory efficacy. Mystics regularly appeal to the spiritual and moral fruits of their experience (typically not just one experience but a continuing series) in support of the claim that they are "from God".[30] Moreover, metaphysical and theological beliefs are obviously behind people's tendency to take certain experiences as awarenesses of the attributes and activities of God. The considerations deployed in section iv can be used here as well to argue that these facts do not serve to show that there is little or no purely immediate justification of M-beliefs. Here too we can find explanations of the epistemic relevance of these beliefs and assumptions even where they form no part of the basis. Nevertheless, it must be admitted that other

[29]One might suppose that experiences undergone while in prayer or worship might be more likely to be veridical than others; but I doubt that solid reasons could be mustered in support of this.

[30]See Chapter 5 for more on this.

beliefs of the subject can, and do, form part of the basis for many M-beliefs. Hence, if M-beliefs are often justified we must recognize both purely immediate justification and partly mediate justification.[31]

One may wonder whether there are any limits on the kinds of predicates the application of which to God can be justified just on the basis of theistic experience. Can one be justified in supposing God to have created everything other than Himself just on the basis of (one's taking it that) God appeared to one as having done so? Can one be justified in supposing God brought the Israelites out of slavery in Egypt by virtue of the fact that God appears to one as having done so? Since purely experiential justification gives us a prima facie justified belief that God is ϕ for any putative experiential appearance of God as ϕ, this is tantamount to asking whether there are any limits on how God can appear to human experience.[32] In Chapter I, section ix, we pointed out that there are no a priori or conceptual limits on comparative appearance concepts.[33] It all depends on our powers of perceptual discrimination, in relation to what they are given to work with. For any property, ϕ, if objects that are ϕ look (usually look, tend to look) a certain way, or a manageable family of ways, then it is possible to form a comparative concept of *looking* ϕ that will pick out a certain mode of appearance. That is not to say that there are no limits here. It is rather that the limits are something we have to learn from experience. We have to learn from sense experience and theories based on that in what ways physical objects can appear to us, and we have to learn

[31]Since mystics engage so much in discussions of the veridicality of their experiences, and bring a variety of pro and con considerations to bear on the issue, it is worth emphasizing that these discussions are aimed at the higher level issue of whether the experiences are veridical, or whether they provide an adequate basis for the perceptual beliefs based on them. Hence it would be a level confusion to suppose that this is incompatible with the M-beliefs themselves being purely immediately justified. When Teresa adduces, in support of the claim that a certain experience is genuinely an experience of God, the fact that the experience brings peace, joy, quietness, humility, detachment from things of the world, and an increase in virtue, she is, of course, supporting a belief by giving reasons for it; she is seeking mediate justification. But the belief in question is not the M-belief, e.g., the belief that Christ was at her side. It is the higher-level epistemic belief that that M-belief was justified or, to use her terminology, that the experience was "from God". It would be a level confusion to suppose that since the latter, higher level belief cannot be justified except mediately, the lower level M-belief is also mediately justified, if at all. The M-belief is not justified unless the higher level belief is *true*. But it does not follow that she must be justified in accepting the higher level belief in order that the M-belief *be justified*—though, of course, to *justify* the M-belief one must adduce reasons. This last point is an application of the crucial distinction, made at the beginning of this chapter, between the state of being justified in believing that p and the activity of justifying one's belief that p.

[32]This question has familiar analogues in sense perception. Can an object *look* distant, attractive, disgusting, or cold, as contrasted with one's merely judging that it has these properties on the basis of some more rudimentary look? Can an object present itself to my experience as a computer or a ballet dancer or a constellation, as opposed to my judging it to be such on the basis of its pattern of simple sensory qualities?

[33]For that matter, there are no a priori limits on how objects can appear phenomenally either. We have to learn that from experience too. There is no way we could have anticipated, just by rational reflection, that physical objects present odors as well as shapes. But here we are specifically interested in the lack of a priori limits for comparative appearance concepts.

from mystical experience and theories based at least in part on that in what ways God can appear to us.

The points made about subject identification in section iv also hold of M-beliefs. Here too there is more of a case for a mediate justification component, since it would seem that one's supposition that it is God that one is perceiving is, always or often, based on certain properties one perceives the object to have or certain actions one perceives the object to be performing. Again, this is not incompatible with taking the basis to be purely experiential, and it may sometimes or often be that way. But the identification is often most naturally construed as based on a belief (recognition) that the perceived object has the property or is performing the action in question. This will be examined in the next section.

The upshot of this section is that in theistic as well as in sense perception a perceptual belief may be based wholly on experience or partly on other beliefs, and hence, if justified, it may be wholly immediately or partly mediately justified in accordance with (I), depending on the details of the actual case. And again the thrust of the discussion is that immediate justification may cover more of the territory than one might think initially.

vi. The Perceptual Identification of God

Many people doubt that it is possible to recognize something one experiences as God. Presumably there can be no doubt that people sometimes believe that what they experience is God; but it is widely doubted that anyone can know, or be justified in believing, this. And there are solid bases for these doubts. How could anything I am directly aware of uniquely identify the creator of heaven and earth, an absolutely perfect being of infinite power and goodness? How can anything that can be displayed to my experience be such that it could attach only to such a being? Even if I can be aware of X as good, powerful, and loving, how could I be aware of X as *infinitely* good, powerful or loving? Don't I read the identification into the experience rather than reading it off the experience?

To come to grips with the serious, unconfused problem here, we will have to cut through some unwarranted assumptions that may be behind these questions. We should not suppose that in order to succeed in perceptually recognizing an object of perception as X (i.e., become perceptually justified in believing, or perceptually know, that the object is X), it is necessary that the object appears to one as ϕ, where ϕ is a property uniquely possessed by X. To perceptually recognize your house, it is not necessary that the object even display features that are *in fact* only possessed by your house, much less features that only your house *could* possess. It is enough that the object present to my experience features that, in this situation or in situations in which I generally find myself, are sufficiently indicative of (are a reliable guide to) the object's being your house. And so it is here. For me to recognize what I am aware of (X) as God, all that is necessary is that X present to me features that are in fact a reliable indication of their possessor's being God, at least in situations of the sort in which I typically find myself. It is, again, not required that these features attach only to God, still less that they be such that they can attach only to God. And it is a matter for detailed investigation what sorts of appearances satisfy that condition, just as in the case of sensorily perceived objects.

Although that is, in outline, the solution of the problem, a further exploration is in order, particularly since it is of interest for our project to look into just how people do suppose themselves to recognize God as the being they are perceiving. What do they go on to make this identification? I will focus on those aspects of the appearance that provide a basis for the identification, though, of course, this presupposes background assumptions that God could reasonably be expected to appear to one in these ways. I will not try to determine whether these features of the appearances are used directly as a basis for the identification or whether they directly support a property attribution to the perceived object, which then functions as a doxastic support for the identification. The material to be presented is usually more smoothly read in the latter way.

Would that our subjects were more explicit as to how they recognize God. If I were instructing them on how to compose their reports, I would enjoin them to always include a statement of the following sort: "I knew it was God because He appeared to me as ———". But those who report mystical perceptions are not concerned primarily with the needs of epistemologists. Typically they just announce that they were aware of God and leave us to figure out how they could tell. But in many cases we can see pretty clearly what they are taking as identifying characteristics. Looking at our battery of reports in Chapter 1, let's begin with some in which the subject is more or less explicit about the basis of the identification.

In (3) after reporting a doubt and lack of "certitude that God is in her", Angela says that "the soul receives the gift of seeing God . . . *for the eyes of the soul behold a plenitude of which I cannot speak; a plenitude which is not bodily but spiritual, of which I can say nothing*. And the soul rejoices in that sight with an ineffable joy; *and this is the manifest and certain sign that God indeed dwells in her*" (my italics). This is certainly explicit. It is, perhaps, not entirely clear whether the "manifest and certain sign" is restricted to the ineffable joy or also includes the plenitude; I shall assume it is the latter. Almost as explicit is (4): "It was, as it were, a manifestation of the sweetness of Eternal Life in the sensations of silence and of rest. Then he said, 'If that which I see and feel be not the Kingdom of Heaven, I know not what it can be". Look also at (12): "I was seized with violent trembling, but had no fear. I knew that what I felt was great awe. This was followed by a sense of overwhelming love coming to me, and going out from me, then of great compassion from this Outer Presence. After that I had a sense of overpowering peace, and indescribable happiness." Later, in a section not quoted in Chapter 1, the author adds, "The sequence of the sensations described have remained very clear, i.e., Awe, Love, Compassion and Peace—in that order. I have never since doubted the existence of a Supreme Power, nor the power of prayer, nor lost a sense of eternity".

Note that both what the object appears as being or doing and the reactions of the subject thereto figure in the identification. Our last reporter takes the object to be a Supreme Power both on the basis of the awe and peace that *he felt* and on the basis of the love shown him by that Power. Likewise, as we just noted, Angela of Foligno makes use both of her joy and the "plenitude" exhibited by the object.

These relatively explicit reports encourage us to suppose that even where the subject does not explicitly say how she knows it is God, we may take it that the main modes of appearance and the main subjective reactions probably figure as bases of identification, at least when they are such as one would naturally expect if it is God they are perceiving. Thus when (1) tells us that God's "goodness and power were penetrating me altogether", we may take it that it was, at least in part, because of this that he took it to be God Who was present. Similar remarks can be made of the "waves and waves of liquid love" in (5).

When God is perceived as communicating a message, whether in audible words or otherwise, then the conviction that it is God speaking will, rightfully, be strengthened if the message is of a sort it would be reasonable to expect to come from God. In (16) the figure says "Mad or sane, you are one of My sheep". In (17) the message is "Be still and know that I am God". Note that although the speaker may identify Himself as God, as in (17), this is not necessary for the content of the message to support the identification.

So the general point is that if the object presents itself as being or doing what it would be natural or reasonable to expect God to be or do, and/or if one reacts as one would expect to react to the presence of God, that supports the claim that it is indeed God Who is perceptually presented. This means that there is a heavy reliance on the background system of Christian belief at this point of perceptual belief formation for principles concerning God's nature and dispositions that will yield conclusions as to how He could be expected to appear to our experience. And these conclusions combine with the reports as to how the perceived object did appear to support the claim that it was God Who was perceived.[34] This leaves the question of what basis the subject or we

[34]This can hardly be supposed to be conclusive support. Even accepting that system, the most we can get is a reasonable assurance that a being appearing in these ways is God; the possibility cannot be foreclosed in any particular case that the subject is aware of an impostor or of something in her own mind. Note that this does not imply that the perceptual belief is based on any part of that background system in such a way as to be, in part, mediately justified, if at all, by the components of that system, though that may be the case. It may be, on the other hand, that the

have for the background principles concerning God's nature and activity, and the implications concerning how God could be expected to appear to us, that are essentially involved here. Before addressing the question, let's be clear as to how and where it arises. Because of the point, already alluded to more than once, that we impose no "higher-level" requirements on perceptual knowledge, it is not the case that S, in order to be justified in the perceptual identification, has to be *justified* in believing that the experience (or property attributions to the perceived object directly based thereon) she takes as a basis for the identification is indeed characteristic of divine appearances. This only has to be true.[35] However, it remains that the epistemologist who asserts that S is justified in the perceptual recognition needs to have sufficient reasons for the adequacy principle (that these appearances support an identification of God). And what might those reasons be?

This question can be raised either "internally" or "externally". Since both will be discussed later in the book, I will now indicate only the character of the treatment. The internal question concerns the grounds within the system of some particular religious belief and practice for the fundamental beliefs about God that indicate that these appearances are characteristic of the divine. This is a large and complex issue that touches on all the bases of religious belief and the interrelations of the components of a religious belief system. Chapter 8 is devoted to this issue, as it arises for the Christian tradition, though a full treatment lies outside the scope of this book. Suffice it to say that we would have to look at experience, revelation, and natural theology, as well as the internal structure of the system of Christian belief, to get a complete picture.

The external question concerns the credentials of the whole complex practice of forming beliefs about God and related matters in the way this is done in the Christian community, or in some other religious community. Granted that some parts of the Christian belief system provide support for other parts, why should we suppose that this whole way of forming and supporting beliefs is at all likely to give us true beliefs about reality? This is the deepest issue to be treated in this book. It will be addressed in Chapters 4–7.

vii. Summary and a Look Forward

In this chapter I have laid out a conception of epistemic justification according to which being jusitifed in believing that p is for that belief to be based on an objectively adequate ground, one that is (fairly) strongly indicative of the truth of the belief. And I have explored the application of this conception to perceptual beliefs—both sense perceptual and theistically perceptual. I have

---

internalization of the background system has been an essential part of the development of certain perceptual skills that enable one to accurately recognize God from perceptual presentations.

[35]Cf. the earlier use of this point, section ivC, to defuse the objection that the empirical justification of adequacy assumptions could never get started.

steered a middle course between holding that perceptual beliefs are based solely on experiential presentations of their subjects and holding that they are always based partly on other beliefs. I have contended that both possibilities are amply realized.

It is against this background that the central issue of the book—the justification of M-beliefs—will be posed. Since I recognize that M-beliefs, like sense perceptual beliefs about the physical environment, are often partly based on "background beliefs", I cannot give as neat a formulation of the issue as I could if they were all based solely on experience. If that were the case, our central issue would simply be one as to the status of a principle like the following, in application to putative experiential appearances of God.

(II) If S's belief that X is ϕ is based on an experience in which, so it seems to S, X is appearing to S as ϕ, then that belief is prima facie justified.

But the recognition that perceptual beliefs can be based partly on other beliefs greatly complicates the matter. As noted earlier, there is no way of giving a general formulation of the way(s) in which other justified beliefs have to be related to a perceptual belief in order to contribute to its justification. Hence we are forced to formulate the issue in less specific terms. How is that to be done? My choice is to appeal to the idea that there are "standard", "accepted", "normal" ways of forming perceptual beliefs—both sense perceptual and mystical perceptual. To anticipate a notion that will be set out in full in Chapter 4, we may speak of various "practices" of belief formation—"doxastic practices"—each of which involves a family of ways of going from grounds—doxastic and experiential, and perhaps others—to a belief with a certain content.[36] I will assume that there are a number of doxastic practices that are socially well established, and hence that we can speak of forming perceptual beliefs in the ways we *generally, normally, standardly* do, where this involves utilizing both experiences and a background system of beliefs as inputs to the "perceptual belief producing mechanism".[37] Even though I will make no attempt to spell out the details of the ways in which this practice utilizes the doxastic component of the input, I believe that reference to our standard, established perceptual-belief-forming practices will identify a sufficiently definite source of perceptual beliefs. We can then ask whether one or another such practice serves as a source of justification, in other words, whether the fact that a perceptual belief stems from such a practice renders it prima facie justified.[38]

[36]As will be made explicit in Chapter 4, this notion of 'practice' is not restricted to spheres of activity that is under voluntary control.

[37]This assumption is much more obvious for sense perception than for mystical perception. In Chapter 5 I will defend it in application to the latter, though I will also be forced to recognize that there is no unique practice of forming theistic perceptual beliefs.

[38]An alternative that confronts us at this point is the following. Should I think of all the products of a certain doxastic practice as having the same (initial) epistemic status, i.e., either prima facie justified or not? Or should we take it to be a live possibility that only some of the

And since I am working with a "truth-conducive" notion of justification, this will involve asking whether the practice is *reliable*, whether it can be relied on to produce mostly true beliefs. This question with respect to the (or a) M-belief forming practice is the form our central issue about the epistemic status of M-beliefs will take. We will be dealing with that in Chapters 5–7. First, however, in Chapters 3 and 4 we will be concerned primarily with our usual sense-perceptual doxastic practice, asking how, if at all, we can show that it is reliable (and hence a source of justification), and if not what we are to say about the situation. The results of this investigation will then be utilized in succeeding chapters in the discussion of M-belief-forming practices.[39]

---

outputs of a given practice are prima facie justified? I think this is basically a bookkeeping issue. Since any prima facie justified belief can fail to be unqualifiedly justified by virtue of being overridden, we can accord all sense-perceptual beliefs, for example, that status without fear of some of them turning out to be clinkers. Any that are suspect will be knocked out at the second stage by overriders. To be sure, if most of the products were to suffer that fate, we might wish to reconsider our decision, though we would be suffering from nothing worse than unnecessary cumbrousness. On the optimistic assumption that most perceptual beliefs, along with beliefs formed in other standard ways, are not overridden, I shall take the simplest course, and suppose them all to have the same initial status—either prima facie justified or not. (Note that we are saved from a plethora of potential clinkers by the fact that we are thinking of a doxastic practice as restricted to "standard" modes of belief formation. If a person should form beliefs about what is perceived in some weird or insane fashion this would not count as the exercise of our standard practice of perceptual belief formation.)

[39]Readers of my earliest essays on this topic (1982, 1983) will have noted that the epistemology I use is quite different in this book. In those essays I was employing a form of a deontological conception of justification that I now consider to be wholly without epistemic merit. And, unfortunately, I suggested that the notion of justification applies primarily to belief-forming *practices* and only derivatively to beliefs. As will become clear from Chapter 4 on, the notion of a belief-forming (doxastic) practice is still central in my epistemology, but I now see that my use of it in those essays was seriously flawed. I believe I am now in a better position to wield effective epistemological tools for the job at hand.

CHAPTER 3

The Reliability of Sense Perception: A Case Study

i. The Problem of This Chapter

At the end of Chapter 2 I said that the basic problem of the book could be formulated as follows. "Is the standard or customary practice of forming M-beliefs a source of prima facie justification for those beliefs?" And since the concept of justification we are using is both truth-conducive and source-relevant, this involves the question "Is that practice a reliable one, one that generally will or would yield true beliefs?"[1] Rather than tackle that straight off, I will approach it indirectly. In this chapter and the next I will concentrate on the parallel question concerning our standard practice of forming sense-perceptual beliefs. In this Chapter I will consider whether it is possible to give adequate reasons for supposing that practice to be reliable. Having arrived at a negative answer to that question, in Chapter 4 I shall consider what we should say, in the light of that result, about the epistemic status of this practice and other basic, universally shared, doxastic practices. Armed with those results I will address our central question about M- beliefs in Chapters 5–7.

There are several reasons for taking this oblique approach. First, sense perception is a much more familiar, intelligible, and well-studied topic. We all constantly form perceptual beliefs on the basis of sense experience, and, in practice, we all take this to be highly reliable. Whatever results we attain here may throw light on the more obscure and controversial area of theistic perception. Second, philosophers typically contrast the epistemic status of M-beliefs unfavorably with the status of sense-perceptual beliefs. It is widely believed that we are in a much better position to judge that sense perception is a source of justification than we are in the case of theistic perception. Many even

[1]The importance of the question about reliability does not hang on how we explicate the notion of epistemic justification. Quite apart from that, the question of whether a given doxastic practice is reliable is an epistemologically crucial question. It is of utmost importance to us to form true rather than false beliefs, and the more important the subject matter, the more important it is for our beliefs to be true.

believe that we can *show* that sense perception is reliable, but not that mystical perception is.[2] These convictions are used as a basis for downgrading the epistemic status of the latter and for denying that beliefs formed on the basis of theistic perception are justified. Looking carefully at attempts to show sense perception to be reliable will put us in a position to assess these views. If we can show that the same or similar problems attach to the vindication of sense perception, that will throw new light on the issue. In this chapter I shall argue that none of the attempts to show that sense perception is a reliable source of belief, at least none that are not otherwise discredited, escape what I call "epistemic circularity". This suggests that, contrary to the usual supposition, the epistemic credentials of sense-perceptual beliefs are not so different from those of M-beliefs. This suggestion will be further developed and modified in the course of the book. I will further suggest that none of our most basic "doxastic" (belief-forming) practices, including introspection, memory, and reasoning of various sorts, can be noncircularly shown to be reliable. This gives rise to a crisis of rationality. What is the most rational attitude for us to take toward these practices, given that we are unable to show that they are reliable? The next chapter will address this question.

But first a disclaimer. It is a long and tortuous job to examine all the attempts, even all the important attempts, to show that sense perception is a reliable source of belief. If I were to do this with ideal thoroughness it would constitute too long a digression from the central concern of this book. On the other hand, since the thesis that we are unable to give an adequate noncircular argument for the reliability of sense perception is an essential link in the overall argument, I cannot shirk the task altogether. Therefore I have compromised. I have selected representative examples of the main types of attempts to validate sense perception, and I will seek to show, in the case of each, that it does not succeed. For a more comprehensive discussion I refer the reader to my *The Reliability of Sense Perception: A Case Study of the Epistemic Status of Our Basic Sources of Belief* (forthcoming from Cornell University Press).

Now for some terminological stipulations. The practice of forming perceptual beliefs about the physical environment on the basis of sensory experience (together, sometimes, with suitable background beliefs) we may term "sense-perceptual practice" ('SP' for short). And the practice of forming M-beliefs about God on the basis of mystical experience (again, sometimes with the addition of suitable background beliefs to the basis) we may term "mystical perceptual practice" ('MP' for short).[3]

[2]See, e.g., Russell 1935, chap. 7; Gaskin 1984, chap. 4; O'Hear 1984, chap. 2.

[3]In asking whether such a wide practice as SP "is reliable", we are obviously presupposing a fair degree of homogeneity in the constituent belief-forming "mechanisms" of the practice, like the tendency to go from something's looking treelike to its being a tree and the tendency to go from something sounding bell-like to its being a bell. That is something that cannot just be taken for granted. It may well be that some sensory belief-forming mechanisms are much more reliable than others. If there are great disparities between large classes of sensory mechanisms, then SP as

Before getting into the main task of this chapter several issues must be addressed. First, we must be a bit more explicit about the constitution of doxastic practices. I have been talking as if the activity of forming perceptual beliefs can by itself constitute a complete doxastic practice. But that supposition will not survive scrutiny. The main reason is that, as pointed out in Chapter 2, the justification that can be claimed on that basis alone is only prima facie. And the concept of prima facie justification is usefully applicable only where there are procedures for determining, in a particular case, whether that initial credibility is overridden by contrary considerations. Prima facie justified perceptual beliefs are subject to further assessment by reference to what we know or justifiably believe about the world, perceivers, and their interrelations. And, of course, in building up that background system we make use of memory and various kinds of reasoning, as well as perception. Thus we can see that other modes of belief formation are involved in the operation of a perceptual doxastic practice, once we realize that the latter involves the second stage of evaluation of perceptual beliefs as well as the initial stage of their formation.

Next some questions about reliability. To call a doxastic practice reliable is to judge that it will or would yield mostly true beliefs. But over what range of employments? Those in which it has been employed up to now? That would be to identify reliability with a favorable track record, but that can't be right. An unreliable procedure might have chanced to work well on the few occasions on which it was actually employed. Anyone can get lucky. If there have been only five crystal-ball readings all of which just happened to be correct, that wouldn't make it a reliable way of forming beliefs; it might still have a poor record over the long haul. Indeed, we can't identify reliability with a favorable record over all past, present, and future employments. A practice, or an instrument, that is never employed might be quite reliable in that it *would* yield mostly true beliefs in the long run. Thus to call something reliable is to say something about the kind of record it *would* pile up over a suitable number and variety of employments. An actual track record is crucial evidence for judgments of reliability just to the extent that it is a good indication of that. But what makes a run of cases suitable? Briefly, the class of cases must be sufficiently varied to rule out the possibility that the results are owing to factors other than the character of the practice. Moreover, they must be cases of sorts that we typically encounter. The fact that sensory experience would not be a reliable source of belief in unusually deceptive environments, or in cases of direct brain stimulation, does not show that standard perceptual belief formation is not a reliable practice. So, in a nutshell, a doxastic practice is reliable provided *it would yield mostly true beliefs in a sufficiently large*

a whole is not an appropriate unit to take; we would do better to concentrate on subgroups of mechanisms that are fairly homogeneous in this respect. For purposes of this discussion I shall assume that both SP and MP are sufficiently homogeneous to make the discussion pertinent.

and varied run of employments in situations of the sorts we typically encounter. This is less than perfectly precise (for example, what does it take for a type of situation to be typical for us?), but it has just the kind of looseness we need for the purpose.

Second, what degree of reliability is in question? Reliability is obviously a matter of degree; one instrument, method, or procedure may be more or less reliable than another. I have been speaking of the reliability of a practice as amounting to the fact that it would yield mostly true beliefs. But how much is "most"? I won't try to give a precise answer; I don't think there is any basis for doing so. The most that can be said in general is that a "high" degree of reliability is required for justification.[4] But just how high may differ for different practices, depending on the degree of reliability it is realistic to expect. For example, the vision of objects directly in front of one is capable of a greater degree of reliability than is the memory of remote events in one's early years. But we shouldn't want to deny that beliefs generated in the less reliable ways can thereby be justified. Perhaps we should distinguish degrees of justification in correlation with degrees of reliability, but I won't get into that. In due time we shall have to recognize that the incidence of conflict in M-beliefs is such as to significantly reduce the degree of reliability one can reasonably expect.

Third, we should not be too fussy about exact truth in asking about reliability. Suppose that, as many philosophers have thought, typical perceptual beliefs are not exactly true as they stand. For one thing, they indefensibly represent qualia like colors and sounds as attaching to the objects themselves. For another, they depict objects as unbrokenly continuous that are actually constituted by many tiny particles moving about in empty space. To be sure, this is highly controversial. Many thinkers deny that ordinary perceptual beliefs are committed to any such construals; others take it that perceptual beliefs as just characterized are strictly true. My aim here is not to settle these issues but to use the view that ordinary perceptual beliefs are not strictly true in order to illustrate a point. That point is that even if perceptual beliefs misrepresent the environment in ways like these, they can still be highly useful guides to that environment. The real facts of the matter can be in a systematic correspondence with the colors and the unbroken surfaces that the perceiver mistakenly attributes to the things in themselves, so that what we believe on the basis of perception can be close enough to the truth for practical purposes. Thus as I construe reliability, SP could be judged reliable if its outputs are usually close enough to the truth, even if they do not strictly hit the mark.

Finally, a terminological note. In the sequel I shall, for stylistic reasons, often speak of the reliability of a *source*, particularly experiential sources. But a given source will, at best, reliably give rise to certain kinds of beliefs and

[4]For some discussion of this issue see Goldman 1986, sec. 5.5.

not others. Nothing is a reliable source for beliefs generally, except an infallible and omniscient authority. Thus talk of the reliability of a source is to be understood as shorthand for the reliability of a certain doxastic practice that takes that source as input, a certain way of going from that source to beliefs related to it in a certain way.

It is important to distinguish our question about the reliability of SP from others with which it might be confused; for a successful answer to one of these other questions will not necessarily answer ours. For one thing, our issue often pops up in attempts to "answer skepticism" or to "resolve skeptical doubts". And one response to skepticism about perception is that it is exaggerated, unreal, artificial, and not to be taken seriously. But our inquiry does not presuppose that there is any real *doubt* about the reliability of SP. We are only seeking to determine what, if anything, can be done to *show* that it is reliable. Hence dismissal of skeptical doubts as impossible or unreal has no bearing on our problem. Second, many of the discussions we will be considering are attempts to demonstrate the existence of the "external world" or the "physical world", starting merely from premises concerning one's own conscious experience (and perhaps a priori truths). But establishing the existence of a world, even a physical world, beyond our experience does not suffice for showing that SP is reliable. Solipsism is not the only alternative to the reliability of SP. It could be that there is a physical world beyond our experience but that our sense perception does not serve as an accurate guide to it. Finally, a number of Wittgensteinian arguments are concerned to show that SP could not *always* be mistaken. But even if successful in that, they fall short of showing that SP is *reliable*. Reliability takes more than the production of the occasional truth.

ii. Simple Empirical Arguments for Reliability

Let us turn to the question of how we might tell whether SP is reliable. The most straightforward way of assessing a practice for reliability is by determining the truth value of selected outputs. If 99 percent of the outputs from a properly selected sample of employments are true, that is strong evidence that the practice is highly reliable. To what extent can we use this method? There is no difficulty in carrying this out where we have an independent cognitive access to the subject matter in question. This condition will be satisfied where we are dealing with a fairly restricted source of beliefs. If we are dealing with the formation of beliefs about temperature or electric charge from the readings of a certain measuring instrument, we will have other, possibly less direct, ways of determining the magnitude of the quantity being measured. That gives us an independent way to determine, at least probably, the truth value of the doxastic outputs in question. Again, if the question concerns the direct visual perception of shapes, we can rely on touch, as well on various more indirect procedures, to check those visual judgments. To be sure, this presupposes that the other modes of access are themselves reliable; not all sources can be checked in this way without falling into circularity or an infinite regress. But, subject to that assumption, we can check a particular source in this manner.

But suppose that the question concerns the whole of our basic access to a certain subject matter, "basic" in the sense that any other access to that subject matter presupposes this one, in the sense that we are justified in supposing the former to be reliable only if we are justified in supposing the latter to be reliable. Suppose that the question concerns the reliability of sense perception in general, not some particular modality or type thereof. Here we are in the situation just described. For ascertaining contingent facts about the physical world we must either rely on sense perception or on some other source that we are entitled to trust only if we are entitled to regard sense perception as reliable. Consider our resources other than sense perception. (1) Reasoning from observed facts. If this is to give us information, observation must be giving us genuine facts from which to reason. (2) Instruments of various sorts. Our trust in these instruments is based on their validation, which will sooner or later involve using our sense organs to determine what is the case. For example, we are entitled to trust a galvanometer only if its output correlates with other indications of electric charge, and we have to use sense perception somewhere down the line to determine what those other indications are.[5] (3) The implications of high level theories. If a theory is to have a claim to give us genuine information about the world it must prove itself by successful accounting for observable data. And, again, we must, sooner or later, rely on sense perception to determine what those data are.

Thus it is futile to try to assess the reliability of sense perception by a simple enumerative induction. To determine whether selected doxastic outputs are true we would have to either take a look, listen, or whatever—to determine whether they are, or use some other procedure that we have reason to think is reliable only if we have reason to think sense perception is reliable. We must either use sense perception as the source of our premises, thereby already assuming that it is reliable, or else get our premises from some other source(s) that we would have reason to trust only if we already had reason to trust sense perception. Any such argument is infected by a kind of circularity. It is not the most direct kind of logical circularity. We are not using the proposition that sense perception is reliable as one of our premises. Neverthe-

[5]It may be thought that the use of instruments presupposes the reliability of sense perception in an even more basic way. For we can't even determine what the reading of the instrument is without using our senses. But just because this point is so basic, it doesn't indicate a way in which the reliability of sense perception is presupposed by the judgment that the instrument is *reliable*, rather than unreliable. On the contrary, it indicates a way in which the reliability of sense perception is presupposed just in setting up the subject of a judgment of reliability or unreliability. We are concerned here with ways in which the reliability of sense perception is presupposed distinctively by the judgment that a certain other access is reliable *rather than* unreliable.

less we are, so to say, assuming the reliability of sense perception in using it, or some source(s) dependent on it, to generate our premises. If one were to challenge our premises and continue the challenge long enough, we would eventually be driven to appeal to the reliability of sense perception in defending our right to those premises. And if I were to ask myself why I should accept these premises, I would, if I pushed the reflection far enough, have to make the claim that sense perception is reliable. For if I weren't prepared to claim that on reflection, why would I, as a rational subject, be prepared to hold perceptual beliefs? Since this kind of circularity involves a commitment to the conclusion as a presupposition of our supposing ourselves to be *justified* in holding the premises, we can properly term it "epistemic circularity".

Epistemically circular arguments would seem to be of no force. If we have to assume the reliability of SP in order to suppose ourselves entitled to the premises, how can an argument from those premises, however impeccable its logical credentials, provide support for that proposition? In section i of Chapter 4 we shall see that it is *possible* to establish the reliability of a doxastic practice by way of an epistemically circular argument, though we shall also see that such an argument fails to satisfy the usual aspirations. In this chapter we will assume that epistemically circular support fails to give us what we are looking for, and we will take epistemic circularity to be disqualifying.

Where are we to turn next? A popular line of thought is that SP proves itself by its fruits, particularly by the way in which it puts us in a position to predict and thereby, to some extent, to control the course of events. It provides us with data on the basis of which we establish lawlike generalizations, which we can then use as the basis for prediction and control. By taking sense experience as a guide to what is around us we can learn in each of a number of instances that milk sours more slowly when cold than when warm. This puts us into a position to predict that a refrigerated bottle of milk will last longer than an unrefrigerated one, and we can use this knowledge to control the condition of our milk. This is the humblest of examples, and the predictive power is greatly increased in scope and precision as we move further into the higher reaches of theory; but the general point is the same. SP proves itself by what it puts us in a position to do. If it weren't usually giving us the straight story about what is happening around us, how could we have so much success in anticipating the further course of events?

That sounds right. But how do we know that we are often successful in prediction? By induction from particular cases of success, obviously. But how do we know that we are successful in particular cases? By using our senses to determine whether what was predicted actually occurred. It is not as if an angel tells us this, or as if rational intuition does the job. But then we are back in epistemic circularity. We can mount this argument for the reliability of SP only by using SP to get some of our crucial premises. Once more the argument establishes the reliability of SP only if SP is in fact reliable. And that still leaves us wondering whether that condition is satisfied.

In the course of our discussion we will find again and again that epistemic circularity rears its unlovely head, sometimes in the most unexpected places.

Having warmed up on the simplest arguments for reliability, let's turn to attempts we can take more seriously. These can be divided into empirical and a priori arguments. The latter have often been developed explicitly to avoid epistemic circularity; and if they are wholly a priori they will succeed in that. The empirical arguments are clearly threatened by epistemic circularity. Some of their authors make strenuous efforts to avoid this, with what success will appear in the fullness of time. It might seem most natural to continue the above discussion by moving on to the more sophisticated empirical arguments, but it will prove most fitting to save them for later.

iii. Descartes' *Meditations*

A historically famous a priori argument is that of Descartes in the *Meditations*. Having produced more than one a priori argument for the existence of God,[6] he goes on in Meditation VI to argue that God would be a deceiver if sense perception were not a more or less reliable source of belief. For, he says, we have a very great inclination to accept the beliefs we normally form perceptually, and we have no resources for correcting this inclination. Since we were put in this situation by God, and since God is no deceiver, we can reasonably conclude that sense perception provides us with a fairly accurate account of the world about us.

We might think of this argument as one form taken by the attempt to validate SP by considering its provenance. A more prominent contemporary form is the idea that the great inclination of which Descartes speaks has been selected by evolution, that this wouldn't have happened unless SP confers an adaptive advantage, and that it wouldn't do this unless it were reliable. But this argument from evolutionary credentials, unlike Descartes' argument, is infected with epistemic circularity. The claims about evolution rest on empirical data.

Descartes' argument, by contrast, is not epistemically circular. No appeal is made in the argument to what we take ourselves to have learned from perception; nor is there any such appeal in the background. On the contrary, everything is made to rest on rational intuition (clear and distinct ideas), one's experience of one's own mind, and deductive reasoning. So if the arguments for the existence of God deployed by Descartes are satisfactory he really has

[6]In the strictest sense only the ontological argument in Meditation V is a priori. The arguments in Meditation III have as crucial premises, one that he has the idea of God, the other that he exists, and both premises are derived from his experience of his own mental states. But that is a source that, according to Descartes, at any rate, is as independent of sense perception as rational intuition is. Hence they may be called a priori in a sense in which we are interested here; they are acceptable prior to any reliance on sense perception as a source of belief.

succeeded in squaring the circle. I won't try to go into a critical discussion of the arguments. Suffice it for present purposes to say that one would be hard pressed to find a defender on the current scene.[7]

Virtually all the recent arguments stem from Kant or Wittgenstein or both. The prime Kantian source is the transcendental deduction of the categories in the *Critique of Pure Reason*, more specifically the attempt to show that a necessary condition of the unity of consciousness is that the categories apply to any objects of experience. The Wittgensteinian sources are more diverse; they include the private language argument, the view that concepts have "criteria" for their application, and, more generally, verificationism. I will reverse the historical order and deal first with attempts that are more or less in the spirit of Wittgenstein.

iv. Verificationism

The simplest of the arguments that I am calling Wittgensteinian is a verificationist one that goes as follows.

> If it is a serious question whether SP is reliable, then it must be a meaningful hypothesis that SP is not reliable. It must be conceivable that our sense experience is just as it is even though the things we take it to reveal are not generally the case. But this is not a meaningful supposition, for there is no conceivable way in which it could be empirically confirmed. What empirical evidence could count in favor of it? We can have empirical reasons for correcting sense perception on points of detail, as has happened repeatedly in the history of science from the seventeenth century. But what possible empirical basis could there be for a wholesale rejection of the deliverances of SP, lock, stock, and barrel? And if there is no possible empirical confirmation for such a view it is without factual meaning. Hence there is no meaningful alternative to the reliability of SP. We can know, just by considering the conditions of meaningfulness, that SP is reliable.[8]

[7]An exception is Clement Dore, who in 1984 defends Descartes' version of the ontological argument. Of course there are notable contemporary defenders of the ontological argument, e.g., Charles Hartshorne, Norman Malcolm, and Alvin Plantinga. But only Dore, to my knowledge, defends Descartes's form.

[8]My justification for calling this argument "Wittgensteinian" is rather indirect. First there is the influence of Wittgenstein on the Vienna Circle, and this argument is the one that made the Vienna Circle famous. To be sure, it is usually more metaphysical theses like "the existence of the external world" or "realism" that the logical positivists attacked on verificationist grounds. (See, e.g., Moritz Schlick, "The Turning Point in Philosophy", and Rudolf Carnap, "The Elimination of Metaphysics Through the Logical Analysis of Language", both reprinted in Ayer 1948). But the arguments could easily be transferred to the question of the reliability of sense perception. Second, Wittgenstein, despite the disavowals of many of his followers, does use verificationist arguments, not infrequently. Later in this chapter we will see a famous one—the private-language argument. Third, the argument is beautifully explicit in Bowsma (in "Descartes'

I have presented this as an argument for the reliability of SP. Another version, more in keeping with the spirit of verificationism, would present it as an argument for the meaninglessness of both sides of the issue—reliability or unreliability. Since no conceivable empirical evidence could decide the matter, there is no real matter of fact at issue. It is a pseudo-question. This version doesn't look like a defense of the reliability of SP, but it has the same effect. Since it forbids us to question something we all take for granted in practice, it leaves that conviction in undisturbed possession of the field.

The most direct way to attack this argument would be to argue against the verifiability criterion of factual meaningfulness, something I am by no means indisposed to do. However, to go into this properly is a long and complicated business, and I shall confine myself here to the following point, which is sufficient for the purpose at hand. The criterion *presupposes* the by and large reliability of sense perception. What would be the point of requiring empirical *verifiability* or *confirmability* of p as a necessary condition of the factual meaningfulness of p unless it were possible to verify or confirm a hypothesis by relating it properly to the results of observation? And that is possible only if the results of observation are by and large correct; otherwise the fact that a hypothesis leads us to expect such results is no reason to suppose it to be *true*. Hence, despite the a priori air of the argument, it turns out to presuppose that which it is invoked to prove.[9]

v. Criteria of Physical Object Concepts

Another Wittgensteinian idea that can be and has been exploited for the validation of sense perception is the view that the terms of our language, or at least terms denoting physical and mental properties and kinds, have "criteria" for their application—where a *criterion* for the use of 'P' is a basis, ground, or reason for supposing it to apply, one that has that status by virtue of the meaning of 'P', or, as Wittgenstein prefers to say, by virtue of the "grammar" of 'P'. For example, if the behavioral criterion for 'upset' obtains, that doesn't logically imply that the person in question is upset; but it is, necessarily, a good reason for supposing that the person is upset, and it is logically impossible that it should not generally be true that a person is upset when the criterion is present. This suggests a way of supporting the epistemic claims of sense perception. If X's looking a certain way is a *criterion* of its being red,

Evil Genius", in 1965), a prominent Wittgensteinian. However, nothing hangs on the Wittgensteinian label. You can discard it if you like.

[9]An antirealist form of verificationism might attempt to disengage the Verifiability Principle from any commitment to what would suffice to verify, or confirm, a proposition, understanding verification and confirmation in terms of a realist conception of truth. But in that case the argument would not support the reliability of SP as I am understanding it. For more on the realist presuppositions of this inquiry, see Introduction, near the end of section i, and Chapter 4, section iii.

or round, or a tree, then it is logically impossible for it not generally to be the case that something that looks this way is red or round or a tree. The by and large reliability of sense perception would be guaranteed by the meanings of terms for perceptually recognizable properties and kinds; and so it could be established just by reflecting on the meaning of those terms. The following passage from the *Philosophical Investigations* (1953) suggests this application.

> The fluctuation in grammar between criteria and symptoms makes it look as if there were nothing at all but symptoms. We say, for example: "Experience teaches that there is rain when the barometer falls, but it also teaches that there is rain when we have certain sensations of wet and cold, or such-and-such visual impressions". In defense of this one says that these sense-impressions can deceive us. But here one fails to reflect that the fact that the false appearance is precisely one of rain is founded on a definition. (P. 354)

Just by knowing the meaning of 'rain' we can know that such-and-such sensory impressions are a good reason for supposing there to be rain in the vicinity; and it is not conceptually possible that such sense impressions should generally fail to be accompanied by rain.

A fuller development of this kind of view is presented by John Pollock. In (1974) he writes:

> To learn the meaning of a concept is certainly not to learn its "definition". It is to learn how to use it, which is to learn how to make justifiable assertions involving it. Thus it seems to me inescapable that the meaning of a concept is determined by its justification conditions. (P. 12)

> . . . when the child has learned to judge justifiably whether a thing is a bird (i.e., he has learned to ascribe the concept and its complement to things justifiably), we are satisfied that he knows how to identify birds and so has got the concept right—he knows what a bird is. (P. 15)

> It was assumed that having once spelled out the justification conditions for a statement, we would have to go on to prove that those are the justification conditions by deriving them from the meaning of the statement (which was identified with the truth conditions). To prove that the purported justification conditions are the justification conditions would be to derive them from something deeper. But in fact there is generally nothing deeper. The justification conditions are themselves constitutive of the meaning of the statement. We can no more *prove* that the justification conditions of "That is red" are the justification conditions than we can prove on the basis of something deeper about the meaning of "bachelor" that all bachelors are unmarried. Being unmarried constitutes part of the meaning of "bachelor" and as such cannot be derived from anything deeper about the meaning of "bachelor"; and analogously the justification conditions of "That is red" or

> "He is in pain" are constitutive of the meanings of those statements and hence cannot be derived from any deeper features of their meanings. There are no deeper features. (P. 21)

Bringing this down to perceptual beliefs, the claim is that it is constitutive of our concepts of perceptually detectable features of the world that they are perceptually detectable in certain ways. It is part of our concept of something's being red or a tree that looking to a subject in a certain way is a "prima facie reason" for that thing's being red or a tree. Hence it is not conceptually possible that I should not be prima facie justified in supposing X to be a tree if X looks a certain way to me.[10]

What are we to say of this position? With respect to "sensory qualities" like colors, shapes, pitch, loudness, and smells, there is much to be said for the idea that at least part of our concept of such qualities of physical objects and events is the way in which they manifest themselves to sensory experience. Surely someone who, because of blindness, has no grasp of how a red or a round object looks under normal conditions to a normal subject is sadly deficient in his grasp of what it is for an object to be red or round. Terms for natural and artificial kinds are a different story, however. The concept *house* is a functional concept. A house is a structure designed for human habitation. The way it looks or feels can vary enormously so long as it was designed for that use. Similar comments apply to articles of furniture, tools, and machines. As for natural kinds like trees, we must take into account the distinction between technical and common-sense concepts. The biologist's concept of a tree is the concept of something with a certain organic structure that carries out certain vital operations. Anything that satisfies these conditions, however it looks, or smells, will be a tree. Perhaps the usual common-sense concept, on the other hand, is one based on perceptual paradigms. In a particular society certain trees are most salient, and it is by reference to these that the concept is taught. At the most primitive level one's concept of a tree is the concept of whatever looks similar enough to the paradigm cases. Obviously, sensory appearance plays a large role in this primitive, common-sense concept. To complicate matters further there can be seepage between the two spheres. Even moderately educated individuals can have a concept of a tree that essentially includes the property of being a vegetable organism.[11]

The moral of all this is that even where the justificatory role of certain

[10]In Chapter 2 I suggested a principle of justification for perceptual beliefs of this general sort. However, I did not say there that such a principle forms part of the meaning of concepts of perceptible properties and kinds, and I will now go on to criticize that view.

[11]Even concepts of sensory qualities may not be exhausted by sensory appearances. Here too there may be seepage from scientific discoveries. Even a moderately knowledgeable person might include in her concept of *red* the fact that it has to do with the frequencies of light waves reflected from the surface of the object.

kinds of sensory appearances plays a role in a physical object concept, it will typically be only a part of that concept, and that raises questions as to how it is related to other parts. We typically suppose that we can perceptually determine that the whole concept of, for example, a tree applies in a particular case, and that supposition does not seem to be supportable purely by the analysis of the concept. Even if X's looking a certain way is guaranteed by the concept of a tree to be one condition of justifiably believing, perceptually that X is a tree, that will fail to guarantee that we can reliably tell by looking that the entire concept applies.

However, in Pollock 1986 we have a more complex doctrine as to how concepts are made up of justification conditions.

> What makes a concept the concept that it is is the way it enters into various kinds of reasoning, and that is described by saying how it enters into various kinds of reasons, both conclusive and prima facie. Let us take the *conceptual role* of a concept to consist of (1) the reasons (conclusive or prima facie) for thinking that something exemplifies it or exemplifies its negation, and (2) the conclusions we can justifiably draw (conclusively or prima facie) from the fact that something exemplifies the concept or exemplifies the negation of the concept. My proposal is that concepts are individuated by their conceptual roles. The essence of a concept is to have the conceptual role that it does. If this is right, the explanation for how there can be such things as prima facie reasons becomes trivial. Prima facie reasons are primitive constituents of the conceptual roles that characterize concepts. (Pp. 147–48)

Thus the justification conditions that make up a concept of a perceivable property or kind may and do include much more than standard looks and sounds. The concept of a tree can include being a vegetable organism. That just means that X's being a vegetable organism is a reason for thinking it is a tree (part of a justification for supposing it to be a tree)—(1) in the last quotation—and/or X's being a vegetable organism can legitimately be inferred from the premise that X is a tree—(2) in the quotation. This will save Pollock from the charge that he illegitimately takes concepts of physical kinds and properties to consist wholly in specifications of the ways in which they manifest themselves sensorily. But it will do nothing for the program of a conceptual, a priori justification of the reliability of SP. For the question remains as to whether the sensory appearance we take to be typical of trees (together with the kinds of background beliefs, if any, that are typically employed here as part of our basis for identifying something as a tree) is a reliable basis for the claim that the whole concept applies to the perceived object. And the mere fact that the concept is made of justification conditions—sensory and non-sensory—will not answer that question for us. It remains to be shown that *the bases we actually employ for a perceptual recognition of something as a tree* consist of items that are guaranteed by our concept of a tree to make up an adequate basis. And neither Pollock nor anyone else has done anything to show this.[12]

Thus Pollock does not succeed in providing an a priori assurance that perception provides justification for beliefs about the physical environment, as we form those beliefs in SP. However, even if he were to succeed in this aim, *given the way he understands 'justification'*, this would still not suffice to show that sense perception is a *reliable* source of perceptual beliefs. How could it? How could the fact that the conditions are satisfied that my concept of a tree lays down as sufficient for justification, imply that my belief is likely to be true? Any sense of 'truth' in which I could guarantee truth just by building justification conditions into my concepts would be a wildly non-realistic conception that I would not dream of taking seriously, nor does Pollock. It can't be that easy to bring it about that our thoughts conform to the way things are. Hence no concept of justification that is such that what it takes for justification depends on the constitution of our concepts can carry any implications for truth or reliability. And hence even if Pollock could show by conceptual analysis that SP provides justification for perceptual beliefs, in his sense of 'justification', he would not have shown this in my truth-conducive sense, in which a doxastic practice confers justification only if it is generally reliable. We are no closer to showing a priori that SP is reliable.

vi. Paradigm Case Arguments

We have been exploring the view that, as a matter of fact, terms for perceivable features of the environment carry perceptual justification conditions as part of their meaning. Now we shall look at the more deeply Wittgensteinian idea that, by the very nature of language, it is necessary that physical object terms have features that guarantee the reliability of SP. One such line of thought would be a verificationist argument. If physical object terms do not carry perceptual criteria as part of their meaning, it would be impossible to have any empirical basis for asserting or denying them of anything; and so they would not be meaningful. But appeals to verificationism having already been set aside, I will consider other versions.[13]

First a form of what has come to be called the "Paradigm Case Argument". The general idea of such arguments is that since we learn the meanings of terms by reference to paradigm cases of what they denote, they couldn't have the meaning they do unless those putative cases were genuine. Our grasp of

[12]Moreover, where beliefs are part of the basis for perceptual beliefs, those beliefs themselves have to be justified if the perceptual belief they support is to be justified. And certainly the perceivable object concept in question cannot guarantee that this is generally the case.

[13]I would also argue if there were time that it is quite possible to have empirical reasons for or against the application of a concept without the relevance of these reasons being built into the constitution of that concept. For an influential statement of such an argument see Chihara & Fodor 1965.

the meaning of 'dog' presupposes that the cases of dogs used to teach us what 'dog' means really are dogs. What we mean by dog is roughly *something similar enough to x, y, z . . .* , where x, y, and z are socially accepted paradigm cases of dogs, and where the "similar enough" part can be spelled out in various ways. Since our access to the paradigms for such terms is perceptual, the argument, if successful, would show that perception does reliably present us with instances of what we believe ourselves to be perceiving, at least in these cases.

Since I do not wish to enter onto the laborious project of extracting something like this argument from the Wittgensteinian corpus, I will work with a version, put forward as distinctively Wittgensteinian in Oldenquist 1971.

> Could everybody be fooled all of the time in their judgments of what is red? . . . I think that this is a conceptual impossibility. If *all* English users were taught 'red' . . . by examples all of which were white things illuminated in red light, and no one ever saw what we now call red things, then it would be a contingent truth that red things were white things illuminated in red light.
> The defense of this anti-skeptical claim lies in showing that it is conceptually impossible that all of the examples by means of which we all learn the meaning of 'red' should be false examples, and that therefore it is a conceptual truth that many of our color judgments are actually true. In learning the word 'red' we are taught that *this* and *that* are red. It makes sense for me to say that a learning example is a false example only if I believe it deviates from the general run of such examples. It is the language game played with the teaching examples that defines . . . what it is to be red. To say something is red is to say it is like the general run of teaching examples, regardless of what features we might later discover or hypothesize the teaching examples to possess. (Pp. 411–12)

Note that Oldenquist cannot suppose that his argument just concerns how we human beings in fact come to learn the meaning of observation terms and that it has no implications for *what* we thereby come to understand, for what the meaning *is*. If the argument had no such implications, it would always be logically and conceptually possible that this meaning could be learned in some other way that did not involve the presentation of samples, or that our knowledge of the meaning is innate. Oldenquist makes it explicit in the above that he supposes there to be a (surely somewhat indefinite) reference to the teaching samples in the meaning that is acquired and that is subsequently used.

In response to this argument I could engage in various quibbles about the ostensive teaching of terms, but I don't feel that to be the heart of the matter. I have no doubt that we do learn at least the simpler and more basic observation terms in this way, and that a reference to paradigms does play a role in their meaning. Instead I will point out that this whole account of how we learn certain terms *presupposes* that perception consistently and reliably presents us with items to which our terms for observable things and qualities are correctly attributable. That is, it once again presupposes that sense perception is a reliable source of belief. For suppose that presupposition is false. Suppose that, unbeknown to us, the items with which we are in effective perceptual contact over a range of alleged ostensive teachings of 'red' are so diverse as to exhibit no perceptually salient characteristic in common. In that case, we would be acquiring no usable meaning for any sensory quality term from this teaching procedure; the term wouldn't have acquired the kind of meaning we think it has. Hence the very supposition that the learning of observational terms is successfully carried out by this kind of procedure *presupposes* that sense perception enjoys a very fundamental kind of reliability. Once more we have run into epistemic circularity.[14]

If Oldenquist should say, "Well, let's not just presuppose this; let's empirically determine whether it is true", that will be of no avail. For he obviously can't empirically determine this or anything else without taking sense perception to be reliable.

Moreover, even if Oldenquist's argument did show that we can't *always* be mistaken in perceptual judgments of color (and other things), that obviously falls far short of showing that sense perception is generally reliable. However exactly the notion of reliability is spelled out, it obviously requires more than just some proportion of true outputs greater than zero, and an argument from teaching examples could never show anything like a preponderance of correct perceptual judgments. Occasions of teaching or learning the meaning of an observation term 'P' will typically constitute a tiny minority of the occasions on which one forms a perceptual belief of some x that it is P. Hence even if all or most of the attributions involved in term learning are correct, it doesn't follow that most attributions generally are. Why isn't it possible for a person, having acquired the meaning of the term in the way specified, to do a poor job of utilizing that semantic knowledge in identifying subsequent examples? This may be unlikely, especially with terms for sensory qualities, but why suppose that it is conceptually impossible? And with respect to kind terms and more complex observable properties, such a pattern may not be terribly uncommon. Hilary Putnam claims not to be able to distinguish elms from beeches. Even if one has undergone a standard course of ostensive teaching one could well wind up in this position. My opponent might claim that someone's being in this position shows that he has forgotten the meaning of the term, even if he once knew it. But there are a number of other possibilities. One's sensory powers may not be sufficient for the required discriminations in

[14]Since I was careful to say that the argument presupposes only that sense perception "enjoys a very fundamental kind of reliability", it may be pointed out that I have not shown that the argument presupposes that perception is wholly reliable, giving us accurate information of just the sort we take it to be giving us. And so I haven't. But neither does the argument succeed in showing that, as Oldenquist, in effect, admits. He claims to have shown only that it gives us correct information about similarity to the paradigms, in whatever way(s) they are markedly perceivably similar among themselves. As he acknowledges, this falls short of showing that being taught 'red' in this way guarantees that anything perceived really is red in the sense we attach to that term. The argument claims to establish just as much as it presupposes, and not a whit more.

many instances; one may be inattentive and uninterested. One may be confronted mostly with situations in which identification is especially difficult. So why suppose that any argument from teaching samples could establish general reliability?

Oldenquist is aware of this objection. What he says in favor of extending his conclusion beyond the teaching samples is the following. "Wittgenstein's view is, I believe, that something like the learning process, or reinforcement of it, continues throughout one's life. . ." (p. 414). But even if something like this is true, it seems clear that initial teaching plus subsequent reinforcement occasions constitute only a small percentage of the total spread of attributions. Moreover, Oldenquist's supposition that the sample included in the meaning I attach to 'red' includes all those involved in subsequent reinforcements seems highly implausible. But why accept any such supposition?

In Putnam 1981 (chap. 1), there is a somewhat similar defense of the reliability of SP, against a skeptical claim that my sensory experience is compatible with my being a brain in a vat and failing to really be perceiving the things I take myself to perceive. The argument appeals to the principle that a term can refer to P's only if my use of it stands in some real causal connection with P's. Assuming that the brain in the vat has always been such, its use of 'desk' has never stood in any real causal connection with desks and hence does not refer to desks. The same, according to Putnam, holds of all other terms used in the expression of perceptual beliefs. Hence the brain in the vat does not have false perceptual beliefs of the same sort as we; rather it has quite different perceptual beliefs, all or most of which might be true. (The terms in these beliefs might refer to brain states or mental images or whatever.) And hence there is no possibility that we, meaning what we do by the terms in our perceptual judgments, might be brains in vats, out of any real contact with the external environment. But again this argument presupposes that we do mean by our perceptual terms what we would mean if we are in genuine perceptual, cognitive contact with the sorts of things we think ourselves to be. And again, if sense perception is not reliable, we are mistaken about that and we are, semantically, in a position more like that of the brain in the vat. Hence what the argument shows is that *if* perception is as we ordinarily suppose it to be and is therefore reasonably reliable, we couldn't mean what we do without sense perception's being that way. And that, of course, falls far short of showing that sense perception *is* that way, or that it *is* reliable. Once again the argument turns out to be circular.

vii. The Private Language Argument

Now to get at the very heart of the later Wittgenstein, let's consider the bearing on our problem of the famous "private language argument". This label is misleading in that it suggests that there is a unique argument properly so called. In fact, one can find in the *Philosophical Investigations* a number of lines of argument that are plausibly so called. To add to the confusion, some true believers stoutly deny that there is any such *argument* at all, since Wittgenstein was opposed on principle to propounding philosophical arguments. However that may be, I shall simplify the present discussion by leaving aside any arguments there may be and simply consider what bearing the Wittgensteinian denial of private languages has on our problem. However, I think it will be useful for our purposes to make explicit what I take to be Wittgenstein's central reason for his denial. It is that language essentially depends on public rules for the use of expressions, rules that are public in the sense that in principle there are ways available to all the members of a community for determining when the rules are being followed or violated. Without such rules no expression has the kind of *use* that makes it possible to employ it to say something meaningful.[15]

First, we must get straight as to just what the antiprivate language thesis amounts to. What Wittgenstein denies is not the possibility of a de facto private language, one that in fact is understood and used by only one person, but rather the possibility of a language that is necessarily private, one that only one person *could* understand.

> But could we also imagine a language in which a person could write down or give vocal expression to his inner experiences—his feelings, moods, and the rest—for his private use?—Well, can't we do so in our ordinary language?—But that is not what I mean. The indivual words of this language are to refer to what can only be known to the person speaking; to his immediate private sensations. So another person cannot understand the language. (1953; § 243)

If it is impossible for another person to understand the alleged language, there can be no publicly available system of rules for the use of the expressions of the language; for if there were such a system, it would be possible for other people to be acquainted with it, in which case they would understand the language.

Suppose there can be no such language. What bearing does that have on our problem? Here is an argument for such a bearing. I take it from some unpublished comments of Peter van Inwagen on a presentation of my "Religious Experience and Religious Belief" (1982) at a symposium of the Central Division of the American Philosophical Association, though the exact shape of the presentation is mine, and van Inwagen should not be held responsible for the details.

Let's use the term 'public language' to cover a language that is used in common by members of a social group (larger than one), a language the terms

[15]See, e.g., Wittgenstein 1953, I, secs. 258–270.

of which mean what they do by virtue of public rules for their use. Now the Wittgensteinian position on private language could be put as follows:

(1) If (alleged) term 'P' cannot figure in a public language it has no meaning.

But:

(2) If sense perception is not reliable there can be no public language.

The reason for this is that a public language gets established by way of social interactions in which the participants find out by perception what other participants are saying and doing. Think of this in terms of a neophyte. If this person is to become a functioning user of the language, she must be able to get reliable perceptual information about the linguistic and other behavior of her fellow group members. Otherwise she would be able neither to learn the language (how could she?!) nor to use it in communication.

But then, by hypothetical syllogism:

(3) If sense perception is not reliable no term can have a meaning.

But in raising the issue of the reliability of sense perception, we suppose ourselves to be using language meaningfully. And if we are not using language meaningfully we have failed to raise that issue, whatever we may suppose.

Hence:

(4) If no term can have a meaning, we cannot raise the issue as to the reliability of sense perception.

Hence:

(5) If it is possible to raise the issue of the reliability of sense perception, then sense perception is reliable.

Thus there is no real possibility that sense perception is not reliable. If it were not, then there could not be so much as a question of its reliability. If there is such a question, it can have only a favorable answer.

Note that this argument exhibits more clearly a feature of all the arguments we have called "Wittgensteinian". They all contend that the hypothesis that sense perception is not reliable is self-defeating. If we try to maintain it, it crumbles in our fingers. Either it is meaningless because not empirically confirmable, or it takes away critical features of the terms we use to formulate particular perceptual judgments—or it would make it impossible for us to learn the meaning of such terms or for such terms to mean what they do, or, as in the present argument, it denies a necessary condition of any term's having meaning.

Although this is the strongest argument for the reliability of sense perception (or for the impossibility of supposing sense perception to be unreliable) from an anti-private language perspective, it too founders on epistemic circularity. This pops up in the support for premise (2). That support consists in pointing out ways in which we have to rely on sense perception in learning a public language. How else can we learn a public language except by getting reliable perceptual information about the linguistic behavior of speakers of the language as that fits onto the physical and social environment? But how do we know that this is the only way? How do we know that we do not have some other cognitive access to the linguistic behavior of others and to the setting in which that is carried on? For that matter, how do we know that our mastery of a public language is not innate, in which case it would not have to be learned at all? Obviously, we know all this because of what we have learned about the world, more specifically because of what we have learned about human beings and their resources for learning, for knowledge acquisition, and for linguistic communication. That gives us good reason for denying that human beings can acquire and use a public language without heavy reliance on sense perception. But we have learned this *by relying on our perception of each other in our physical and social environment and by reasoning from that perceptually generated information*. It is not as if we can know a priori that we have no other cognitive access to these matters. Quite the contrary. A priori it seems quite possible that the requisite knowledge should be innate, or that we should have other, non-sensory modes of access to the linguistic behavior of others and to the stage setting of that behavior. Hence we are relying on sense perception in arguing that a public language presupposes the reliability of sense perception. Epistemic circularity has once more vitiated what looked like a purely a priori argument.

viii. Transcendental Arguments

The next item on the agenda is "transcendental arguments". This label has been much in vogue of late, though as pointed out by Jonathan Bennett (1979, pp. 50–51), it has been variously employed. The contemporary use of the term stems from Kant. In *The Critique of Pure Reason* (1929) he wrote: "The term 'transcendental' . . . signifies such knowledge as concerns the *a priori* possibility of knowledge, or its *a priori* employment" (A56; B80). And again: "The explanation of the manner in which concepts can thus relate *a priori* to objects I entitle their transcendental deduction" (A 85; B117). More specifically, Kant's famous transcendental deduction of the categories sought to show that their applicability to objects of experience is necessary for any experience of objects, since it is necessary for that experience to be attributed to a subject, which in turn is necessary for an experience of objects. We might think of the contemporary use of 'transcendental argument' as broadening out from the Kantian argument in various ways: extending to any argument designed to show that the applicability of certain concepts is required for experience of an objective world, or for self-consciousness, or for experience of the past, or for having any experience whatsoever. The term has also been stretched to cover arguments to the effect that something or other is necessary for the possibility of language or judgment or the possession of any concepts. Thus the label might be applied by some to all or most of the "Wittgensteinian" arguments we have been considering. Again, since Kant's transcendental deduction was directed at Humean skepticism, the label has been applied to any argument that seeks to show that something the skeptic acknowledges suffices to undermine his skepticism. For present purposes I shall stick fairly closely to Kant and restrict myself to arguments designed to show that the applicability of certain basic, physical object concepts is a necessary presupposition of any possession of experience by a subject.

Fortunately the consideration can be brief since even if the Kantian argument, or any like it in the specified respect, is wholly successful in its announced aim, it will fail to establish the reliability of sense perception. What such arguments are designed to show is that certain fundamental concepts, such as *causality* and *substance*, are applicable to the objects of sense experience. But even if that is so, the question still remains as to whether perceptual beliefs are mostly true. After all, what we come to believe on the basis of perception is almost always much more specific than that we are confronted with substances that are interrelated causally. Hence even if perception is right in representing its objects as substantial and causally connected (and subject to various other categories), it could be wrong in most of the (alleged) information it provides.

This judgment of irrelevance to our problem applies not only to Kant's transcendental deduction of the categories, but also to the (more or less) Kant-inspired arguments for the applicability of concepts that we find in part II, chapter 2 of Strawson 1966, in Bennett 1979, and in chapter 2 of Grayling 1985. The same is to be said of other well-known arguments of Strawson's that have been called "transcendental", such as the argument that one can attribute conscious states to oneself only if one can attribute them to others (1959, chap. 3). Here too we can derive from the conclusion no positive epistemic evaluation of any particular way of forming beliefs about the conscious states of others. Strawson does, indeed, argue that we have the other-attribution capacity in question only if we are able to identify other persons, and that that, in turn, requires that something we can observe constitutes sufficient bases for such identification. But even if we accept that, it does not follow that our customary ways of forming beliefs about the conscious states of the persons so identified can be relied on to produce mostly true beliefs. More generally we can say that when recent Anglo-American philosophers have been engaging in producing arguments they call "transcendental", they have been concerned with establishing the applicability of certain concepts, or the real existence of certain types of entities, or the possession of certain conceptual or judgmental capacities. They have not been concerned with the reliability or other epistemic properties of modes of belief formation. In a word, they have been doing metaphysics rather than epistemology. And so, despite initial impressions to the contrary, we can set their efforts to one side here.

This brings us to the end of our discussion of a priori arguments for the reliability of SP. The chief morals to be drawn from this survey are the following. (1) Apparently a priori arguments frequently contain hidden empirical assumptions that rely on sense perception for their justification. (2) It is all too easy to assume (falsely) that by establishing various other things, such as the existence of the physical world or the application of certain categories to the objects of experience or the falsity of solipsism or the impossibility of all perceptual belief's being false, we can thereby show sense perception to be reliable.

ix. The Explanation of Sensory Experience

I now turn to a consideration of avowedly *empirical* arguments for the reliability of SP. First, a point made in section ii, since we are looking for arguments that do not exhibit epistemic circularity, we are blocked off from using what is most usually termed "empirical evidence", viz., what we learn about the environment from perception and what is based on that. This means that simple track-record arguments, appeals to the predictive and control successes of SP, and evolutionary arguments are off limits.[16] Indeed, at first glance it seems impossible to mount any a posteriori argument for the reliability of SP without relying on its outputs to do so. For where else would we get the empirical premises we need for such an argument? However there is at least one other source of knowledge that deserves to be called 'empirical', namely, introspection, our awareness of our own conscious states. Perhaps this could be used to provide the empirical premises of an a posteriori argument. If we could find some way to go from facts about our sensory experience to external facts putatively perceived via those sense experiences, without the conclusion depending on an appeal to other external facts, that would give us an effective noncircular argument. For it would show us how to establish for a given perception that what we take ourselves to have learned therein really is (probably) the case. But how would such an argument go? As has been repeatedly pointed out since the time of Hume, it can't proceed by appealing to sensory experience-external fact correlations that have been established inductively. For to perform such inductions we would have to have established by experience in a number of particular cases that when one has a sensory experience of type ϕ there is a red object before one. Since we can ascertain the latter part of this conjunction only by relying on sense perception, epistemic circularity creeps back in. However, there is another way. When high-level scientific theories are established (confirmed, tested, supported . . .) it is not by inductive correlations of the sort just mentioned, and

[16]At least appeals to predictive success as these are generally carried out, in terms of the success of SP in predicting the course of events in the physical world. In the next section we shall see that a different kind of prediction, prediction of sensory experience, can be appealed to without epistemic circularity.

for reasons analogous to those just appealed to. Consider a theory of chemical compounds in terms of the structure of constituent molecules. We cannot establish by induction that whenever we have something with the surface properties of salt, the molecular structure is thus-and-so; for apart from this or some other equally high-level theory, we have no way of knowing what kind of molecular structure we have there. We have no cognitive access to molecular structure that is independent of a theory, just as in the former case we have no cognitive access to the putatively perceived facts independent of reliance on sense perception. However, this by no means leads scientists to throw up their hands in despair. On the contrary, they have recourse to a form of argument called "hypothetico-deductive", or "argument to the best explanation". Rather than seeking some inductive support for the theory, they try to show that it constitutes the best explanation of the empirical facts in question—in this case, inductively established, lower-level, lawlike generalizations. Similarly, it has often been suggested that the physical world as we normally suppose it to be provides the best explanation for our sensory experience or for certain introspectively ascertainable facts concerning our sensory experience. It is this project that we will be examining in this section.

Before considering specific versions of the argument, it will be useful to remind ourselves how difficult it is to avoid epistemic circularity in the enterprise. Consider John Locke's famous discussion in the *Essay Concerning Human Understanding* (1975), which runs in part as follows.

> But besides the assurance we have from our Senses themselves, that they do not err in the Information they give us, of the Existence of Things without us, when they are affected by Them, we are farther confirmed in this assurance, by other concurrent Reasons.
>
> First, 'Tis plain, those Perceptions are produced in us by exteriour Causes affecting our Senses: Because *those that want the Organs of any Sense, never can have the Ideas belonging to that Sense* produced in their Minds. . . . The Organs themselves, 'tis plain, do not produce them: for then the Eyes of a Man in the dark, would produce Colours, and his Nose smell Roses in the Winter: but we see no body gets the relish of a Pine-apple, till he goes to the Indies, where it is, and tastes it. (P. 632)

This is blatantly circular. How does Locke know that those without the use of their eyes never have visual ideas, except by relying on what he has learned through perception, including what other people say about their experience? Indeed, so sweeping a generalization could not be based solely on what he has observed, but requires crediting the testimony of others, which itself is known about only through perception. For that matter, how does he know that anyone has, or lacks, eyes? The same point applies to such claims as that the eyes of a man in the dark do not produce colors, and that nobody gets the taste of a pineapple without putting that fruit in his mouth.

Attempts to show that the course of our sensory experience is best explained in terms of physical causes differ both in how they construe the explanandum and in how they construe the explanans. I shall begin with the former.

First, note that we can't get any mileage at all out of considering particular bits of experience one at a time. If I take a particular visual experience and consider what is responsible for my having that experience, without taking into account how it fits into some overall pattern, I will have no basis for choosing between possible explanations, apart from whatever differential credibility they have from other sources. Later we will consider claims to the effect that one explanation out of all the competitors (of this or some other explanandum) is clearly superior on grounds of simplicity or some other way of choosing between empirically equivalent explanations. But the present point is that so far as throwing light on the fact that this experience occurs, so far as *the connection between explanans and explanandum* is concerned, one explanation is as good as another when the explanandum is this impoverished. If I can make the effort of will necessary to leave out of account everything else I think I know about the course of my sensory experience and whatever I base on that, I will be completely at a loss in choosing between the usual physical-physiological-psychological explanation, the Cartesian demon explanation, the self-generation-by-unconscious-psychological-processes explanation, and others. What possible basis could there be for such a choice? I have a reason for picking one explanation of X rather than another after some lawlike generalizations have been established connecting states of affairs like X with others. If I have established the necessary or sufficient conditions of combustion I have something to go on in determining how to explain a fire. But at this stage of our inquiry we are quite without any such resources. Thus we are well advised to choose a richer explanandum, such as recurrent patterns we find in our sense experience.

On the side of the explanans it also turns out that the simplest choices fail to do the job. A minimal explanatory gesture in the direction of an external cause would be that some (relatively) permanent and stable entity or entities is causally responsible for our sensory experience. But even if that were true it would fail to show that these entities are as they perceptually seem to us. That explanation is compatible with the cause being God, a demon, Kantian things-in-themselves (with the ban on causal efficacy lifted), or Leibnizian or Whiteheadian centers of psychic force. The explanation could be enriched with the stipulation that the causes(s) is physical in character, but that would have no tendency to show that sense perception gives us the correct story about those causes. It could be that our sensory experience results from the causal impact of physical things on us, but not in such a way as to yield generally correct beliefs about those causes. This could either be because the same external state of affairs does not, even usually, produce the same kind of sensory experience (because of the preponderant influence of factors internal to the subject), or because of peculiarities in the perceptual belief-producing mechanism. In the latter case, the experience itself could be as sensitive an indication as you like of the nature of its causes, but the belief-producing mechanism(s) fails to exploit this fact sufficiently.

Thus in order to have a chance of reaching our goal, we must enrich the explanans still further. Rather than a bare supposition that sensory experience is caused by something(s) physical, we must build in the supposition that sensory experience is caused in pretty much the way it is thought by contemporary science to be caused. That will give us a much richer and more detailed explanatory hypothesis, one that is open to continual development and even modification but that is clear enough in its general outlines.

Does this explanation imply that SP is reliable? One thing is clear. If our sense experiences are produced in the way current scientific thinking has it, that experience does consistently, though not perfectly or invariably, reflect differences in the objects putatively perceived. But that by itself does not guarantee that the perceptual belief-producing mechanism will itself register those experiential indications in such a way as to reliably produce true beliefs about the perceived objects. Therefore, the assumption that it does so will have to be built into the explanans. Second, we will also have to build in the assumption that our sense perceptions usually occur in "normal situations", situations that "fit with" the capacities of the perceptual apparatus so that the latter yields mostly true beliefs. Even if things are with perception and perceptual belief as we ordinarily suppose, we could hardly expect people to have mostly true perceptual beliefs if they were confronted mostly with extremely clever look-alikes, or if their sensory experiences were produced by direct brain stimulation in a laboratory. It must be confessed that this second assumption could hardly lay claim to being part of a scientific account of perception and perceptual cognition. It is no part of physics and psychology to map the whereabouts of this or that person. But that is neither here nor there. Our enterprise of validating SP is not a scientific one. It depends on science only for suggestions for an explanation of sense experience.

We are now in a position to assess the explanation under consideration. Contrary to what one might naturally suppose, it cannot assume the form typical of theoretical explanations in science, in which a body of lower-level, inductively established, lawlike generalizations are explained by hypotheses concerning the underlying structure and/or mechanisms that are responsible for these regularities. Consider, as a modest example, the vast body of lawlike regularities in the chemical interaction of substances, where the characterization of the substances are in terms of empirically accessible "surface" properties like color and weight or in terms of common-sense natural kinds like milk and salt, and where the interactions and their products are also described in observational or near-observational terms. These interactions include combustion and other forms of oxidation, the reduction of metallic ores, corrosion, and the like. A theory is then developed that identifies elements by atomic weight and the like, and describes compounds in terms of molecular composition. None of the latter is directly accessible to observation, even with the help of instruments (unless the instrumental readings are informed by the high-level theory). Acceptance of the theory is justified by the fact that it makes possible a systematic unification and explanation of a vast body of otherwise heterogeneous and unrelated empirical generalizations.

The present explanatory enterprise cannot be construed in these terms just because there are no genuine lawlike regularities at the purely phenomenal level. We cannot ascertain any regularities that we have reason to think will hold up under any and all circumstances, so long as we stick strictly to sensory experience. The first point to note here is that we cannot identify even rough regularities so long as we leave out of account the behavior of the subject. I am looking at my desk in my study with a cork bulletin board behind it on the wall. By what will this visual display be followed? That all depends, obviously, on what I do. If I remain motionless with eyes open I will continue to be presented with an an almost identical visual field, at least until some sensory satiation point is reached. If I turn my head in one direction something different will follow; if I turn my head in another direction or if I move into another room, still different visual experiences will ensue. It is hopeless to try to find regularities in changes of sensory experience without taking into account the movements of the subject. But to take those into account we will have to abandon purely phenomenal description, will we not? Well, insofar as kinesthetic and other sense experiences are an accurate reflection of bodily movement, something may be done. By factoring these phenomenal shadows of the subject's locomotion into the equation, we may be able to sketch out rough regularities. Thus my visual experience as if looking at the wall behind my desk plus certain characteristic kinesthetic sensations will be followed regularly by a visual experience as if seeing the door of my study with a full bookcase to its right. And so on.

However, no such regularities have any title to lawlikeness. They are eminently subject to exception even when the phenomenal antecedents are as specified. If the bookcase to the right of the door has been moved the visual consequent in the above will not be forthcoming. If my neighbor across the street cuts down his trees the visual scene to the right of my desk will have changed. When I open my eyes in the morning I am confronted with a typical visual experience of my bedroom. But I have lived in other houses, where what I experience under those conditions is quite different. All such regularities—constancies as well as successions—are at the mercy of transactions in the external environment that are not registered in my experience. Moreover, there is no pattern to these exceptions that would give us a handle on taking account of them in some principled fashion.[17]

It may be thought that we will achieve lawlikeness if we turn from the

[17] I owe this last point to Robert Audi.

"local" regularities just exemplified to the phenomenal shadows of physical lawlike connections. A visual experience as of putting a lighted match to some newspaper will be followed by a visual experience as of the newspaper catching fire. A tactile experience as of grasping a door handle and turning it will be followed by a visual experience as of a door opening. A tactile experience as of a gust of wind plus a visual experience as of leaves on the ground in the vicinity will be followed by a visual experience as of leaves moving. And so on. But here too there is not enough in the phenomenal shadows to effect lawlike connections. The newspaper may be flame resistant in ways not detectable by just looking, or the apparent flame of the match may be an optical illusion. Doors notoriously sometimes fail to open when we turn the knob and pull. The leaves may be firmly stuck to the ground or the wind may not be strong enough to move them. Perhaps we could get rid of all these exceptions by suitable enrichments of the phenomenal antecedents. But further exceptions are always waiting in the wings.[18]

The closest we can come to genuine phenomenal laws concern variations in visually sensed shape and other spatial properties with variations in relative position and distance of observer and object. Suppose we really can take care of observer movement in terms of kinesthetic and other sensations. Then it is a plausible candidate for a lawlike regularity that as the observer moves away from a position directly in front of an object that presents a round appearance, that object will appear more or less elliptical. To be sure, this is complicated by constancy mechanisms, and there is persistent controversy over whether there is an increasing *experienced* ellipticality that is masked by belief and other nonperceptual, cognitive factors. But even if there are a few phenomenal laws of this sort, they are too few and too isolated to provide the explanandum base for an explanatory theory rich enough to bring in what it takes to support the reliability of SP.

Even if there are no, or few, lawlike regularities within the phenomenal realm, that is not necessarily the end of the explanatory enterprise. It would be a narrow, dogmatic scientism that would allow as explanations of sensory experience only what conforms to the pattern of theoretical explanation in the most advanced sciences, where we have genuinely lawlike, empirical generalizations with which to work. We often seek to explain rough regularities in everyday life, and such explanations often genuinely throw light on the matter. We seek to explain the fact that Jim is often so moody on weekends, we ask why the furnace tends to break down when the weather is coldest, why

[18]It may be pointed out that even with physical descriptions, practically any laws we are able to work with hold only within a "closed system", closed against any effective influences not taken account of in the law. But the point is that with physical variables we are able to specify connections that are so close, for all practical purposes, to holding no matter what, that it is at least close enough to the truth to think of ourselves, much of the time, as working within a closed system. Such is decidedly not the case with the kinds of putative phenomenal laws we have been illustrating.

people catch colds more in winter than in summer, and so on. Why shouldn't we seek an explanation of the rough, and even local, regularities we find in our sensory experience? Perhaps the best explanation we can find is one that will imply the reliability of SP.

This brings us to the question of whether the standard explanation of patterns in sensory experience is superior to its competitors. Remember that ultimately we are interested in an explanatory hypothesis that not only involves the standard suppositions about the production of sense experience but also contains the assumption of a standard mode of perceptual belief formation, as well as an assumption of the by and large normality of situations in which perceptual beliefs are formed. However, we will be best advised to focus on the production of sensory experience. Since virtually all the discussions in the literature are confined to the explanation of sense experience, this will enable us to make contact with that literature. Since the claim to superiority for this part of the explanation is fundamental to this venture, if that claim cannot be made out, that will subvert the whole enterprise.

At the risk of belaboring the obvious I will make explicit just how it is that the standard explanation of sense experience bids fair to throw light on the kinds of patterns cited earlier. First, consider the constancies and regularities of succession in my visual experience when certain kinds of kinesthetic sensations do (or do not) occur (i.e., though we can't explicitly say this, when I remain at rest or move in certain ways). When I have a visual experience as if seeing the desk in my study, this will remain constant, then be followed by certain other visual experiences, and reappear, depending on the kinesthetic sensations that occur. These patterns are naturally explained by the supposition that the experiences are produced in the standard way, thereby revealing an external environment that is relatively stable and structured in such a way as to yield visual experiences of the sorts specified depending on what visible objects are in the line of sight and close enough when I turn my open eyes in one or another direction. Again, the *spread of fire* and other rough "causal" regularities in experience mentioned earlier receive a ready explanation if we suppose these experiences to be caused by environmental happenings in such a way as to reflect the character and causal interactions of the physical realities involved. Finally, consider the continuous deformation of visually sensed shape as we get the sensory correlates of movements away from looking straight on to an object, and the fact of increasing apparent size as we, so it seems sensorily, move closer and closer to an object, with a typical set of tactile experiences becoming available as the object looms largest in the visual field. All such patterns are naturally understood in terms of the experiences being produced in the standard way by external objects that are spatially disposed in a certain way at each moment vis-à-vis the moving observer. I take it that there is no question that the standard theory has explanatory force with respect to these explananda.

But the question remains as to whether it is a better explanation than its competitors. Just what competitors are there? Discussions of the issue have been almost hypnotically fastened on the Cartesian demon or the Berkeleyan God, according to theological taste. It has been argued, as we shall see in a moment, that the standard explanation better satisfies certain generally accepted constraints on explanation than do these alternatives. But even if that is so, we are not home free unless other live alternatives have been excluded. What others deserve consideration? The phenomenalist view that patterns of experience are ultimate, requiring no explanation in terms of anything else, is often mentioned; but I will summarily dismiss this null hypothesis, on the grounds that this takes us outside the "explanation game".[19] Another group of explanations that is rarely given so much as a nod is made up of those that represent sense experience as due to the causal impact on the subject of a variegated environing world of finite substances on roughly the same scale as physical substances, but differ in not taking these substances to be physical in character. The most familiar views of this sort are Leibnizian and Whiteheadian panpsychism. According to both there is no such thing as (completely) dead matter. Every existing entity engages in *perception* (Leibniz) or *feelings* (Whitehead), albeit these rise to a conscious level only in such high-grade existents as human minds. What perception inaccurately presents to us as a field of inert, lifeless things (except for the plants and animals therein) is really a continuum of enduring, perceiving substances (Leibniz) or a four-dimensional continuum of "occasions" of experience (Whitehead). Our interaction with these beings gives rise to our sense perceptions, which, taken uncritically, lead us to form false beliefs about perceived entities.[20] But these beliefs do serve us well, practically, since the envisaged spatial field in which physical substances display themselves is, in Leibniz's phrase, a *phenomenon bene fundatum*, a well-founded phenomenon. Here we do have a class of explanations that are genuine alternatives to the standard explanation and that do not imply that SP is reliable—in fact they imply that it is unreliable.[21]

Another alternative that does not get the innings it deserves is the self-

[19]Actually the situation here is more complicated, since the usual phenomenalist account is in terms of patterns of actual *and possible* experiences; and the appeal to possible experience raises problems of its own. These problems will, however, do nothing to nullify the reason for which I dismissed such accounts.

[20]This talk of "interaction" does not represent Leibniz with strict accuracy; he denies that substances can affect each other causally, though because of the preestablished harmony their successive states are correlated as they would be if they did causally affect each other.

[21]To this it may be objected that so long as perceptual beliefs serve us well as guides to action, we cannot properly take SP to be unreliable. But we can. Reliability, after all, requires a preponderance of *true* beliefs, not just practically useful beliefs; and that is precisely what we do not have on the panpsychist explanation. To be sure, I said earlier that I would not take reliability to require a preponderance of strictly true beliefs; sufficient approximations to truth would be enough. But if all our beliefs about rocks, trees, and air generated by SP represent them as insentient and if they are, in fact, sentient, that hardly counts as a close approximation to the truth, even if the distinctions we make perceptually between different objects and states of affairs closely correlate with the real distinctions between them.

generation hypothesis. It is conceivable that my sense experiences are wholly generated by myself. To be sure, I am not conscious of doing so; but then I do lots of other things I am not conscious of doing—for example, I digest my food. Obviously, this explanation would not imply that SP is reliable, and if we exclude preestablished harmony it will imply that SP is unreliable.

Let's say then we are working with the following alternatives to the standard explanation.

(1) Cartesian demon explanation.
(2) Berkeleyan God explanation.
(3) Panpsychist explanation.
(4) Self-generation explanation.[22]

Contemporary discussions of this problem typically assume that all these competitors are empirically equivalent in that they all explain the same range of experiential data. The task of choosing a winner boils down to determining which candidate best satisfies other criteria for the comparative evaluation of explanations. Those most commonly cited are economy and simplicity. But it is not at all clear that the alternatives all score worse in these respects. These criteria are notoriously subject to various construals, but let's say that economy is a matter of the number of entities, or, better, the number of basic kinds of entities, to which the explanatory hypothesis commits us. On this score it would seem that (1), (2), and (4) win hands down over the standard theory and panpsychism. Each of the former postulates only a single kind of explanatory factor, indeed only a single individual factor, whereas the standard view is recklessly prodigal in the kinds of things it invokes: as many kinds of things as we currently recognize to inhabit the physical world. Simplicity is a more difficult notion to make precise. In default of a thorough discussion, let's say that it is a matter of the complexity of the connections between the ultimate explanatory factors and the terminal explanandum. On this reading, (1), (2), and (4) are again clearly superior, or can easily be construed as such. Let's say that God or the demon or the subject herself produces sensory experiences directly. In the first two cases a simple act of will suffices. In the third case, some unconscious analogue of an act of will can be deemed sufficient. But perhaps simplicity is something like the complexity of the whole story that

[22]The reader may be surprised that I did not include the currently popular "brain in a vat" hypothesis, according to which all my sensory experiences are produced by direct brain stimulation, I myself being just an isolated brain kept alive in an appropriate nutrient solution. The reason is that such a hypothesis inevitably raises the question of the status of the perceptions of the scientists and technicians who are thus manipulating me. Presumably, in order to make the hypothesis readily intelligible and not intolerably implausible they will have to be credited with normal perception. But then the hypothesis does not imply that SP is *generally* unreliable. Even if other sentient subjects are in the same unhappy situation as I, there would have to be some normal percipients to keep the thing going. Thus, for deliberate deception I will restrict myself to the good old Cartesian demon, who can merrily deceive all humankind evenhandedly.

has to be told in order to complete the explanation. On that understanding, it has been argued that the demon hypothesis is less simple than the standard one; for to bring it about that the hypothesis does suffice to explain our experience we must represent the demon as using the standard scheme as a model so as to achieve his deceptive aim, to give us a pattern of experiences that will lead us to believe we are perceiving a physical world. But it is not at all necessary that a demon proceed in this way. Why couldn't he simply intend to produce in us experiences that exhibit the kinds of internal patterns we have already noted, along with giving us the penchant to go from such patterns to beliefs about physical things supposedly perceived in these experiences? The demon need not spell out in advance all, or even any, of the details of the particular physical world scheme we end up with, though of course it is conceivable that he should do so.[23] Thus the prospects for justifying the standard explanation by an appeal to economy or simplicity do not look promising.

Alan Goldman, in "The Inference to Physical Reality" (1988, chap. 9), appeals to "explanatory depth" as a criterion for goodness of explanation. Initially he compares the standard explanation with the view that phenomenal regularities are ultimate, and rightly points out that the former is deeper in that it answers questions (why does our experience exhibit just these regularities?) that the latter refuses on principle to raise (pp. 206–7), as well as explaining deviations from the regularities, not just the regularities themselves (p. 208). But, more to the present point though he recognizes that alternatives like the ones we are considering also provide deeper explanations than phenomenalism (pp. 209–10), he objects to deceiver hypotheses like (2) on similar grounds.

> If God caused all the lawlike regularities in our experience without creating physical objects, then, as Descartes pointed out, he would be a deceiver. At least his motives would be far from clear, as unclear as the mechanisms by which he worked this enormous deception. The same obscurities as to motives and mechanisms, that is, as to any attempt to carry the purported explanations to deeper levels and make them more explicit and detailed, infect the superbeings of the skeptic's imagination. Not only do we not know why or how they produce the sequences of appearances for us that they do; we also have no idea why they make it seem to us as if there are physical objects. The latter question, natural here, does not arise given the initial explanation of appearances that we all naturally accept, and accepting the explanation as true leads to deeper and more satisfying theories to explain physical interactions. Certainly whatever psychology and programming apparatus one could dream up for the superbeings could not be as rich or testable as the theories of physical science and neurophysiology. (P. 212)

[23]It may well be that *we* cannot set out the demon's program without using our standard, physical world scheme as a model for the patterns of sense experience he aims to produce in us. But there is no reason to suppose the demon to be restricted in this way.

There seem to be a number of points jumbled together here. First, ". . . we do not know why or how they produce the sequences of appearances for us that they do . . .". If this means that we do not have independent information as to this why and how, that is irrelevant. As we noted earlier, we can't make use of such independent information with respect to the standard theory either, or any other alternative, without epistemic circularity. When we are at this basic a level, we may concoct any explanatory hypothesis we choose, *without antecedent evidence for its truth*, and then let its relative explanatory efficacy decide whether it is to be accepted. But perhaps the point is that even though the standard theory is enormously rich and complex, the alternatives, as developed thus far, consist merely in bare suggestions as to how an explanation might be developed in detail. Thus, in comparing actually existing theories, the standard one is miles ahead on richness and detail. This is an important point. But what bearing does it have on the question of which explanation is the true one? Obviously, the reason the other alternatives have not been significantly developed is that we all accept the standard explanation and are quite satisfied with it. No one is motivated to carry out the enormous labor that would be involved in developing one of the alternatives to anything like the same extent. But to build this superiority of the standard explanation into an argument for its truth, we would have to be justified in supposing that (1) none of the other alternatives could be developed into something equally rich and detailed and (2) of two explanations the richer and more detailed is more likely to be true, *ceteris paribus*.

(2) may be defensible. This is one form of the general question as to whether these "good-making" properties of explanations should be thought of as indications of *truth*, or of other desiderata: fruitfulness, ease of operation, intellectual satisfaction, or whatever. Perhaps this question should be answered differently for different criteria. The truth conducivity of simplicity and economy is often questioned. Why should we suppose that reality is maximally simple or maximally economical? We can readily understand the appeal of these criteria without supposing them to be indicative of truth. A simpler theory is easier to grasp and easier to work with; a more economical theory presents us with fewer factors to keep track of. One might say something similar about *depth* in the sense in which I first reported Goldman as using it, a sense in which it amounts roughly to pushing explanation as far as possible. (And who is to say how far is possible?) Again, we can understand the appeal of this without supposing that it has anything to do with truth. If explanation is our game, we want to keep doing it for as long as possible, or we are out of business. But why suppose that an explanation in terms of a further level, realm, or domain is more likely to be true, *ceteris paribus*, than one that stays modestly at home? There is more to be said for the desideratum currently under consideration, also termed 'depth' by Goldman, but better termed 'detail'. This is, in a way, the opposite of simplicity. On one natural

understanding of 'simplicity', detail and simplicity are contraries; the simpler the hypothesis the less detail and vice versa. Before considering whether *detail* is truth indicative, we should render our understanding of it more detailed. Are we speaking of detail in the explanans or detail in the connection? If it is only the former, then if we compare two hypotheses that are unequally detailed but have equal explanatory power, I think we must prefer the less detailed one; it gives us more bang for the buck. To have a clear ground for preferring more detail, I think that will have to be construed in terms of the explanatory connection. That sort of detail would enable us to explain more aspects of the explanandum. Here we have a clear superiority and one that arguably increases the probability of truth, *ceteris paribus*. But note that this superiority is simply a consequence of the greater explanatory power. It is not the detail as such, but the resultant explanatory power that makes it a better explanation. That may be what Goldman was thinking: that the standard theory can throw more light on why we have patterns of each of a number of different sorts, and can differentially explain each by specifying the causal antecedents peculiar to it; the demon hypothesis can do only a bit of hand waving with its talk of an intention to deceive.

Although we have finally identified a superiority that carries with it some presumption of truth, the first assumption, "none of the other alternatives could be developed into something equally rich and detailed", will not fare so well. Granted that none have been so developed, why suppose that none *could be*? Why suppose that "whatever psychology and programming apparatus one could dream up for the superbeings could not be as rich or testable as the theories of physical science and neuronphysiology"? How do you know till you've tried? As pointed out earlier, we can easily understand why no such development has taken place, and this explanation has no tendency to show that the development is impossible. I would say that whereas unequal richness in the sense that implies unequal explanatory power, *where equal effort has gone into development*, is arguably a token of greater probability of truth, that is not the case where the developmental effort is grossly unequal. If you've just won the Heisman Trophy, that doesn't show that you have more athletic ability than I if I haven't done much to use what ability I have and there is no reason to think I couldn't develop into that good a football player if I tried hard enough.[24]

For a consideration of other attempts to show that the standard explanation is superior, and thereby to show that SP is reliable, see my forthcoming monograph on this subject mentioned earlier (*The Reliability of Sense Perception*). My examination reveals that they either fall into epistemic circularity, or they fail to support an attribution of by and large truth to the output of SP, or they suffer from other crippling defects. At bottom the reason that so many

[24]In the next section we will continue the discussion of whether alternative explanations could be developed further.

acute philosophers have failed to do this job is the ban on epistemic circularity. When we are precluded from making use of anything we take ourselves to have learned from SP and whatever is based on that, we have little to go on in deciding which explanation of experience is mostly likely to be true. The various "nonevidential" criteria of explanations may be useful in certain choices between scientific theories, but when we have as little else to throw into the scales as we do in this radical a situation, they fail to pick a winner, especially when reliability is the goal. The idea that we can validate the epistemic claims of SP by considering how best to explain facts about our sensory experience turns out to be a nonstarter.

x. Explanations of Our Success in Predicting Our Experience

Before abandoning explanatory approaches to our problem we must look at one that is clearly superior to those we have scrutinized in the last section. This new tack will involve a different explanandum. Instead of confining ourselves to sense experience and patterns therein, we enrich it to include as well the following facts. (1) We use a certain physical and social world scheme to conceptualize what we perceive and we use a certain procedure, SP, for forming perceptual beliefs. (2) By accepting the perceptual beliefs so formed and by developing systems of belief from them we are enabled to effectively predict *the course of our experience*. We can foresee with an amazing degree of accuracy what sensory experiences we will have at a given moment. Furthermore, it is not just that we do this by relying on SP; that in itself would be noteworthy, but hardly a decisive support for SP, provided it were possible for us to do the same thing in other ways—for example, by basing our predictions on observed regularities within sense experience. However, the clinching point is that, so far as we can tell, reliance on SP, along with memory and reasoning based on that, is essential to the enterprise. We are simply unable to do the job just on the basis of patterns within sense experience, the most obvious alternative. Even if there are enough stable regularities within sense experience to serve as a basis for the predictions, something we have already seen ample reason to doubt, they would be too complex for us to spot, store, and utilize. Think back on some of the earlier points. We can see from our familiar, physical world scheme that what prevents simple regularities in sense experience is that what I experience at a given moment is a function not just of what I have previously experienced but also of various details of the physical setting, including the behavior of my body. Thus if there are to be any dependable phenomenal regularities, they will have to take into account not just the immediately preceding phenomena but also whatever sensory basis I have, in present and past experience, for supposing the physical environment and my body at that time to be so-and-so. The complexity this would assume is so staggering that one cannot even form a plausible sketch of how it would go. Thus it is not only that these predictive achievements are made possible by the use of SP; it looks as if we couldn't bring them off in any other way.

The argument is, then, that far and away the best explanation for this complex fact is that the scheme we use to bring off these predictions does fit the reality we perceive, and that the procedure we use to form perceptual beliefs is a reliable source of belief. If our perceptual beliefs are not mostly an accurate rendering of what we take ourselves to be perceiving, why is it that the forecasts of future experience we make on the basis of those beliefs should so often be borne out? It would be an incredible run of good luck. And so an inference to the best explanation assures us that SP is indeed reliable.[25]

Let's note several crucial features of this argument.

(1) The reader will remember that an earlier argument from predictive success was dismissed in section ii as infected with epistemic circularity. This argument is specifically designed to avoid that disability. The earlier argument appealed to our success in making accurate predictions of external, physical states of affairs. Hence it required reliance on SP to determine that those predictions are often correct. But this argument appeals to our success in predicting *the course of our sense experience*. It trades on our ability to anticipate that, for example, *it will be just as if we are seeing a maple tree in front of us*, rather than on our ability to anticipate that there will be a maple tree in front of us. Hence no reliance on the perception of external states of affairs is presupposed by the argument.[26]

(2) The argument avoids epistemic circularity at another point by merely appealing to the fact that *we use SP and associated doxastic practices involving the physical world scheme*, rather than itself working *within* those practices and thereby presupposing their reliability.

(3) It is clearly superior to the argument that is based on the standard explanation of patterns in our sense experience, superior in several respects. First, it doesn't require that any patterns or regularities can be found *within* sense

[25]It is amazing that this line of argument is not represented, or hardly represented, in the literature. Perhaps it would be if people were more often concerned specifically with our problem—the reliability of SP—as contrasted with such problems as the existence of the physical world and/or its characteristics and constituents.

[26]At least that's the way it appears on the surface. That appearance will be challenged by any view that, like Wittgenstein's, takes it that we cannot refer to sensory experience unless we are in possession of a public language that itself presupposes the reliability of sense perception. (For some consideration of this see section vii.) For another example of views that don't allow this argument to escape epistemic circularity, see Jonathan Bennett's argument (1966, pp. 204–9) that it is impossible to have beliefs about one's own past sensory states unless one also takes them to be perceptions of objective states of affairs. More generally, we can say that this argument escapes epistemic circularity only if it is possible to think and speak about one's own experiences without already being au courant with a public physical world in a way that presupposes the reliability of sense perception. I shall assume that this is indeed the case. I believe it to be the case, but even if I didn't I would assume it in order to give this line of argument a run for its money.

experience. Its explanandum is rather the predictive success we attain when we abandon that search and seek patterns in the objective states of affairs we take ourselves to perceive through sense experience. The whole point of the argument is that by taking individual sense experiences as revelatory of external physical realities and connecting up our sense experiences through a detour into the physical world, we can do an incomparably better job of predicting those experiences than we could by looking for purely phenomenal patterns.

(4) The argument is also superior in that the desired conclusion, the reliability of SP, is built into the explanans that we are claiming to provide the best explanation. We don't, as we did earlier, have to argue from the explanatory claim to the epistemological conclusion of reliability by means of additional premises. Thus the argument, if sound, directly establishes the reliability of SP. This point is, of course, intimately connected with the previous one. It is because the explanandum concerns the predictive success we attain *when using SP* that the explanans features the reliability of SP.

(5) Finally, the argument is superior in that the favored explanation seems clearly to be preferable to its alternatives. What better explanation of effective prediction on the basis of premises obtained by a certain doxastic practice, than the reliability of that practice? More generally, what better way to explain the fact that the employment of certain methods and/or a certain view of things consistently leads to predictive success than to suppose that that method and that view of things puts us into accurate cognitive contact with the realities that are responsible for the events predicted? And, as just noted, the argument is greatly strengthened by the fact that there is no other way in which we could achieve the same results. It is standard scientific procedure to reason in this way. If a particular account of the underlying structure of matter enables us to predict surface phenomena far better than any alternative account we have developed or can envisage, that is taken to be a decisive reason for taking this account to be correct. What better reason could we have, given that this underlying structure is not itself observable?

Recall that the proponents of earlier explanatory arguments were forced to try to show that the favored explanation was superior on grounds of simplicity or economy or detail, or some other "nonevidential" grounds. We saw reason to reject some of these claims of superiority; in other cases we saw no reason to suppose that the superiority in that respect carried with it a greater probability of truth. But here, it would appear, we can dispense with appeals to such criteria. The argument is quite straightforward: we can effectively anticipate our experience by taking it as revelatory of the external world in accordance with SP; therefore, SP is probably quite reliable. What could be more direct or convincing?

But despite these advantages all is not clear sailing. The most obvious defect of the argument is the restricted character of the explanandum. If we are to avoid epistemic circularity I cannot appeal to the success of other people in predicting their sense experience. For apart from reliance on SP I have no reason to think that there are other people, much less that they make use of SP and enjoy predictive success thereby. Hence the explanandum is restricted to *my* predictive success when using SP. And how can we base so enormous a conclusion on so slender a thread? So far as the argument goes, I might be the only person who enjoys such success from using SP; or I might be the only person to use it. Let's concentrate on the former. If that were the case, if all the other billions of human beings who have existed have failed to reap such results from the use of SP, we could hardly conclude that SP is reliable. It would not be an incredible run of luck for one out of billions to experience predictive success. Of course, I am not suggesting that this is actually the case. The point is that if I am to avoid epistemic circularity I can't assume either that it is or that it isn't. Behind my veil of ignorance I cannot suppose myself to know anything at all about the matter. Hence the argument is an exceedingly weak one, since it is in no position to rule out a possibility that, if realized, would render it impotent. So long as we have nothing but one case to go on, we are in no position to choose between *Sp is reliable* and *I am an exceptionally lucky case*.

It may be thought that this objection amounts simply to pointing out that no inductive argument is conclusive, that any such argument can be overturned by unexamined cases. Not so. This is not an an enumerative induction at all. It is an argument to the best explanation. And the point is that the narrow compass of the explanandum prevents us from showing that the suggested explanation is in fact the best one.

I feel that the above is sufficient for rejecting the claim that I can become justified in accepting the reliability of SP by noting that it best explains my success in predicting my sense experiences by using SP. Nevertheless, I will set the above objections aside for the nonce and consider how matters stand with respect to another component of the argument, the claim that the predictive success cannot be attained in any other way. We have seen that, so far as we can tell, we are incapable of taking a purely phenomenal route to effective prediction. But we have not yet explored alternative objective routes, via the demon or panpsychism. Why shouldn't we employ one of those alternatives in the following way. The demon, let's say, directly produces our sense experiences, together with inclinations to employ SP and other components of the physical world scheme, in such a way as to lead us to make accurate predictions of our sense experience. In other words, the demon sets everything up in just such a way as it would be set up if there really were a physical world with which we are in effective cognitive contact via SP. (And we can envisage an exact parallel for the panpsychist and self-generation hypotheses.) Why isn't this just as good an explanation of our predictive success as the standard hypothesis?

There is a good answer to that question. These "alternatives" are obviously riding piggyback on the standard theory. They haven't been developed independently; that would require, for example, developing a theory of demonic psychology on the basis of which we could predict what sense experiences we would have, given the current and past states of the demon's psyche. We don't have anything like that, nor do we have the analogues for the other alternatives: for example, a theory of the internal structure, operations, and interactions of Whiteheadian actual occasions that would enable us to predict future experiences on the basis of detailed descriptions of the external environment in those terms. Instead we just latch onto the way all this has been developed in detail for the standard theory, and lamely say that, for example, the demon produces experiences so that things will come out this way when we employ SP. This means, first of all, that these alternatives are less simple, for they contain, if fully spelled out, all the complexity of the standard account, plus something extra.[27] And, worse, the alternatives suffer from being ad hoc. There is no serious theoretical motivation or justification for tacking the demon or self-generation onto the detailed standard theory.

But not so fast. Granted that these alternative explanations, *as we are presently capable of developing them*, are markedly inferior to the standard explanation, why should we suppose that a consideration of what is possible for us in the way of explanation can tell us what reality is like? After all, the fact that we human beings cannot mount an effective prediction of our experience with, e.g., purely phenomenal means is at least as much a fact about us as about what the rest of the world is like. And the same is to be said for our inability to do the job independently in terms of a demon or a panpsychist scheme. Indeed, we have not even argued that it is *impossible* for us to carry through these jobs in a satisfactory way, and I don't see how such an argument would go. It is impossible to predict, or set limits on, theoretical developments; remember Comte's notorious example of an empirically undecidable question: the chemical composition of the stars! The fact that a given theoretical development has not been carried out is a weak argument for its impossibility. To be sure, the fact that the standard theory has been developed in detail and these putative rivals have not is itself a fact that requires explanation, but our cognitive successes and failures in dealing with reality are due to an interaction between us and the subject-matter. If either factor were sufficiently different, the outcome would be different as well. If the course of our experience were such as to present sufficiently simple lawlike phenomenal regularities we might never have so much as thought of the standard view and, even if we had, it would have had much less to recommend it. Even given the internal irregularity of our sense experience, the relevant facts might still not have been such as to permit the development of the relatively simple

[27]Recall that a similar charge against the demon theory was rebutted earlier, on the grounds that the demon need not be using the standard theory as a model. But that was before we built *our predictive success when using the standard theory* into our explanandum. But since we have done so, reference to the standard theory in the alternative explanations is unavoidable.

physical object scheme we actually have. And from our side, if our cognitive powers had been quite different the epistemic situation would have been correspondingly different. If we had intuitive powers of the sort ascribed to angels by Aquinas, we could have known about the physical world in a way unmediated by sense experience; and the issue with which we are dealing would not have arisen. Again, we might have been without our innate tendencies to form perceptual beliefs about an external physical world, in which case what is in fact the standard external world theory would perhaps never have occurred to us. I am engaging in this science-cum-theological fiction to sharpen the point that when we try to assess the ontological and epistemological significance of the fact that we do an impressive predictive job with the standard scheme, and can't or don't do so with any alternative, we are faced with the question of how much this is due to the subject matter and how much it is due to our cognitive powers. Suppose it were true that a cognitive subject with much greater computing capacity—one who could note, store, combine, reason, and otherwise work with much more complicated formulations—could do at least as good a job of predicting sense experience as we do, working purely with phenomenal patterns? Wouldn't that cast doubt on the claim that our inability to do the job with the purely phenomenal, but our ability to do it with the standard scheme, is a good reason for thinking that the standard scheme captures the determinants of our experience? Admittedly this would still be compatible with the truth of the standard scheme; but the current argument for that scheme would be greatly weakened, since our cognitive situation would be revealed as the result of limits on our powers, whether reality is as we ordinarily think it is or not. Contrariwise, if it is impossible for any subject, however complex, to do the job in phenomenal terms, that would strengthen the reasons for thinking that our success betokens the accuracy of the scheme employed. The same point holds for the other alternatives. If it is possible for some cognitive subject, perhaps even one such as we, to develop the demon hypothesis or panpsychism independently as a basis for successful prediction, then the fact that we have actually done so with the standard scheme, but not with these others, looks to be due to our proclivities, or accidents of our history, rather than to the constraints that stem from the nature of things. We should not rush into ontological or epistemological conclusions from our cognitive successes and failures without further consideration of how they are best accounted for.

Thus the crucial question is whether it is possible, for ourselves or for other cognitive subjects, to successfully predict sense experience on bases other than the standard theory. In considering this question let's declare out of bounds appeals to an essentially omniscient God, Who can predict anything infallibly on no basis whatever. Since the predictive success of such a being is equally compatible with any view about the subject matter, it is irrelevant to our present concerns. Confining ourselves to finite subjects of limited capacity, it would seem that we have little enough to go on. How can we tell what is possible, for some finite cognitive subject, by way of theoretical-cum-predictive achievements? As just pointed out, it is notoriously impossible to predict actual future theoretical developments; just as impossible, and for the same reasons, as it is to predict future artistic developments. The point in each case is that in order to predict those achievements, even in outline, I would have to have envisaged them myself and have had good reason to suppose that they could be carried out. Thus I would have done the most basic theoretical/artistic work already, and so, except for detailed implementation, I would have already carried out these developments, instead of predicting them. But then we are not in a good position to determine whether it is *possible* for us, much less for radically different cognitive subjects, to do an equally effective job of predicting sense experience without working through the standard physical world scheme. We can be assured that none of us is at present able to do so and that the motivation to develop such an ability is lacking. But to have a solid basis for attributing our predictive success to the fact that the scheme we work with is basically *correct*, we would need good reasons for thinking that no fundamentally different scheme would do as well. And we have no such reasons.

It may be felt that I am unfairly placing the burden of proof on my opponent. "Why", she might say, "do I have to show that it is impossible for any cognitive subject to predict sense experience on a different basis? Why isn't it up to you to show that this is possible, or at least to give reason to take the possibility seriously? Why do I have to assume the burden of eliminating every hare-brained scheme that anyone mentions?" Well, where the burden of proof lies depends on who it is that is making a claim. The claim under discussion here is that SP is reliable, and the argument for that claim is that our success in predicting sense experience on the basis of SP and associated practices is best explained by supposing SP and the associated practices to be reliable. That argument provides adequate support for the claim only if it is adjoined to an adequate argument that the success in question, and our failure to do the job in any other way, reflects the accuracy of the practices employed, and not just our cognitive limitations. So the reason it is incumbent on my opponent to show that a more powerful cognitive subject couldn't do as good a job on a quite different basis is that this is needed to shore up her argument for the claim under discussion.

Indeed, it is not just that we find ourselves unable to show that it couldn't be done otherwise; there are positive reasons for supposing it can, though these could hardly be deemed conclusive. When we think about the project of proceeding solely on the basis of phenomenal regularities, what appears to be the main bar to carrying this through? The regularities we can actually formulate are, as noted earlier, too "local", too much at the mercy of shifts in the external environment; they have no claim to be regarded as lawlike. When we consider how this might be overcome by further elaboration, including in the antecedents enough sensory evidence for the physical environment being just right for the production of the consequent, things soon become too complex for us to handle, we get dizzy, and we give up. But this gives rise to the suggestion that *a subject with sufficient cognitive capacity would not have to give up at this point, and could proceed to put in enough phenomenal detail to ensure that the phenomenal consequent is as specified.* At least, *so far as we can see*, this is a live possibility for a subject with sufficient computational capacity.

Moreover, even if no one could do it differently, there are considerations that can legitimately inhibit us from inferring that the subject matter must be in accordance with the way we have to think of it. There are many cases in which a certain scheme serves us well, predictively and explanatorily, but where there are reasons to think that the scheme does not accurately capture the intrinsic nature of the subject matter and that another scheme does so, or could if developed properly, even though we are unable to work out the latter approach in detail.[28] First, think of the much maligned "folk psychology". We, not only we humble laypersons but social scientists as well, work for the most part with our familiar scheme of perceptions, beliefs, desires, intentions, attitudes, emotions, and other intentional psychological phenomena, in seeking to explain and predict behavior. And it works reasonably well. It doesn't give us the degree and precision of prediction that we have in chemistry or physics, but it gives us much more than we get with any other approach. On the other hand, various philosophers and psychologists have given reasons for thinking that this familiar "folk psychological" scheme is radically defective in ways that debar it from serious consideration as a literal account of the way things are with us. I won't try to go into those reasons here, but they include such things as the ontological baggage involved, the assumptions we must make to determine the intentional psychological states of others, the limitations on the development of theories involving such concepts, and the requirements of materialism. Still less will I undertake to assess these reasons. Suffice it to say that some case has been made for the thesis that what we human beings are actually like is captured only in more hardheaded physiological concepts. I put this forward as an example of a not obviously false and not obviously ill-supported claim that the predictive success we enjoy with a scheme is not a sufficient support for its literal accuracy.

Again, consider the frequent recourse to idealization in science. Physicists and engineers work with notions of perfectly rigid rods, frictionless planes,

[28]I may as well acknowledge in advance that some of my examples will be philosophically controversial, but I am not using them to establish an actuality, only to illustrate the way in which we can have grounds for suspecting the literal truth of a scheme that serves us much better in prediction and explanation than any alternative available to us.

and the like, even though they realize there are no such things. By proceeding in this way we can spell out formulas that are simple enough to work with for prediction and design, formulas to which many actual situations are close approximations. Likewise, in many applications it is much more useful for predictive and applied purposes to use a simpler approximation to the truth, like Newtonian physics, rather than a more complex true (or closer to being true) theory like relativity theory. In all these cases there is widespread agreement that we use the scheme we do because of our cognitive limitations, that the reality we are dealing with is not that way, and that a more powerful intellect could do an equally effective predictive job, while representing things as they really are.

Thus the fact that we can effectively predict our sense experience by using SP is, at best, a weak reason for supposing SP to be reliable. Hence even the strongest nonepistemically circular argument for the reliability of sense perception falls considerably short of giving adequate support to that thesis.

xi. Establishing the Reliability of Mystical Perception

I have examined a large number of attempts to show in an noncircular fashion that sense perception is a reliable guide to the external environment. None has survived scrutiny. Unless and until someone comes up with a more successful alternative we will have to conclude that we are unable to give a noncircular demonstration, or even strong supporting argument, for the reliability of SP. That presents us with a pressing question as to what attitude it is reasonable to take toward SP, a question we shall be dealing with in Chapter 4. First I want to take a briefer look at the prospects for an effective noncircular support for the reliability of MP.

There is an important reason why it is not necessary for me to go into this question in the same detail. It was incumbent on me to examine samples of all the promising-looking arguments for the reliability of SP, because I was concerned to contest the common supposition that we have sufficient reason to trust SP, but not MP. By showing that any otherwise impressive argument for the reliability of SP suffers from epistemic circularity, I have rebutted this attack. *Any* doxastic practice that is not grossly internally inconsistent can be strongly supported if epistemic circularity is allowed. We just use the practice to determine the facts reported by the practice; since it will agree with itself, it will turn out that it is invariably correct. Hence if the reliability of SP can be (strongly) supported only with circularity, it cannot be claimed to be superior to any other practice, including MP, in this respect. But my grand design does not require that I show that MP cannot be noncircularly shown to be reliable. If it can, then so much the better for the program of supporting its credentials. It will be sufficient for my purposes just to *assume* that its reliability cannot receive strong non-circular support; if that assumption is false, so much the better for my position. That is, I will be defending the rationality of engaging in MP on the more unfavorable hypothesis that it cannot be noncircularly shown to be reliable. But rather than blindly assuming this, I will indicate that the assumption is not without plausibility.

The most obvious candidates for a noncircular support for the reliability of MP come from natural theology and revelation. We could use these sources to try to establish certain points about the existence and nature of God and His relations to us that lend credence to the claim that putative direct experience of God is a reliable source of information about Him. The trick comes in extracting enough from these sources for this purpose, without relying at all on mystical perception. As for natural theology, the cogency of various arguments for the existence and attributes of God has long been hotly disputed, but let's leave that aside and consider how useful they are in the present application. Note that appeal to arguments for the existence of God to establish the reliability of MP is quite on a par with an appeal to arguments for the existence of the "external world" to support the reliability of SP. This comparison also reveals a weakness of the appeal to natural theology to establish the reliability of MP, even if the arguments are perfectly in order. We noted earlier that even if we can prove the existence of the external world without circularity, that conclusion by no means implies that sense perception is a reliable guide to that world. Similarly, even if we can establish the existence and basic nature of God without reliance on MP, how do we get from that conclusion to the informational efficacy of MP? Natural theology operates at too high a level of abstraction to enable us to do this job. The standard arguments for the existence of God give us no reason to think that God is interested in displaying Himself to our experience. And even if He is, how can we make the further step to the very specific conclusion that God is (usually or often) displaying Himself to our experience on those occasions when people are strongly convinced that He is doing so? I don't see how we can get any such conclusion from the properties of aseity, omnipotence, omniscience, perfect goodness, and the like.

Revelation would seem to be a more promising place to look, for it purports to give us more specific information, to tell us about God's purposes, requirements, how He has acted in history for our salvation, and the destiny He has prepared for us. Depending on just how the story goes, it might be argued that God has Himself assured us that we can be directly aware of Him when we satisfy certain conditions ("Blessed are the pure in heart, for they shall see God"), or when He chooses to reveal Himself. But the appeal to revelation is threatened with epistemic circularity, for it can be argued that revelation, as a source of information about God, is just one kind of theistic perception. Confining ourselves here to revelation in the form of messages transmitted to us by God through human messengers, it seems clear that the human messenger must have perceived God as saying so-and-so to him in order to function as a conduit for the message.[29] Hence in appealing to revelation I am simply appealing to someone else's perception of God.

This brief discussion will have to suffice as a support for the thesis that MP cannot be shown noncircularly to be reliable. If this thesis is false, all the better for the claims of MP. I shall proceed to defend those claims on the worst-case scenario that no otherwise effective argument for its reliability escapes epistemic circularity.

[29]In Chapter 8 we shall explore other forms of revelation.

CHAPTER 4

A "Doxastic Practice" Approach to Epistemology

i. The Problem

At the end of the last chapter we were confronted with what looked to be a desperate situation. The course of the argument led us to the conclusion that with respect to even those sources of belief of which we are normally the most confident we have no sufficient noncircular reason for taking them to be reliable. Concentrating on sense perception, we examined the most impressive of the many attempts to show that the belief-forming practice we labeled 'SP' is reliable, and we found that all those that were not otherwise disqualified were vitiated by epistemic circularity.

How widely does this problem extend? What sources of belief are such that we can provide no otherwise impressive argument for their reliability without falling into epistemic circularity? I won't be able to go into this issue properly here, but it is a familiar story that our best attempts to establish the reliability of memory, introspection, deductive reasoning or inductive reasoning will make use of premises derived from the practice under consideration, and so fall into epistemic circularity. Thus it seems plausible to suppose that the most fundamental of our sources of belief are faced with the very problem we pointed out for sense perception in Chapter 3.

Furthermore, even if we were mistaken in Chapter 3, and SP or memory or introspection can be noncircularly shown to be reliable by reflection on concepts or by rational intuition, we would still not have escaped the necessity of dealing with the problem of what to do about doxastic practices we all engage in without being able to show that they are reliable. For what about the practice we employ to show that SP is reliable—rational intuition, let's say? Can we mount a noncircular proof of its reliability? If we can't, we have the same problem at a second remove. If we can, then if that proof depends on using SP we are involved in a very small circle. If we do not have to use SP here, let's consider the practice we do use. Can we give a noncircular proof of its reliability? If not, our original problem has been postponed to this point. And so on. We are faced with the familiar dilemma of continuing the regress or falling into circularity. Whatever the possibilities of a noncircular proof of reliability for one or another source, if we pursue the question far enough we will either (a) encounter one or more sources for which a noncircular proof cannot be given or (b) we will be caught up in circularity, or (c) we will be involved in an infinite regress. Since the number of basic sources is quite small for human beings, we can ignore (c), and for the same reason any circle involved will be a small one. Thus in practice we can say that, whatever the details of our epistemic situation, either there are some doxastic practices for which we cannot give a noncircular demonstration of reliability, or in giving such demonstrations we involve ourselves in a very small circle.

Epistemic circularity thus would appear to be inescapable. But surprisingly enough, as I argue in "Epistemic Circularity"[1], that does not prevent our using such arguments to *show* that sense perception is reliable or to *justify* that thesis. Nor, pari passu, does it prevent us from being justified in believing sense perception to be reliable by virtue of basing that belief on the premises of a simple track record argument. At least this will be the case if there are no "higher-level" requirements for being justified in believing that p, such as being justified in supposing the practice that yields the belief to be a reliable one, or being justified in supposing the ground on which the belief is based to be an adequate one. And, though I cannot defend the position here, I have not been thinking of justification as subject to any such requirements. According to the account laid out in Chapter 2, a belief is justified if and only if it is based on an adequate ground. That is, it is necessary only that the ground *be* adequate, not that the subject know or justifiably believe this, much less that the subject know or justifiably believe that all requirements for justification are satisfied.[2] But then I can be justified in accepting the outputs of a certain doxastic practice without being justified in believing that the practice is reliable. I need not already be justified in supposing SP to be reliable in order to be justified in various perceptual beliefs. SP must *be* reliable if I am to be justified in holding perceptual beliefs, but I don't have to be justified in supposing this to be the case. But then *if SP is reliable*, I can use various (justified) perceptual beliefs to show that SP is reliable, for I need not already be

[1]Alston 1989b.

[2]For a defense of this position see "An Internalist Externalism", in Alston 1989b and 1991a. A conclusive reason for avoiding such higher level requirements is that they imply that one is required to have an infinite hierarchy of justified beliefs. For if to be justified in the belief that p one has to be justified in believing that *the ground of the former belief is an adequate one* (call the italicized proposition, 'q'), then a parallel condition will be put on the belief that q; to be justified in holding it one must be justified in believing that *the ground of the belief that q is an adequate one*. And to be justified in that belief, one will have to have a still higher level justified belief that the ground of that belief is adequate. And so on ad infinitum. Since it seems clear that no human being can possess an infinite hierarchy of beliefs—justified or not—to impose any such requirement will imply that no human being justifiably believes anything, and our subject matter will have disappeared.

justified in holding the conclusion in order to be justified in holding the premises. The argument would still be *epistemically circular*, for I am still assuming *in practice* the reliability of SP in forming normal perceptual beliefs. Nevertheless, I don't have to be justified in making that assumption, in order to be justified in the perceptual beliefs that give me my premises. Hence the epistemic circularity does not prevent justification from being transmitted from the premises to a conclusion that would have been unjustified except for this argument. This applies even to a simple track record argument.[3]

If it is possible to establish the reliability of sense perception and other basic sources of belief by simple track-record arguments, why is the situation so desperate? The reason is this. What I pointed out in the previous paragraph is that *if sense perception is reliable*, a track-record argument will suffice to show that it is. Epistemic circularity does not in and of itself disqualify the argument. But even granting that point, the argument will not do its job unless we *are* justified in accepting its premises; and that is the case only if sense perception is in fact reliable. And this is to offer a stone instead of bread. We can say the same of any belief-forming practice whatever, no matter how disreputable. We can just as well say of crystal-ball gazing that if it *is* reliable, we can use a track record argument to show that it is reliable. But when we ask whether one or another source of belief is reliable, we are interested in *discriminating* those that can reasonably be trusted from those that cannot. Hence merely showing that *if* a given source is reliable it can be shown by its record to be reliable, does nothing to indicate that the source belongs with the sheep rather than with the goats. I have removed an allegedly crippling disability, but I have not given the argument a clean bill of health.

So the situation is fairly desperate after all. What options are there for the epistemologist? For one thing, she might weaken the concept of justification, disembowel it of its implications of likelihood of truth. In that case our inability to satisfactorily establish the reliability of SP would not prevent us from showing SP to be a source of justification.[4] But apart from attachment to my theory of epistemic justification, I do not choose to take this way out. The main reason is that, apart from the question of how to think about *justification*, the question of the reliability of whatever doxastic practice we are concerned with is itself a matter of the highest importance, since our chief concern, after all, in belief formation, and in cognition generally, is to get the truth.[5]

Second, one might "hang tough". That is, one might take the position that

[3]See "Epistemic Circularity" for more detail on this.

[4]It would still be a further question whether on one or another weaker concept of justification it is possible to show this.

[5]Near the end of this chapter I will suggest a way of formulating my position in terms of a conception of justification that does not entail likelihood of truth. But, as will appear, this by no means amounts to throwing in the towel at the outset.

in considering any question, including epistemological ones, a person is free to make use of anything one knows (or justifiably believes). And since we know a lot on the basis of SP, we can make use of that in determining what to say about any issue with which we are concerned, including the reliability of SP. This is to bite the bullet, embracing epistemic circularity. It is to take a purely *internal* approach to the situation, denying the need for any *external* support. We take our stand *within* SP and other familiar practices that have become firmly established, psychologically and socially, in our lives, and we feel free to use their output without non-epistemically circular validation thereof.[6] We take it as a rock-bottom conviction that these practices are reliable, a conviction that is not to be questioned.

I find this attitude quite attractive, and, as will appear, it has definite affinities with the position to which I finally come in this chapter. Nevertheless, I do not agree that nothing significant can be said about the epistemic status of SP and other basic doxastic practices without relying on their outputs. Shortly I shall seek to support those reservations by delineating an approach to the problem that stands between a purely internal reaction, and a supposition that the matter can be definitively resolved from a purely external standpoint.

One other reaction to our dilemma should be mentioned, namely one based on coherence theory. I have already given a brief indication of my reasons for setting coherence theory aside (Chapter 2, section ii). But it should be mentioned in this context that a coherence theorist will not be at all disturbed by the pervasiveness of epistemic circularity, since circularity (of the right sort) holds no terrors for him. The thesis that the components of a total belief system stand in relations of mutual support is fundamental to coherence theory. Hence if it turns out that the belief in the reliability of SP stands in a relation of mutual support with the products of SP, that is just a particular application of a principle that the theory warmly embraces.

ii. The Autonomy of Doxastic Practices

As just indicated, I am going beyond the purely internalist reaction to the menace of epistemic circularity by exploring what can be usefully and defensibly said, in general, about the epistemic status of our established ways of forming and evaluating beliefs. The basic point is this. Given that we will inevitably run into epistemic circularity at some point(s) in any attempt to provide direct arguments for the reliability of one or another doxastic practice, we should draw the conclusion that there is no appeal beyond the practices we find firmly established, psychologically and socially. We cannot look into any issue whatever without employing some way of forming and evaluating be-

[6]This reaction is typical of the "naturalized epistemology" found, in different forms, in such sources as Quine 1969 and Goldman 1986.

liefs; that applies as much to issues concerning the reliability of doxastic practices as to any issue. Hence what alternative is there to employing the practices we find ourselves using, to which we find ourselves firmly committed, and which we could abandon or replace only with extreme difficulty if at all? The classical skeptical alternative of withholding belief altogether is not a serious possibility. In the press of life we are continually forming beliefs about the physical environment, other people, how things are likely to turn out, and so on, whether we will or no. If we could adopt some basic way of forming beliefs about the physical environment other than SP, or some basic way of forming beliefs about the past other than memory, etc. (and it seems unlikely this is within our power), why should we? What possible rationale could there be for such a substitution? It is not as if we would be in a better position to provide a non-epistemically circular support for the reliability of these newcomers. The same factors that prevent us from establishing the reliability of SP, memory, and so on without epistemic circularity would operate with the same force in these other cases. Hence we are just not in a position to get beyond, or behind, our familiar practices and criticize them from that deeper or more objective position. Our human cognitive situation does not permit it.[7] Again, we cannot take a step in intellectual endeavors without engaging in some doxastic practice(s) or other, and what reasonable alternative is there to practicing the ones with which we are intimately familiar?

These considerations seem to me to indicate that it is eminently *reasonable* for us to form beliefs in the ways we standardly do. Lest it be supposed that this is too uncritical an endorsement of the status quo, let me say by way of anticipation that when the position is fully worked out there will be a specification of various grounds for criticism of existing practices, as a result of which they can be rationally modified or, in extreme cases, abandoned.

Perhaps we have concluded too hastily that we have no reasonable alternative to forming beliefs in all the ways that are firmly entrenched in our lives. Why shouldn't we take our stand on one or more of these, and hold the others subject to judgment on that basis? This is what has often happened in the history of philosophy. Descartes takes his stand on what is rationally evident on reflection and takes sense perception to be under suspicion until it vindicates itself to rational intuition. Hume takes his stand on the awareness of "impressions and ideas" and relations among them, and takes sense perception of the external world and inductive reasoning to be questionable pending a verdict of innocent before the bar of impressions and ideas. Nevertheless,

[7]Alvin Plantinga has suggested to me that this is not something distinctive of our human situation. Even God couldn't turn the trick. Even God couldn't *establish* the reliability of some belief-forming practice without using some doxastic practice to do so. And then the above regress argument would apply. However, granting that point, I, unlike Plantinga, think that God's situation in this regard is radically different from ours. Since, as I see it, God does not have *beliefs*, this whole problem could not come up for God. See my "Does God Have Beliefs?" in (1989a).

such theorists are vulnerable to a charge of "undue partiality". Here are two expositions of this point by Thomas Reid.

> The author of the "Treatise of Human Nature" appears to me to be but a half-skeptic. He hath not followed his principles so far as they lead him; but, after having, with unparalleled intrepidity and success, combated vulgar prejudices, when he had but one blow to strike, his courage fails him, he fairly lays down his arms, and yields himself a captive to the most common of all vulgar prejudices—I mean the belief of the existence of his own impressions and ideas.
>
> I beg, therefore, to have the honour of making an addition to the skeptical system, without which I conceive it cannot hang together. I affirm, that the belief of the existence of impressions and ideas, is as little supported by reason, as that of the existence of minds and bodies. No man ever did or could offer any reason for this belief. Descartes took it for granted, that he thought, and had sensations and ideas; so have all his followers done. Even the hero of skepticism hath yielded this point, I crave leave to say, weakly, and imprudently . . . what is there in impressions and ideas so formidable, that this all-conquering philosophy, after triumphing over every other existence, should pay homage to them? Besides, the concession is dangerous: for belief is of such a nature, that, if you leave any root, it will spread; and you may more easily put it up altogether, than say, Hitherto shalt thou go and no further: the existence of impressions and ideas I give up to thee; but see thou pretend to nothing more. A thorough and consistent skeptic will never, therefore, yield this point. To such a skeptic I have nothing to say; but of the semiskeptic, I should beg to know, why they believe the existence of their impressions and ideas. The true reason I take to be, because they cannot help it; and the same reason will lead them to believe many other things. (1970, V, 7, pp. 81–82)

> The skeptic asks me, Why do you believe the existence of the external object which you perceive? This belief, sir, is none of my manufacture; it came from the mint of Nature; it bears her image and superscription; and, if it is not right, the fault is not mine: I even took it upon trust, and without suspicion. Reason, says the skeptic is the only judge of truth, and you ought to throw off every opinion and every belief that is not grounded on reason. Why, sir, should I believe the faculty of reason more than that of perception?—they came both out of the same shop, and were made by the same artist; and if he puts one piece of false ware into my hands, what should hinder him from putting another. (1970, VI, 20, p. 207)

Reid's point is that the only (external) basis we have for trusting rational intuition and introspection is that they are firmly established doxastic practices, so firmly established that we "cannot help it"; and we have exactly the same basis for trusting sense perception, memory, nondeductive reasoning, and other sources of belief for which Descartes and Hume were demanding an external validation. They all "came out of the same shop", and therefore if one of them is suspect so are all the others.

A defender of Descartes' or Hume's procedure might well point to differences between say, introspection and rational intuition on the one hand, and sense perception and nondeductive reasoning on the other. It will be claimed that whereas the latter practices not infrequently lead to incompatible results, this does not, or even, it is sometimes claimed, *cannot* happen with the former. It has been a familiar thesis that we are infallible with respect to our current states of consciousness, or at least that nothing should show that one has made a mistake about such matters.[8] And similar claims have been made for rational intuition. Reid himself recognizes important differences (1969, II, 20, p. 296). However, I cannot see that such differences as exist warrant our accepting some of our firmly established doxastic practices without external support and not others. First, it is not at all clear that a judgment of infallibility or incorrigibility is justified for any of them. This has been a hotly debated topic with respect to introspection in recent decades[9], and powerful arguments have been levelled against the ascription to it of incorrigibility, much less infallibility. For example, it seems *possible* that neurophysiology should progress to the point that we should have public evidence of a neurophysiological sort that a person's sensations, feelings, or thoughts, are different from what he sincerely believes them to be. As for rational intuition, one would be hard pressed to find a contemporary defender of its infallibility or incorrigibility, and for good reason. It can hardly lay claim to complete consistency of output. To some philosophers it has seemed self-evident that every event is causally determined; to others it has seemed self-evident that humans have free choice in a sense in which that is incompatible with the causal determinism of such choices. To some it has seemed self-evident that temporally backward causation is impossible; to others it has seemed self-evident that it is possible. And so it goes. If the deliverances of rational intuition contradict each other it cannot be that they are all correct. Nor does it seem at all impossible, in some cases, to determine which party is correct. But if the strongest candidates for these "epistemic immunities" do not really enjoy them, then any epistemic superiority that some of our basic practices enjoy over others is just a matter of degree and hardly warrants our taking some for granted and requiring others to justify themselves by the output of the privileged few.

Moreover, even if certain practices never, so far as we can tell, issue mutually contradictory outputs, though others do suffer this disability from time to time, this will still not justify the Descartes-Hume procedure of taking the former, but not the latter, without external validation. For the fact remains that, however *internally* consistent the former may be, they still share with the

[8]See, e.g., Hume 1888, I, iv, 2; Lewis 1946, pp. 182–83; Ayer 1959, p. 59; Shoemaker, 1963, pp. 215–16. For other examples see my "Varieties of Privileged Access", in 1989a.

[9]For the negative position see, e.g., Armstrong 1968, chap. 6, sec. 10, and Aune 1967, chap. 11, sec. 1.

latter the crucial feature of being insusceptible of a noncircular proof of reliability; and it is the latter with which we are centrally concerned. We have already pointed out, in our brief comments on coherence theory (Chapter 2, section ii), that internal consistency, or even a stronger kind of internal coherence, is radically insufficient to guarantee that the constituents of a belief system are by and large true. Hence, where it is *reliability* that is in question, we lack sufficient excuse for treating different practices in a fundamentally different way.

Thus we will follow the lead of Thomas Reid in taking all our established doxastic practices to be acceptable as such, as innocent until proven guilty.[10] They all deserve to be regarded as prima facie rationally engaged in (or "acceptable", as we shall say), pending a consideration of possible reasons for disqualification, reasons we shall go into in due course. First, however, I want to give a more extended treatment of the nature of established doxastic practices than I have done thus far. Having done so, we can proceed to complete our account of their epistemic status.

iii. The Nature of Doxastic Practices

First a caveat. The term 'practice' will be misleading if it is taken to be restricted to voluntary activity, for I do not take belief formation to be voluntary.[11] I am using 'practice' in such a way that it stretches over psychological processes like perception, thought, fantasy, and belief formation, as well as voluntary action. A doxastic practice can be thought of as a system or constellation of dispositions or habits, or to use a currently fashionable term, "mechanisms", each of which yields a belief as output that is related in a certain way to an "input". SP, for example, is a constellation of habits of forming beliefs in certain ways on the basis of inputs that consist of sense experiences.

When I suggest that our epistemic situation may be illuminated by thinking of our beliefs as formed by various *practices*, the reader may be struck by the similarity to what Wittgenstein is up to in *On Certainty* (1969), though, as will become clear, I am far from a slavish follower. Wittgenstein is concerned with the epistemic status of propositions of the sort G. E. Moore highlighted in his "Defence of Common Sense" and "Proof of an External World"[12]—such propositions as *This is my hand, The earth has existed for many years*, and *There are people in this room*. The gist of Wittgenstein's position is that the acceptance of such propositions is partially constitutive of participation in

[10]This amounts to a kind of "negative coherentism" for socially established practices; they do not require positive support in order to be (prima facie) acceptable, but only the absence of sufficient reasons against them. I am not at all tempted by a negative coherentism with respect to beliefs. But the considerations of this chapter provide powerful support, I believe, for such a position for doxastic *practices*.

[11]See "The Deontological Conception of Epistemic Justification", in Alston 1989b.

[12]Both in Moore 1959.

one or another fundamental "language game".[13] To doubt or question such a proposition is to question the whole language game of which it is a keystone. There is no provision within that language game for raising such doubts. In fact, there is no provision within the language-game for justifying such beliefs, exhibiting evidence for them, or showing that we know such matters, as Moore tried to do. Hence we cannot even say that we know or are certain of such matters. They are too fundamental for that. By accepting these and other "anchors" of the game we are thereby enabled to question, doubt, establish, refute, or justify less fundamental propositions. Nor can we step outside the language game in which they figure as anchors and critically assess them from some other perspective. They have their meaning only within the game in which they play a foundational role; we cannot give sense to any dealings with them outside this context.

Thus, if we ask why we should suppose that some particular language game is a reliable source of belief, Wittgenstein would respond by denying the meaningfulness of the question. The concept of a trans- or inter-language game dimension of truth or falsity is ruled out on verificationist grounds. We can address issues of truth and falsity only within a language game, by employing its criteria and procedures to investigate issues that are within its scope. There is no room for raising and answering questions about the reliability of a language game as a whole. To be sure, language games are not sacrosanct or fixed in cement. It is conceivable that they should be abandoned and new ones arise in their place. But even if we should have some choice in the matter, something that Wittgenstein seems to deny, the issue would be a practical, not a theoretical one. It would be a choice as to what sort of activity to engage in, not a choice as to whether some proposition is true or false.[14] The foundation of the language game is action, not intuition, belief, or reasoning.

This, then, is Wittgenstein's reaction to the epistemological crisis generated by the results of Chapter 3. There is no perspective from which the question of the reliability of SP can be intelligibly raised. This is a sphere of activity in which we are deeply involved; "this language game is played".[15] Since we continue to be whole hearted participants, we would be guilty of duplicity in pretending to question, doubt, or justify the practice.[16]

[13]What Wittgenstein called a "language game" is something much more inclusive than the term would suggest. It involves modes of belief formation and assessment (the aspect we shall be concentrating on under the rubric "doxastic practice"), characteristic attitudes, feelings and modes of behavior toward certain sorts of things, as well as ways of talking. The Wittgensteinian term "form of life" is better suited to suggest the richness of the concept.

[14]There is a striking similarity here to Rudolf Carnap's distinction between questions that are internal to a conceptual framework and hence theoretical, and questions that are external to a conceptual framework and hence practical. See his 1950.

[15]Wittgenstein 1953, I, sec. 654.

[16]These denials of meaningfulness distinguish Wittgenstein's approach from the superficially similar "internalist" approach of "naturalized epistemology", referred to in fn. 6. Quine and

Now I do not accept for a moment Wittgenstein's verificationist restrictions on what assertions, questions, and doubts are intelligible. There is no time here for an attack on verificationism. I will simply testify that I can understand perfectly well the propositions that *sense perception is (is not) reliable*, that *physical objects do (do not) exist*, and that *the earth has (has not) been in existence for more than a year*, whether or not I or anyone else has any idea of how to determine whether one of these propositions is true. This confidence reflects a realistic concept of truth, on which a proposition's being true is not a matter of anyone's actual or possible epistemic position vis-à-vis the proposition. Hence I cannot accept Wittengenstein's solution to skepticism about perception, and his answer to the question of the reliability of basic doxastic practices, the solution that seeks to dissolve the problem by undercutting the supposition that it can be meaningfully posed.[17] With this realist orientation I am ineluctably faced with the question of whether a given practice is a reliable source of true beliefs, and hence with the question of whether it is rational or justified to suppose this. Moreover, since from this perspective it is not the case that each practice creates its own reality, but rather seeks to tell it like it is with respect to the one reality (or some segment thereof), there is a live possibility that the outputs of one practice contradict those of another. We will exploit this possibility in taking interpractice inconsistencies as a reason for disqualification.

If I differ this sharply from Wittgenstein on the status of doxastic practices, how can I look to him for inspiration? I shall explain by setting out the basic features of the view of doxastic practices I have arrived at, partly inspired by Wittgenstein and also by Thomas Reid. Some of these features are not stressed by Wittgenstein and some are only hinted at. But I believe that all of them are in the spirit of his approach.

A. A System of Belief-Forming Mechanisms

As I have already made explicit, I think of a doxastic practice as the exercise of a system or constellation of belief-forming habits or mechanisms, each realizing a function that yields beliefs with a certain kind of content from inputs of a certain type. Such functions differ in the width of the input and output types involved. The input type could be something as narrow as a certain determinate configuration of specific sensory qualia, and the output type something as narrow as a belief to the effect that the object in the center of the visual field is Susie Jones. Again on the narrow side, the input type might be a belief of the form 'X is an American citizen' and the output type a belief of the form 'X is not an Israeli citizen'. Or the function could be wider

---

Goldman by no means deny that it makes sense to ask whether SP, for example, is reliable, though, like Wittgenstein, they refuse to hold it subject to any external validation.

[17]See Chapter 3, sections iv–vii, for allied anti-Wittgensteinian arguments.

in scope. In thinking about perceptual belief formation we have been thinking of a very wide function that takes inputs of the type *an experience of the sort S would be inclined to take as a case of X's appearing* ϕ *to S*, and yields outputs of the correlated type *a belief of the form "X is* ϕ". Among inferential mechanisms we have functions corresponding to each form (invalid as well as valid, I am afraid) of inference. Thus we can have a modus ponens function that takes as input a belief of the form 'If p then q, and p', and yields an output of the correlated form 'q'. It is a difficult question in cognitive psychology as to just what belief forming mechanisms there are in the psyche and how wide or narrow they are. But for epistemic purposes we can think of individual mechanisms as quite narrow in scope. If one can reliably go from a certain specific pattern of sensory qualia to the attribution of a certain property to the current object of perceptual attention, then that attribution will be justified whether the most adequate psychology would ascribe that particular transition to a separate mechanism or construe it as a particular application of a more general mechanism. In any event, however we individuate belief-forming mechanisms, what we are calling "doxastic practices" will each involve large aggregations or families of mechanisms rather than a single mechanism. How are individual mechanisms properly grouped into such families? Since mechanisms are defined by their constituent functions, the most basic ground for such groupings will be similarities in constituent functions. These similarities may be more or less strong. The theory of appearing gives us a way of construing all direct perceptual belief formation (where there are no other beliefs in the input) as exhibiting a single function that goes from an experience as of X's appearing ϕ to X to the belief that X is ϕ. This even extends over direct M-belief formation, though, as we shall see later, there are other reasons for denying that MP belongs to the same practice as SP. Introspective practice can be equally tightly specified as made up of mechanisms that go from a current conscious state to the belief that one is in that state.[18] But the mechanisms constituent of a practice are not always that tightly unified. For deductive inference we can say that all input types are in terms of "formal" or "logical" features of beliefs rather than their "content". Thus, in describing the *modus ponens* mechanism, we specified input and output types in terms of forms of propositional logic. This bond that holds together the deductive inference practice is only as tight as the distinction between logical form and "content", or between logical and nonlogical terms; and there are difficulties about these distinctions. Nevertheless, it would be rash to deny that they are usable. Inductive inference is, notoriously, more difficult to handle. It is not even clear whether we should reckon all nondeductive inference as belonging to the same wide-ranging practice, and if not

[18]Memory practice can verbally be given a very tight unity. It consists in going from a "memory impression" that p to a belief that p. But persistent unclarity as to what counts as a memory impression clouds this picture somewhat.

it is unclear just what and how many the more restricted practices are. In summary, doxastic practices are bound together by some commonality in the functions that make up the constituent mechanisms, including the specification of input and output types.

B. Generational and Transformational Practices[19]

Generational practices produce beliefs from nondoxastic inputs; they can be the source of radically new information coming into the doxastic system. Transformational practices yield belief outputs from belief inputs. As we saw in Chapter 2, a given belief can stem from both doxastic and nondoxastic inputs. To simplify the discussion let's classify a mechanism that operates on both sorts of inputs as generational. That will enable us to continue to speak of two types of mechanisms.

One reason it is important to make the distinction is that generational, but not transformational, practices each typically involve a distinctive subject matter and a distinctive conceptual scheme. A (basic) generational practice gives us our access to a certain sphere of reality—SP to the physical and social environment, introspective practice to one's own states of consciousness, MP, so I claim, to God. Since each is fitted to form beliefs about a different mode of reality, it will utilize a conceptual scheme suited to that mode. That is not to say that there will be no overlap. The practices just mentioned share, to a greater or lesser degree, the basic "grammar" of subject and attribute, state and process, disposition and actualization.[20] But the matter that is poured into these forms will differ markedly from one practice to another. For example, the concepts of physical properties and spatiotemporal distribution that plays a major role in the framework of SP finds no place in the others.

Transformational practices, on the other hand, are designed to deal with beliefs about any subject matter, utilizing any conceptual frameworks. The forms of deductive and inductive inference will work, whatever the specific content of the beliefs that figure as premises and conclusions.[21] That is what makes inference so useful. Memory, which we might think of as a "preservative" rather than strictly a "transformational" practice, is not quite so neutral. Consider what we might call "event memory". If it is true that the only events I can remember are those I have experienced, then beliefs derived (in their

[19]This parallels the distinction between "belief-independent" and "belief-dependent" processes made in Goldman 1979, p. 13.

[20]There is extensive disagreement as to how to understand our thought and talk of God, but in my view there is considerably more overlap with other spheres of thought and talk than many contemporary philosophers and theologians are disposed to recognize. See my "Can We Speak Literally of God?" and "Divine and Human Action" (both in 1989a).

[21]In this brief summary I ignore the possibility that there are various subject matter specific forms of inference, e.g., one that goes from a premise of the form *X is a square* to a conclusion of the form *X is a plane figure*.

current incarnation) from event memory can utilize concepts from any of the experiential generational practices, which gives it a very wide, though perhaps not unrestricted, range. What we might call "propositional memory", on the other hand—remembering that something is the case, remembering what one has learned—is as neutral as inferential practices. What one has learned can deal with any subject matter and can utilize any of our concepts.

C. *The Evaluative Side*

Thus far we have been presenting doxastic practices in their purely factual guise, as utilizations of families of psychological mechanisms for belief formation. But there is an evaluative side to them too, as Wittgenstein emphasized. They also involve distinctive ways of assessing and correcting the beliefs so formed. When we acquire these practices, the evaluative system is as much a part of what we learn as the sheer habits of going from a type of input to a correlated type of output. In part these assessment procedures are just the reverse side of the coin we have already presented. What is, factually, a more or less fixed habit of going from inputs of type I to a belief output of correlated type B, is also, evaluatively, a principle of justification for beliefs so formed. The principle says that when a belief of type B is formed on the basis of an input of type I, that belief is thereby (prima facie) justified.[22]

So far we have added no new content to our description of practices but have only put an evaluative frosting on the descriptive substance of the cake. But there is more. With all or almost all our doxastic practices the justification accruing to a belief by virtue of its generation is prima facie only.[23] As noted earlier, beliefs can have this status only if the subject has the capacity for determining when the prima facie justified status is overridden, for determining whether the belief is true (whether there is a "rebutter") and whether in that situation the basis has its usual justificatory efficacy (whether there is an "underminer").[24] This requires a backlog of other justified beliefs and investigative procedures that can be called on to do these jobs. Put more concretely, to determine whether a given perceptual belief is true or whether there is anything in the situation to cast doubt on the justificatory efficacy of its basis, we have to know a fair amount about the sphere of reality the belief is about and we have to know how to get more knowledge as needed. If we are

[22]As Philip Quinn has pointed out to me, one could acquire bad habits of belief formation, e.g., paranoid tendencies, of which one disapproves and which one does not take to confer justification. Nevertheless, I believe that the statement in the text holds in the overwhelming majority of cases.

[23]The only possible exceptions to this "prima facie only" status for belief outputs would be practices that are infallible, which therefore leave no place for further checking. Philosophers have often regarded introspective practice and rational intuition as infallible, but the matter is controversial. In Chapter 2 we emphasized the point that perceptual justification is always only prima facie.

[24]See p. 72 for an explanation of these terms.

looking into the credentials of S's perceptual belief that there was a lion on his property, we have to know the likelihood of a lion's being there, know how to carry out further investigation, and know how to look into S's condition as an observer.[25]

Since these background systems of belief and knowledge and these background capacities are required for participation in the doxastic practice in question, it is natural to count them as a part of the practice. Let's say then that attached to each practice is an "overrider system" of beliefs and procedures that the subject can use in subjecting prima facie justified beliefs to further tests when that is called for.

A further word is needed as to when, in a practice with this two-level structure, a belief can be said to be justified unqualifiedly. Does this require it to have been examined in a second-stage process and passed the tests? No, that is not required in each instance, or generally. Further checking is needed only when there is some special reason to doubt the truth of the belief or the efficacy of its basis; normally that will happen only rarely. A belief is unqualifiedly justified (by the standards of the practice in question) provided it is prima facie justified (formed on the right kind of basis in accordance with the built-in principles of the practice), and there are no sufficient overriders (rebutters or underminers). It is not necessary for unqualified justification that the subject has *determined* that there are no sufficient overriders, only that there *are* none. That requirement is not perfectly precise. We can't restrict there being an overrider to its already being present in the subject's existing system of belief. We must also allow that an overrider exists provided it is something that the subject could ascertain fairly easily. How easily? That's where the vagueness enters. Nevertheless, this criterion is, I believe, sufficiently precise to be usable.[26]

D. *Mutual Involvement of Practices*

It would be a mistake to think of doxastic practices (individuated in terms of constituent mechanisms) as operating independently of each other. There are several reasons for this. Some were touched on briefly in section i of Chapter 3.

(1) Reasoning is beholden to other belief-forming practices for its premises.

[25]The *extent* to which one is master of all this can vary greatly from one subject to another. Considerable success in forming justified beliefs is compatible with only a rudimentary mastery of checking procedures.

[26]If this were a treatise in general epistemology we would have to go into overriding much more thoroughly. For one thing, can a prima facie justification be overridden by an unjustified rebutter or underminer, or must the overrider be a justified belief or a piece of knowledge? We must also take account of the fact that overriders may themselves be overridden by further components of the subject's doxastic system. I will not be able to pursue the matter further in this book.

We can, of course, reason from the output of previous reasoning, but somewhere back along the line we must have reasoned from beliefs otherwise obtained.[27] Ultimately, transformational practices are dependent on generational practices.

(2) Consider the overrider system for SP. It consists of knowledge (belief) about the physical environment that is relevant to the correctness of perceptual beliefs and to what it takes for such beliefs to be prima facie justified by sensory experience. It also includes ways of finding out more about these matters. How do we obtain the knowledge in question? Since that knowledge concerns the physical world, we must, of course, use SP. But it is not enough to form individual perceptual beliefs. They must be stored in memory and retrievable therefrom if they are to be of use. We must reason from them in various ways if we are to extend our knowledge beyond a mere collocation of individually perceived situations. Thus memory and various inferential practices are called on to assist in the development of the overrider system for SP. And the ways of finding out more about relevant matters will draw on these other practices as well as on SP. The general point here is that just because an overrider system is an essential part of a particular doxastic practice, no practice can function without a considerable dependence on other practices.

It is worthy of note that there could be an experiential doxastic practice without an overrider system. There could be a practice in which perceptual beliefs are formed without any provision for a second, "censor" stage that filters out some beliefs as incompatible with what we already firmly believe. Here prima facie and unqualified justification would not be distinguished. This would be a more primitive kind of perceptual practice than we actually have in mature human beings, but it is possible, and may well be actual in very young children and lower animals. Moreover, even our mature "introspective" practice of forming beliefs about our feelings, sensations, and thoughts is of this independent sort if, as may well be the case, beliefs about such matters do not normally face any test of compatibility with what we believe otherwise.[28]

(3) More generally, when we use the outputs of a given doxastic practice for cognitive or practical purposes, to extend our knowledge or to guide our activity, we typically use them in tandem with other practices. To make use of what we have learned from SP or introspection or rational intuition or reasoning, we have to have stored it in memory, retrieved it therefrom, and reason from it. Thus a given practice depends on others for its utility.

(4) There is another way in which SP, for example, is dependent on other

[27]This is a psychological rather than an epistemic regress argument. See Audi 1978.

[28]This is clearly not true of beliefs about many sorts of psychological states, e.g., emotions. As many recent writers have emphasized, to be in a certain emotional state, e.g., being indignant at Jones for having done A, requires having certain beliefs about Jones and attitudes toward him, and various things one knows may count for or against the supposition that such beliefs and attitudes are involved.

practices. Recall that SP is a practice of forming perceptual beliefs, sometimes on a purely experiential basis, but sometimes on a mixed basis that includes other beliefs of the subject. In the latter case SP will often be dependent, in part, on other practices for the beliefs in question just as much as reasoning practices are. In particular, where the doxastic portion of the basis of a perceptual belief includes generalizations, memory and reasoning will have been involved in the formation and justification of that general belief. In fact, we might think of the mediate component of perceptual belief formation as being itself a form of reasoning that is blended with the "registration" of sensory appearance to form the complex I have been calling "mediate perceptual belief formation".

(5) A given practice is generally beholden to the outputs of other practices, as well perhaps as to its own outputs, for the conceptual scheme it employs. Sticking with SP, let's consider the concepts we use to identify perceived objects. I can recognize my wife just by the way she looks. But the conception of her I employ when I realize that what I see is my wife draws from other things I know or believe about her—for example, features of her personality and her characteristic patterns of activity. And, again, those beliefs depend on memory and reasoning, as well as on perception, for their formation and their justification. Thus even where the basis of a particular perceptual belief—for example, that my wife is awake—is purely experiential, other beliefs may be found in the background of the conceptions employed.

(6) Another mode of dependence has to do not with the functioning of a practice but with its assessment. If we attempt to determine whether SP is reliable or how reliable it is, or if we abandon that enterprise and simply scrutinize the practice with an eye to deciding whether it is rationally engaged in, we will, of course, have to make use of information stored in memory and, as with any intellectual activity, we will have to reason. Even if we can't carry out an assessment of SP without relying on SP itself for relevant information, we can't depend on that alone. A particular practice depends on others for its validation as well as for its functioning.

These modes of interdependence may lead one to reconsider the distinctions between practices with which we have been working. If SP is that intimately entangled with memory and reasoning, perhaps we should reconsider treating it as a distinct practice. Perhaps we should think rather of a general empirical doxastic practice with SP, memory, introspection, and various kinds of reasoning as components. But there are reasons for not taking this course. It is still true that the distinctions I have made represent ways of forming beliefs that are different in fundamental respects. There are important differences between input types and between input-output functions. These differences have to be recognized somehow or other, and I have chosen, I believe, the most natural way of doing so. So long as we are alive to the various modes of interdependence, we can enjoy the advantages of distinguishing doxastic practices without suffering the disadvantages.

E. Irreducible Plurality of Practices

One of Wittgenstein's emphases, stressed at least as much by Reid, and one that I am very much continuing in my approach, is the irreducible plurality of doxastic practices. The fact that doxastic practices differ in the ways we have been laying out has important implications for epistemology as well as for cognitive psychology. Each practice, as we have seen, carries its own distinctive modes of justification, its own distinctive principles that lay down sufficient conditions for justification, not only prima facie justification but also, through its overrider system, unqualified justification as well. These conditions differ markedly from one practice to another. A belief's being based on a sensory appearance is quite different from its being based on a set of premises. In one way this is boringly uncontroversial; most epistemologists will accept the letter of what I have just said. The thrust of the position is in the "irreducible" qualification. Epistemologists have traditionally sought to reduce different modes of justification (evidence, knowledge . . .) to as few basic types as possible. This has often led to a drastic narrowing of the scope of knowledge and/or justification, as with Descartes's "clear and distinct perception" and Locke's "perception of the agreement or disagreement of ideas".[29] A currently popular mode of unification has to do with explanation; at bottom, it is said, whenever we are justified in any belief it is because the truth of that belief would be the best explanation of what is taken as the ground of the belief.[30] We saw a manifestation of this in Chapter 3, when we noted the popularity of the idea that SP can be shown to be reliable by showing that in most cases the truth of the perceptual belief in question is the best explanation of the sensory data on which it is based. This explanatory approach is a good example of the way in which philosophers seek to combine a unified account of epistemic justification with a recognition of the diversity of grounds of belief. An attempt is made to show that whatever the nature of the proximate ground of the belief, its justificatory efficacy is always due to an application of a single principle. Thus the contemporary view just alluded to is that whether the basis of the belief is sense experience, introspection, memory, or inference, that basis is justifying only because the truth of the belief is the best explanation for its ground.

Following Reid and Wittgenstein, I mean the thesis of the irreducible plurality of doxastic practices to run counter to this claim of an underlying unity. I do not deny that the aim at unification and systematization is a laudable one. The only question concerns when or to what extent it is possible. The discussion of Chapter 3 showed, I believe, that we cannot rest SP on some deeper mode of justification that is common to most or all other practices. I am

[29]Philosophers who take a hard line on knowledge are often saved from the worst consequences thereof by a felicitous abstention from practicing what they preach. This is especially true of Locke and, to a lesser extent, of Descartes.

[30]See, e.g., Alan Goldman 1988 and Moser 1989.

convinced that a similar argument could be carried through for other basic doxastic practices. Ultimate diversity is a fact of our epistemic life, however humbling this may be for our pride as theoreticians.

F. Pre-Reflective Genesis

A point emphasized by Wittgenstein is that doxastic practices are acquired and engaged in well before one is explicitly aware of them, and subjects them to criticism. When one arrives at the age of reflection one finds oneself ineluctably involved in their exercise. Here especially the owl of Minerva flies only at the gathering of the dusk. Practice precedes theory; the latter would be impossible without the former. This is a recurrent theme in *On Certainty*. If we hadn't learned to engage in inference, more or less critically, we could never develop a system of logic; we would have nothing either to reflect on or to reflect with. If we had not learned to form and evaluate perceptual beliefs, we would have no resources for formulating the philosophical problems of the existence of the external world and of the epistemic status of perceptual beliefs.

G. Involvement in Wider Spheres of Practice

We learn to form perceptual beliefs along with, and as a part of, learning to deal with perceived objects in the pursuit of our ends. Our practice of forming beliefs about other persons is intimately connected with interpersonal behavior. And, as we shall see in the next chapter, the practice of forming perceptual beliefs about God is thoroughly interwoven with orienting oneself to God in attitude, feeling, and action.

H. Socially Established

Doxastic practices are thoroughly social: socially established by socially monitored learning, and socially shared. We learn to form perceptual beliefs about the environment in terms of the conceptual scheme we acquire from our society. This is not to deny that innate mechanisms and tendencies play a role here. We still have much to learn about the relative contributions of innate structures and social learning in the development of doxastic practices. Of my predecessors in this approach, Reid places more stress on the former, Wittgenstein on the latter. But whatever the details, both have a role to play; and the final outcome is socially organized, reinforced, monitored, and shared.

I. Subject to Change

We should not suppose that doxastic practices are immutable. They can and do change. For example, the overrider system of SP has changed as we have learned more about sense perception. Change is obvious in religious doxastic practices. The background belief system of Christianity, for example, has undergone marked development, especially in its early centuries, and that has repercussions for its M-belief forming practice, both for its overrider system and for its identification of the object of theistic experience.

J. Distinctive Presuppositions

An idea that bulks large in *On Certainty* is that each practice possesses its own distinctive set of foundational presuppositions. I feel that Wittgenstein is much too generous in according this status to beliefs. It seems clear to me that *This is my hand* and *The earth has existed for more than a year* are propositions for the truth of which I have a great deal of empirical evidence within SP (or rather within some combination of that with memory and reasoning), rather than a basic presupposition of the practice. However, I do recognize this latter category. The existence of physical objects and the general reliability of sense perception are basic presuppositions of SP; we couldn't engage in it without at least tacitly accepting those propositions. Similarly the reality of the past and the reliability of memory are basic presuppositions of the practice of forming memory beliefs.

At the beginning of this section I said that my doxastic-practice approach to epistemology is inspired by Reid and Wittgenstein. So far, little has been said about the former. But only the name has been absent. The conception of doxastic practices just outlined is, in its essentials, the view of Reid, even though the terminology is different.[31] Where I speak of various doxastic practices, Reid speaks of various kinds of "evidence", "the evidence of sense, the evidence of memory, the evidence of consciousness, the evidence of testimony, the evidence of axioms, the evidence of reasoning".[32] "We give the name of evidence to whatever is a ground of belief."[33] Alternatively he speaks of "general principles of the human constitution" by which we form beliefs of certain sorts under certain conditions.[34] Reid stresses the plurality of these principles or sorts of evidence, and the impossibility of reducing them to a single supreme principle. ". . . I am not able to find any common nature to which they may all be reduced. They seem to me to agree only in this, that they are all fitted by nature to produce belief in the human mind . . .".[35] Again, Reid often stresses the point that we utilize these principles in practice long before we are explicitly aware of them as such. As mentioned above, he stresses the contribution of innate structure, where Wittgenstein stresses social learning—but in both cases there is emphasis on the point that we have them

[31]For a discussion of Reid that stresses this point, see Wolterstorff 1983.
[32]Reid 1969, Essay II, chap. 20, p. 291.
[33]Ibid.
[34]Reid 1970, VI, 24, p. 237.
[35]*Essays*, II, 20, pp. 291–92.

and use them before we reflect on them. Reid, much more than Wittgenstein, goes into the way in which belief forming dispositions, once established, can be modified by experience.[36] On the other hand, Reid does not stress the way in which cognitive practices are set in the context of practices of overt dealings with the environment. Reid's perspective is that of a purely cognitive, mentalistic psychology. Finally, one reason my account is closer to Reid's is that Reid had the advantage of philosophizing before the advent of verificationist and other antirealist philosophies. Reid never suggests that there is anything unintelligible about the idea that, for example, sense perception is or is not reliable, or that we cannot meaningfully raise the question of whether this is so, however difficult it may be to find a way to answer the question. This leaves Reid and me free to look for ways of evaluating basic doxastic practices.[37]

iv. The Individuation of Doxastic Practices

Since a doxastic practice is essentially the exercise of a family of belief-forming mechanisms, the unity of a doxastic practice is most centrally a function of important similarities in the constituent mechanisms. And since a belief-forming mechanism is simply the realization of an input-output function, the unity of a doxastic practice most basically consists in important similarities in input, in output, and in the function connecting the two.

There is no one uniquely right way to group mechanisms into practices. A doxastic practice has only "conceptual" reality. It proves convenient for one or another theoretical purpose to group particular mechanisms into larger aggregations, but a "practice" is not something with an objective reality that constrains us to do the grouping in a certain way. One way of cutting the pie will be best for some purposes and other ways for other purposes. I am assuming that any plausible mode of individuation will group mechanisms into a single practice only if there are marked similarities in inputs and functions, but that still leaves us considerable latitude. Thus we could think of each sensory modality as determining a separate doxastic practice, so that there is a

[36] 1970, VI, 24.

[37] As should be clear from the above, my theory of doxastic practices differs radically from the various nonrealist, verificationist, and relativistic versions of Sprachspielism now current, represented by writers like D. Z. Phillips and Richard Rorty, and by such rumblings as deconstructionism that emanate from Europe. I am far from supposing, with many of these writers, that each "language game", "conceptual scheme", "discourse", or what have you, carries its own special concept of truth and reality, that each defines a distinct "world", or that truth is to be construed as "what one's linguistic peers will let one get away with" (Rorty). My theory of doxastic practices is firmly realistic, recognizing a single reality that is what it is, regardless of how we think or talk about it. The doxastic practice is a source of criteria of justification and rationality; it does not determine truth or reality. In other words, for me doxastic practices are crucial epistemologically, not metaphysically.

visual perceptual-belief practice, an olfactory perceptual-belief practice, and so on. Or we could cut the pie still finer and distinguish within visual perceptual beliefs between color attributions, shape attributions, position attributions, and so on, counting each of these as stemming from a different practice. Or we could do as we have been doing and lump all sense-perceptual belief formation into the same practice. The wider the practice, the less overall similarity between sensory inputs. There is no overlap in phenomenal qualia between one sensory modality and another; such intrinsic similarity as there is in input will be more abstract, residing in the "directly experiential" or "presentational" character of all sensory experience, the fact that it all involves something's being "given" to the subject as bearing certain qualities. Again, an important part of what is responsible for our having a general category of *sense perception* is the fact that all sensory experience is due to the stimulation of sense receptors and that the character of the experience closely reflects features of that stimulation. This is not an intrinsic similarity of inputs, but it is an important similarity, and we are not debarred from taking it into account. As for the choice between a single visual-belief practice and separate practices for color attributions, object identifications, and so on, these distinctions can be made partly on differences in sensory input, but they mostly hang on differences in the content of belief outputs.

As for functions, we have already pointed out that function type can be construed more or less generically. A visual color-attribution function can be formulated very specifically in terms of the features of sensory experience that give rise to the attribution of a particular color, or we could think more generally of a function that leads from any of a number of distinguishable sensory input aspects to a correlated color attribution. At the other end of the spectrum, we can think with maximum generality of a perceptual belief function that goes from *an experience of X's appearing as* ϕ to a belief that X is ϕ. That function type ranges over both sense perception and mystical perception, and any other variety there be.

The last two paragraphs may have given the impression that it is completely arbitrary how we individuate doxastic practices. But thus far we have only considered input-output functions; other constituents have to be taken into account as well, as we shall see in the next paragraph. And there is also the point, mentioned in passing above, that there may be theoretical reasons for doing it one way rather than another, even if we are confining our attention to the input-output relations. From an epistemic point of view, we want to work with practices that are as homogeneous as possible with respect to reliability, given the other constraints on individuation. For we want practices to be subject to epistemic evaluation in terms of reliability; and unless the constituent mechanisms of a practice are close in degree of reliability, the practice as a whole cannot be judged markedly reliable or unreliable. The qualification, "given the other constraints on individuation" is important. If epistemic homogeneity were the only consideration, we would try to individuate practices in such a way that every one turns out to be either very reliable or very unreliable. But that is not the best way to proceed, just because various psychological facts—function similarity, similarity in causal genesis, similarity in psychological function, similarity in physiological underpinnings—constitute strong reasons for grouping certain mechanisms together. Quite apart from considerations of reliability, we will want to distinguish between perceptual, memory, introspective, and inferential practices, just because they involve such different psychological states and processes. However, epistemic homogeneity can come into the decision as to how finely to carve up each of these domains. Comparisons of the reliability of perceptual belief formation from different sensory modalities can properly influence the decision on whether to work with a single perceptual-belief-forming practice, and the same is true of comparisons between the reliability of various nondeductive modes of inference.[38]

Still another influence on individuation comes from a second feature of doxastic practices, the overrider system. Before going into this let me bring out the hitherto suppressed point that it is only generational practices that have distinctive overrider systems. Since they each deal with a distinctive subject matter, the overrider system is made up of relevant facts about that subject matter, together with ways of finding out more when needed. The overrider system for SP concerns the perceivable physical and social environment, the system for introspection concerns conscious psychological states, and the system for MP concerns God and His relations to His creation—whereas transformational practices like inference and preservative practices like memory can produce beliefs about anything whatsoever. Therefore, their overrider systems are unlimited; in principle, they range over anything we can know and any ways we have of finding out about things. Hence, practices of the latter kinds cannot be distinguished from other practices by their overrider systems, while generational practices can. This is an important point for this book, since this is one of the chief bases for distinguishing between SP and MP. As we have seen, we can give a formulation of an input-output function that applies to both. No doubt, they have qualitatively different experiential inputs; but that is equally true of different sensory modalities. The experiential input for MP does not, so far as we know, stem from the stimulation of physical sense receptors, but since we understand so little about the input of MP, that is a rather shaky basis for differentiation. The most important basis for treating SP and MP as distinct practices is that our beliefs about the physical world and about God constitute systems each of which is complexly inter-

[38]Still, when all is said and done, someone may legitimately want to know about the reliability of some grouping of mechanisms that in fact exhibits an intermediate range of reliability. We cannot proscribe such interest. I have been talking as if internal variation is always due to differences in the reliability of constituent mechanisms, but such is not the case. It could also be due to the fact that all or most of the constituent mechanisms themselves are neither very reliable or very unreliable.

related but only tenuously related to the other. The two systems of belief, in addition to differences in subject matter and conceptual scheme, have different sources, different criteria of assessment, and different ways of hanging together. In Chapter 5 we will see that differences in overrider systems not only lead us to distinguish MP from SP but also force us to distinguish different MP practices.

v. Practical Rationality

Let's return to the thesis of the epistemic autonomy of established doxastic practices. I said in section ii that it is rational for us to engage in such practices. Indeed, I claimed that there is no rational alternative to this. It is a kind of practical rationality that is in question here. In reflecting on our situation—what considerations are available to us, what we can and can't know, can and can't prove, what alternatives are open to us—we come to realize that we are proceeding rationally in forming and evaluating beliefs in ways that are established in our society and that are firmly embedded in our psyches. Or rather it is *prima facie* rational for us to proceed in this way, with this initial presumption subject to being overridden or strengthened in ways I will be exploring shortly. I call this rationality "practical" to differentiate it from the rationality we would show to attach to a belief if solid grounds for its truth were adduced, or to attach to a doxastic practice if sufficient reasons were given for regarding it as reliable. I have foresworn the attempt to carry out anything like that for our familiar doxastic practices. I only claim that we cannot be faulted on grounds of rationality for forming and evaluating beliefs in the ways we normally do (absent any sufficient overriding considerations), since there are no alternatives that commend themselves to rational reflection as superior.

One objection to thinking of this as *practical* rationality is that it is not clear, in many cases, that it is possible for us to adopt any other course. It is dubious that we have any real choice as to whether to form perceptual, memory, introspective, and simple inferential beliefs in ways we ordinarily do. If I seem to see a chair across the room, do I have any choice as to whether to form the belief that there is such a chair across the room? To be sure, even if I lack the capacity to inhibit perceptual belief formation on the spot, I might be able to modify perceptual and other belief tendencies in the long run by a systematic program of education or conditioning. But that doesn't appear to be feasible either, at least as far as large scale modifications are concerned. However, the point of raising the question of rationality, as I have been understanding it, does not depend on the real possibility of alternative courses of action. It is sufficient to consider alternative modes of belief formation, whether we are capable of realizing them or not, and ask whether it would be rational for us to stick with what we have, *if we had a choice*. And, so I claim, the considerations I have been adducing support an affirmative answer to that question.

Note how some of the features of doxastic practices enumerated in section iii contribute to this practical-rationality argument. First consider the rootedness of these practices in our lives. Our basic doxastic practices are firmly entrenched long before the age of reflection (F). Thus they are a much more ineluctable part of our lives than are habits, dispositions, and practices that are acquired by deliberate effort later in life. Even if it were possible to abandon or alter them, it would be a very arduous task. Hence, in the absence of extremely good reason to do so, the effort would be ill advised.

The point that doxastic practices are intertwined with wider spheres of practice (G) also contributes to their rootedness. Just because SP is part and parcel of our ways of interacting with the physical and social environments, it could not be abandoned or changed without a corresponding shift in the ways we respond to things and people about us. If we didn't acquire the information we get from SP, we wouldn't relate ourselves to the environment or engage in intercourse with other people as we do. This greatly magnifies the changes in our lives that would be entailed by abandoning SP, and it correspondingly ups the requirements for a justification of such changes.

How widely should we consider this defense to apply? We have been speaking in terms of "socially established" practices, more specifically those that the individual acquires early in life and that are intimately intertwined with other spheres of practice. Should we extend our defense to all such practices or should we restrict it to those practices that are common to all normal, adult human beings? This question is crucial for the main concern of this book, for MP, though rooted in lives in the ways we have been considering, is by no means engaged in by all normal, adult humans. I will have a bit more to say about the bearing of universality in Chapter 5. Here let me just say this. Why suppose that the outputs of a practice are unworthy of acceptance because it is engaged in by only a part of the population? Why this predilection for egalitarianism in the epistemic sphere, where its credentials are much less impressive than in the political sphere? Why suppose it to be an a priori truth that truth is less likely to be available to a part of the population than to the whole? We are familiar with many areas in which only a small percentage of the population has developed the perceptual sensitivity to certain features of the world,—for example, the distinctive qualities of wines and the inner voices of a complex orchestral performance. I can see no good reason for excluding deeply rooted epistemic practices that are engaged in by only a part of the population. (Here we depart from Reid, who restricted himself to universal practices.) Provided that MP is firmly rooted in its devotees from early in life, interconnected with other practices in a form of life, and socially established, there will be the same argument against abandoning it as there is for more widely distributed practices.

My judgment may also be assailed as not permissive enough. "Why not take *all* practices to be prima facie acceptable, not just socially established ones? Why this prejudice against the idiosyncratic? If Cedric has developed a practice of consulting sun-dried tomatoes to determine the future of the stock market, why not take that as rational too unless we have something against it?" Now I think that we will almost always have something decisive against idiosyncratic doxastic practices; and in that case it would do no harm to let all of them in as prima facie acceptable. Nevertheless there is a significant reason for doing it my way. When a doxastic practice has persisted over a number of generations, it has earned a right to be considered seriously in a way that Cedric's consultation of sun-dried tomatoes has not. It is a reasonable supposition that a practice would not have persisted over large segments of the population unless it was putting people into effective touch with some aspect(s) of reality and proving itself as such by its fruits. But there are no such grounds for presumption in the case of idiosyncratic practices. Hence we will proceed more reasonably, as well as more efficiently,[39] by giving initial, ungrounded credence to only the socially established practices. Newcomers will have to prove themselves.

vi. Overriders of Prima Facie Rationality

What can knock out the prima facie rationality enjoyed by established doxastic practices? The simplest and least controversial candidate is internal consistency. If two perceptual beliefs contradict each other, at least one is false. The existence of even one such pair is sufficient to show that SP is not perfectly reliable. A large number of such pairs, relative to the total output, would show that SP is not sufficiently reliable to be a source of justification for the beliefs it generates and hence that it is not rational to engage in it, or would not be rational if we had a choice in the matter. There is no doubt but that SP and other basic practices do generate mutually contradictory beliefs. Witnesses to crimes and automobile accidents often disagree as to what happened, and there are undoubtedly many other cases of disagreement that go unnoticed because they are of no practical importance. It is notorious that people's memories often conflict. And it is equally notorious that investigators not infrequently draw contradictory conclusions from the same data concerning such matters as the health hazards of a given pesticide. As noted above, it has often been claimed that introspection and rational intuition are in principle immune from any discrepancies in their output, but the claim has as often been disputed.

Nevertheless, I doubt that any of our most basic doxastic practices yield enough mutually contradictory pairs to be disqualified as a rational way of forming beliefs. It is only on a fantastically rigoristic epistemology that one would be deemed irrational in holding perceptual beliefs just on the grounds that those beliefs were formed by a sort of mechanism that sometimes yields

[39]As for efficiency, contrast the procedure of accepting all applicants to a graduate program and then flunking out the unqualified ones, with the procedure of carefully screening the applicants and accepting only those whose records ground a prima facie presumption of success.

mutually contradictory beliefs. To be sure, what I am condemning as fantastic has often been held in the history of philosophy. Plato and Descartes, to name only two of the most prominent, have refused to allow that sense perception can be a source of knowledge on just that ground.[40] Nevertheless, along with most contemporary epistemologists, I take it to be the better part of wisdom to allow that sources of belief can be rationally tapped and can be sources of epistemic justification even if they sometimes yield mutually contradictory pairs of beliefs, provided this is a small proportion of their output. However, the present point is that sufficiently extensive and persistent internal contradictions in the output of a practice would give us a conclusive case for regarding it as unreliable.

Second, and for similar reasons, a massive and persistent inconsistency between the outputs of two practices is a good reason for regarding at least one of them as unreliable. It has been alleged that the whole of the output of SP comes into conflict with what has been established by rational intuition and deductive reasoning. Parmenides and Zeno took it that since SP represents things as multiple and as moving it conflicts with what reason assures us about the nature of reality. F. H. Bradley argued that since SP represents its objects as interrelated spatiotemporally, none of its products are strictly true, since we can prove that any alleged relational complex is shot through with contradictions. I mention these historically famous cases not to endorse them but to illustrate claims to a massive interpractice inconsistency. Even if there are such inconsistencies, that does not tell us which is to be condemned. Rationalistic philosophers like those cited take it that SP is the loser, but that should not be taken for granted. To argue that it is self-evident that rational intuition should be trusted rather than SP when they conflict is obviously epistemically circular, and we certainly can't suppose that SP will support the choice of its rival. But where there is such conflict at least one of the contestants is unreliable.

What can we do to choose between the disputants in such a case? The only principle that suggests itself to me as both non-question-begging and eminently plausible is the conservative principle that one should give preference to the more firmly established practice. What does being more firmly established amount to? I don't have a precise definition, but it involves such components as (a) being more widely accepted, (b) having a more definite structure, (c) being more important in our lives, (d) having more of an innate basis, (e) being more difficult to abstain from, and (f) its principles seeming more obviously true. But might it not be the case in a particular conflict that the less firmly established practice is the more reliable? Of course that is conceivable. Nevertheless, in the absence of anything else to go on, it seems

[40]Neither of these people used anything very like our contemporary concept of *justification*. Perhaps if they had they would not have denied justification to perceptual beliefs; it is hard to say.

the part of wisdom to go with the more firmly established. It would be absurd to make the opposite choice; that would saddle us with all sorts of bizarre beliefs.[41]

What about interpractice conflicts that are less sweeping than those alleged by the likes of Parmenides and Bradley? Well, just as a modicum of intrapractice inconsistency is compatible with a degree of reliability sufficient for justification, so it is with interpractice contradiction. We do find quite a bit of this. Memories are not infrequently at variance with perceptible traces left by past events. "I would have sworn that I turned off the coffee pot, but I can't doubt the evidence of my senses that it is still on." Predictions arrived at inferentially are fairly often disconfirmed by direct perception; otherwise science would be much easier. But so long as these conflicts are no more frequent than is actually the case we can live with them. They do not entail such a degree of unreliability as to inhibit the justificatory force of both practices. Thus I would judge that none of the familiar practices we have been discussing are discredited by conflict with other practices.

However, doxastic practices have fallen by the wayside in the course of history and prehistory through being undermined by conflict with more firmly established rivals. This is what has happened with a great variety of magical practices and practices of divination. Predicting the future by scrutinizing the stars, tea leaves, or the entrails of sacred beasts, one forms beliefs that frequently come into conflict with what can be observed. The priest consults the entrails and predicts that enemy forces will appear before the city on the morrow, but the morrow comes and, as everyone can see, no enemy is there.[42] Predicting the future, especially apocalyptic events, on the basis of supposed communications from God, have also fell into discredit with the vast majority of the population, and again frequent empirical disconfirmation has played a key role. In this latter case it seems best to take such predictions to constitute a peripheral feature of a more general, religious-belief-forming practice, rather than a separate practice on its own. Hence the abandonment of this kind of prediction in large segments of religious communities should be thought of as a purification of a doxastic practice rather than as abandonment.

The same diagnosis (purification rather than abandonment) is to be given of the way in which religious beliefs have progressively given way to scientific beliefs in the last few centuries. When *some* religious beliefs contradict *some*

[41]To be sure, there is no advance guarantee that when two practices are in total or massive conflict with each other, one will be more firmly established than the other. But that is just an example of the general point that the human condition provides no guarantee that we will not be faced with questions we have no way to settle.

[42]In saying that such practices have fallen by the wayside, I am not claiming that no one engages in them or considers them to be reliable. The recrudesence of magic, witchcraft, and superstition of all kinds is a much advertised feature of our times. I am, rather, making a normative statement concerning their epistemic status. And even on the factual side it is true that such modes of belief formation are much less prevalent now than several thousand years ago, which is in no small part a result of the frequent disconfirmation of their output.

scientific beliefs, the less firmly established practice, the religious one, can be preserved by sacrificing some of its beliefs and/or by modifying its belief-forming procedures. This is what has happened in our culture over the last few centuries. What we may term the "Judeo-Christian doxastic practice" has been modified by, for example, changes in biblical interpretation, so that it no longer generates a belief structure that is massively inconsistent with the belief structure generated by the "scientific doxastic practice". Many churchmen in the sixteenth and seventeenth centuries took Copernican astronomy to come into conflict with a passage from the Psalms: "The earth is stablished that it shall not be moved (93:1)". But most Jews and Christians nowadays, at least those who have considered the matter, would take the Psalmist to be poetically expressing a sense of the stability of the earth relative to a human life, rather than propounding an astronomical hypothesis. Thus the Judeo-Christian doxastic practice is modified, not abandoned.

vii. Significant Self-Support

Next I want to consider a way in which the prima facie claims of established doxastic practices can be strengthened. We get the key to this by noting that not all epistemically circular arguments fall under the ban against track-record arguments for being equally available for any doxastic practice. There are epistemically circular arguments that will help us to discriminate between practices since they cannot automatically be used for any practice whatever. To illustrate this consider the following ways in which SP supports its own claims. (1) By engaging in SP and allied memory and inferential practices we are enabled to make predictions many of which turn out to be correct, and thereby we are able to anticipate and, to some considerable extent, control the course of events. (2) By relying on SP and associated practices we are able to establish facts about the operation of sense perception that show both that it is a reliable source of belief and why it is reliable. Our scientific account of perceptual processes shows how it is that sense experience serves as a sensitive indicator of certain kinds of facts about the environment of the perceiver. These results are by no means trivial. It cannot be assumed that any practice whatever will yield comparable fruits. It is quite conceivable that we should not have attained this kind or degree of success at prediction and control by relying on the output of SP; it is equally conceivable that this output should not have put us in a position to acquire sufficient understanding of the workings of perception to see why it can be relied on. To be sure, an argument from these fruits to the reliability of SP is still infected with epistemic circularity; apart from reliance on SP we have no way of knowing the outcome of our attempts at prediction and control, and no way of confirming our suppositions about the workings of perception. Nevertheless this is not the trivial epistemically circular support that necessarily extends to every practice. Many practices, like crystal-ball gazing, do not show anything analogous. Since SP supports itself in ways it conceivably might not, and in ways other practices do not, its claims to reliability are thereby strengthened; and if crystal-ball gazing lacks any comparable self-support, its claims suffer by comparison. Analogous points can be made concerning memory, introspection, rational intuition, and various kinds of reasoning. The results we achieve by engaging in these practices and by using their fruits are best explained by supposing these practices to be reliable.

We must be careful not to suppose that a practice can be nontrivially self-supported by its fruits only in the SP way. The acceptability of rational intuition is not weakened by the fact that reliance on the outputs of these practices does not lead to achievements in prediction and control. The point is that it is, by its very nature, unsuitable for this use; it is not "designed" to give us information that could serve as the basis for such results. Since it does not purport to provide information about the physical environment, it would be unreasonable to condemn it for not providing us with an evidential basis for predictive hypotheses concerning that environment. As I will argue in Chapter 5, it is equally inappropriate to expect predictive efficacy from the practice of forming beliefs about God on the basis of mystical perception, and equally misguided to consider the claims of that practice to be weakened by its failure to contribute to achievements of this ilk. On the other hand, we can consider whether these practices yield fruits that are appropriate to their character and aims. It would seem that the combination of rational intuition and deduction yields impressive and fairly stable, abstract systems, while the religious perceptual practice, as we shall point out in Chapter 5, provides effective guidance to spiritual development.

Since even significant self-support exhibits epistemic circularity, I will refrain from taking it to be an independent reason for supposing the doxastic practice in question to be reliable. Because self-support requires assuming the practice in question to be a reliable source of belief, it provides evidence for reliability only on the assumption of that reliability; and that is hardly evidence in any straightforward sense. Hence I am taking significant self-support to function as a way of strengthening the prima facie claim of a doxastic practice to a kind of practical rationality, rather than as something that confers probability on a claim to reliability. But as such it is by no means a negligible consideration.

Let me sum up the ways in which a concentration on doxastic *practices*, rather than *principles* of justification or adequacy of *grounds* of belief, is crucial for the treatment we have provided in this chapter. It is obvious that the argument to and from *practical* rationality depends on our focus on practices. A question of practical rationality arises only when we are dealing with what we *do*. If we were speaking of the truth (validity, acceptability . . .) of principles or the adequacy of grounds, then there could be no question of what it is rational to do, since we would not be discussing doings. But the other components of the argument also presuppose, less obviously, that we are dealing with practices. First a general point. Self-support of all kinds can be enjoyed only by modes of belief formation that are actually utilized; otherwise the mode would not "do" anything to support itself. As for a *principle* that lays down conditions of justification for beliefs of a certain kind, the only way it could support itself would be via an inference from itself to the proposition that it is reliable; and even if such an inference were cogent, it would hardly constitute *significant* self-support, since exactly the same inference could be mounted from any principle of justification whatever. We can say the same about consistency. If we haven't actually been forming beliefs in accordance with a principle, we will not have much to go on in considering whether the body of beliefs that would be formed by following that principle is internally consistent, and consistent with the beliefs that would result from following other principles.[43]

viii. The Overall Status of Established Doxastic Practices

To summarize, it is *prima facie* rational to engage in established doxastic practices. That prima facie acceptability can be overridden by such considerations as the internal and external inconsistency we have been discussing. To put it into a formula, *a firmly established doxastic practice is rationally engaged in unless the total output of all our firmly established doxastic practices sufficiently indicates its unreliability*. In other terms, *a firmly established doxastic practice is rationally engaged in provided it and its output cohere sufficiently with other firmly established doxastic practices and their output.*[44] On the other side, the prima facie rationality of a practice can be strengthened by what we have called "significant self-support". I have suggested that our most familiar and basic doxastic practices pass all these tests. They are sufficiently socially established to be accorded the status of prima facie rationality. They escape disqualification by massive and persistent internal or external contradiction. And their claims are reinforced by significant self-support.

It remains to consider where epistemic circularity is to be found in this case I have been making for the rationality of doxastic practices. It obviously attaches to "significant self-support". That is the reason for the term "self-support". But what about the basic claim of social establishment? And what about the judgment of the absence of anything that could be termed "massive and persistent" internal or external contradiction?

[43]It is also relevant that by conducting the discussion in terms of practices we can raise questions about areas of belief without being able to give adequate formulations of principles of justification that apply to those areas (a difficult undertaking). For we can effectively identify practices just by indicating the crucial range of inputs (SP) or outputs (scientific theorizing).

[44]Lest we fear that this will commit us to approving patently irrational modes of belief formation, let us note that if a mode is "patently irrational" that will in itself constitute a substantial reason to the contrary.

Beginning with social establishment, it does seem that we have to make use of what we may call the "standard package" of SP, introspection, memory, rational intuition, and various forms of reasoning to determine the social establishment of the practices we have been considering. How else would we learn that these practices are deeply rooted socially, that they are established in the individual at a very early age, and that they are embedded in wider spheres of practice? How else except from our observations of ourselves and others, the examination of historical records, and reasoning from all this?[45]

Thus the practical-rationality argument from social establishment will have to be categorized as one more instance of "significant self-support".[46] Even if it is *self*-support, it can qualify as significant, since a parallel argument cannot be mounted for any doxastic practice whatever. Even if such practices as reading the entrails of sacred beasts were at one time intimately involved in a form of life, their degree of rootedness was significantly less than that of the standard package, as shown by the fact that the former, but not the latter, was abandoned. And even the former degree of rootedness is not enjoyed by all doxastic practices, even on their own showing. If crystal-ball gazing yields the information that this very practice is widely established, news of this has not reached me.

What about the overriders having to do with consistency? Can one show a practice to be consistent or inconsistent, internally or externally, with no taint of epistemic circularity? Yes, to a point. We don't have to use SP to determine the incidence of contradiction in SP's output.[47] Nor do we need to use

[45]Although this is undoubtedly the case, it might be claimed that in using these practices we do not have to assume, even in practice, that they are rationally engaged in (as we do have to assume that they are *reliable*) and hence that there is no epistemic circularity in this argument, as there is in the straightforward argument to reliability. I find it difficult to assess this claim. In any event it is not necessary to do so, since, as we will be pointing out shortly, we are interested in practical rationality as a support for a claim of reliability. Since the reliability of the practices is the ultimate conclusion, we will still run into epistemic circularity even if we reach that conclusion by way of an intermediate conclusion of practical rationality.

[46]It may reasonably be claimed that you do not have to use MP to show that MP is socially established, entrenched before the age of reflection, etc. Hence this may be taken to be a way in which MP is in a stronger position than SP; the argument for the practical rationality of engaging in it does not fall into epistemic circularity. However, this difference dissipates on further consideration. Although we do not have to employ mystical perception itself to determine social establishment, the *practice* we have been calling 'MP' involves an associated background belief system; and in building up that system we have to make use of SP, reasoning of various sorts, and so on. Hence in showing the place of MP in our lives we have to rely on practices involved in MP, at least by reason of MP's background belief system. And so epistemic circularity is not totally absent after all.

[47]Well, perhaps we have to use SP to determine what that output is, over and above one's own case. We have to listen to the perceptual judgments people make. But that is a different use from the ones we have been considering. Let's take the output as given. The question concerns the balance of truths and falsehoods. It is here that we have to use SP to provide otherwise strong evidence for reliability but not to show internal or external consistency or inconsistency, and so not to give such support for a reliability claim as is forthcoming from the absence of internal or external contradiction.

memory to discover contradictions between memory beliefs. The same goes for inconsistencies between, for example, the outputs of memory and perception. But this is true only for detecting each individual contradiction, and only in one's own case. To pile up a record of contradictions I will have to rely on memory at some point. And to bring the memory and perceptual beliefs of others into the reckoning I will have to rely on SP to find out what those are. Moreover, if we are examining more purely intellectual belief-forming processes it is a different story. We can't spot contradictions without utilizing rational intuition and, except for the simplest cases, without using reasoning. Hence we can't establish consistency or inconsistency for *these* practices without epistemic circularity. There will be no harm in generalizing this point and thinking of considerations of consistency as yet one more form of significant self-support.

But if the practical-rationality argument is infected with epistemic circularity, how does it differ from what I called the "internal" or "hang tough" reaction to our dilemma, a reaction from which I sought to differentiate my approach by claiming that the latter involves taking a sort of external look at the status of doxastic practices? To answer this question I will have to make some further distinctions.

The most fundamental stratum of my "doxastic practice" approach is the claim that there is no appeal beyond the doxastic practices to which we find ourselves firmly committed. That claim is based solely on the pervasiveness of epistemic circularity in attempts to show those practices to be reliable. The only reliance here is on reasoning, including rational intuition, something we perforce rely on in any intellectual activity whatever. It does not require any sociological or psychological investigation into the status SP and the like have in our personal and corporate lives. It doesn't require the theory of doxastic practices set out in section iii. Hence, so long as it isn't reasoning or rational intuition that is in question, no epistemic circularity is involved in this appeal.

The rest of my case—the appeal to social establishment, to the absence of sufficient overriders, and to what I called "significant self-support"—I have admitted to exhibit epistemic circularity and so to constitute "significant self-support" in a wider sense.[48] Nevertheless my approach is still distinguished from the purely internal one by the fact that it involves a general reflection on doxastic practices and the vicissitudes of trying to show them to be reliable, an "external" perspective that is most prominent in what I called the basic stratum of the position—the thesis that there is no appeal beyond the doxastic practices with which we find ourselves.

[48]When I use 'significant self-support' in contrast to, e.g., 'social establishment', I am restricting it to the use of facts about the outcome of using the practice to provide (epistemically circular but significant) evidence for the reliability of the practice. I will continue to use the term in this restricted way, but it must be remembered that the term is naturally and felicitously applied to any argument in support of the epistemic claims of a practice that exhibits epistemic circularity.

ix. Practical Rationality and Reliability

So far I have been arguing that it is (practically) rational to engage in SP and other standard, basic doxastic practices.[49] But the original question was whether SP is reliable. In addition to the intrinsic interest of that question, we got into it because we wanted to know whether SP is a source of epistemic justification, and the concept of justification we were using is such that a practice will issue justified beliefs only if it is by and large reliable. Does the (practical) rationality of engaging in a practice have any bearing on whether it is reliable.

This may well be doubted. First, it is clear that the rationality of a practice does not *entail* its reliability. The claim to practical rationality was that where doxastic practices are firmly rooted in our lives, it would be folly to cease practicing them without very strong reasons for doing so; and we have no such reasons. This could be the case even if the practice were in fact unreliable. Moreover, the practical rationality of SP does not even provide nondeductive but sufficient grounds for supposing it to be reliable. I fail to discern any evidential tie; how could the practical rationality of engaging in SP be *evidence* for its reliability?[50] But, then, it looks as if the judgment that the practice is "rational" has no bearing on the likelihood that it will yield truths, in which case the argument for rationality will not advance our original aim of determining whether one or another practice is reliable.

Nevertheless, I believe that in showing it to be rational to engage in SP I have thereby not shown SP to be reliable, but shown it to be rational to suppose SP to be reliable. Let me explain. In what follows I will abbreviate 'it is rational to engage in SP' as 'SP is rational'.

In judging SP to be rational I am thereby committing myself to the rationality of judging SP to be reliable. Note the carefully qualified character of this claim. I did not say that in judging SP to be rational I was thereby *judging* it to be rational to suppose SP to be reliable, much less that I was thereby *judging* that SP is reliable. One can make the former judgment without making the latter; much less are the judgments identical. I may make the

[49]This defense of the rationality of (engaging in) SP amounts to a defense of the rationality of the "adequacy principles (beliefs, assumptions)" discussed in Chapter 2. These were the principles that embody our customary ways of going from phenomenal presentations to beliefs about the external environment. Such a principle lays it down that a certain kind of phenomenal presentation constitutes an adequate basis, a justifying ground, for the correlated objective belief formed on the basis of that presentation. Such principles are constitutive of the doxastic practice we have been calling 'SP'. Hence in making a case for the rationality of SP we have been making a case for the rationality of accepting principles that epistemically approve the modes of belief formation that are involved in SP.

[50]If it were we would have to give up the conclusion of Chapter 3 that there can be no adequate, nonepistemically circular argument for the reliability of SP and other fundamental doxastic practices.

judgment of rationality without ever having raised the question of reliability and, hence, without having taken any stand on that issue. When I say that in judging that p I am thereby *committing* myself to its being the case that q, what I mean is this. It would be irrational (incoherent . . .) for me to judge (assert, believe) that p and deny that q, or even to abstain from judging that q, *if the question arises*. The judgment that p puts me in such a position that either of those reactions would be irrational. There is no way in which I can both judge that p and take a doxastic attitude toward q other than acceptance.

It is in this sense that judging SP to be rational *commits* me to its being rational to suppose that SP is reliable. But how can this be? How can taking a stand on the practical rationality of SP put me in such a position? Won't the same considerations that led me to deny that the rationality of SP is *evidence* for its reliability also work against this claim of commitment? No, they will not. The reason is that we are dealing with *doxastic* practices, belief-forming practices. With many sorts of practices I can take it to be rational to engage in them without supposing them to enjoy the kind of success appropriate to them. I can take it to be rational to engage in playing squash for its health and recreational benefits, without thereby committing myself to the proposition that I will win most of my matches. But to engage in a doxastic practice is to form beliefs in a certain way. And to believe that p is to be committed to its being true that p.[51] But what is true of individual beliefs is also true of a general practice of belief formation. To engage in a certain doxastic practice and to accept the beliefs one thereby generates is to commit oneself to those beliefs being true (at least for the most part), and hence to commit oneself to the practice's being reliable. It is irrational to engage in SP, to form beliefs in the ways constitutive of that practice, and refrain from acknowledging them as true, and hence the practice as reliable, if the question arises.

But if one cannot engage in the practice and refuse to admit that the practice is reliable if the question arises, then in judging that the former is rational one has committed oneself to the latter's being rational, in the sense of 'is committed to' we have been explaining. For I cannot hold that X is rational and coherently deny (or abstain from judging) that Y is rational, where accepting (engaging in) X commits me to accepting Y. If pursuing a Ph.D. commits me to the belief that it is possible for me to get a Ph.D., then I can't rationally hold both that it is rational to pursue a Ph.D. and that it is not rational to suppose that I can get a Ph.D. The rationality of a practice (action, belief, judgment . . .) extends to whatever that practice . . . commits me to. But, then, if I judge SP to be rational and deny that it is rational to regard it as

[51]Again this 'is to be committed to' rather than 'is to believe that', for the very reason brought out in the last paragraph: one could believe that the sun is shining without having ever raised the question of truth, and even without having the concept of truth. But if one does raise the question it is irrational to assert that p and abstain from asserting that it is true that p.

reliable, I would be in an incoherent situation. Thus we may conclude that in judging SP to be rational I am committed to judging it to be rational to suppose SP to be reliable.[52]

But, then, if I have shown, by my practical argument, that it is rational to engage in SP I have thereby shown that it is rational to take SP to be reliable. For since the acknowledgment of the rationality of the practice commits one to the rationality of its reliability, to provide an adequate argument for the former will be to provide an adequate argument for the latter. Hence our argument from practical rationality, though it does not show that SP is reliable, does show that it is rational to take it to be reliable. No doubt, it would be much more satisfying to produce a direct demonstration of the truth of the proposition that *SP is reliable*. But since that is impossible, we should not sneer at a successful argument for the rationality of supposing SP to be reliable.[53]

It may be claimed that there is less than meets the eye in this conclusion. We have shown, at most, that engaging in SP enjoys a *practical* rationality; it is a reasonable thing to do, given our aims and our situation. But then it is only that same practical rationality that carries over, via the commitment relation, to the judgment that SP is reliable. We have not shown that it is rational in an *epistemic* sense that SP is reliable, where the latter involves showing that it is at least probably true that SP is reliable. This must be admitted. We have not shown the reliability attribution to be rational in a truth-conducive sense of rationality, one that itself is subject to a reliability constraint. But that does not imply that our argument is without epistemic significance. It all depends on what moves are open to us. If, as I have argued in Chapter 3, we are unable to find noncircular indications of the truth of the reliability judgment, it is certainly relevant to show that it enjoys some other kind of rationality. It is, after all, not irrelevant to our basic aim at believing the true and abstaining from believing the false, that SP and other established doxastic practices constitute the most reasonable procedures to use, so far as we can judge, when trying to realize that aim.[54]

[52]Note that this is a case of what has been "pragmatic implication". Indeed, pragmatic implication is felicitously characterized in just the terms we have used: it consists of the fact that *asserting* that p commits one to asserting that q, even though the *proposition*, p, does not entail, or otherwise imply, the proposition, q. Thus in asserting that my car is in the garage I pragmatically imply that I believe that my car is in the garage, even though the propositions *my car is in the garage* and *I believe that my car is in the garage* are logically independent. This is just the situation we have with *SP is rational* and *it is rational to take SP to be reliable*.

[53]This is analogous to the "fideist" move in religion. Pessimistic about the chances of directly establishing the truth of the existence of God, one seeks to show that it is rational for one to believe in God, as a postulate of pure practical reason, as a requirement for fullness of life, or whatever. But only *analogous* to fideism.—I don't wish to wear that label.

[54]The point that it is a practical rather than an epistemic rationality that has been established (where it is a distinguishing mark of the latter that it implies likelihood of truth) enables us to meet an objection to our procedure from some recent attacks on the idea that a justification (or

x. Practical Rationality and Justification

Now we must relate the conclusions of this section to the discussion of justification in Chapter 2. There we took the concept of epistemic justification to embody a "reliability constraint", such that if a belief is epistemically justified it is thereby conceptually implied that the belief is at least likely to be true. In Chapter 3 we found severe difficulties in showing that familiar doxastic practices like SP are sources of justification in this sense. And now we have moved to arguing that the claim of reliability (and hence of being a source of justification in the Chapter 2 sense) for SP enjoys a certain kind of practical rationality, a kind that doesn't entail a likelihood of truth for that claim and hence does not entail a likelihood of truth for the outputs of SP and other established practices. Thus, despite the initial tough talk about justification entailing reliability, it would seem that, as far as this argument goes, we have finally settled for an epistemic status for SP (and derivatively for the epistemic status of perceptual beliefs) that falls short of likelihood of truth. So why didn't we begin with a weaker notion of justification, instead of initially holding out hopes that were eventually to be dashed? Why didn't we begin with a more "internalist" notion of justification that does not entail the likelihood of truth?

So far as this charge is applied to perceptual beliefs, it is vitiated by a level confusion. The lower epistemic status we have settled for attaches to the *higher-level* claim that SP is reliable, not for the particular perceptual beliefs that issue from that practice. As for the latter, what we are claiming is still the full-blooded (prima facie) justification of Chapter 2 that involves likelihood of truth. To be sure, the fact remains that the higher-level claim that they enjoy that status has not itself been shown to enjoy such a status (one entailing likelihood of truth), and we have despaired of being able to show that it does.[55] At the higher level we have settled for showing that it is (practically) *rational*

sufficient reasons, evidence, or grounds) for the belief that p is also a justification . . . for anything entailed by p. Dretske 1970 argues that my adequate perceptual evidence for "That's a zebra" is not also adequate evidence for "That's not a donkey with stripes painted on it", even though the former entails the latter. One might have parallel qualms about my claim that an adequate argument for p is also an adequate argument for everything to which the assertion of p commits one. If we were thinking of the rationality involved in my discussion as guaranteeing likelihood of truth, this would be a serious objection. But since it is practical rationality that is involved, the situation is different. Dretske's point is that what renders probable the supposition that it's a zebra does not also render probable the supposition that it's not a donkey with stripes painted on it. But what I am thinking of the rationality of SP as committing one to is not the likelihood of the truth of the claim that SP is reliable (or anything entailing that), but rather the practical rationality of taking SP to be reliable, the thesis that, given what I have to go on, I am well advised to make and act on this assumption. Thus the qualms expressed by Dretske and Nozick (1981, chap. 3) do not apply here.

[55]This does not, of course, imply that the higher-level claim is not justified in the truth-conducive sense. It is just that we have given up on *showing* that it is.

to take SP to confer justification in the full-blooded sense. But it would be a level confusion to suppose that this implies that perceptual beliefs themselves are not justified in the stronger sense. Once more, according to our account of justification, the justification of perceptual beliefs requires that it is *true* that SP is reliable, not that we are truth-conducively justified in believing this. Moreover, though I do not claim to have shown that SP is reliable, and that its products are prima facie justified in my strong sense, I do claim to have shown that it is *reasonable* to take SP to be reliable, and hence reasonable to suppose that its products are prima facie justified in that strong sense.[56]

But even so one might suggest that a simpler procedure would have been to work from the beginning with a weaker sense of 'justified', such that we might have a better chance of *showing* that the products of SP and other established doxastic practices are justified in this sense. This is the kind of approach I took in my first essays on this topic (1982, 1983). Such a sense might be that these beliefs have an adequate ground, *so far as we can tell*, or that we would take it, on mature reflection, that they have an adequate ground.[57] This would spare us the rather complicated multilevel view we have come to and would still give us a significant sense in which the products of established doxastic practices might be shown to be justified.

I have not chosen this route because I feel that when we wonder about the credentials of mystical perception we are interested in whether it is a source of knowledge, or true beliefs, about God, not just whether it enables us to form *justified* beliefs in some non-truth-conducive sense of 'justified'. Since we have to tackle the question of reliability sooner or later, I have felt that it is more candid and more revealing to highlight it from the outset.

Nevertheless, my results could be couched in terms of a weaker, non-truth-conducive concept of epistemic justification, and I have no objections to doing so provided the rest of the picture is not neglected. Indeed, the very considerations I have adduced to construct my practical-rationality argument could be utilized to construct such a concept. Let's say that a belief is prima facie justified in this new sense provided it stems from a socially established doxastic practice that is not discredited by the total output of such practices. Unqualified justification will then be a function of the relation of the belief to other beliefs justified in the same way. In that sense I claim to have shown, or at least provided good reasons for supposing, that standard sense perceptual beliefs, memory beliefs, and so on, are prima facie justified. For I have argued that the practices from which they issue do have the status just specified.

[56]It is also worth pointing out that it is only when we are raising the most ultimate questions that we are in the position of having to settle for practical rationality. Typically, in fact invariably when we are not probing the ultimate foundations of epistemology, we are operating in a context in which we take enough for granted to provide us with grounds for what we believe that provide adequate reasons for the truth of these beliefs, as judged from the context defined by those assumptions.

[57]This last suggestion is developed in Foley 1987, chaps. 1, 2.

Hence I am willing to put part of my results in these terms. But I would also insist that, as made explicit in the last section, I have shown that it is rational to take SP and other established doxastic practices to be reliable, and hence rational to suppose that standard perceptual beliefs are justified in the stronger, truth-conducive sense. It is crucial for the argument of this book not to omit that further step. That is the final conclusion I want to take from this chapter for use in the rest of the book—*for any established doxastic practice it is rational to suppose that it is reliable, and hence rational to suppose that its doxastic outputs are prima facie justified.*[58]

[58]Alston 1989c is an earlier version of some of the basic ideas of this chapter.

CHAPTER 5

The Christian Mystical Perceptual Doxastic Practice (CMP)

After our long excursus into general epistemology, we are ready to return to the central topic of the book, the epistemic status of M-beliefs. Let's summarize briefly the main results of the last three chapters, results we will now apply to our central problem.

In Chapter 2 we first developed a conception of epistemic justification in terms of a belief's being based on an (objectively) adequate ground. Applying this conception to perceptual beliefs, we saw that although some are based in part on other beliefs, the range of beliefs based purely on perceptual experience is larger than one might think. However, in thinking about our standard ways of forming and evaluating perceptual beliefs, our perceptual doxastic practices, we must range over both immediate and (partly) mediate belief formation and both immediate and (partly) mediate justification.

In Chapter 3 we tackled the question of why we should suppose our usual ways of forming perceptual beliefs to be reliable. Focusing on *sense* perception, we reviewed the most promising attempts to show in a noncircular fashion that our standard sense perceptual doxastic practice, SP, is reliable. We concluded that all such attempts have failed, and we saw little hope for the enterprise. This result engenders an epistemological crisis. Why, if all noncircular arguments fail, should we repose more trust in SP than in entrail reading or crystal-ball gazing? In Chapter 4 we provided an answer to that question by developing a theory of doxastic practices and their epistemic assessment. We concluded that it is rational to engage in any such practice that is socially established, that yields outputs that are free from massive internal and external contradiction, and that demonstrates a significant degree of self-support. This implies that it is rational to take any such practice to be reliable and hence a source of justification for the beliefs it engenders. It is this result that I now wish to apply to the practice of forming M-beliefs on the basis of mystical experience. That is, I will be contending that the "mystical experience belief forming practice" (MP)[1] satisfies the above conditions for rational acceptance.

i. The Individuation of Mystical Perceptual Doxastic Practices

Before turning to the exposition and defense of that contention let us note the ways in which the points about the individuation of doxastic practices set out in Chapter 4 apply to MP. First, we said that such practices are distinguished most centrally by differences in inputs and in the input-output functions. A doxastic practice *is* the utilization of a "family" or input-output mechanisms, each of which is sensitive to inputs of a certain kind and goes from such inputs to outputs in accordance with a certain function. What binds a certain group of mechanisms together into a "family" is an important similarity between the kinds of inputs and between the kinds of functions involved. For the sense-perceptual doxastic practice (SP) the inputs are similar in that they are all, at least in part, direct awarenesses of objects as displaying basic sensory qualia; and the most common functions are of the form *an experience as of X's appearing as* ϕ *(plus perhaps certain relevant beliefs)* $\rightarrow$ *a belief that X is* ϕ. As we construe MP, the most common functions are of the same form. In both spheres perceptual beliefs are typically formed by taking the perceived object to have the characteristics it experientially presents itself as having.

Is there a single distinctive type of experiential input for MP generally, or must we distinguish different forms of MP on the basis of differences in inputs? This is a difficult question. First, as noted in detail in Chapter 1, we are not in nearly as good a position here to specify phenomenal similarities and differences between experiences as we are with SP, since we are not in a position to isolate and catalog the simple phenomenal qualia involved. But though we lack intersubjective stimulus control, and hence lack a theoretical grasp of phenomenal content, it seems clear that the experiences on the basis of which M-beliefs are formed are similar in something like the ways in which sense experiences are similar. If you look back over the samples presented in Chapter 1, you will see important commonalities in the ways the subjects describe their experiences, both in terms of how the object is appearing to them and in terms of the subjective character of the experience. That is not to say that there is any one or more features that are common to all cases. It is rather that there is a sizable list of typical features, each of which is found frequently, so that the cases exhibit a "family resemblance". In section ix of Chapter 1 we made a list of what God is reported as presenting Himself to one's experience as being or doing. There are also characteristic affective

[1] Remember that 'MP' is to be read not in the most natural way, as an acronym for 'mystical perception', but as an acronym for the practice of forming beliefs directly on the basis of mystical perception.

reactions: awe, bliss, ecstasy, joy, calm, delight, peace. At least we get typical features within a single religious tradition, such as the Christian tradition from which our examples have been drawn. The cross-cultural situation is much less clear. There is a considerable literature devoted to exhibiting cross-cultural commonalities in *mystical experience*, in the distinctive sense of that term explained in section iv of Chapter 1;[2] but it is not at all clear that this holds of the wider category of mystical experience with which we are dealing. Indeed, another large body of literature is devoted to arguing that this is not the case.[3] Be all this as it may, the crucial point for our present concerns is that a marked phenomenal similarity between experiential inputs is not required to treat the formation of beliefs on the basis of those inputs as falling within a single doxastic practice. After all, there is no discernible phenomenal similarity across sense modalities; odors and colors, for example, are lumped together as sensory qualia only because they are both produced by the stimulation of sensory receptors. But this does not prevent us from thinking in terms of a single practice of sense-perceptual belief formation. With MP we are not in a position to group inputs together on the basis of proximate causal origin. Nevertheless, we can group phenomenally diverse experiences together, as we have been doing, in terms of the content of beliefs to which they give rise: beliefs about perceivable features and activities of God. This puts us in a position to form the concept of a single doxastic practice, the inputs of which are experiential, and the outputs of which are M-beliefs. Because of the specific features of the concept of God the practice so defined does not extend into all religions; but it corresponds to the territory on which we are concentrating in this book.

To be sure, to discern a commonality in phenomenal content, we must be able to distinguish this from the conceptualization to which it is subjected. And, as pointed out in section viii of Chapter 1, the impossibility of doing this has almost attained the status of a dogma in the current intellectual climate. It has been claimed repeatedly that there is and can be no perception without conception, and even that perception is just a particular way of applying concepts, or a particular mode of belief formation. Those who deny cross-cultural universals of mystical experience have generally based their position on such a "conceptualist" or "judgmental" theory of perception.[4] But as I made explicit in section viii, Chapter 1, at the heart of perception, on my view, is a direct awareness of something's appearing to one as so-and-so. This fact of X's appearing to S as ϕ is, in principle, independent of any conceptualization or judgment, independent of S's *taking* X to be ϕ or believing or judging X to be ϕ, or even thinking of X as ϕ. Sensory appearance is a

[2]See, e.g., Otto 1932; Stace 1952, 1960.
[3]See, e.g., Steven T. Katz, "Language, Epistemology, and Mysticism", in Katz 1978.
[4]See, e.g., Katz 1978, Proudfoot 1985.

more rudimentary constituent of the total phenomenon of perception than anything involving judgment. Adult perception is typically shot through with conceptualization and belief, but that is a further development; it goes beyond the minimal requirement for there being a case of perception. For the likes of Katz, on the other hand, if subjects in different cultures construe the objects of mystical experiences quite differently, then their experiences are quite different; if there is no interesting commonality in the conceptualization, there is no interesting commonality in the experiences.

Thus, if we adopt the theory of appearing that gives us a *chance* to find common phenomenal features of mystical perception across cultures, but the task of determining whether there are such features is a delicate one, rendered still more difficult by our lack of any nonanalogical way of specifying the basic phenomenal qualia involved. Fortunately, we don't have to decide this issue, since we will find ample reasons in other quarters for distinguishing different MP's for different religions.

We can easily verify that MP displays certain other features that we said in Chapter 4 are characteristic of doxastic practices.

(1) Like SP, MP is normally acquired and engaged in well before one is explicitly aware of the practice as such and before one comes to reflect critically on it, if one ever does. This is not as invariable as in the case of SP, where hard wiring is more prominent. Although learning and socialization play a role in both practices, it presumably plays a larger role in MP. But keeping in mind these differences, the normal situation in religious communities (and our fragmented and spiritually impoverished society is not at all typical in this respect) is for the young to learn how to perceptually recognize God well before any critical reflection on the process. But just because the practice is so much at the mercy of social influences, it is possible for a person to take up the practice after arriving at the age of reason, though this remains the exception rather than the rule.

(2) MP involves procedures for evaluating its outputs as well as for forming them. This requires an "overrider system" against which to check those perceptual beliefs we have specific grounds to doubt. Since I will be discussing overrider systems later in this section, and since in section iii I will consider reasons for denying that any such evaluation procedures are widely shared, I will say no more about this point here.

(3) As with SP, the belief-forming practice is set in the context of wider spheres of practice that involve interacting with the perceived objects—forming relationships, developing attitudes and feelings toward them, and so on. One does not learn to perceive God as a detached observer. One learns to pray to God, worship God, hear and respond to His voice, ask God for forgiveness, and see one's life and the environing world in the light of its creation, sustenance, and providential ordering by God. This is an exact analogue to the way in which one learns in SP to perceive and to form perceptual beliefs

as a way of orienting oneself toward the external environment and of guiding one's attitudes and behavior toward that environment.

(4) I have already pointed out that MP is socially transmitted by socially monitored learning and is socially shared. This is even more obvious than in the case of SP.

(5) In the last chapter we pointed out ways in which one doxastic practice depends on, and is connected with, others. This is richly exemplified by MP. An individual cannot acquire the background system of doctrine involved in the overrider system without using sense perception—to read sacred writings, for example—memory, and various kinds of reasoning. And just as with other socially established practices, one must perceive other people, understand what they are saying, remember it, and reason from it, if one is to learn the practice. Moreover, as noted in Chapter 2, we draw on a wider system of belief in identifying objective realities and attributing objective properties to them on the basis of phenomenal content. What we are calling MP is best viewed as a fragment of the cognitive aspect of a larger religious practice that, on its cognitive side, makes use of all a person's faculties and wide stretches of the person's belief system.

(6) We had already noted in Chapter 4, when laying out basic features of doxastic practices (section iiiI), that religious doxastic practices are obviously subject to change.

(7) MP clearly has its distinctive set of presuppositions, particularly the existence of God and the reliability of this way of forming beliefs.

A consideration of how the other basic features of SP apply to MP brings us to a very important difference between the two spheres. The other features in question are a distinctive subject matter, a distinctive conceptual scheme, and an overrider system. The point is that whereas SP presents virtually an identical picture in these respects across cultures, this is by no means the case with MP.

(A) First the conceptual scheme. Whether it is a Manhattan stockbroker or an Australian bushman, the perceived environment gets conceptualized in pretty much the same terms. This uniformity may not have always held good. Although this is very controversial, many anthropologists have supposed there to be, or to have been, a great deal of diversity in the ways in which different cultures conceptualize sensory input. In some cultures, perhaps in all cultures if we go back far enough, what we consider inanimate nature is or was perceived as animated. Rocks and springs and plants and the earth were perceived as alive, ensouled, possessing intentions and emotions and acting purposefully. When this mode of perception was dominant in some cultures and not others, there was not the uniformity in SP that seems to obtain today in our thoroughly westernized world. Be that as it may, it is clear that MP presently exhibits a much greater degree of cross-cultural diversity than does SP. The ways in which theists, Hinayana Buddhists, Mahayana Buddhists, and Hindus of one or another stripe think of the objects of their worship (and of what they take to be Ultimate Reality) differ enormously.[5] The differences are as great as that between personal and impersonal, positive and negative, concerned and unconcerned about morality, all-inclusive and related to others. There are also differences in the ways God is conceived in the different theistic religions, but they seem like family squabbles compared to the differences between all of them and the nontheistic religions.[6] Thus if the use of a uniform conceptual scheme, with only minor deviations, is required for a single doxastic practice, we will have to deny that there is any single MP. We will have to distinguish as many MP's as there are different conceptual schemes for grasping Ultimate Reality.

(B) The situation with respect to subject matter is less clear-cut. The natural way to specify the sphere of reality with which a cognitive system is dealing is to use the concepts employed by that system. We use our physical-object conceptual scheme to specify the reality we learn about from sense perception. If that is the right way to proceed, we will have to deny that radically different religions are dealing with the same subject matter. However, the usual assumption is not that Hinduism, Buddhism, and Christianity are, or even may be, dealing with different subject matters all of which are real, but rather that no more than one of them is dealing with anything that really exists. If Christianity has the right line on Ultimate Reality, the others are wrong. In that case, either Hinduism and Buddhism have no real subject matter at all, or they have the same subject matter as Christianity, but it is incorrectly characterized. Because of these complications I shall not employ this factor in distinguishing forms of MP.

(C) Overrider system. Here, as with (A), we have a clear case for Balkanization, indeed a more compelling case. Provided there were uniformity in experiential input and input-output functions, we could absorb a fair amount of difference in conceptual scheme and still count MP as a single belief forming practice. But differences in overrider systems are more crucial. The overrider system determines how we go from prima facie to unqualified justification; as such it has a crucial bearing on the what outputs are ultimately approved. Hence we cannot count practices with quite different overrider systems as different branches of one practice.

For SP, the overrider system concerns what we have learned or can learn, from SP together with other practices, about the subject matter and about the conditions of veridical perception thereof. This general statement holds equally for MP, the most important difference being that here there is more of

[5]I must ask the reader's indulgence for the extremely crude nature of my appeals to the comparative study of religions. I am concerned only to make the point that there is diversity in certain respects, and therefore I need not go into the careful distinction of, e.g., different forms of Hinduism that would be required for a different purpose.

[6]Theistic religions, and even different sects of the same religion, differ sharply on such matters as the requirements God makes of us, God's purposes, that from which we need saving, and the nature of that salvation. We are not concerned with any of that at this point.

a possibility of input to the system from sources that are independent of perception. Even if the perception of God plays as important a role in the grounds of religious belief as I believe it to, it is by no means the only contributor. There is also God's self-revelation, where this comes in other ways than through human perception of God as communicating a message, and there is natural theology. In Chapter 8 we will be considering the place of MP vis-à-vis other grounds of religious belief. But whatever the basis for the background scheme, such a scheme is operative wherever there is a well established form of MP. It will include both a general picture of the nature of Ultimate Reality and our relations thereto, and some generalizations concerning the conditions under which mystical perception is likely to be veridical or the reverse.

Consider how this might work in a particular case. James Jones reports that God told him that it is His will that all the members of Jones's sect commit suicide. God, according to Jones, gives no reason for this. Since it seems very unlikely, given the account of the nature, purposes, and pattern of activity of God in the Christian tradition, that God would command any such thing, we (almost everyone in the mainline Christian community who considers the matter) reject the claim. Smith reports that God told him that the world will end on July 14, 1977, and that he and his fellow sect members should make certain preparations for this. Since this claim does not tie into anything else in the tradition and since many such claims have been empirically disconfirmed, it should be rejected. On the other hand, consider the following report, (6) in Chapter 1.

> (6) I attended service at a church in Uppsala. . . . During both the Confession of Sin and the Prayer of Thanksgiving which followed Communion, I had a strong consciousness of the Holy Spirit as a person, and an equally strong consciousness of the existence of God, that God was present, that the Holy Spirit was in all those who took part in the service. . . . The only thing of importance was God and my realization that He looked upon me and let His mercy flood over me, forgiving me for my mistakes and giving me the strength to live a better life. (Anonymous report in Unger 1976, p. 114)

What the person claimed to have experienced here is not discordant with anything in the Christian tradition. Moreover, the conditions under which s/he had this experience are not such that the pooled Christian experience in these matters indicates that it is likely to be hallucinatory. That doesn't show that the experience was verdical, but it leaves undisturbed the justification the experience provides for what is reported.

Having come this far, the next step will be obvious. This background scheme differs widely across different religions. The Hindu, Buddhist, and Judeo-Christian-Moslem stories about the nature of Ultimate Reality and our relations thereto, and about the marks of an accurate perception of that reality, differ greatly. We certainly wouldn't have the *same* reasons for rejecting Jones's and Smith's reports in most other major traditions (though I am not suggesting that those claims would pass muster elsewhere). And among theistic religions there are enough differences—contrasting emphases on God's justice or love, quite different stories as to what God expects and requires of us, as to what His plans for us are, and as to His activities in history—to make a significant difference to the associated overrider system. Two pictures of the subject matter don't have to differ in their most fundamental features in order to make an important difference to the overriding function. Anything in the overrider system that might be contradicted by a perceptual report can serve as a corrective to that report; and since reports of the perception of God can deal with what God said, that can bring in any material whatever. Even if, say, Christianity and Islam have the same basic conception of God and share a common doctrine on Creation and other matters,[7] if they have different stories as to what God's plan for human salvation is, what God has done and is doing to implement this, and what God's requirements on us are, then they will function differently as a corrective to reports as to what God told someone about these matters. Hence anything in the doctrinal system of a religion can make a difference to the overrider system.

Remember that overriders of the justification for a belief that p are of two kinds. First there is the presence of not-p, or of something that renders p improbable, in the "overrider system". These we have called *rebutters*. Second, there are reasons for supposing that the justification for the belief that p does not have its usual efficacy in this instance. With perceptual justification this would involve reasons for supposing the situation of perception to be abnormal in some way that would prevent the perceptual experience from functioning as a reliable sign of what is believed. These we have called *underminers*. Thus far, in pointing out how doctrinal differences can make a significant difference to the overrider system, I have been concentrating on rebutters. But doctrinal differences can also affect underminers. For example, in the Catholic mystical tradition great stress is laid on the consequences of one's experiences for one's moral and spiritual development. The idea is that if one really is in contact with God, this will influence one in the direction of what God would have one become. But this depends on what God wills for us, and that in turn depends on what God is like. If one takes a given perceptual justification to be overridden because the subject's experiences are reinforcing pride rather than humility, one is working within a system in which humility is an important part of what God wants us to exhibit; and religious traditions will differ on this.

The upshot is that we have as many different MPs as there are importantly different doctrinal systems. In a moment we shall consider how far this Balkanization is to be carried. How about the situation of SP in this respect? We

[7]I don't mean to be committing myself as to whether this is the case.

have already noted that in SP we are not confronted with the diversity of conceptual schemes that we have in the religious sphere. How about the differences in the background beliefs that make up the overrider system? There might be significant differences here even if the conceptual scheme is uniform. After all, incompatible beliefs can be formed with the same repertoire of concepts. But again it is clear that, whatever may have been the case in ages past, we are now confronted with no such sharp diversity in beliefs about the physical world as we have in religion. There are no college courses, much less whole academic departments, that deal with "Comparative Common Sense"; nor are there councils, commissions, or international agencies that are devoted to breaking down the differences between beliefs about the physical world in different cultures. But we should not suppose that there is perfect uniformity either. The most obvious source of difference is the development of science. Scientific conceptions, discoveries, and ways of thinking seep into popular culture, often in a bowdlerized form, and play a role in the background beliefs of Everyperson. This happens to different extents, at different times, and at different rates in different cultures and subcultures. Whereas basic chemistry, physics, and biology might form part of the overrider system of an educated Manhattan business consultant, they may be totally lacking in the belief system of a Tibetan sheepherder or an Appalachian farmer. This could make a difference to the second-stage treatment of a putative perception of spontaneous generation of insects. Nevertheless, these differences will be peripheral. For all practical purposes, we may think of a single worldwide overrider system for SP; and hence we may continue to think of SP as a single doxastic practice that is shared by all normal, adult human beings.

As for the other side, we have seen that we must make at least as many cuts between forms of MP as there are different religions. Can we stop there? How about differences between sects of what is commonly regarded as the same religion? Are these sufficient, in some cases, to force us to distinguish different doxastic practices? Don't Roman Catholics and Pentecostalists differ enough in their doctrinal systems to warrant us in attributing to them different forms of MP?

This question is tied up with prickly issues concerning what it takes for different religious communities to be different sects of the same religion, rather than different religions, and I don't want to get into that. Common origin plays a large role here, though there are constraints on how far one can depart from the origin while remaining a part of that same religion. Other modes of commonality come into the equation, and perhaps the cultural bias of the classifier plays a role as well. Thus the Hinayana and all forms of the Mahayana are counted as forms of Buddhism, while Christianity is not counted as a form of Judaism. In this book I will not attempt to determine how many, and what, distinct MPs there are in the world at present. My excuse is that this is not a work in the comparative study of religions but in the epistemology of religious experience and belief. From that standpoint any actual practice is brought in only as an illustration of general philosophical points. Insofar as the book is concerned with a particular practice it is one that is in the main stream of the Christian tradition. Combining these two points, I shall proceed as follows. The discussion will focus on the practice of forming perceptual beliefs about God that is standard in what we may think of as mainline Christianity. I will arrogate to this practice the title "Christian mystical perceptual practice" ('CMP' for short). CMP takes the Bible, the ecumenical councils of the undivided church, Christian experience through the ages, Christian thought, and more generally the Christian tradition as normative sources of its overrider system. Since this brief description touches on hotly controverted points and is, in any event, not perfectly precise, I had better provide some commentary.

The thorniest issue has to do with how much disagreement on these sources we allow within CMP, or, to put it the other way round, how much disagreement it takes to spawn two distinct doxastic practices. Obviously there is a lot of disagreement on the status and interpretation of the Bible, and on how to use the Bible as a source of belief. There is also disagreement on what conciliar, episcopal, papal, or other pronouncements to take as authoritative, and also on what kind of authority these individuals or bodies have for us today, as well as on how much latitude one has in interpreting or reinterpreting what they say. Christian experience and Christian thought present even more choices. The raw mass of Christian experiential reports presents many contradictions, particularly in reports of messages from God, and different groups and individuals, will make different choices as to what is central and what is peripheral. Christian thought is notoriously of more than one mind on various issues, such as the Atonement and the person of Jesus Christ. If we count a different doxastic practice for every difference on these issues, we will wind up with an enormous proliferation of practices and the concept will be of no use. I think that the following attitude is a defensible one. Let's say that an individual or group that forms perceptual beliefs about God engages in CMP provided she/he/it stands unmistakably in the Christian tradition—that is, provided it takes its overrider system from the sources mentioned above and does so in a way that does not alter their traditional significance to such an extent as to make a mockery of them. This is not a perfectly precise stipulation. Just how much reinterpretation or accommodation to contemporary modes of thought can be engaged in without "making a mockery" of ones allegiance to the tradition? When does allegiance become mere lip service? And so on. But we must recognize that the concept of a particular doxastic practice is not, and cannot be, a perfectly precise concept. There will always be borderline areas. If we try to precise the concept too much we end up with an unmanageable plurality of practices. Moreover, Christian groups and individuals that differ in their understanding and use of the traditional sources can and do function together in a common enterprise. And although I argued above that any doctrinal difference can make a difference to the overriding function, this point should not be overblown. Many differences are rarely called upon in this capacity. Hence groups that differ on certain doctrines may in fact use the same criteria for testing putative divine perceptions.

More concretely, what Christian denominations am I thinking of as included within CMP? I will try to give some answer to this question, even though denominational distinctions are too crude to capture all the significant distinctions in doxastic practice. Not all members of a denomination will be involved in forming perceptual beliefs about God; of those that are, there may be important differences in how the practice goes. In some subgroups an "anything goes" attitude will prevail, whereas others will utilize a strict overrider system. Nevertheless, we can make some rough statements about the extent of CMP in denominational terms. Certainly it includes vast stretches of the center of traditional Christianity—the Orthodox, Roman Catholic, and Anglican churches—as well as the more conservative strands in the Reformed, Lutheran, Baptist, and Methodist traditions. I won't try to be more exact than this. The crucial test of involvement in CMP for an individual or group is the set of stipulations given above, not the official denominational affiliation.

ii. The Defense of CMP

My main thesis in this chapter, and indeed in the whole book, is that CMP is rationally engaged in since it is a socially established doxastic practice that is not demonstrably unreliable or otherwise disqualified for rational acceptance. If CMP is, indeed, a socially established doxastic practice, it follows from the position defended in Chapter 4 that it is prima facie worthy of rational participation. And this means that it is prima facie rational to regard it as reliable, sufficiently reliable to be a source of prima facie justification for the beliefs it engenders. And if, furthermore, it is not discredited by being shown to be unreliable or deficient in some other way that will cancel its prima facie rationality, then we may conclude that it is unqualifiedly rational to regard it as sufficiently reliable to use in belief formation. That is the position I will be endeavoring to support in this and the next two chapters.[8]

Since, as I fancy, I have already made a prima facie case for CMP's being a socially established doxastic practice, I will proceed as follows. First I will consider reasons for denying that it is a genuine, full-fledged experiential doxastic practice to which the conclusion of Chapter 4 applies. That will occupy me for the rest of this chapter. In Chapters 6 and 7 I will enter onto

[8]In arguing in this way for the rationality of engaging in CMP and taking it to be reliable, I will be assuming, as I pointed out at the end of Chapter 3, where I was still speaking in terms of an undifferentiated concept of MP in general, that CMP cannot be noncircularly shown to be reliable, in order to defend the rationality of CMP on a worst-case scenario. (If it can be noncircularly shown to be reliable, so much the better for my case.)

the second stage of the evaluation of a doxastic practice, the assessment of putative overriders of prima facie rationality, and consider reasons for denying that CMP is sufficiently reliable to be rationally engaged in, as well as considering whether CMP exhibits a significant degree of self-support. Having, as I will take it, disposed of the strongest objections to my position, I will take its prima facie claims to have been vindicated, and the rationality of regarding CMP as a source of epistemic justification to have been established, so far as this is possible for us.

Before entering onto this investigation, let me distinguish my defense of CMP from closely allied positions in the recent literature. Perhaps the closest neighbor is Swinburne's "principle of credulity", which he formulates as follows. "I suggest that it is a principle of rationality that (in the absence of special considerations) if it seems (epistemically) to a subject that x is present, then probably x is present; what one seems to perceive is probably so. How things seem to be is good grounds for a belief about how things are".[9] In our terms, its seeming to S that x is present renders the belief that x is present prima facie justified.

There are minor deviations between Swinburne's principle of credulity and our thesis. For example, his principle is limited to the belief that *x is present*, while ours is of much wider scope. Again, we are dealing with (putative) direct presentations to experience, rather than mere epistemic appearings (the experience's tending to give rise to a belief-forming tendency). However, the difference I want to emphasize is this. Swinburne's principle applies to experience-belief pairs individually, in isolation, while in my approach a principle of justification that applies to individual beliefs is grounded in a defense of the rationality of socially established doxastic practices. This provides support for my position that is unavailable to Swinburne. None of my arguments in Chapter 4 for the rationality of socially established doxastic practices is available to him. He can appeal only to the intuitive plausibility of his principle. I can, of course, recognize that too, and then provide the additional support that comes from thinking in terms of doxastic practices. Put another way, by recognizing the embeddedness of individual experiential beliefs in a socially rooted practice, I can thereby put the burden of proof on one who would deny the rationality of such belief formation. However, Swinburne's account is, within his chosen terms, well set out and well argued, and I welcome him as an ally.

Another close relative is Alvin Plantinga's view that certain kinds of beliefs about God (which largely overlap my M-beliefs) are "properly basic".[10] A basic belief is one that is not formed on the basis of other beliefs, and it is *properly* basic if the subject is justified in so forming it. It is clear that beliefs

[9]Swinburne 1979, p. 254.

[10]See Plantinga 1983 for the latest formulation of this view to date. Earlier formulations include 1979 and 1981.

formed solely on the basis of a putative experience of the subject of the belief count as basic, and, in Plantinga's terms, I am contending that many such beliefs (including many M-beliefs) are properly basic. But, of course, properly basic beliefs include more than those formed on the basis of experience—for example, beliefs in what is self-evidently true. Moreover, it seems that not all the beliefs about God that Plantinga would count as properly basic are formed on the basis of an experiential presentation of their subject. For example, he takes the beliefs about God a young person acquired from his parents to be properly basic. However, many of his examples would seem to fall within my category of M-beliefs.

> Upon confession and repentance I may feel forgiven, forming the belief *God forgives me for what I have done*. A person in grave danger may turn to God, asking for his protection and help; and of course he or she then has the belief that God is indeed able to hear and help if he sees fit. (1983, p. 80)

This does not make it explicit that the person takes God to be experientially *appearing* to her as doing these things, but that would be a natural way to fill out the examples. However, others cited in the same place are less naturally construed in my terms.

> . . . there is in us a disposition to believe propositions of the sort *this flower was created by God* or *this vast and intricate universe was created by God* when we contemplate the flower or behold the starry heavens or think about the vast reaches of the universe. (1983, p. 80)

At most, these beliefs are based on an indirect perception of God. Thus Plantinga's properly basic beliefs about God cannot be wholly assimilated to my M-beliefs. And where they deviate, I feel that there is a much stronger prima facie case for the justification of M-beliefs. There the subject has something quite explicit to go on, something she can "point to", namely the putative direct presentation of God to her experience as so-and-so. But in the Plantingian cases that are not of this sort, what we have is simply a strong tendency to form a certain belief in certain circumstances without any capacity to specify anything (doxastic or nondoxastic) that it is intuitively plausible to take as a basis. Plantinga does deny that his properly basic beliefs about God are without grounds; the grounds, he says, consist of the circumstances that elicit the belief. But if the only thing that fills this slot (elicits the belief) in the two cases last cited is seeing the flower or looking up into the sky, there is no intuitive plausibility to the claim that these experiences constitute grounds for the beliefs about divine agency. Why should *merely* seeing the flower give one a sufficient basis for believing that God created it? With the M-beliefs that God is sustaining me in being, on the other hand, there is a very definite intuitive plausibility to the supposition that the basis of that belief does provide a solid ground for supposing it to be true, for that basis consists in (what seems to the subject as) God presenting Himself to the subject as doing just that.[11]

We may also profitably compare the supports Plantinga and I give for our respective epistemological positions concerning properly basic beliefs about God. Plantinga supports his position in two ways. First, he launches an internal criticism of "classical foundationalism", which restricts the properly basic to propositions that are "self-evident, incorrigible, or evident to the senses", thus freezing beliefs about God out of the foundations (1983, pp. 59-63). Second, in addition to answering certain objections to his position, he claims that the proper method for developing principles of justification is inductive, proceeding from clear individual cases of justified or unjustified belief (pp. 75–78). Thus Plantinga takes it to be clear on reflection, in some cases, that beliefs about God are properly basic. He acknowledges that many people will disagree, but notes that we are accustomed to widespread disagreement in philosophical matters (p. 77).[12]

Plantinga's defense of his position is carefully crafted and very much to the point. Nevertheless, except for negative critiques, the defense is an internal one. It consists of taking one's stance within the doxastic practice in question and defying all comers to dislodge him. This is valuable, but it would also be worthwhile to have some positive reasons in support of the practice that appeal to more widely shared assumptions. This is what I have tried to do with my defense of the rationality of socially established doxastic practices.[13]

iii. Reasons for Denying that CMP Is a Full-fledged, Experiential Doxastic Practice

A. Partial Distribution of Mystical Perception

First, there is the point touched on in Chapter 4 (section v) to the effect that CMP, and indeed MP generally—unlike SP, and memory, introspective, and reasoning practices—is not universally engaged in by normal adult human

[11]Plantinga holds that God has instilled in us dispositions to form certain beliefs in certain circumstances. In the above, however, I was not going into possible theological reasons for the position but rather considering whether the experiential basis provides an intuitively plausible support. I should point out that Plantinga objects to my *general* account of epistemic justification in terms of *adequate grounds*. He points out that memory beliefs and beliefs in what seems self-evident, beliefs that are often justified, would not seem to owe that justification to any "grounds". And, with respect to this particular paragraph, he has suggested that his examples I quoted last might be analogized to memory or a priori beliefs rather than to sense-perceptual beliefs.

[12]More recently, Plantinga has been working out a new, general epistemology according to which epistemic "warrant" is a matter of beliefs being formed by the proper functioning of one's cognitive faculties. (The actual formulations are much more complicated.) And this will undoubtedly form a new basis for taking certain beliefs about God as properly basic. However, sufficient unto the day are the published versions thereof.

[13]For a fuller statement of my reactions to Plantinga's view see Alston 1985,

beings. That was brought up in Chapter 4 in connection with the question of whether social establishments should be allowed to confer prima facie rationality only on universal practices. There I argued that there is no reason to suppose that a practice engaged in by some proper part of the population is less likely to be a source of truth than one we all engage in. No doubt, this fact of partial distribution makes for various difficulties in discussing the problems of this book. When we are doing the epistemology of sense perception or memory or inductive reasoning, we can proceed on the assurance that all our readers are fellow participants. No such assumption can be made here. Nevertheless, I see no real reason for supposing that the partiality of participation derogates from the epistemic claims of a doxastic practice. Indeed, I do not find this consideration bulking large in the writings of my opponents, though it may exercise a sub rosa influence on unfavorable evaluations of MP. Thus it is worth pointing out that a priori it seems just as likely that some aspects of reality are accessible only to persons who satisfy certain conditions not satisfied by all human beings, as that some aspects are equally accessible to all. I cannot see any a priori reason for denigrating a practice either for being universal or for being partial. We have to learn from experience which features of the world are equally open to all and which are open only to an elite. Moreover, quite apart from the religious case, we can see many belief-forming practices, universally regarded as rational, that are practiced by only a small minority. Higher mathematics and theoretical physics certainly satisfy this description. But what about *experiential* doxastic practices? Well, in acknowledging SP to be universal we were speaking too roughly. There are large stretches of the territory that are open to all normal human beings, but there are also restricted domains that are available only to a chosen few. Only the connoisseur can perceptually discriminate the taste and smell of wines so finely as to be able to tell by tasting a wine from what Burgundy commune or Bordeaux chateau it originated. Relatively few persons can follow inner voices in complex orchestral performances. But such belief-forming practices are not denied epistemic credentials on the grounds of narrow distribution.[14]

Moreover, the belief-system ingredient in CMP provides explanation for the partial distribution. This will differ somewhat with the particular theological orientation, but the most basic point is that God has set certain requirements that must be met before He reveals Himself to our experience, at least consistently and with relative fullness. "Blessed are the pure in heart for they

[14]At this point the reader might protest. "In those sensory discrimination cases there are universally available ways to authenticate the alleged discriminatory power. It can be independently determined whether the wine our expert assigned to Chateau Margaux really was made there. But no such public validation is possible for MP." (See, e.g., Daniels 1989, Gale 1991.) That's as it may be. I am by no means claiming that MP is like these sensory-discrimination practices in all epistemically relevant respects. Here I am only making the point that an experiential doxastic practice should not be held suspect just on grounds of partial distribution. The question of the kinds of intersubjective checks available will be addressed later in this chapter.

shall see God." Again, the details of this vary, but it is generally acknowledged in the tradition that an excessive preoccupation and concern with worldly goods, certain kinds of immorality—particularly self-centeredness and unconcern with one's fellows—and a mind that is closed to the possibility of communion with God, are all antithetical to an awareness of God's presence. This being the case, and given well-known facts about human predilections, it is the reverse of unexpected that not all people should participate in mystical perception.

We can see this criticism from partial distribution to exhibit two vices, each of which we will encounter repeatedly in the ensuing discussion. First, in denigrating CMP for not exhibiting a certain feature of SP, namely, universal distribution, the objector is guilty of what I shall call *epistemic imperialism*, unwarrantedly taking the standards of one doxastic practice as normative for all. The "unwarrantedly" qualification is crucial. Some features of SP are de rigueur for any respectable practice,—for example, embodying certain distinctive input-output functions. But universal distribution, so I claim, is not one of those. On reflection we can see no reason for supposing that every reliable doxastic practice will be engaged in by all normal, adult human beings. Second, in pointing to uncontroversial examples of reliable doxastic practices with quite restricted distribution—theoretical physics and wine-tasting—I show the objector to be guilty of using an (unwarranted) double standard. CMP is being condemned for features shared by other practices that are approved. This is to apply *arbitrarily* a double standard, as when one takes whites to be innocent until proved guilty but takes blacks to be guilty until proved innocent, or when one requires a higher level of achievement for women than for men in executive positions. Again the qualifiers, "unwarrantedly" and "arbitrarily", are important. There is nothing wrong with applying different standards to two candidates if there is sufficient reason to do so. It is quite in order to require a higher level of education for executives than for manual laborers. But no reason can be given for accepting some doxastic practices that extend only to a certain elite as epistemically in order, and then rejecting CMP *on the very ground* that it is so restricted. Thus the objection from partial distribution is particularly rich in vices. It exhibits two that we shall be encountering repeatedly: (1) *imperialism*, unwarrantedly taking features of one practice to be normative for others, and (2) *double standard*, unwarrantedly making requirements of one practice from which others are exempted.

B. Extent of the Organized Practice

Second, there are doubts as to whether there really is any widely shared *practice* of forming perceptual beliefs about God, as we have depicted doxastic practices. This may be based on a doubt that the formation of such beliefs is widely dispersed in the population. I have already spoken to this in Chapter

1, where I cited sociological studies that indicate that an experiential awareness of God is not at all uncommon (fn. 24). But even if many people form M-beliefs, there is still the question of whether there is a widely shared *practice* of the sort I have labelled 'CMP'. Isn't it more accurate to say that for the most part people who take themselves to perceive God are each "going it alone", doing it on their own, without reliance on the kind of socially established procedures required for a full-blown doxastic practice? No doubt, in Catholic, monastic mystical circles, there is a well-organized practice of cultivating union with God, including putative direct experiential awareness of God, and a standardized set of criteria for distinguishing the real thing from the spurious. But why suppose that other Christians who take themselves to perceive God and who form M-beliefs on that basis are involved in any such practice?

We must be careful not to suppose that the structure of a doxastic practice has to be explicitly formulated in the minds of the participants. Here, as with many other things, the tacit is the normal and the explicit the exception. Just as people internalize and utilize systems of semantic and syntactic rules without ever becoming explicitly aware of them as such, and just as they reason and criticize reasoning in accordance with principles they never explicitly formulate, so it is with doxastic practices. One picks up the mastery of a language from one's social surroundings without any explicit formulation of the structure of the language, and one picks up ways of perceptually recognizing chickens and dogs and houses and apples without anyone ever saying in so many words what the identifying marks are. In the same way one picks up ways of recognizing God and His activities, and criteria for separating verdical perception of God from counterfeits, without any of this ever being explicitly formulated. If rules of speech and of belief formation could not be operative without being verbally articulated, our voices would be stilled and our minds emptied of cognitive content. We are bound together by ties that take hard digging to bring to light. This is not to say that what is internalized in learning CMP is as definite and as uniform across the population as is the structure of a natural language or the marks of sense-perceivable items. But the existence of a socially shared practice is compatible with a certain degree of looseness and individual variation in the constituent rules and criteria.

Considerations like these are sufficient to show that the absence of explicit awareness of the constitutive principles of a doxastic practice on the part of S does not show that S is not a participant. But they do not show that CMP *is* widely engaged in outside monastic circles. An ideally convincing case for this would be difficult to bring off. We would have to show that a significant proportion of mainline Christians who form M-beliefs on the basis of experience mostly do so in accordance with common principles for going from features of the experience to belief contents, and share common grounds for the criticism of such beliefs. The former task is rendered difficult, if not impossible, by our lack of an adequate vocabulary for basic phenomenal qualities of mystical experience. Nevertheless, a survey of reports like those cited in Chapter 1 strongly suggests that people in the Christian community do tend to make the same or similar attributions to God on the basis of similar experiences. The latter task, determining whether there are common principles of criticism, is somewhat more manageable, though the practical problems of subjecting an adequate sample to the required tests is staggering. But just by doing a survey of the relevant literature we can verify the claim that an overrider system of the sort I have been describing is often operative. Let's begin with professed mystics in organized monastic communities, who are very much preoccupied with distinguishing genuine from spurious experiences of God and often explicitly discuss criteria. I will restrict myself here to passages from St. Teresa's *Autobiography* (1957). First an expression of concern as to whether certain experiences are genuine.

> His Majesty began to give me the prayer of quiet very frequently, and often the prayer of union too, which lasted for some time. Since there have been cases lately of women who have been grossly deceived and subjected to great illusions through the machinations of the devil, I was very much afraid. For I felt very great delight and sweetness, which it was often beyond my power to avoid. On the other hand I was conscious of a deep inward assurance that this was of God, especially when I was engaged in prayer, and I found that I was the better for these experiences and had developed greater fortitude. But as soon as I became a little distracted, I would be afraid again, and would wonder whether it was not the devil that was suspending my understanding and making me think this a good thing, in order to deprive me of mental prayer, to stop me from my meditating on the Passion, and to prevent my using my mind. (P. 162)

From time to time St. Teresa identifies some criteria or marks by which the genuine presence of God can be recognized.

> I believe that it is possible to tell whether this state comes from the spirit of God or whether, starting from devotion given us by God, we have attained it by our own endeavours. For if, as I have said before, we try of our own accord to pass on to this quiet of the will, it leads to nothing. Everything is quickly over, and the result is aridity. If it comes from the devil, I think an experienced soul will realize it. For it leaves disquiet behind it, and very little humility, and does not do much to prepare the soul for the effects which are produced when it comes from God. It brings neither light to the understanding nor strength to the will. (P. 108)

> I think it possible that a person who has laid some request before God with most loving concern may imagine that he hears a voice telling him whether his prayer will be granted or not. This may well be, though once he has heard some genuine message, he will see clearly what this voice is, for there is a great difference between the two experiences. If his answer has been invented by the understanding, however subtly it may be contrived, he perceives the intellect ordering the words and speaking them. It is just as if a person were composing a speech . . .and the understanding will then realize that it is not listening but working, and that the words it is inventing are imprecise and fanciful; they have not the clarity

of the real locution. In such cases it is in our power to deflect our attention, just as we can stop speaking and be silent. But in the true locution, this cannot be done. Another sign, which is the surest of all, is that these false locutions leave no results, whereas when the Lord speaks, words lead to deeds; and although the words may be of reproof and not of devotion, they prepare the soul, make it ready, and move it to tenderness. (P. 175)

By now I have had so much experience of the devil's work that he knows I can recognize him and so torments me less in these ways than he used to. His part in an experience can be detected by the restlessness and discomfort with which it begins, by the turmoil that he creates in the soul so long as it lasts, also by the darkness and affliction into which he plunges it, and by its subsequent dryness and indisposition for prayer or anything else that is good . . . In true humility, on the other hand, although the soul knows its wretchedness, and although we are distressed to see what we are, there is no attendant turmoil or spiritual unrest. True humility does not bring darkness or aridity, but on the contrary gives the soul peace, sweetness, and light. (P. 215)

. . . I merely believed the revelation to be true in the sense that it was not contrary to what is written in the Holy Scriptures, or to the laws of the Church, which we are obliged to keep. (P. 239)

If it proceeded from our own mind, not only would it not have the great effects that is has, but it would have none at all . . . instead of being restored and fortified, the soul will become wearier; it will become exhausted and nauseated. But it is impossible to exaggerate the riches that accompany a true vision; it brings health and comfort even to the body. I advanced this argument, amongst others, when they told me—as they often did—that my visions were of the devil and were all imaginary . . . I once said to some of these people whom I used to consult: "If you were to tell me that someone I knew well and to whom I had just been talking is not really himself, and that I was imagining things and you knew what the truth really was, I would believe your statement rather than my own eyes. But if this person had left me some jewels as a pledge of his great love, and if I were still holding them, and if I had possessed no jewels before and now found myself rich where I had been poor, I could not possibly believe that this was delusion, even if I wanted to." I said too that I could show them these jewels, for everyone who knew me saw clearly that my soul had changed . . . I could not believe, therefore, that if the devil were doing this in order to deceive me and drag me down to hell, he would adopt means so contrary to his purpose as to take away my vices and give me virtues and strength instead. For I clearly saw that these visions had made me a different person. (P. 202)

From such passages spiritual directors and mystical theologians have distilled criteria of genuine perceptions of God. Here is a selection from a list given in de Guibert (1953).[15]

[15]See also Parente 1945. These two are simply plucked from a large number of books of

True	False
Intellect	
1. Not concerned with useless affairs	Futile, useless, vain preoccupations
2. Discretion	Exaggerations, excesses
Will	
1. Interior peace	Perturbation, disquiet
2. Trust in God	Presumption or despair
3. Patience in pains	Impatience with trials
4. Simplicity, sincerity	Duplicity, dissimulation
5. Charity that is meek, kindly, self-forgetful	False, bitter pharisaical zeal

I know of no canonical systematization of these criteria, but it seems to me highly plausible to take the moral criteria to be the most fundamental. The criteria of conformity to the tradition (Scripture and the Church) are obviously derivative. For how was that tradition built up, except by taking some phenomena rather than others as involving genuine perception of God? As for the way in which the locutions or whatever are presented, it seems plausible to suppose that whatever phenomenal character we fasten on—distinctness, seeming to come from beyond oneself, or whatever—this could possibly be a result of psychological processes within oneself if those processes are sufficiently blocked off from consciousness. But the fruits of the experience in the way of sanctification of the individual are another matter. As Teresa says, if a pledge of jewels has been left, it is difficult not to believe that this is the real thing. We might think of mystics as learning from experience which phenomenal features are regularly correlated with the kinds of results (humility, love, joy, peace, etc.) that would be expected from prolonged contact with God; these features can then be taken as derivative marks of genuineness.

Thus "professional" mystics, more generally, persons under spiritual direction, do recognize and use a fairly definite set of criteria of genuineness. With "amateurs", whose participation in the practice is not explicitly organized, the picture is not so clear. For one thing, the reports here are very sketchy. Even if one or another of these persons is sufficiently reflective to articulate her overrider system, they have not written extensively enough to communicate it to us. Moreover, there is no doubt but that they take a less critical attitude toward their mystical experiences than do monastics. Not being under the supervision of a spiritual adviser and lacking contact with others who have had longer experience in the things of the spirit, they are not so sensitized to the possibilities of delusion and the need for external criteria; hence they tend

spiritual direction that say essentially the same thing. For a famous Protestant treatment see Jonathan Edwards, *A Treatise Concerning Religious Affections* (1746), ed. John E. Smith (New Haven, Conn.: Yale University Press, 1959).

much more to repose complete confidence in their spontaneous understanding of their experiences.

Nevertheless, it is unlikely that a contemporary educated believer should suppose it to be impossible that what seems to be a direct awareness of God is delusory. Our contemporaries are more likely, if anything, to suppose that the chances are against such experiences being veridical. Hence when such a person finds herself spontaneously believing that she is experiencing God, she is unlikely to be unaware of the possibility that the experience may not be what it seems, even if in the heat of the moment this idea does not occur to her. And it is quite plausible that if she goes so far as to explicitly raise the question of genuineness, the kinds of criteria mentioned above would appeal to her as the right ones to use: conformity with the tradition, concordance with what God could be expected to be, do, or say, and fruits in the way of spiritual development. Hence, though direct evidence is in short supply, I think it quite plausible to suppose that CMP, as I have described it, is widespread at various levels of explicitness within the Christian community. However, I want to emphasize that the extent of distribution is not crucial for my central contentions. Even if CMP were confined to monastics or to other very restricted groups, it would still be worthy of consideration as a possible source of epistemic justification.

To provide a bit of evidence for the claims of the previous paragraph, I will quote some unpublished remarks of Robert M. Adams, made in the course of commenting on a precursor of Chapter 1.

> . . . I would like to reflect on a religious experience of my own adolescence. I wanted to feel God's presence in prayer. After a time of looking for it, I noticed a certain feeling that I commonly had when I prayed. It was in some ways rather like a sensation. I wondered whether this could be the experience of the presence of God. I think I sometimes took it to be so. But was it really so? Did I perceive God in that experience? I had my doubts then, and I have them now.
>
> The experience certainly did have a content that went beyond anything I could convey discursively. One who had not had a similar experience could not know exactly what I felt . . . I do remember some of my misgivings about it, however. One main misgiving I would express, in the context of my present remarks, by a question about what I felt that went beyond anything I could grasp or express discursively. Was it something about *God*, or only something about *me*? Of course, in those moments when I believed the experience to be genuine I took myself to be feeling the presence of a God who had all the attributes I believed God to have—but that's discursive content. . . .
>
> A more disturbing doubt about my adolescent feeling of God's presence in prayer has to do with its causes. Was it something I was doing to myself? Was it perhaps a distinctive complex bodily sensation caused by squeezing my eyelids shut very hard and unconsciously controlling my breathing in a certain way? Or was it simply begotten of my imagination by my desire to feel God's presence?

I certainly do not wish to suggest that a brilliant, sophisticated philosopher like Robert Adams, even as an adolescent, is typical of the amateur mystic. Nevertheless, I find in this account a nice presentation of doubts that would naturally occur to a person in the contemporary world who tends to suppose himself to be directly aware of God. And though Adams does not get so far here as to excogitate ways of resolving his question, it would be natural to go from his questionings to criteria not unlike those of Teresa.

C. Not a Genuine Source of New Information.

But even if CMP is admitted to be a genuine doxastic practice, there may still be doubts as to whether it is one that is capable of forming new beliefs from experiential input. It may be suspected that what the practice amounts to is just reading one's prior religious beliefs into a cognitively indifferent experiential matrix, rather than forming new beliefs on the basis of experience, plugging into a genuinely new source of information.

> Even when we discount all the identifiable conditions in which illusions, dreams, deceptions and mistakes occur . . . one influence is likely to remain which disposes him or her to have or to interpret numinous experience in a particular way. That influence is the cultural and religious environment of the person; the possession of one world view rather than another, or at the very least, familiarity with, or concern with, one system of ideas rather than another. Now there is ample evidence to show that numinous religious experiences are frequently received as, indeed are normally articulated by means of, the religious forms, symbols and figures with which one is familiar, and these may be as incompatibly different as a feeling of union with the god at a Dionysian festival on an Aegean island, or a vision of the Blessed Virgin Mary in a Dublin suburb. To put it baldly: one encounters what one has been brought up to expect to encounter. This, not the independent existence of multiple and incompatible external objects, seems to account for the similarities of what is reported as the object of religious experience within a given community, and for differences between communities with differing world views.[16]

This claim is closely connected with a similar charge I considered in Chapter 1 to the effect that mystical experiences are not genuinely perceptual, even phenomenologically, since the subjects are just reading antecedent beliefs into essentially subjective experiences. The difference between the two claims is this. In Chapter 1 we were considering whether our subjects were correct in taking their experiences to be phenomenologically of a perceptual sort, involving an experiential presentation of something or other to one's awareness

[16] J. C. A. Gaskin, *The Quest for Eternity* (New York: Penguin Books, 1984), pp. 101–2. Gaskin is making a number of points simultaneously here, including the problem posed by the plurality of incompatible forms of MP. Here I am concerned with the point that the content of the experience is determined by one's antecedent beliefs.

as so-and-so. We may take that question to have been settled in the affirmative. That is the way the experience presents itself to its subjects. Now we are asking about the belief formation that stems from that experiential presentation. To what extent is it a source of new information, and to what extent does it just read back to the subject the beliefs the subject brings to the experience?

Even though the questions are different, we can draw on some of the same points in answering this one. First let's separate the charge that one brings an antecedently possessed conceptual scheme to one's experience from the charge that one acquires no new beliefs. The former clearly holds as much for SP as for CMP. When I look around me I typically make use of my familiar and much used concepts of houses, trees, grass, and so on, in recognizing what I see and forming beliefs about them. And so it is with CMP. The Christian typically brings the conceptual framework of Christian theology to her putative experience of God and makes use of it in construing what she is perceiving and how that is presenting itself to her. To be sure, perception *can* lead to conceptual development, in both SP and MP. People and societies do acquire new concepts and modify old concepts over time, and presumably their experience plays some role in this. Indeed, how did the individual acquire the concepts that she possessed prior to a particular experience? Past experiences played some role in this unless the concepts were purely innate. Nevertheless, I dare say that the overwhelming majority of perceptual situations, both SP and CMP, involve the application of antecedently possessed concepts. The main point I want to make is that in neither case does this have any tendency to prevent one from genuinely perceiving objective realities or gaining new information about them. If it did we would rarely learn anything in sense perception. Indefinitely many specific bits of information can be formulated by the same conceptual scheme, and the fact that I antecedently possess the concepts that I use to articulate a given perception has no tendency to show that I already had the information I claim to derive from that perception.

But what about the second charge? Does the alleged mystic perceiver learn anything genuinely new in her perception, or is she just reading antecedently held beliefs into it? In considering this question we can usefully distinguish two relations of a particular perceptual belief to the perceiver's prior stock of beliefs. First, the belief may represent a net addition to the stock. This is frequently the case in both SP and MP. As for the latter, remember that M-beliefs often concern God's specific relation to the individual perceiver at the moment, and this kind of information obviously was not in the background belief system. I don't already know or believe, prior to the experience, that God is comforting or upbraiding me at that moment, or that God tells me then what I ought to concentrate on now. Second, the perception may present what one already knows or believes, save for updating. I look at my house as I approach and it presents itself to my experience as shingled. But

I already knew that it was shingled; the only possibility for a net increment is that I learn from the perception that it is still shingled. Likewise, in MP God may appear to me in an experience as supremely loving, but I already firmly believed that. There isn't even any significant updating to be derived here, if one can assume that changes in the divine nature are out of the question. Even so, the experience can add to my total sum of justification for believing that God is loving, even if it doesn't add to the firmness of the belief.[17] And of course, there are obvious noncognitive advantages in experiencing God's love in addition to just believing or knowing "at a distance" that it is there.

But though these considerations draw the teeth of the claim that CMP cannot be a source of new beliefs, it must be acknowledged that CMP does not typically alter the major outlines of a person's faith. Ordinarily the subject already has a more or less firm Christian faith, which is left largely unchanged by mystical experience. What the experience does yield, cognitively, is: (a) information about God's particular relations to the subject; (b) additional grounds for beliefs already held, particularly the belief that God does exist; (c) additional "insight" into facets of the scheme. Examples of the latter range from the more to the less controversial. On the former end are reports by St. Teresa to have gained new understanding of such doctrines as the Trinity and the Incarnation by having "seen" how God is three persons or how the divine and human natures of Christ are united.[18] On the less controversial side is the fact that one has more of a grasp of what a certain fact is like by having experienced it, rather that just believed it. I may believe on general grounds that my wife loves me, but I have a much fuller sense of what this love is like if I have experienced a variety of manifestations. And so it is here.

I would like to stress that even if one acquired no new beliefs at all from CMP, it could provide additional justification for old beliefs. In the final chapter I will address the question of how mystical perception interacts with other grounds for religious belief in the total spectrum of such grounds. There we will note how perceiving God can shore up the belief system at points at which it would otherwise be a bit shaky.

D. Obvious Differences between Sense Experience and Mystical Experience

In Chapter 1, section viii, I pointed out some of the obvious and important differences between mystical experience and sense experience. Sense experience is continuously, insistently, and unavoidably present during all our wak-

[17]If a belief is already maximally firm, them obviously, any additional support I acquire for it will not make it firmer.

[18]St. Teresa 1957, chap. 39, pp. 304–5.

ing hours; mystical experience, except for a few choice souls, is a rare phenomenon. Sense experience, especially vision, is vivid and richly detailed, bursting with information, more than we can possibly encode; mystical experience is usually but dim, meager, and obscure. The net effect of these differences is to render MP much less useful as a source of information, even if its epistemic credentials are in order. One might think that these differences could not possibly be adduced by any reasonable person as a reason for refusing to take seriously the idea that MP is a genuine source of knowledge and/or justified belief; but that would be a mistake. Daniels (1989) points out that whereas sense perception reveals indefinitely many trivial and unimportant facts about its objects, along with things of interest to us, mystical perception reveals only what is of such supreme importance as to call forth affective reactions of ecstasy, joy, and peace.

> People with sight notice and can attest to complexes of things whose presence or absence is indifferent to their desires: like the textures and gradations of hues and shades of color on the ceiling of an office they find themselves in or the pattern of cracks in a sidewalk. . . . Gifted musicians, judging contests of their juniors, may hear in great detail aspects of performances that, while not thoroughly abysmal, are quite undistinguished and forgettable. (P. 493)

On the other hand:

> Those who claim to have religious experiences tend not to acquire complexes of trivial, unimportant beliefs from them. This lack is a very significant one. Claims of religious experience tend to be just too important and too narrowly focused and simple. Is it that the religious simply fail to report to the rest of us or to each other the trivial yet complex webs of facts their religious experiences reveal? If the answer is no, then we must begin to entertain suspicions that the explanation for these experiences does not lie in any perceived religious reality, but is rather the effect of some other cause - perhaps excessive emotion and fervor, perhaps the belief that since God causes everything, His hand will be seen in the exceptional experiences life does bring. (Pp. 498–99)

Daniels has identified one possible explanation of the difference cited. But perhaps this explanation will seem less compelling when we reflect that the difference in question is simply one aspect of the difference I have already noted as to the amount of informational content. Since SP, particularly vision, carries such an overload of information it is not at all surprising that much of it will be trivial and uninteresting. Whereas, given the meager content of mystical experience, there is no room, so to speak, for a lot of surplus baggage. If I'm walking to California from New York, I won't take along all the unnecessary frills I would take if I were driving. Of course, it is *conceivable* that a much thinner mode of experience would carry the same proportion of the uninteresting, but it seems much more plausible that details unrelated to our needs would be found in modes of cognition that are overloaded with information. Whether we think of perception as designed by God, or as "selected" by evolution, its basic function is to give us information that we need for the conduct of life. A meager source would have to concentrate on what is important, or it would not be chosen or selected at all. Only the rich source can "afford" to give us lots of extras. Hence I can't see that the restriction of MP to what is of interest counts against its epistemic pretensions.

E. Checks and Tests of Particular Perceptual Beliefs

We have been making much of the fact that overrider systems are essential to doxastic practices, and we have brought out something of the character of the overrider system to be found in CMP. Interestingly enough, a favorite criticism of MP has been its lack of an effective overrider system. A much-discussed statement of this criticism is found in Martin 1959.

> There are no tests agreed upon to establish genuine experience of God and distinguish it decisively from the nongenuine. Indeed, many theologians deny the possibility of any such test or set of tests. (P. 67)

> It is only when one comes to such a case as knowing God that the society of tests and checkup procedures, which surround other instances of knowing, completely vanishes. What is put in the place of these tests and checking procedures is an immediacy of knowledge that is supposed to carry its own guarantee. (P. 70)

> Because "having direct experience of God" does not admit the relevance of a society of tests and checking procedures, it tends to place itself in the company of the other ways of knowing which preserve their self-sufficiency, "uniqueness", and "incommunicability" by making a psychological and not an existential claim. For example, "I seem to see a piece of blue paper", requires no further test or checking procedure in order to be considered true. (P. 72)

> . . . the religious statement "I have direct experience of God" is of a different status from the physical object statement "I see a star" and shows a distressing similarity to the low-claim assertion "I seem to see a star." (P. 75)

A terminological note before we proceed. I have taken Martin's reference to "a society of tests and checkup procedures" to be equivalent to my "overrider system". And yet tests can have a positive as well as a negative outcome; they do not always override. Actually I have been thinking of my "overrider systems" in this way all along, though the term fails to indicate that. From now on, whether I speak of "checks and tests" or "overrider systems", I should be taken as thinking of procedures and criteria for testing beliefs for correctness and putative justifications for efficacy, where these tests may have either a positive or a negative outcome.

As these quoted passages indicate, Martin takes the lack of such checking procedures to cancel out any objective truth claim that goes beyond a report of one's present conscious experience. I won't spend any time on this charge; it is based on a public empirical verifiability criterion of meaningfulness that I see no reason to accept. Apart from reliance on such a criterion the lack of checks and tests cannot prevent one from *claiming*, as an objective truth, that God is, or is doing, so-and-so. The charge I will take seriously is epistemic. The lack of a system of checks and tests prevents M-beliefs from being experientially justified. We find this version in Rowe (1982), where he alleges that the absence of effective checking procedures prevents the application of Swinburne's "principle of credulity" to mystical experience, where the principle of credulity is roughly equivalent to our claim that established experiential doxastic practices confer prima facie justification on their outputs.[19]

> . . . there is an important difference between (1) knowing how to proceed to find positive reasons, if there should be any, for rejecting an experience as probably delusive, and (2) not knowing how to proceed to find such positive reasons if there should be any. When we are in situation (1), as we clearly are in the case of those who habitually drink alcohol to excess and report experiences which they take to be of rats and snakes, the application of the principle of credulity is clearly in order. But when we are in situation (2) as we seem to be in the case of religious experience, I am doubtful that the application of the principle of credulity is warranted. Since we don't know what circumstances make for delusory religious experiences . . . we can't really go about the process of determining whether there are or are not positive reasons for thinking religious experiences to be probably delusive. (Pp. 90–91)

But, contra Martin and Rowe, there are, as we have seen, such checking procedures. How can Martin and Rowe have missed this?

Well, Martin makes it explicit that the targets of his criticism are people who represent "religious experience" as "self-authenticating."[20] In one of the passages quoted above he says: "What is put in the place of these tests and checking procedures is an immediacy of knowledge that is supposed to carry its own guarantee" (P. 70). To claim that my experience is self-authenticating is to deny that there is any point to external tests of its veridicality. What Martin did not realize is how atypical of the religious tradition such claims of self-authentication are. The great mystics of the Middle Ages and Counter-Reformation almost weary one with their incessant talk about the difficulties of distinguishing genuine from counterfeit perception of God. They are keenly aware that we cannot uncritically accept any old claim to be directly aware of God; these experiences might be due to the devil or to an overheated imagination. As we have seen, they devote much thought to the articulation of criteria that will enable us to tell when we have the real thing. "Self-authentication" is

[19]For a discussion of differences between Swinburne and myself on this, see section ii.
[20]See Chapter, 2, section iii.

the furthest thing from their mind. And it is they, rather than the proponents of "self-authentication", that are typical of CMP.

If confronted with this criticism Martin might say that the situation with MP is still quite different from SP in that there is a single overrider system for the latter but not for the former; and we have seen that this is undeniable. This would be a form of the general problem of the plurality of incompatible religious traditions that we will tackle in Chapter 7. But that does not negate the fact that each form of MP does have a working overrider system.

Perhaps Martin's next complaint, if he were available to continue the discussion, would be that the overrider system for CMP and other forms of MP is of no real value since it is, at least in part, based on the very kinds of perceptual beliefs it is designed to correct, and since it employs the very modes of belief formation the outputs of which it is used to check. If we appeal to the doctrinal system of Christianity to check the accuracy of a particular report of divine perception, we are appealing to beliefs that we have reason to accept only if that mode of perception is a source of justification. And if we, more directly, check one person's reported experience of God by determining its consonance or dissonance with other persons' reports, we are relying directly on just the source of belief that is in question. Now, as we have seen and will see in more detail in Chapter 8, there are other sources of a religious belief system, but the point to be made here is that even if the overrider system were based solely on MP and what can be inferred from its products, it would be in just the same situation as SP. How do we proceed when seeking to determine whether to accept S's report that he saw a fighter plane flying over his house at 11:40 A.M.? We consider, on the basis of what is known about air traffic in that area at that time, what the likelihood is that a fighter plane would be in that spot at 11:40. If necessary we can carry out tests on S's visual apparatus. In both cases we are tapping into our general background-belief system that was built up on sense perception, precisely the source of the belief under investigation. Or, more simply, we can determine whether others in the area saw a fighter plane at that time. Here we are relying more directly on perceptual beliefs to check another perceptual belief. So even if the system for checking the outputs of CMP rely on the use of CMP itself, Martin cannot make that a reproach to CMP unless he is prepared to flush SP down the drain as well.[21] The *double standard* again.

I want to underline the point that in SP our procedures for checking a particular perceptual belief make use of what we have learned about the world from SP, together with memory and reasoning; that is, they make use of what we have learned from within the very doxastic practice being tested. Indeed, we have to make use of what we have learned from SP to determine what tests are relevant. We don't know a priori what conditions must be satisfied in

[21]This point is made effectively in Peter Losin's "Experience of God and the Principle of Credulity: A Reply to Rowe", *Faith and Philosophy*, vol. 4, no. 1 (Jan. 1987).

order for a particular perceptual report to be acceptable, nor was this revealed to us by an angel. And once we have established the tests we have to make use of perceptual information to determine whether the conditions are satisfied in a particular case. Although I won't take time for a survey, I believe this to be true of all our basic sources of information. We can't critically evaluate deductive reasoning without using, or relying on the results of, deductive reasoning; we can't assess a memory claim without using, or relying on the results of, memory; and so on. Thus CMP is in very good company when it exhibits this feature.[22]

As long as we are putting words into Martin's mouth, let's give him one more shot. What makes CMP unacceptable, he might say, is that its system of tests is markedly inferior to that of SP. Let's agree that in both cases a perceptual report can be checked for conformity with a background system of belief as to how things are in that sphere of reality; in both cases we can, relying on what we have learned from the doxastic practice in question, determine whether the subject is, in general, an accurate observer, or likely to be such. But although such considerations can serve to disqualify a candidate they are hardly decisive on the positive side. Even if what I report is the sort of thing that *could* be the case, given our general knowledge, and even if I don't exhibit any features that we have learned to inhibit accurate observation, it is still an open question whether what I report was in fact the case. In SP, but not in CMP, we have a more decisive test in the confirmation or disconfirmation by other observers of the same scene. Suppose I report seeing a morel (a particularly delicious wild mushroom) at a certain spot in the forest. It can be determined in various ways whether I really did see a morel at that spot. A number of other observers can take a good look at that spot at (approximately) that time and report whether they saw a morel. If it is clear that there is something there that looks like a morel, further tests, including microscopic examination, can be made to determine whether the object really is a morel, rather than some other wild fungus. Tests like these are capable of providing strong confirmation as well as strong disconfirmation for a perceptual report in SP.

But in CMP none of this is available. Let's focus on the testimony of other observers, since it is overwhelmingly obvious that nothing like microscopic examination or chemical tests can be carried out on God. The crucial point here is not that not all persons report experiences of God. Not all persons report having seen morels either. The point, rather, is that for SP, but not for CMP, we can specify conditions under which the experience of one subject is *relevant* to the testing of the report of another subject. If S does (doesn't) see a morel in some other place, or at the same place in some other year, that has

[22]Note the connection of this point with the thesis of Chapter 3 that any otherwise effective argument for the reliability of SP, and other basic sources of belief, will fall into epistemic circularity.

no bearing (at least no crucial bearing) on whether my report was accurate. It is only visual perception of that spot at (approximately) that time that can provide a maximally decisive test. For SP we are able to determine which perceptions have what bearing on the credibility of the report in question. We can't always do this in as simple a fashion as the "same time, same place" formula. If the alleged object is, unlike a morel, something that moves around a lot, like a human being or other animal, or like the plane in the previous example, then the recipes will be more complicated. With respect to the plane report, what perceptions of others are relevant will depend on the direction in which the plane was moving and at what speed. Where we have to take into account the modifications undergone by an object over a considerable period of time, as we do with a seventeenth-century traveler's report of a Cambodian temple, the recipes are still more complicated. But whatever the complexity, we have a considerable capacity to discriminate between relevant and irrelevant experiences of others in the critical examination of a particular sense-perceptual report.

There is nothing comparable to this in CMP. God is always present everywhere, if present anywhere, and so the whereabouts of a subject has no bearing. If a CMP report were to be assessed on the SP model, we would have to say that S really perceived God at t only if every normal subject perceives God all the time. But no participant in CMP would take this to be an appropriate test. "Why should we expect God to be perceivable by everyone all the time even if He is present everywhere all the time?" he might ask. To be sure, in what I said above I seriously oversimplified the SP test. Another observer at the right time and place will not serve as a check if his sensory apparatus is not in proper working order or if he is too distracted by other matters. And so it might be suggested that other persons' experiences or lack thereof count toward the assessment of my putative perception of God only if the other person is sufficiently "receptive" to the presence of God, is "spiritually attuned", and the like. But in SP we have tests of the condition of the sensory apparatus and of the mental and emotional condition of the subject that are independent of whether the person reports a given object. How about CMP? Well, it's not that we have no tests of spiritual receptivity. Those who address such matters typically lay down such characteristics as the possession of certain virtues (humility, compassion) and a loving, obedient attitude toward God as productive of openness to the presence of God. But no alleged perceiver of God would take the veracity of her claims to be determined by whether everyone (or almost everyone) who passes the tests for spiritual receptivity is always aware of God.[23] That is still an unreasonable requirement.

[23]Since the condition of the observer is an independent check on perceptual reports, as well as being involved in the check by other observers, these considerations show that the former is also not as tight a check in CMP as in SP. But in the present discussion we are confining ourselves to SP checks that can decisively confirm as well as disconfirm; the condition of the observer, like the background belief system, can serve as a decisive check only on the negative side.

If I continue to insist that I saw a morel in the face of massive disconfirmation by observers at that time and place who pass the standard tests for competence, then I would be branded as irrational by community standards. But nothing analogous can be said for religious communities. The reports are not held subject to community consensus *in that way*. There are no clear-cut conditions such that we are prepared to admit that God exists and is perceived by me if and only if a person who satisfies those conditions perceives God whenever God is present to him, that is, continuously.

We have put all this into the mouth of C. B. Martin,[24] but that is hardly necessary, since there is no dearth of writers who have gone on record as making these points. Thus Rowe, as quoted above, says "we don't know what circumstances make for delusory experiences" but then goes on to add a phrase I deliberately suppressed at that time, "and we don't know what the conditions are which, if satisfied, one would have the experience of God if there is a God to be experienced"—a formulation almost word-for-word like some of those in the last paragraph. Here are some other samples. First from O'Hear 1984.

> The likelihood of an objective reality being causally related to certain experiences will be very much increased if (i) we are able to predict accurately further experiences of our own or others due to our assuming the existence of the reality, (ii) some of these future experiences of our own are experiences of senses other than the original sense involved, and (iii) other people can corroborate what we are perceiving. . . . Condition (iii) reflects the not unreasonable presumption that if something is objectively real, it will have similar effects on other similar observers similarly placed. . . .
> The religious interpretation of religious experience, however, comes off quite badly under all three conditions. (Pp. 45–46)

> This does not show that there is no religious sense, of course, nor that the non-religious are right to reject the idea. After all, as Ayer has pointed out (1976, p. 6), the sighted man might have been unable to correlate his visual experiences with tactile or auditory experiences, yet he would still have every right to insist on his extra sense, and the blind people would be wrong to reject his claims. But the argument for such a dissociated sense, giving insight into a real world, even for the sighted man himself, would surely depend on his visual experience having a degree of consistency, regularity, and predictability, features which are mostly absent in the case of religious experience. (P. 47)

[24]Actually, though Martin does not say in so many words that checks and tests of the SP sort are required for the making of *justified* claims, he does say things that suggest that is the way he is thinking of the matter. " . . . if Jones wanted to know whether it was really a star that he saw, he could not only take photographs, look through a telescope, and the like but also ask others if they saw the star. If a large number of people denied seeing the star, Jones's claim about the star's existence would be weakened" (p. 73). This is then contrasted with a case in which a person's conviction that he has experienced God is held to in the face of a lack of any such corroboration.

> What I am suggesting, then, is first, that religious experiences lack either that degree of independent testability or the degree of regularity which in the case of sensory experience allows us to speak of the experiences supporting our physical object scheme. (P. 48)[25]

Here are some other authors who make similar points.

> But why can't we have an argument based upon religious experiences for the existence of the apparent object of a given religious experience and its bearing the right sort of causal relation to the experience? There can be such an argument only if religious experiences count as cognitive. But they can count as cognitive only if they are subject to similar tests to those which sense experiences are.[26]

> But whereas questions about the existence of people can be answered by straightforward observational and other tests, not even those who claim to have enjoyed personal encounters with God would admit such tests to be appropriate here.[27]

> If, as seems clearly to be the case, a person can in all ways be a normal observer (relative to our culture, of course) and still not have a glimpse of Heaven, a vision of God, or other religious experience under any known objectively specifiable set of circumstances, then there is no reason to suppose that a general defense of the empirical foundations of knowledge requires that we assign any evidential value to religious experience.[28]

The specific theses of these authors differ somewhat. I have already noted that O'Hear, for example, is pursuing a line that takes explanatory efficacy to be epistemologically crucial. But they all take it that the lack in CMP of the kinds of checks from other observers that is characteristic of SP is a serious epistemological defect and that it prevents us from supposing M-beliefs based on mystical perception to be in a strong epistemic position. I shall be discussing this charge in my own terms, taking it to amount to the claim that since CMP lacks this kind of check by other observers it does not have the kind of overrider system that a doxastic practice must possess if it is to confer prima facie justification on its outputs. Experientially based beliefs must be subject to test by the experience of other observers in the SP way if they are to count as prima facie justified by that experience. The price of justification for an objective claim about the world is subjection to an appropriate objective scrutiny by other members of the community. *Objective* epistemic worth requires

[25]In these passages O'Hear speaks of predictive capacity as well as of corroboration by independent observers. In a bit we shall address the former issue. It should also be noted that this discussion is set in the context of a claim that the epistemic credentials of a mode of putative experience of objects depend on the explanatory efficacy of that range of objects vis-à-vis that experience. This is an issue that will be addressed in the next chapter. For now we are concerned with the epistemic bearing of CMP's lack of the kind of check by other observers typical of SP.

[26]Gale 1991. This quotation is set in an elaborate discussion that involves a list of 11 tests of the veridicality of sensory experiences.

[27]Flew 1966, pp. 138–39.

[28]Clark 1984, p. 192.

intersubjective validation. Otherwise we are left with only the subject's predilection for a particular interpretation.

This is a powerfully tempting position. Our conviction that sense perception puts us in effective cognitive contact with a surrounding world is intimately tied up with the fact that when we compare our perceptual beliefs with those of relevant others, they exhibit a massive commonality. And if we can have no such interpersonal confirmation how can we distinguish veridical perception from dreams and fancies? Nevertheless, I am going to resist the temptation. The argument rests on an unjustified, and unjustifiable, assumption: that reports of perception of God are properly treated in the same way as reports of perception of the physical environment, so that if the former cannot be validated in the same way as the latter they have no epistemic standing as objective claims. But there is no reason to suppose it *appropriate* to require the same checks and tests for them as for sense-perceptual reports, and every (or at least sufficient) reason to suppose it inappropriate. Here we have what is perhaps our most glaring example of epistemic *imperialism*, unwarrantedly subjecting the outputs of one doxastic practice to the requirements of another.

The first step in this defense is to point out that CMP is a different doxastic practice from SP and to ask why we should suppose that beliefs from the one practice should be subject to the same tests as beliefs from the other in order that the former be rationally respectable. We do not generally accept such cross-practice extrapolations. Consider an analogous critique of introspective reports—for example, that I now feel excited. Here too the report cannot be assessed on the basis of whether other people experience the same thing under the same conditions. Even if they don't that has no tendency to show that I didn't feel excited. But this will not lead most of us to deny that such beliefs can be justified.[29] We would simply point out that we should not expect beliefs about one's own conscious states to be subject to the same sorts of tests as beliefs about ships and sealing wax. Tests of a public sort can be given to determine the subject's mastery of mentalistic language and her general reliability as a reporter. But as for particular reports, if we can assume general competence, there is no appeal beyond her word. The formation of beliefs about one's own conscious states belongs to a different doxastic practice with a different range of inputs, different input-output functions, a different conceptual scheme, a different subject matter, and different criteria of justification.[30]

[29]It is true that the behaviorist movement in psychology sought to ban introspective reports from the data base of psychology precisely on the ground that they were not intersubjectively testable in the way sense-perceptual reports of the environment are. But this behaviorist ruling concerned what should be required of data for purposes of science; it was not a question of general epistemic status. In any event, if my opponents' case is supported by behaviorist psychology, I take that to be a point in my favor.

[30]I do not follow Martin in supposing that since CMP does not make provision for the same kind of intersubjective corroboration as SP, its outputs are like those of introspection in their

This example is designed to suggest the *possibility* that it is just as inappropriate to subject perceptual beliefs about God to the tests of SP as to subject introspective beliefs to such tests, and that the inability to do so will have no more epistemic significance than the inability to use perceptual checks on mathematical statements, or mathematical checks on perceptual reports. But so far I have only adumbrated a possibility. To get beyond this we must look into CMP itself for some internal reason why confirmation by other observers, as we have it in SP, is not to be expected here.

To do this I must return to the point that the checking system of a practice is typically built up, in good part, on the basis of what we have learned from that practice itself. In particular, in experiential practices like SP and CMP, the general picture of the subject matter that forms an important part of the checking system, is constructed, at least in part, on the basis of what that very practice has taught us. And whatever we know about the conditions that make for accurate or inaccurate perception, we have come to know by relying on the deliverances of perception. How could we know anything about what makes for accurate perception of the physical environment except by using perception to determine what the environment is actually like at a given time and place, what a given subject perceives it to be then and there, and how it is with that subject at that time. If we couldn't rely on sense perception we would never find out anything about these matters. Likewise, in CMP we would have no basis for judgments as to the conditions that make for accurate or inaccurate perception if had no knowledge of the nature and purposes of God to go on; and this knowledge is derived, at least to a considerable extent, from CMP itself. Thus, to a large extent at least, the practice supplies both the tester and the testee; it grades its own examinations. There is a certain circularity involved in supporting the choice of tests. One has to use the practice, including the tests in question, to show that these tests are the right ones to use. Choosing tests in an "inside" job. And this circularity attaches as fully to universal practices like SP that are taken, in practice, to be unproblematic, as it does to controversial practices like CMP.

Note the difference, as well as the connection, between this point and the earlier point that in checking a perceptual report we make use of what we have learned perceptually. Here we are making a similar point concerning judgments as to what tests are appropriate in a given practice. Putting the two points together, we can say that we perforce make use of what we have learned from a given practice, both in deciding how to go about checking particular outputs of the practice, for accuracy and for epistemic status, and in carrying out such checks in particular cases.

Now let's apply the general point about what is involved in choosing a test

subject matter. I introduce introspective practice simply to illustrate the point that one cannot assume that the same sorts of tests are available in all doxastic practices, even in all experiential doxastic practices.

for a practice, to the consensual validation test that CMP does not share with SP. And let's begin by asking what SP has taught us about its subject matter that makes it possible and appropriate to hold perceptual beliefs subject to such a test. The basic point is this. We have learned from SP that there are dependable regularities in the behavior of physical objects, including their interaction with the human perceptual apparatus, and we have learned what some of these regularities are. To take some modest examples, we have learned that plants mostly just stay where they are, open to the observation of anyone who is in the right place in the right conditions, whereas animals move around a lot and you can't depend on one staying at the same place over a long period of time. We have gained a lot of empirical knowledge of the dependence of visual perception on lighting, distance of the object from the observer, angle of observation, and other factors. It is because we are cognizant of regularities like this that we are in a position to spell out the conditions under which an observer will perceive a reported object if it really is there. And, to repeat, it is from SP itself that we have learned all this. Hence it is on the basis of what SP has revealed about the nature of its subject matter that we take its deliverances to be subject to assessment in terms of the perceptions of properly qualified others.

A quite different picture of the subject matter of CMP (God and His relations to His creation) has been built up on the basis of CMP and other sources, including revelation[31] and natural theology. God has not revealed to us, nor have we discovered by mystical perception or natural theology, any dependable regularities in divine behavior, particularly regularities in God's interactions with human perceivers. The Christian scheme does include certain basic points about the character and purposes of God, and about patterns in His behavior toward us in the course of history. God can be depended on to work for our salvation from sin, to keep His promises, and to see to it that the church continues to proclaim His message to mankind. Moreover, the scheme does include, as we have seen, some identification of factors that tell for or against openness to the awareness of God. But all this is far from yielding usable recipes for what God will do under certain circumstances. No amount of knowledge of God's essential nature will enable one to predict just when He would punish the Israelites by delivering them to their enemies, or just when He would deliver them from captivity. It is part of the Christian picture that God will forgive those who sincerely repent; but woe to one who supposes that some conditions ascertainable by us will infallibly lead to divine forgiveness. The sufficient condition, "true repentance", is itself such that no effectively ascertainable set of conditions guarantees that it obtains. And most germane to the present concern, such awareness as we have of what is conducive to spiritual receptivity, definitely does not provide any assurance that one

[31]Revelation might or might not be a form of mystical perception. See Chapter 8 for a discussion of this.

who satisfies certain effectively identifiable requirements will experience the presence of God. A constant refrain of the great Christian mystics is that the direct awareness of God is not within our control; we can help to make ourselves receptive, but it is God Himself who determines the time and place, and even whether it will occur in this life.[32]

Moreover, it is not just that we have not discovered any such dependable regularities; the scheme implies that we should not expect to do this. The nature of God and our relations thereto are such that this is simply not in the cards. The rationale for this thesis differs somewhat in various theologies, but both the following themes appear frequently. (1) Divine transcendence. God is infinite; we are finite. How can we hope to attain as adequate a cognitive grasp of the nature and activity of God as we do of finite substances? Our intellect is suited to the knowledge of finite things; there we can discern regularities that enable us to predict and control and to set up tests of the sorts we have been discussing. But why should we expect any such cognitive achievements with respect to an infinite creator? (2) It is presumably true that God could reveal more than He has about regular patterns in His behavior. But it would be contrary to His sovereignty to do so. He is not subject to natural laws, for He is their author. Any regularities in His behavior are due, at least in large part, to His free choice. Moreover, it is essential to His status as Lord of all that He is not beholden to any creature to respond to conditions in one way rather than another. It would thus be contrary to the fundamental conditions of the divine-human relationship that God should put into our possession a set of recipes that could be used to predict and control His actions. That would be to give us a degree of control highly unbefitting our place in reality.[33]

The upshot of all this is that while what we have learned about the physical world from SP gives us the wherewithal to hold particular perceptual reports subject to a decisive test in terms of what relevant others perceive, what we have learned about God and His relations to His creation, from CMP and other sources, gives us reason to suppose that no such tests are available here. And lest one think that this is just an ad hoc move to escape a difficulty, the features of the Christian scheme that imply this were basic to the scheme long

[32]Even if there are regularities in divine appearances to our experience, the sufficient conditions of such appearances are not at all within our control, or even effectively recognizable by us. Thus a knowledge of such regularities would not put us in a position to carry out decisive tests by other observers, for we would not be in a position to get other observers in the right position or even to determine when they are.

[33]Another idea along this line is that if God were to allow us to have as much knowledge of Him as would be required for checks of the SP sort, that would destroy His "epistemic distance" from us, which is itself a necessary condition of our having a free choice as to whether to believe in Him and live according to His commandments. The idea is that if the existence, nature, purposes, and activities of God were to become obvious to us, we would not have a choice as to whether to trust in Him and live the kind of life he enjoins on us. (See Hick 1966, chap. 6, for a well-known exposition of this view.) I have not included this point in the text because I find it unpersuasive. Even if we were as certain of the basic outlines of Christian doctrine as we are of the physical world, I fear that not all of us would automatically lead the new life of the Spirit.

before anyone thought of making unfavorable epistemic comparisons with SP. Thus it is an unthinking parochialism or chauvinism, or epistemic *imperialism* as we have been saying, to suppose the CMP is properly assessed in terms of the checks and tests appropriate to SP. Judging CMP outputs on the basis of SP tests is no more appropriate than evaluating introspective, memory, or mathematical beliefs by the same tests. The objection to CMP I have been considering is guilty of the same kind of chauvinism as Plato's and Descartes's low assessment of SP as lacking the precision, stability, and certainty of mathematics and Hume's low assessment of inductive reasoning as lacking the conclusiveness of deductive reasoning. These last analogues highlight the way in which I have been stressing the irreducible plurality of doxastic practices in the tradition of Reid and Wittgenstein. Like them, I have been insisting that the criteria of justification are quite different for different doxastic practices, and only confusion results from an attempt to subject the outputs of one practice to the standards of another, without good reason for supposing that those standards carry over.

An even more striking manifestation of SP imperialism is to simply proceed on the assumption that SP is normative without even making the assumption explicit. A particularly glaring example of this is found in Gaskin 1984 (chap. 4). He begins by distinguishing between *experience of an externally existing object* and *experience of an internally existing object*. He *defines* the former as "experience such that any other person rightly and possibly situated, with normally functioning *senses*, powers of attention, and a suitable conceptual understanding, will have the same or a closely similar experience" (P. 80; my italics). He then has no difficulty in showing that mystical experiences are not "experiences of an externally existing object"! The game has been rigged from the start.

I am quite prepared to recognize that a checking system of the sort we have in SP is an epistemic desideratum. If we were shaping the world to our heart's desire, I dare say we would arrange for all our fallible doxastic practices to include such checks.[34] It certainly puts us in a better position to distinguish between correct and incorrect perceptual beliefs than what we have in CMP. But though this shows that CMP is epistemically inferior to SP in this respect, that is not the same as showing that CMP is unreliable or not rationally engaged in, or that its outputs are not prima facie justified. These conclusions would follow only if the possession of a checking system of the SP sort were not only *a* way of being epistemically acceptable, but the only way. And there is no reason to make the stronger claim. I have already given examples of

[34]Actually, if we had our druthers, we would undoubtedly arrange for our doxastic practices to be much less fallible than SP, so as to stand in no need for an elaborate overrider system. This observation provides another reason for resisting SP imperialism. Since SP itself is not as epistemically ideal as it might conceivably be, why should we take its constitution to be obligatory for other experiential doxastic practices?

practices universally regarded as intellectually respectable that involve no such tests. My opponent may still insist that any acceptable *experiential* doxastic practice that issues beliefs about what goes beyond the subject's experience must provide for its outputs being checkable in this way. But what is the basis of this requirement? How can it stand in the face of the fact that the system of belief associated with CMP and built up, at least in part, on its basis, implies that no such checking system is to be expected even if CMP is as reliable as you please?

The point that the standard tests within a doxastic practice are based on the account of the subject matter that is developed within that practice is crucial to the pluralistic epistemology I am employing here. Once this point is fully appreciated it should break the hold exercised on us by our most deeply rooted and widely shared practices like SP. Because we have been so thoroughly immersed in this practice since long before the age of reflection, since it is second nature to us and no doubt contains many elements of first nature as well, we naturally fall into thinking that any objective experiential claims must be subject to *its* tests and must successfully pass them if they are to be intellectually respectable. But once we realize that the relevance of these tests to sense-perceptual beliefs is not an a priori truth but rather is based on empirical results obtained within SP, we can be open to the possibility that a different structure of the same generic sort is to be found in other experiential doxastic practices, a possibility that is realized in forms of MP. The tests that have been built up within CMP have the same *sort* of justification as the tests of SP, namely being based on the picture of the subject matter that is associated with the practice and that is, in whole or part, built up on the basis of the output of that practice. Thus when CMP does not utilize some test that is crucial in SP, that is no reason to condemn CMP as lacking in justificatory force, any more than the fact that SP does not utilize some test that is crucial in CMP is a reason to downgrade SP epistemically. It is because of the central place SP occupies in our lives that we are drawn to set it up as judge over practices like CMP and not vice versa. But, on rational reflection, we can see that colonial rule is no more appropriate in the one direction than in the other. Once we realize the internal source of the checks and tests of any doxastic practice, we will lose our tendency to entrust imperial control over its fellows to any of these essentially sovereign spheres of cognition.

To put the point most succinctly, the character of CMP is such that even if it is as reliable a cognitive access to God as you like, it still would not make provision for an effective check on particular perceptual beliefs by the perceptions of others. Hence the absence of any such provision cannot be used to cast doubt on its cognitive reliability or on the rationality of engaging in it. Since what it purports to give us information about is not such as to allow for usable formulations of the conditions an observer must satisfy in order to serve as a relevant check on the observations of another, we would still not have any such checks available, however accurate a picture CMP is giving us of that sphere of reality. Hence the lack of such tests is no basis for a criticism of its epistemic pretensions.

F. Predictive Efficacy

I have noted that the difference of CMP from SP in the matter of checks and tests is rooted in a difference in the extent to which the outputs of the two practices give us a handle on prediction. This latter difference itself is taken by some as a reason for denying that CMP can reasonably be regarded as a reliable source of belief.

> The judgment that one has had a divine experience is quite unlike the judgment that one has seen a table in that it appears to lead to no testable independent predictions. Moreover, in many religious traditions, it is a key aspect of religious experience that it is unpredictable. Christians, for example, tend to explain this unpredictability by saying that these experiences are a gift of God. This may be so, but saying it certainly weakens attempts to argue from the experience to the reality.[35]

We need not spend time countering these asseverations. To do so would be to rerun our response to the "checks and tests" objection. What we have here is simply another bit of epistemic imperialism. A distinctive achievement of SP is arbitrarily elevated into a requirement for any experiential doxastic practice and used as a club to beat CMP into submission. And this despite the fact that the picture of the subject matter involved in CMP leads us to expect that prediction is not in the cards, however reliable a source of belief CMP is. Again, this need not be taken seriously.

Here is another way of formulating our response to these unfavorable comparisons of CMP with SP. If we were to accept predictive efficacy and effective testing by other observers as a necessary condition for any acceptable experiential doxastic practice, we would foreclose the possibility of cognitive contact with any sphere of reality that does not allow for these achievements, *no matter what can be said in favor of the idea that people do succeed in establishing effective contact with such a sphere*. But this is intolerably restrictive. How can we, in good conscience, assume that there is no realm of reality so structured and so related to us that it is impossible for us to get the kind of predictive handle that is required for the tight control of perceptual reports typical of SP? Or if my opponent admits the possibility that there are such realities but merely denies that we can establish effective cognitive con-

[35]O'Hear 1984, p. 44. See also the quotations from O'Hear in section iiiE. Note that O'Hear is objecting to an *argument* "from the experience to the reality. I have already pointed out that in claiming that M-beliefs are prima facie justified, I am espousing no *argument* from the occurrence of an experience to the existence or nature of God.

tact with them, how can he be justified in ruling out that epistemic possibility? I take it that more openness is required than that. Let us humbly wait for what experience teaches us about what there is and how we can find out about it, and not be so eager to draw in advance the boundaries of being and knowledge.

If one supposed that my argument for the rationality of CMP were most basically an analogical argument, trading on analogies between CMP and SP, it might be contended that the disanalogies I have acknowledged in the matter of checks and tests greatly weaken, if they do not destroy, the analogy, *whatever the explanation of these disanalogies*. Thus Gale.

> Wainwright and Alston admit these disanalogies but try to neutralize them by claiming that they are due to a difference in the categoreal nature of the apparent object of sense and religious experience. . . . This explains why the Agreement and Prediction tests will not apply to religious experience in the same way that they do to sense experience. . . . There are two difficulties with this response. First, to explain why the tests for sense and religious experiences are not analogous is not to explain away the disanalogies; and these disanalogies are devastating to the Analogical Argument. . . . A second difficulty . . . is a tension, if not inconsistency, in Alston's work. It is between his demands, on the one hand for parity of treatment of the religious and sense experience doxastic practices and, on the other, that we not be chauvinistic, that we not uphold the epistemological principles of one practice as a standard by which to judge the adequacy of others. Alston's demand for parity of treatment of the two practices is based on the claim that the religious experience doxastic practice is sufficiently analogous to the sense experience doxastic practice so as to be subject to all of the cognitive rights and privileges thereunto appertaining to the latter. . . . Therefore it would be most inconsistent of him to charge an objector with being an objectionable chauvinist when it is charged that the religious experience doxastic practice fails to count as cognitive because its tests are quite disanalogous to those of the sense experience doxastic practice.[36]

I could respond to this by denying that my argument is an argument from analogy, or any kind of "parity" argument to the effect that we cannot consistently downgrade CMP while approving of SP. It is true that I sometimes point out that critics of CMP are employing a double standard, criticizing it for features that it shares with SP, which they accept. However, responses to criticisms aside, the positive argument for CMP is based on my theory of doxastic practices. The basic contention is that it is prima facie rational to engage in CMP, not because it is analogous to SP in one or another respect, but because it is a socially established doxastic practice; and that it is unqualifiedly rational to engage in it, as we shall argue in the next chapter, because we lack sufficient reason for regarding it as unreliable or otherwise disqualified for rational participation. It is true that it is rational to engage in SP for

[36]Gale 1991.

precisely analogous reasons, but no explicit reference to SP is required to present the case for CMP, any more than it is necessary to bring in an analogy with swimming to present the case for the legality of jogging. It is true that swimming is legal for precisely the same reason that jogging is legal (it violates no laws), but it would be grotesque to suppose that the case for the legality of jogging depends essentially on an analogy with jogging.

However, this response might reasonably be taken to be a shuffling evasion. After all, whatever the logical possibilities for our argument, we have been trading throughout on certain analogies between CMP and SP, for example, that neither can be shown noncircularly to be reliable, that both are socially established, that both possess an overrider system, and so on. Hence it will not be irrelevant to show that Gale's response lacks cogency even if my argument is as he represents it. The point is very simple. Any argument from analogy depends on certain points of resemblance and not on others. The analogies between CMP and SP that are needed to yield the conclusion that CMP is rationally engaged in and rationally taken to be reliable if SP is, are the ones just noted: being a full-fledged socially established doxastic practice with distinctive input-output functions, having a functioning overrider system, the lack of sufficient reasons to take the practice as unreliable, and a significant degree of self-support. (The last two are treated in the next chapter.) If these analogies hold, then CMP enjoys basically the same epistemic status as SP, though it may well be less firmly established, less informative, and its output may well enjoy a lesser degree of justification. (Again, this will be taken up in the next two chapters.) The crucial questions concern what analogies are required for analogy in epistemic status, and whether *these* analogies hold. I have just stated my position on this. Gale could, of course, argue that effective intersubjective corroboration and a predictive test must be available if any practice, or any experiential practice, is to be a rational way of forming beliefs about objective reality, but he does not do so. O'Hear argues that the availability of these tests is a necessary condition of practice's satisfying the explanatory efficacy condition for epistemic respectability, but I see no reason to adopt any such condition as the latter. But Gale himself gives us no reason for supposing that the availability of SP-type checks and tests is a necessary condition for being a source of epistemic justification for objective beliefs. Nor can I see any reason for holding this that is not based on a public empirical verifiability criterion of meaning. If one utilizes such a criterion one can argue that in the absence of tests of the sorts we have been discussing, one's statements are deficient in cognitive meaningfulness and so fail to express genuine beliefs in objective states of affairs.[37] But, as I made explicit in Chapter 3, I find no merit in any such criterion. It seems clear to me that I can form beliefs that make claims about objective reality, and thus possess a truth value, without having any idea of how they could be tested by sense percep-

[37]Cf. the quote from Martin on pp. 27–28.

tion—by the reports of various observers or by deriving empirically testable predictions from them or in any other way. The belief that there are no indivisible bits of matter is just such a belief, and that God is pouring out His creative love into me at this moment is another. I have discovered from presenting my views on this topic to various groups that it is widely, and confidently, held that tests of the SP type are required for the epistemic respectability of a practice of forming objective beliefs on the basis of experience; but I have yet to find a serious basis for this conviction, or indeed any explicit basis at all, except the one involving a verifiability criterion of meaningfulness.

iv. Conclusion

Let's take it, then, that CMP is a functioning, socially established, perceptual doxastic practice with distinctive experiential inputs, distinctive input-output functions, a distinctive conceptual scheme, and a rich, internally justified overrider system. As such, it possesses a prima facie title to being rationally engaged in, and its outputs are thereby prima facie justified, *provided we have no sufficient reason to regard it as unreliable or otherwise disqualified for rational acceptance*. In the following two chapters we will consider alleged reasons of this sort.

CHAPTER 6

Can the Christian Mystical Perceptual Doxastic Practice Be Shown to Be Unreliable?

In the last chapter we consider various objections to the thesis that CMP constitutes a full-fledged, socially established experiential doxastic practice and as such serves as a source of prima facie epistemic justification for its outputs—M-beliefs. We found substantial merit in none of those objections and concluded that the claim of M-beliefs to prima facie justification by virtue of their origin remains unshaken. We will now turn to the second stage of the evaluation of established doxastic practices. Are there sufficient reasons for taking CMP to be *unreliable* or otherwise unworthy of rational acceptance, despite its being a fully equipped, socially established practice? And does it exhibit a significant degree of internal self-support? This chapter will be devoted to those questions.

i. Some Old Reasons for the Unacceptability of CMP

First here are two alleged reasons for the unacceptability of CMP, which I have already, in effect, answered.

(1) "If we are to take seriously a claim to acquire knowledge, or justified belief, from the perception of God, we will need sufficient reason for supposing that anyone ever does really perceive God. In order for S to perceive God it would have to be the case that (a) God exists, (b) God is related to S's experience in such a way as to be perceivable by S, and (c) this possibility is sometimes actualized. Only after we have adequate reasons for all that can we proceed to scrutinize the claim that beliefs formed on the basis of perceptions of God are thereby justified. And no such reasons are to be found".[1]

As pointed out in section i of Chapter 1, if this is a demand for *external*

[1]This imaginary objector does not claim that it has to be true that God exists and that we genuinely perceive Him in order that the perceptual justification of M-beliefs can be taken seriously, and he was wise not to do so. Provided we have an established practice of forming beliefs about X on the basis of what seems for all the world to be perceptions of X, a practice that also passes any further tests for acceptability, then it is rational to engage in the practice even if, unbeknown to us and unknowable by us, its putative objects do not exist or we do not actually perceive them. How could it fail to be rational for us to form beliefs in this manner if, so far as

support for these claims, support from outside the practice of forming beliefs on the basis of this mode of perception, then it cannot be met, either for mystical perception or sense perception. In Chapter 3 I argued that the reliability of SP cannot receive any sufficient external support, and I indicated the plausibility of a like conclusion with respect to our other basic doxastic practices. A parallel argument could be mounted for the three assumptions just mentioned. We are no more able to show that physical objects exist and that we perceive them, without relying on the output of SP to do so, than we are able to provide an external demonstration for the reliability of SP. I leave it to the reader to construct an analogue of the argument of Chapter 3 for attempts to give nonepistemically circular arguments for these claims. But then if we suffer a like incapacity with respect to CMP, that practice is thereby in no worse an epistemic condition than SP. And there is no dearth of internal, epistemically circular support in either case. Both SP and CMP generates plenty of perceptual evidence for the existence of its object(s) and for the claim that we perceive it (them).

In section i of Chapter 1, I also indicated that, although we are unable to find external considerations that strongly probabilify the theses that we genuinely perceive the object(s) of CMP and of SP, we can show that it is *rational* to engage in these perceptual practices in question and to regard them as reliable. That line of argument was presented in general terms in Chapter 4, and we are now in the process of spelling it out for CMP. This carries out the program adumbrated in Chapter 1: defending the genuineness of the perceptions by defending the reliability of forming beliefs on the basis of those putative perceptions, rather than vice versa. By showing that it is rational to take CMP as a (reasonably) reliable mode of belief formation, we thereby show that it is rational to suppose that God is genuinely perceived in CMP. For if this were not the case, why should it be that we form largely true beliefs on the basis of these putative perceptions? If we are not really perceiving what we think we are perceiving, how are we able to use these experiences to form mostly true beliefs about this supposed object? And a precisely parallel argument can be mounted for SP. Thus, contrary to what might seem to be the most natural procedure, we must defend the genuineness of perceiving X on the basis of the rationality of forming beliefs on the basis of such a putative perception, rather than vice versa. And, again, this is because of the epistemic circularity into which we fall in seeking to carry out the vice versa.[2]

we can tell, it is a reliable way to do so? To be sure, it has to be true that God exists and that we genuinely perceive Him if we are to gain *knowledge* of God from that perception. But here we are restricting ourselves to the question of *justification* of M-beliefs, which is logically compatible with the falsity of those beliefs, though it tells powerfully against that supposition.

[2]Actually the SP-CMP contrast is a bit more complicated than this. As pointed out Chapter 4, the doxastic-practice argument for the rationality of regarding SP as reliable is more heavily entangled in epistemic circularity than the parallel argument with respect to CMP. Nevertheless, in both cases we are, at least, less involved in epistemic circularity in the argument for the

(2) "It is rational to form beliefs about the physical environment in accordance with SP because we have reason to take it to be reliable. But we have no such reasons to suppose CMP to be reliable".

Here we can appeal directly to Chapter 3, where we presented strong reasons for denying that we have strong external reasons for regarding SP as reliable. Hence the absence of such reasons for CMP does not imply that its epistemic status is lower than that of SP. And, again, there is an abundance of internal support for reliability in both cases. The objector is once more arbitrarily applying a double standard.

ii. The Objection from Naturalistic Explanations of Mystical Experience

Now I will turn to a reason for the unreliability of CMP that is new to the discussion and that I am prepared to take more seriously.

It is widely held that mystical experience can be adequately explained naturalistically, whether in terms of psychodynamic mechanisms à la Freud, in terms of social or economic forces à la Marx or Durkheim, in terms of neurophysiological functioning, or otherwise. But, as was pointed out in Chapter 1, it is plausible to hold that an experience can be an experience of an objective reality only if that reality is among the causes of that experience, only if that reality figures importantly in an adequate causal explanation of that experience. Normal visual experience can justifiably be taken to be an experience of items in the field of vision just because we can't understand why the visual experience occurs as it does without taking into account the causal influence of those items (in this case their reflection of light which then strikes the retina . . .). But if the occurrence of mystical experience can be adequately explained solely in terms of this-worldly factors, God need never be mentioned in an adequate explanation. Nous n'avons pas besoin de cette hypothèse. Hence we have no justification for supposing that God is causally involved in the generation of the experience and thus no justification for supposing that the experience is a perception of God.

> If we have grounds other than the experiences themselves for believing that God exists, then his selective revelation of himself would account for the solitary and frequently unshared experiences which people have of him. On the other hand, if we do not have other grounds for believing in his existence, then it will remain a more simple and obvious explanation for the selective experiences if we take them to be internal, and caused by social and psychological factors.[3]

---

rationality of taking the practice to be reliable than we are in arguing directly for the truth of the thesis that the practice is reliable.

[3]Gaskin 1984, p. 100.

> It is not at all difficult, however, to construct a plausible explanation not consisting of mere possibilities like the machinations of demons, why people should come very strongly to believe there to be a divinely populated religious reality which is perceived in religious experiences even when there is none . . . we very much *want* there to be an understandable order to the universe, we very much *want* our lives to be of consequence, and we very much *want* to know in practical detail what's right and wrong. Religion addresses what we very much want. The universe has an intelligible order because there is an intelligent powerful God who made it. We are important because God made us (as Christians say, "in His image") and gave us the faculties of understanding and free, intelligent action. And God, being knowledgeable and perfect, is the ultimate moral authority—if He says it's right, *it's right*! People are known to let their desires, hopes, and fears color and cloud their critical faculties. No wonder they believe in a religious reality![4]

> The issue is whether the hypothesis that there objectively is a something more [revealed in mystical experience] gives a better explanation of the whole range of phenomena than can be given without it. James himself thinks that it does; yet he gives no real argument to support this opinion. This is, obviously, a less economical hypothesis than its naturalistic rival, and in fact such argument as James gives undermines it: 'the theologians contention that the religious man is moved by an external power is vindicated, for it is one of the peculiarities of invasions from the subconscious region to take on objective appearances and to suggest to the Subject an external control' (1902, p. 488). . . . But this clearly 'vindicates' the theologian's contention only by reducing it to the rival naturalistic view. . . . The undeniably real causal source of these impulses may be normally 'unseen' and not understood or articulately reported; but it is eminently understandable, and it belongs well within the same 'dimensions of existence' as other, wholly familiar, mental phenomena.[5]

Would the (alleged) fact that the causal requirement for perception of God is not met show CMP to be unreliable or would it disqualify it on some other basis? I think the most natural construal is in terms of unreliability. If, so far as we can tell, we are not genuinely perceiving God in mystical experience, then there is no reason to regard that experience as a source of information about God. After all, our conviction that sense experience provides reliable indications of how things are in the immediate physical environment is intimately dependent on the conviction that in normal sense experience items in the physical environment are presenting themselves to our experience, the conviction that in such experience we are genuinely aware of those items as being and doing so-and-so. If this latter conviction were undermined, we would cease to regard SP as reliable. Hence, if we are justified in supposing mystical experience not to be a genuine perception of God, we are left without any coherent way of maintaining that CMP is reliable.

[4]Daniels 1989, p. 497.
[5]Mackie 1982, pp. 183–84.

I should say a word about the relation of this criticism to my discussion of the causal requirement for the perception of God in Chapter 1. There I was only aspiring to argue that it is possible that human beings sometimes perceive God. I did this by pointing out that it is basic to Christian belief that God figures in the causal chain leading up to every occurrence in His creation, and that there is no a priori reason to suppose that the particular causal contribution God makes to mystical experience is not of the sort to qualify Him as an object of that experience. Since I was confining myself there to arguing for the real possibility of the perception of God, that was sufficient to do the job. But now we are concerned with what reason we have to think that such perception does or does not actually occur. And so we can't just appeal to what follows from Christian belief with respect to its *possibility*; we have to consider reasons from whatever quarter that bear on its actuality. And at the moment we are considering a reason for a negative answer.

The first thing to consider is whether mystical experience *can* be given an adequate explanation in terms of purely natural causes. If we consider the actual attempts to do this (and this is not a popular research field for social and behavioral scientists), we must judge them to be highly speculative and, at best, sketchily supported by the evidence. Mystical experience poses severe problems for empirical research. In addition to the difficulties in determining when we have a case thereof, it is something that cannot be induced at the will of the researcher and so is not amenable to experiment. Attempts to get around this by substituting drug-induced analogues are of little value, since it is an open question whether findings concerning these analogues can be extrapolated to spontaneous cases. Since the states are usually short-lived, the researcher must rely on autobiographical reports; we can't expect a researcher to hang around a person on the off chance that he might happen to have a mystical experience. Hence the data are subject to all the well-known problems that attach to such reports. Moreover, the most prominent theories in the field invoke causal mechanisms that themselves pose thus far insoluble problems of identification and measurement: unconscious psychological processes like repression, identification, regression, and mechanisms of defense; social influences on ideology and on belief and attitude formation. It is not surprising that theories like those of Freud, Marx, and Durkheim rest on a slender thread of evidential support and generalize irresponsibly from such evidence as they can muster. Nor do the prospects seem rosy for significant improvement.[6]

In considering this matter we must avoid a tempting fallacy. Let's say that experiences phenomenologically indistinguishable from genuine mystical experience[7] are induced by drugs or psychosis, and thus are adequately explain-

[6]A variety of naturalistic explanations of mystical experience is discussed in Davis 1989, chap. 8.

[7]"Genuine" in the modest sense that they satisfy my criterion for mystical experience: that the subject be disposed to take the experience to be a direct experience of God.

able naturalistically. The fallacy consists in inferring from this that all experiences with this phenomenology are a result of natural causes, or, more boldly still, of natural causes of just these sorts. But this doesn't follow, any more than the fact that hallucinatory sensory experiences can be phenomenologically indistinguishable from the real thing implies that no sensory experiences are veridical. The fact that hallucinatory experiences can exactly mimic the real thing certainly complicates the philosophy and psychology of perception, but it does not imply a general skepticism about perception.

If all my opponent is looking for is a set of purely this-worldly conditions that are causally sufficient for mystical experience, she need not get hung up on dubious psychoanalytic, behaviorist, Marxist, or sociological claims. She can turn to neurophysiology. There is overwhelming support for the thesis that every conscious experience is proximately caused by neurophysiological happenings in the brain, and caused in such a way that every difference in experience can be traced to some difference in the neurophysiological underpinning.[8] Unless we have sufficient reason to make an exception for mystical experience, this general principle applies here as well. There are metaphysical and theological systems that invoke reasons for making the exception. St. Thomas, for example, takes mystical experience to exceed the natural capacities of the human psyche, and gives that as a reason for denying that it is entirely due to natural causes. But those systems were developed long before the emergence of twentieth-century physiological psychology.[9] It looks as if we will have to admit that mystical experience can be adequately explained naturalistically.

But if this is what our opponent is driven to in order to make her case, that case is thereby subverted. Turning to SP again, we have at least as strong reasons for holding that sense experience is proximately caused by brain processes alone. So long as those processes are going a certain way, it doesn't matter what is the case elsewhere, including the putatively perceived segment of the external environment; the sensory experience will still be the same.[10] So if the fact that God is not among the proximate, sufficient causal conditions for a mystical experience shows that God is not perceived in that experience, then by the same token the fact that a certain book is not among the proximate, sufficient causal conditions for a certain visual experience shows that that book is not perceived in that visual experience. But no sensible person draws that conclusion in the latter case. And the reason is close at hand. Even though the book is not among the *proximate* causes of the visual experience, it can still figure further back along the causal chain leading to the experience,

[8]In speaking of "underpinning" I appear to be assuming that the experience can be distinguished from the neurophysiological processes that produce it. But I could make the same points on an "identity theory" according to which the conscious experience simply *is* the neurophysiological process in question.

[9]Remember that the most influential philosophical psychologies before the eighteenth century or so also regarded abstract thought as beyond the power of any physical mechanism.

[10]This is another factor that makes life difficult for the philosopher of perception.

as it does if this is a normal case of visual perception; that is sufficient to satisfy the causal condition for the book's being perceived. That condition should not be construed as requiring that the object be among the *proximate* causes of the experience, but only that it figure somewhere in the casual chain. To require that the object of *mystical* experience be among the proximate causes of the experience, while not making a parallel requirement of *sensory* experience, would be, once more, to arbitrarily impose a double standard.[11] And none of the data at our disposal have any tendency to show that mystical experience does not satisfy the requirement that God figure somewhere among the causal conditions of mystical experience. Indeed, it is an essential part of the Christian scheme that God figures among the causes of any occurrence whatsoever; and so, according to Christian belief, mystical experience could not fail to satisfy the causal requirement. In the present context I don't want to stress this epistemically circular reason for supposing the requirement is satisfied. Since my concern is to answer an objection, I only want to claim that we have no sufficient reason for supposing that mystical experience does not satisfy the requirement. The mere fact that mystical experience can be explained in terms of causally sufficient, *proximate* natural factors has no tendency to show that it does not constitute veridical perception of God.

To be sure, as pointed out in Chapter 1, section xi, the requirement that the putatively perceived object figure somewhere in the causal chain that leads up to the experience is too weak; many items satisfy that requirement without being perceived. Happenings in the central nervous system and the transmission of light from object to retina are to be found in the causal chain that leads up to visual experience; but none of this is *seen* in normal vision. But if we try to beef up the requirement to specify some particular causal contribution, then, as also pointed out there, we run into the difficulty that this contribution differs widely for different modes of perception. In vision it is something like *reflecting or generating light that then reaches the retina without additional reflection*; for audition it is something like *generating or reflecting sound waves that strike the ear drum*; and so on. For mystical perception it will be something different, the exact nature of which is obscure to us. Furthermore, the causal contribution that is required for objecthood in each case is something we can learn only from experience, including the experience involved in that case. We must have a number of cases of genuine perception of X in that modality before we are in a position to discover inductively what distinctive causal contribution the perceived object makes to perceptual experience in that modality. There is no a priori way of determining this. Thus we are in no

[11]This double standard may be encouraged by talk of mystical experience as a "direct" awareness of God, one so direct that it even obliterates the subject-object distinction. But, as pointed out in Chapter 1, the kind of mystical perception on which we are concentrating in this book is best thought of as being no more direct than normal visual awareness of objects in the environment, on a direct realist construal of the latter. And that is compatible with causal intermediaries.

position to rule that the causal contribution God makes to mystical experience, according to Christian doctrine, is *not* the sort of contribution it would have to make in order to be genuinely perceived in that experience.

The above considerations make things even more difficult for the critic. Since we are in no position to say what kind of causal contribution is required for objecthood until we have some genuine cases of object perception to work from, one can't even embark on the project of specifying the necessary causal contribution until one recognizes that there are authentic cases of object perception. And by then the game is lost.

At this point the critic might recur to what we might call *disreputable* explanations of mystical experience. "I concede", he might say, "that the mere fact that mystical experience is proximately produced by neural processes in the brain has no tendency to show that it is not an authentic perception of God. But if it is produced in the way Freud or Marx or Durkheim suggest, that will surely rule out the idea that God authentically reveals Himself there. To take one Freudian theory, if mystical experience is the upshot of a regression to one's infantile way of experiencing one's parents, how could it be a veridical awareness of the infinite source of all being? Pathological regression naturally issues in hallucination or at least in severely distorted experience, not in veridical perception."

The most basic reply to this is that since, as noted above, all these disreputable accounts rest on slender evidence at best, there is no occasion to worry about them until that evidential base is considerably enriched. But for the sake of argument let's take Freud seriously and see what follows for our central problem. Can we rule out the perceptual status of mystical experience if it is generated in the way just adumbrated? I don't see how. Why suppose that this is not the mechanism God uses to reveal Himself to our experience? Because it seems very odd that God would choose such a means? But much of what happens in the world seems to us to be not the sort of thing the Christian God would choose. Hence the problem of evil, and hence the paradoxicality of the cross (to the Jews a stumbling block and to the Greeks foolishness). Because regression to earlier levels of psychic organization is not the way to get accurate perceptual information about the physical environment? But why suppose that the conditions that make for accurate (inaccurate) perception of God are the same as those that make for accurate (inaccurate) perception of the physical environment?[12] On a typical hot sunny day in the Arizona desert a pair of sun glasses is an aid to accurate observation; but they have quite the reverse effect on a cold foggy day in the Aleutians. And surely God is more different from the physical world than the Aleutians are from Arizona.

"Still", the critic may continue, "you have only broached the possibility

[12]Cf. William James. "If there were such a thing as inspiration from a higher realm, it might well be that the neurotic temperament would furnish the chief condition of the requisite receptivity" (1902, p. 26).

that God is among the remote causes of mystical experience in such a way as to figure as an object of that experience. You have given no nonepistemically circular reason for supposing this to be the case." This particular critic has obviously not read the earlier parts of this book. If he had, he would realize that we have already argued at length, in Chapter 3, that in the case of SP also we have no nonepistemically circular reasons for supposing that putatively perceived physical objects are among the remote causes of sense experience in such a way as to count as being perceived in those experiences. Hence, if we make the lack of noncircular support a ground for dismissing CMP, while accepting SP as a rational mode of belief formation, we are, once again, guilty of arbitrarily imposing a double standard. And if we insist that any acceptable reasons for supposing that mystical experience (sometimes) satisfies the causal requirement must come from SP and other universal doxastic practices, we are guilty of epistemic chauvinism.[13]

I conclude from all this that the appeal to naturalistic explanations of mystical experience has no tendency to show that CMP's prima facie claim to rational acceptance is overridden.

iii. Inconsistencies in the Output of CMP

In Chapter 4, I distinguished intrapractice inconsistency and interpractice inconsistency as grounds for a judgment of unreliability. Let's look first at the former.

A practice internally displays unreliability when it persistently yields massively inconsistent outputs. The inconsistencies in question might occur between outputs or between outputs and the background system of belief constitutive of the overrider system, or within that background system itself. I will concentrate on inconsistencies of the first sort. Here we are faced once more with the question of how rigoristic to be in our epistemic requirements. This has been an issue throughout the history of epistemology. Utopian theorists from Plato through Descartes to Prichard have plumped for the exclusion, from knowledge if not from rational or justified belief, of everything that fails to meet the highest conceivable standards. Thus Plato ruled out any empirical knowledge based on sense perception because it lacks the precision and stability that we seek in knowledge and find in pure mathematics and, Plato thought, in the knowledge of the Forms. Descartes made a similar ruling, countenancing as knowledge only what we "clearly and distinctly perceive" in

[13]The critic may protest that if God exists His existence would make a noticeable difference to what we can perceive of the natural world. But there is no a priori guarantee that this is the case. We have to learn from experience whether or not we find unmistakable traces of God in what we can perceive of nature. And without denying all probative value to natural theology, I think it must be conceded that the verdict of history is that the natural world does not speak of God in an unambiguous fashion.

such a way that we cannot doubt that what we perceive is as we perceive it. Spinoza, Leibniz, Locke, and Hume talk in the same vein, though in some cases, notably that of Locke, the tough talk is tempered in application by a robust sense of reality. Prichard restricts knowledge to what is presented to us with absolute certainty, and acknowledges that this implies that the boundaries are narrowly drawn.

There has also been an undercurrent of healthy protests against these exorbitant demands, based on a nagging sense that we do know much more than rigoristic theories allow. Sometimes the opposition has been over the extent of knowledge and sometimes over rational or probable belief, or, in contemporary lingo, *justified* belief. Since the latter is our specific concern, I'll focus on that. In the early modern period the protest movement was spearheaded by Thomas Reid, who, as we saw in Chapter 4, insisted on the irreducible plurality of sources of knowledge, even when they yield something less than absolute certainty. If we join Descartes in rejecting fallible belief sources we cannot tolerate any inconsistency, for that is one way in which a source displays its fallibility. But, in line with the avoidance of Cartesian perfectionism by Reid and twentieth-century fallibilists, I too will insist that a modest degree of internal inconsistency will not disqualify a doxastic practice. If we were to take it to do so, we would be left with few if any sources of belief. Certainly SP displays a modicum of inconsistency in its results. Witnesses to a crime or an automobile accident not infrequently contradict each other. Not even Descartes' chosen sources will escape the stigma. Rational intuition can be found to be wholly at one with itself only by carefully editing its deliverances so as to filter out one member of each contradictory pair. If we include in the pool every case of something's seeming self-evident to someone, it is notorious that we will wind up with a number of such pairs. To some it seems self-evident that a human being could not possibly become a cockroach while remaining the same individual; to others it seems self-evident that this is a possibility.[14] And so it goes. Since an absolute ban on inconsistency in output will deprive us of all sources of justification, it is clearly the better part of wisdom to require only that the source not generate "persistent and massive inconsistency". Sporadic and occasional bursts of internal inconsistency can be tolerated. And even a perennial tendency to minor pockets of inconsistency need not be disqualifying.

We can be a bit more precise than this. Remember that we are thinking of a doxastic practice as a two-stage operation: (1) generation of prima facie justified beliefs; (2) the assessment of such beliefs (and the possibility thereof) in terms of the background "overrider system". Now the basic rationale for allowing internal inconsistency, so long as it is not too "persistent and/or massive" is that inconsistencies that do not exhibit those features can be handled sufficiently by the overrider system, whereas if they are too massive they will

[14]For other examples see Chapter 4, section ii.

overwhelm it, flood it with a volume of inconsistency greater than it can deal with. And if they are too persistent, at least in too considerable a quantity, the overrider system has repeatedly failed to do its job well enough. Thus the criterion is best put by saying that a practice is disqualified as insufficiently reliable provided it generates significantly more inconsistences that the overrider system can handle. This is still less than ideally precise, but it is precise enough to be usable.

How does CMP fare in this regard? It undoubtedly generates more inconsistencies than SP, or rational intuition, or memory, or any of the other basic secular practices. The magnitude of this difference is going to depend, in part, on bookkeeping decisions. How much inconsistency we get within a practice, rather than between practices, will depend on how we individuate them. If we lump all MP that takes place within Christianity into one practice, we will get more internal inconsistency than if we follow my recommendation and distinguish a "mainline Christian" MP from outlying districts. And if we count all MP as a single practice we will purchase immunity from competition between different forms of MP at the cost of maximizing internal inconsistency. Internal and external inconsistency vary inversely. The problems of incompatibilities in religious perceptual beliefs will not go away, however practices are individuated; they just take different forms. Therefore, we may as well make our individuation choices on the basis of other considerations, as we did above, and let the problems fall where they may.[15]

Thinking then of CMP as we have specified it, we will find a considerable incidence of incompatible pairs in the outputs. Especially when it comes to perceptions of communications from God, we get a wild diversity, many mutually inconsistent. The reports people give as to what God told them about His plans, especially eschatological ones, and reports as to what assignments God has given them, could not possibly all be true unless God is incredibly confused, vacillating, or inconsistent Himself. Moreover, in many cases pairs of alleged communications are such as to evince radically incompatible divine attributes. Some represent God as bloodthirstily eager for revenge; others represent Him as infinitely forgiving. Some represent God as demanding a high

[15]I should not suppress the fact that it is not always clear how to assign belief formation to a practice. In explaining CMP I said that it would include any MP that employs a certain kind of overrider system. But what does it take for such a system to be "employed"? That may be fairly clear-cut for a group that has an officially promulgated doctrinal system; but what about an individual, whether a member of a tightly organized group or not? Does the individual have to consciously appeal to that system, or be disposed to do so? Or is it sufficient that her MP has formed by a group in which that system plays a key role? Suppose that John, a practicing Roman Catholic, takes himself to have received a message from God that would be disallowed by Catholic doctrine and procedure, but John is either unaware of this or doesn't think of it or chooses to ignore it, and believes that this is a genuine message from God? Is this belief formation taking place within CMP? I think we have to allow a certain looseness here. If we knocked out all cases in which the individual does not actually use (is not actively disposed to use) the group overrider system, we would get rid of many discordant perceptual beliefs within the practice, but at the cost of intolerably proliferating practices. In cases of doubt I will lean to the side of inclusiveness.

degree of ascetic withdrawal from worldly delights; others represent Him as wanting His creatures to enjoy the delights of His creation. And so on. In addition, there will be a significant number of incompatibilities on matters concerning which the system does not speak authoritatively, or on which its voice is not unambiguous. There are many disputed issues such that one can find biblical and patristic warrant for both sides.

Thus it cannot be claimed that the inconsistencies in CMP's output are merely minor ripples in a placid sea. As is indicated by the reference to the difficulty of extracting a single unambiguous picture from the Christian tradition, it cannot even be claimed that the overrider system suffices to resolve all incompatibilities, though it will knock out many. In particular, it will eliminate all reports that represent God in ways that are incompatible with the main lines of tradition. But there will be many inconsistencies that stubbornly continue to confront us. In the light of this, can we hold that CMP is rationally engaged in?

Once again, we must remember to avoid puritanical rigorism. Not even the more unambiguous overrider system of SP will resolve all inconsistencies. Just exactly what happened in that automobile collision? Each witness continues to maintain his story. Even if another witness should be found, that would only add one more voice to the chorus. We don't always have "instant replays". General considerations concerning the laws of nature, human motivation, or the usual distribution of objects in that vicinity will not settle the matter. We have to leave the matter unresolved. A certain amount of unresolved dissonance is compatible with viability, in matters epistemic as well as musical. How large an amount? I don't think there is any precise answer to that question. Apart from the inevitable vagueness that attaches to such discriminations, there are the following points. (1) the *number* of unresolved inconsistencies is not the only relevant factor; there is also the importance of the issues involved. (2) Since it is reasonable to expect more closure, as well as more certainty and precision, on some matters than on others, the amount of inconsistency that is tolerable may well vary in different areas. Our knowledge of the physical world is much more detailed, precise, structured, and extensive than our knowledge of human history, human social interactions, or God and salvation history. Hence it is reasonable to expect less resolution of disagreements in the latter fields, even if we are in genuine cognitive contact with them. Given the incomplete and shaky character of our cognitive grasp of the subject matter, it is the reverse of surprising that there should be numerous disagreements we are incapable of resolving.[16]

Taking all this into account, I think we can say in good conscience that the

[16]To be sure, this judgment can be questioned as based on circular reasoning and as self-serving. For in what I just said I was using CMP itself to determine how much we know about its subject matter. But this is just another example of the epistemic circularity that plagues all the issues we have been discussing.

incidence of inconsistencies in perceptual beliefs stemming from CMP that are not resolved by the overrider system are not so numerous or so central as to override the prima facie claim to rational acceptance that CMP enjoys by virtue of being a socially established doxastic practice. However, I do agree that these considerations indicate that the degree of reliability it is reasonable to assign to CMP is less than it is reasonable to assign to SP and other basic secular doxastic practices.[17] Is that degree too low for us to be rational in engaging in it? Again I can't say anything very definitive, both because we have no usable metric for degrees of reliability (we lack both the necessary statistical data and the conceptual resources for deriving usable degrees of reliability from them) and because there is no determinate answer to how much reliability is required for rational participation. (With respect to this latter point, the degree of reliability required may well vary, depending on our reasonable expectations for one or another subject matter.) If we had sufficient reason to judge that the degree of reliability is quite low, say 50–50 or less, that would show that the practice is not rationally engaged in. But I see no grounds for any such judgment. Hence I will take it that internal inconsistency gives us no reason to assign so low a reliability to CMP as to override its prima facie rationality.

iv. Conflicts between CMP and Other Practices

But even if CMP is not disqualified by internal inconsistency, it may fall victim to an excessive inconsistency of its output or overrider system with that of other, more firmly established doxastic practices, like SP or current empirical science or historical research.[18] The latter meet a number of the conditions spelled out in Chapter 4 for being more firmly established. They are more widely practiced, have a richer and more definite structure, are more difficult to abstain from, and their principles seem more obviously true to more people. If there is such conflict it would seem to be sufficient to disqualify CMP.

It is a complex question whether this is the case. First, remember that it is only massive inconsistency that is disqualifying. Minor inconsistencies between even the most respectable practices are a fact of life. Scientific theory is always running into conflict with observation and vice versa. That is one of the necessary conditions for progress in science. Memories often fail to jibe with the evidence of current sense perception. But none of this concerns the most basic principles associated with the contenders; nor does it affect more than a small proportion of their output. The conflicts take place against a

[17]This serves as a correction of certain extravagant statements I have made. For example: "I conclude that CP [Christian mystical practice] has basically the same epistemic status as PP [sense perceptual practice]" (1982, p. 12).

[18]We have thrown in the background belief system as well as the output of the practice as an alternative just because the former, as we have seen, may draw on more than the latter.

background of general consonance. That is what keeps our cognitive life in good order and our total system of epistemic principles coherent. Similarly, if the output of CMP, or the background system of Christian belief, conflicts here and there with scientific results or the best judgment of historians or with what we can see in front of our eyes, that again could be but an isolated bit of turbulence in a generally calm sea. So we won't be worried by the fact that Christians have believed things on the basis of an overly literal reading of the Bible (Joshua made the sun stand still instead of moving about the earth as it ordinarily does; the physical universe came into existence about 6,000 years ago) that conflict with scientific results or historical investigation. To be sure, if some Christian individual or group refuses to modify its beliefs when they are flatly contradicted by a more firmly established practice, we cannot regard this reaction as rational. But that does not show that CMP in general is not, or cannot be, rationally engaged in. It only shows that this particular individual or group is not practicing a rational form of CMP.

Are there more fundamental and/or more massive conflicts between CMP and more firmly established doxastic practices? Here I will restrict consideration to suggestions that CMP comes into serious conflict with (1) natural science, (2) history, (3) naturalistic metaphysics. I will take them in that order.[19]

To be sure, these are by no means the only possibilities for serious conflict. One obvious set of candidates is constituted by the other major world religions, with their perceptual belief forming practices and background belief systems. I am going to reserve that topic for separate consideration in Chapter 7, partly because it poses a much more serious difficulty for my claims, and partly because it differs from the possible competitors we will be considering here in that with the former, unlike the latter, there is no clear superiority as to firmness of establishment. As we shall see in Chapter 7, that makes a big difference to the situation. To anticipate my conclusions, there turns out to be no serious conflicts with the secular belief sources and systems treated in this section. As for other religions, there are serious conflicts, but they do not imply that any of the competitors thereby lose their claims to rational acceptance.

A. Natural Science

The relations of religion and science, logical and otherwise, is an enormous topic that has spawned whole libraries. Here I can only hit the highlights in a

[19]As noted in Chapter 4, section v, my version of a doxastic-practice epistemology makes room for interpractice conflict because, unlike the related views of Wittgenstein and his followers, it takes the realist view that there is a basic (roughly, "correspondence") concept of truth, and a single concept of reality, that is common to all doxastic practices. They all aim at forming correct beliefs about a common reality, and so it is quite conceivable that they should contradict each other as to the nature of this reality.

mostly dogmatic fashion. Let's distinguish three areas of conceivable serious conflict. (1) Particular scientific results, hypotheses, or theories versus particular religious doctrines. (2) Scientific and religious methods or procedures. (3) Religious doctrines and basic assumptions of science.

As for (1), I cannot see that there are any contradictions between established scientific results and central Christian doctrines. It is true that putative conflicts of this sort have occupied center stage throughout the postmedieval period. First, there was the battle over Copernican astronomy, with the Church doggedly clinging to the old Ptolemaic picture. Then there was bitter ecclesiastical opposition to both the claim that all current forms of life, including the human, have evolved from simpler forms, and to the Darwinian explanation thereof. But it cannot be seriously maintained that any of this involves matters of central concern to the Christian faith. No doubt, the Christian picture of God, creation, man, and salvation had long been set in the context of Ptolemaic astronomy, so that it was a a wrench to rethink it in other terms. It is also true that an astronomy that puts the earth at the center of the universe is more imaginatively suitable to the Christian drama of salvation. But nothing at the heart of the Christian faith is contradicted by Copernican or any other astronomy, as even the most conservative Christians now realize. The same story is to be told of the other skirmishes in the "warfare of science and religion". With respect to battles over evolution, it can hardly be supposed essential to the Christian faith to take the account of creation in Genesis as a chronology that is accurate when construed in the most literal terms. Nor does it contradict the idea that man is created in the image of God to suppose that that creation takes place through the intermediary of evolutionary mechanisms.

I will not go so far as as to maintain that there *can* be no contradiction between scientific results and central tenets of Christianity. The most obvious possibility concerns the human sciences. It undoubtedly is crucial for theistic religion that it work with a conception of man as capable of being addressed by God, capable of responding to God, capable of freely deciding whether or not to follow God's behests, capable of eternal loving communion with God after the death of the body. And some views about human nature do not allow for any such possibilities. Extreme behaviorist theories, like that of B. F. Skinner, depict human beings as wholly subject to laws of conditioning, and leave no room for free will. Freudian theories, as well, would seem to leave no room for human self-determination, though their state of development is such as to to make it impossible to say anything with assurance on this point. But though one can see the possibility of a serious conflict here, there is no such conflict at present, and the chances appar to be small. No theories of human nature and behavior sweeping enough to generate conflicts with religious belief are, or have any prospects of becoming, well enough established scientifically to give cause for concern.

While on this subject, let me underline the point that it would take conflict with established scientific *results* to discredit CMP, not conflict with scientific *hypotheses* that have not been thoroughly confirmed. Degree of confirmation is, trivially, a matter of degree (as well as being a thoroughly controversial subject), and I am not prepared to specify a minimal degree of confirmation that would cause trouble, even if I had the terms in which to do so. But that is not a serious problem. No scientific hypotheses or theories that come into serious conflict with the Christian faith have reached even the lowest level of confirmation that could sensibly be suggested here, nor, in my judgment, do they show any promise of doing so. This judgment applies not only to general theories of human nature and behavior, like those just mentioned, but even more so to their application to religious thought, feeling, and behavior. The Freudian theory of religion does definitely contradict the Christian faith, for it contradicts the claim that this faith was initiated by God's self-revelation. But I doubt that even the hardiest Freudian would suppose that this theory is to be counted among the assured results of science.

Even if some scientific result should contradict something central to the Christian faith, the question would remain as to whether that faith could be reconstructed so as to be compatible with the result in question and still be distinctively Christian. After all, the faith has undergone many such modifications in the past. Today most Christians are inclined to think that the features that were discarded or changed were not essential to the faith, but that is a retrospective judgment. They seemed essential to many at the time, and perhaps an analogous fate is in store for some features that seem essential to us today.

We should not ignore the various respects in which scientific developments have been felt by many to support, or at least to fit in well with, Christian and other theistic belief. I can't get into that in this book, but, just to take one example, the shift in astrophysics from the beginningless universe to the big bang obviously harmonizes with the idea that the physical universe was brought into existence by God some finite period of time ago.

I have been arguing that we do not in fact find serious conflicts between scientific results and the Christian faith. Is that just an accidental feature of the present situation, or are there deeper reasons for this? I think that there are such reasons. Science is essentially concerned with the structure of the physical universe, including embodied human beings and their social organization. It seeks to determine both the nature of its constituents, in as fine-grained a fashion as possible, and the laws of their behavior and interaction. That is, science is concerned to determine the taxonomy and the lawlike connections that hold *within* the physical universe. It is not concerned to determine what external source, if any, that universe depends on, or what that source is like and how it is related to its creation. This latter, by contrast, is the special purview of theistic religion; an account of this, together with practical implications thereof, lies at the heart of its mission. Its account will inevitably be couched in terms of some conception of the nature of the universe and the way its constituents work, and in this respect the religious account can come into conflict with science. But this is quite peripheral to the essential concerns of religion, which are with God and His purposes, activities, and requirements vis-à-vis His creatures, especially human beings. The basic message of Christianity can be recouched in terms of a different physics, astronomy, or biology without losing anything of its religious significance. It matters not a whit to the dependence of everything for its existence on God, the need of man for salvation from sin, or God's plan of redemption through Jesus Christ, whether the sun goes around the earth or vice versa, or whether the physical universe was created in six days 6,000 years ago or in a millisecond 5 billion years ago.

The only thing that mars the beautiful simplicity of this picture is the abstract possibility (one form of which, concerning the human sciences, was mentioned earlier) that the religious account of God's relation to certain parts of His creation might be such that it could be true only on certain views of the nature of those parts. And it is abstractly conceivable that incompatible views on these matters might be scientifically established. I can only say again that no such views seem to me to be scientifically established, nor do I see any reason to anticipate such a development.

What about (2), methodological conflicts? Here we must be careful to distinguish conflict from difference. It is true, of course, that Christian belief cannot be supported in the same way as scientific hypotheses and theories. But that by no means implies that there is any conflict or incompatibility between the two. It is only that they are different. Neither can the results of pure mathematics be established in the same way as the hypotheses and theories of empirical science; but that by no means implies that they are incompatible, only that they deal with different subject matter and different problems, and hence that they must proceed in correspondingly different ways. Indeed, my beliefs about my own conscious experience cannot be justified, established, or tested in the ways characteristic of empirical science; but again that has no tendency to show a conflict. There would be a conflict only if the the two parties made claims to the superiority of different methods for settling the same questions, but that is not the case here. Science has no business getting into the question of how to settle religious questions; and the same point is to be made in the reverse direction, despite the fact that certain ecclesiastical authorities forgot this during the rise of modern science. Scientistic philosophers often make the claim that the methods of science constitute the only way of finding out anything. But that is a bit of epistemological imperialism. It is not the sort of thing that could itself be established, or even supported, by the procedures of science; it does not fall within the purview of science.

As for (3), conflicts between religious doctrines and basic assumptions of science, that would seem to be more promising. It has often been said to be essential to science to assume (a) causal determinism, (b) materialism, and (c) mechanism. To be sure, (a) and (c) are a bit out of date. With the triumph of quantum mechanics, very few physicists adhere to determinism any more. As for mechanism, if it amounts to anything more than the denial of any indispensable teleological explanations, it presumably involves a commitment to the claim that every explanation must be in terms of mechanical forces (as contrasted with, e.g., gravitational or electromagnetic forces), in which case it is a relic of the seventeenth and eighteenth centuries. However, to come to grips with the question of whether there could be this kind of conflict, we need to consider just what assumptions like these amount to, where they are made, and whether they do generate a conflict with Christianity.

So far as I can see, when science, a science, or a scientist, is said to assume determinism or materialism, what is involved, at most, is that it or she proceeds on the working assumption that this is true of what it is investigating, or at least close enough to being true to justify giving the investigation one direction rather than another. Thus in looking for the causal determinants of a certain phenomenon, one assumes, at least provisionally, that there are causal determinants; otherwise there would be no point in looking. Again, in restricting one's attention to material features of one's subject matter, one is assuming that they are the only ones that matter, at least for the kinds of problems under investigation. Notive the qualifications involved here. The doctrine in question,—for example, determinism—is true *of the subject matter being investigated*, or at least *close enough to being true to make the investigation a sensible one*. Because of the first qualification, science cannot come into any conflict with religion over the existence and nature of God. Even if science assumes materialism and determinism for its subject matter, and these do not hold of God, there is no conflict, for God does not form any part of the subject matter of science.[20] The second qualification blocks what otherwise looks like a conflict between determinism and the religious belief that God acts in His creation outside the natural order of causes. This is the belief in *miracles*, construed as instances in which God directly acts on the world to bring about an outcome different from what it would have been if only natural causes were operative. Thus, let us say, God brings it about that Robinson recovers from a disease from which he would have died if nature had taken its course.[21] Now there is, undoubtedly, a direct logical contradiction between the belief in miracles, so construed,[22] and the claim that every

[20]Again scientistic philosophers will claim that everything that exists falls within the purview of science; anything that is alleged to fall outside the domain of scientific investigation is thereby doomed to dismissal as nonexistent. But again it is no part of science to make imperialist claims like this.

[21]I use a made-up example here because I don't want, for purposes of this discussion, to commit myself to the reality of any particular, famous biblical miracle. I want to consider only the general belief that such things do occur.

[22]This is the traditional construal. Lately various thinkers have sought to revise the concept of miracle so that the occurrence of miracles is compatible with complete natural-causal determinism. See, e.g., Tillich 1953, p. 130; Macquarrie 1977, p. 250. In this discussion I am concerned only with the more traditional understanding.

event in the physical universe is determined to be just what it is by natural causes. However, it does not seem to me that it is any part of science to make the latter claim. I can see that a scientist, when engaged in a search for causes of X,[23] will proceed on the assumption that X is at least fairly close to being what it is because of the operation of natural causes. But I can't see that the assumption has to be any more rigid than that. Indeed, if it were it would come into conflict with quantum theory. Moreover, and this is really the crucial point, what is of importance to scientific inquiry is that one can assume that it is *generally* true that a certain kind of phenomenon is determined by natural causes in a certain way. I can't see that it would significantly impede scientific research if a given phenomenon were occasionally to occur in a way that deviates from the general rule; and since, as it is usually supposed religiously, miracles are most uncommon, the odd miracle would not seem to violate anything of importance for science. It would be quite a remarkable coincidence if a miracle should be among the minute proportion of the cases of X that are examined for scientific purposes.[24] Thus it would appear that the belief in miracles fails to contradict anything that is of crucial concern for science.

B. History

I must consider, all too briefly, whether a historical religion like Christianity could come into fundamental conflict with the results of historical research. This is, obviously, possible in principle. It is conceivable that historians might turn up hard evidence—documentary and/or archaeological—that Jesus' tomb was not empty shortly after his death, that the resurrection narratives were faked, and that the whole thing was an elaborate scam. No doubt, this evidence would be subject to diverse interpretations like any other, but I will suppose for the sake of argument that it could be overwhelming in probative force. Indeed, some scholars seem to think that this possibility has already been realized, though I find that view too extreme to be worth notice. But though sticks and stones will break my bones, mere possibilities will never harm me. And as for actualities, I can see no conflict between actual historical results and any central Christian doctrine, nor do I see that any such conflict is looming on the horizon. To be sure, there is no independent historical confirmation of what is reported in the Gospels, but that is quite another matter. I suspect that most of the opposition of historical scholars to accept-

[23]Contrary to philosophical mythology, this is by no means all the time or even most of the time. Scientists are very much taken up with considering how best to categorize their subject matter, what the structure of certain things is, what mechanisms are employed in certain transactions, and so on.

[24]It is pertinent to point out in this connection that medical research goes merrily along, and makes dramatic advances, despite the fact that, by common consent, many cures occur for reasons no physician or researcher is in a position to specify. There are more than enough routine cases to form the needed inductive evidence for generalizations that turn out to be useful.

ing, for example, the resurrection as historical fact comes from an attachment to scientific determinism and a consequent denial of miracles. This is often claimed to be a tenet of historical methodology (though I would deny that it is required for historical research), but it can hardly be claimed to be a *result* of historical investigation.

C. Naturalistic Metaphysics

Here there undoubtedly is a conflict. Naturalism defines itself by contrast with what Christianity most centrally affirms—the dependence of the world of nature (the physical universe) on a transcendent spiritual being that has knowledge and acts to fulfill His purposes. God is, paradigmatically, *supernatural*, however much current Christian theologians may deplore the term because of various connotations from which they wish to disassociate themselves; and naturalism is, naturally, committed to oppose *super*-naturalism. Materialism is equally opposed to theistic religion. God is most definitely not a material entity; and so the belief in the existence of God, as central as you can get, runs directly counter to the view that everything that exists is material. Moreover, material things, according to naturalism, are subject to the rule of natural law. But God is subject to no such constraints. God is supremely sovereign over all things other than Himself, including the laws of nature. He is the free creator of such laws (or, if you prefer, the free creator of beings as subject to laws); they hold at His pleasure. Hence it would be incoherent to suppose that His activity, including His creative activity, is necessarily subject to such laws. There is no doubt, then, that Christian belief runs smack into contradiction with naturalism and materialism.[25] If such a metaphysics is correct, CMP gives us a radically distorted picture of the way things are.[26]

[25]Naturalism is largely a matter of giving an unrestricted metaphysical application to the assumptions that science is often said to make concerning its subject matter: materialism, determinism, and so on. In spite of this I hold that there is no conflict between Christian doctrine and the assumptions of science, while also recognizing serious contradictions between Christianity and naturalism. The reason for this difference is that by metaphysically generalizing the assumptions science makes for its own domain, naturalism gets into the business of legislating for the same territory occupied by religion; hence the conflict.

[26]In making this judgment I am *not* assuming that Christian belief or doctrine consists, even in part, of a metaphysical system or theory, or a world view, or any such thing. Beliefs can be incompatible with certain metaphysical theories without themselves being, or being part of, a metaphysical theory or system. If that were not the case, then every time I believe something about something other than myself I would be involved in developing or applying a nonsolipsistic metaphysics. But surely innumerable persons totally innocent of metaphysics constantly have beliefs about things other then themselves. The supposition that one is engaged in metaphysics whenever one believes anything that some metaphysical view would rule out has been a source of a great deal of mischief that has darkened our understanding of religious belief. Religious belief, like commonsense belief, can have metaphysical implications while lacking the theoretical and speculative character of metaphysical thinking.

How much of a worry this is for CMP depends on the status of these contrary metaphysical systems. And how about that? Again, I will have to state and defend my position briefly. In doing so, I will avoid the awkwardness of constantly dealing with the disjunction 'naturalism-materialism' by confining attention to the materialist form of naturalism, which is in any event the most common form and particularly prevalent at present. Moreover, to keep the discussion within reasonable bounds, I shall confine myself to the bearing on Christian doctrine of the thesis that everything that exists is material in nature, using the term 'materialism' for that thesis alone. It is in line with the position I defended earlier with respect to the religion-science relationship to hold that the bite of materialism, vis-à-vis CMP, comes from what it denies rather than from its treatment of the natural world. Although this is highly controversial, I believe that Christianity could accommodate itself to a purely materialist account of the creation, including human beings. This is not a perfectly precise issue because of the notorious indeterminacy of the concept of the material. But, pretending that we have workable criteria for a process or state being purely material, could Christianity accept the claim that human beings are purely material organisms? Obviously, this is not the view of the matter (no pun intended) most congenial to the Christian tradition, but the question is whether anything essential to Christianity would be lost on this view of human nature. I will focus on just one possible loss: the life of the world to come. None of the currently prominent eviscerations of Christian belief will have any trouble here, since they don't take "eternal life with God" to involve a literal continuance of human life after death. But I am asking about Christian belief as more traditionally understood. Can that coexist with a purely materialist account of human beings? Yes; the doctrine of the resurrection of the body performs exactly that function.[27] If the life of the world to come is a life lived by a resurrected body, then even if that body has usually been taken in the Christian tradition to differ markedly from our present bodies, there is no reason to deny that it will be *material*, especially given the nebulousness of the concept of materiality.

I take it, then, that the force of materialism, vis-à-vis CMP, lies in its denial that anything other than the purely material universe exists and exerts any influence on the course of events. Here it undeniably stands in flat opposition to CMP, for reasons given above. However things are with us, God cannot be construed as a material being, and Christian belief could not be recognizably itself without committing itself to His existence and His influence on the course of events. Thus we must ask what reasons there are to accept materialism.

Very few. Historically and at present the strength of materialism lies in the

[27]I am not suggesting that the doctrine was developed to accommodate materialism, for nothing like modern materialism was dreamed of at that period. Nevertheless, ancient Hebrew conceptions of man were perhaps closer to modern materialism than to modern dualisms.

impressive achievements of science. Modern science has shown, to an extent hitherto undreamt of, that the physical world, including to some extent human beings and their activities, can be understood, charted, predicted, and explained when we think of them as purely material. And, by contrast, no such achievements have stemmed from nonmaterialist construals. Materialist physics from the seventeenth century on far outstripped the previously dominant, Aristotelian physics with its built-in teleology and other nonpurely materialist features. But this support extends only to the materialist construal of the natural world. It has no tendency to show that there are no other orders of being that fall outside the materialist net. How could it? Recall the earlier discussion of science. Science is fitted for the exploration of the natural world that is accessible to sense perception. How could its procedures throw any light on whether or not there are orders of reality not cognitively accessible in the same way? That would be like expecting mathematical thought to tell us whether life evolved, or aesthetic sensitivity to tell us about the constitution of galaxies.

This point is liable to be obscured because of its entanglement with other issues we have been discussing, particularly the science-religion relationship. If one thinks that scientific results contradict Christian belief at fundamental points, or that it is crucial for science to assume that everything conforms to causal determinism or mechanism or materialism, one will naturally suppose that science can support materialism against theistic religion. And if one thinks that the sciences of man have decisively refuted a conception of man needed for Christian belief, one will naturally suppose that these sciences provide support for a metaphysics that is an alternative to Christian belief. I will not repeat the above arguments against these ways of thinking.

Can the denial of the nonmaterial be supported in any other way? Materialists commonly appeal to such desiderata of theories as economy and simplicity. The success of science does make it clear that we have to use materialist categories to understand the natural world. We get a much simpler and more economical metaphysical theory if we assume that everything that exists is amenable to full understanding in the same way. Sure! We always get simpler and more economical accounts by leaving out additional complexities. And it is no doubt intellectually satisfying to do so. But what is more important, intellectual satisfaction or adequacy to the subject matter? I think it would be universally agreed that the latter desideratum should have priority. But then the crucial question is whether there are realities not adequately construable in materialist terms. If we have no other basis for answering this question, the preferred course would be a negative answer, on grounds of simplicity. But do we have some other basis? CMP puts itself forward as supporting an affirmative answer. We can't dismiss that claim just on the grounds that a negative answer would be more intellectually satisfying. That would be like dismissing the claims of psychoanalytic investigation, or telescopic observation, or the study of fossils, on the grounds that if we admit data from these sources it will greatly complicate things. I am not saying that it is obvious that CMP is a source of knowledge or justified belief. I am merely pointing out that its prima facie claim to this cannot be overthrown just on the grounds that it would make life more complicated for metaphysicians.

Similar remarks are to be made about appeals to coherence by materialists. Whether and how strongly a given thesis is supported by coherence considerations depends on what there is for it to cohere with. Again we are faced with the question of whether there are any beliefs about nonmaterial facts in the system with which a given proposition must cohere in order to be justified. We can't rule out that possibility by pointing out that if the system includes only beliefs about material facts then materialism coheres with that very well.

On the metaphysical front I have been considering only the possibility that CMP might be discredited by a naturalistic metaphysics. I have said nothing about the possibility that it might be undermined by a nontheistic, nonnaturalistic metaphysics, such as those excogitated by monistic Hindus and by Buddhists. Nor have I said anything about the possibility of support for CMP from a theistic metaphysics. The reasons are somewhat different in the two cases. I have eschewed the latter because I have been concerned to determine how well CMP conforms to the model of a socially established, undefeated doxastic practice. In Chapters 5–7 I am arguing that CMP is rationally accepted (engaged in) *just by virtue of being a socially established doxastic practice that is not disqualified by severe internal or external incompatibilities*. The question of what other support is forthcoming for it is a further question, on which I shall (barely) touch in Chapter 8. As for the former abstention, I can plead no such principled ground. I must admit that conflict with a monistic Hindu metaphysics is, in principle, as relevant as conflict with a naturalistic metaphysics and that an ideally complete treatment would go into this. In explanation, if not extenuation, of my failure to do so I can only plead lack of expertise and the fact that a proper treatment of the whole range of opposing metaphysical systems would far exceed the limits of this book.

v. Summary

In this and the preceding chapter we have considered a number of alleged reasons for supposing that the prima facie claim of CMP to rational acceptance by virtue of its being a going concern is overridden by one or another crippling defect. I have concentrated on three lines of criticism. (1) CMP doesn't have the kind of overrider system that provides checking and testing procedures that are required if it is to be a respectable doxastic practice. (2) Mystical experience can be adequately explained in terms of purely natural factors. (3) CMP can be shown to be unreliable either by internal contradictions in its output or by conflicts between its output and that of more firmly established practices. We have argued that in none of these cases do we have a sufficient reason to cancel the prima facie claim to rationality CMP enjoys by virtue of being a socially established doxastic practice.

Having identified certain intellectual vices exhibited by one or another of the objections canvassed, it may be useful to classify the main objections by the vice predominantly exhibited.

A. Epistemic Imperialism

(1) "The so-called checks on particular perceptual claims in CMP aren't genuine checks, since there is no specification of the conditions under which a qualified observer would perceive the same thing if it is there to be perceived." This is to unwarrantedly take features of the checking system typical of SP as the norm for all perceptual belief forming practices.

(2) "CMP cannot claim to give us effective cognitive contact with objective reality. If it did it would put us into position to make accurate predictions of that reality." Ditto. SP gives us predictive power because of the kind of reality with which it puts us into touch. We cannot assume that any veridical access to any reality, no matter what it is like and no matter how we are related to it, will yield just that kind of fruit.

(3) "If the putative object of CMP really existed we would have adequate reason for this (from "secular" practices), since it would have some impact on the natural world from which its existence could be inferred." Why suppose that God must reveal Himself to the SP-memory-inference package if He really exists? That is no more compelling than the assumption that the atomic structure of matter must reveal itself to CMP if it really obtains. We are in no position to assume a priori that the object of one practice will reveal itself through some other practice if it does exist.

B. Double Standard

(1) "We have no non-circular reason to believe that CMP is a reliable source of belief." Neither do we have such reason for SP and for other basic secular doxastic practices.

(2) "The checking system of CMP is of no epistemic significance since its claim to provide effective checks rests on support from CMP itself." Exactly the same is true of SP. We have to use SP to determine what tests a particular report must be able to pass in order to be unqualifiedly justified and whether that report passes them.

(3) "CMP yields mutually inconsistent beliefs." So does SP.

(4) "Mystical experience can be given an adequate causal explanation without mentioning God." Likewise sense experience can be adequately causally

explained in terms of neural processes in the brain without mentioning the putatively perceived external object.

vi. Self-Support of CMP

In Chapters 5 and 6 we have completed the easy part of rebutting objections to our central thesis. In the next chapter we will turn to the thorny problems posed by the existence of a plurality of mutually incompatible systems of religious belief and associated perceptual belief-forming practices. But first I want to apply to CMP another general feature of doxastic practices listed in Chapter 4, namely, "significant self-support". I pointed out there that not all self-support exhibits the kind of triviality we get when we simply use the same output twice, once as testee and once as tester. Obviously any practice can support itself in that way. But our most fundamental and widely dispersed practices support themselves in other ways that are by no means trivial. SP, as we pointed out, supports itself in the following nontrivial ways, among others. (1) By engaging in SP and reasoning from its output, we are enabled to make predictions many of which turn out to be correct, and thereby we are able to exercise considerable control over the course of events. (2) On the same basis we are able to establish facts about the operation of sense perception that show that it is a generally reliable source, why it is reliable, and the conditions under which it is less reliable. These results are by no means trivial. Not every doxastic practice exhibits something similar. The fact that we have achieved these results by using SP and associated practices goes some way toward justifying our confidence in its reliability.

I now want to suggest that CMP supports itself in an analogously nontrivial way. We should not suppose that the self-support will be of just the same sort. Indeed, we have already seen that no predictive fruits of the SP sort are forthcoming from CMP, and we have achieved some insight into why this should be so. However it is reasonable to think that the self-supporting fruits of CMP would be related to *its* basic aim and structure in a similar way. The basic function of SP in our lives is to provide a "map" of the physical and social environment and thereby enable us to find our way around in it, to anticipate the course of events and to adjust our behavior to what we encounter so as to satisfy our needs and achieve our ends. Part of the self-support we have noted for SP constitutes the successful carrying out of this aim. To discover an analogous self-support of CMP we have to ask what its basic function in human life is. It is not primarily a theoretical or speculative function, any more than with SP, but it is not the same kind of practical function either. It is an analogous function, namely, providing a "map" of the "divine environment", providing guidance for our interaction with God. CMP, along with the other sources that are drawn on to build up the Christian scheme of things, has the function of giving us a picture of God, His purposes, activities, requirements on us and plans for us, a picture that will guide us in our interactions with Him. That is a large order, of course. To give the discussion a bit more focus, I will concentrate on one aspect of this, namely, the spiritual development of the individual, the transformation of the individual into what God intended her to be, into the sort of person that is capable of entering into the loving communion with God for which we were created. We may as well use the traditional Christian term for this process, *sanctification*. Thus CMP proves itself, if at all, by the fact that it provides guidance in the all important enterprise of sanctification, guidance in the pilgrimage that leads, if things go right, to eternal loving communion with God. This story is a long one. It involves a radical turning (conversion) of oneself from preoccupation with the satisfaction of desires for sensory gratification, creature comforts, keeping up with the latest trendy consumer goods, one's own peace and serenity, one's status and reputation, and other self-centered aims; it involves turning away from this in the direction of an aim at loving communion with God and with one's fellows. It involves letting go of one's insistence on controlling one's destiny and opening up oneself to the Spirit, receiving the fruits of the Spirit—love, joy, peace, and so on—as free gifts, not as something one has earned by one's industry or one's own merits. It involves living one's life in the presence of God, following whatever vocation is given one by God. It involves opening oneself up to other people and loving them, to the measure of one's capacity, as God does. This is just a quick sketch. I can't embark here on a treatise on the spiritual life; that's all right, for it has been done many times by people much better equipped to do so than I. I merely want to give some indication of the sorts of fruits of participation in CMP that provide a self-support for CMP that is analogous, in a way appropriate to CMP, to the kind of self-support we have seen SP to generate.

A more comprehensive treatment would reveal the modes of self-support I am emphasizing as simply the most prominent and noteworthy examples of a much more general phenomenon—the support provided some components of the practice (including outputs, background belief system, overriding procedures, etc.) by others, sometimes in both directions. Thus the self-support exhibited by SP involves not only the items we have mentioned, but also all the ways in which observational results support general beliefs, all our successes in explaining certain facts revealed by the practice in terms of other things we have learned in the practice, and all the ways in which our perceptions generally fit into a unified coherent picture of the physical world. Likewise the self-support of CMP includes the ways in which putative perceptions of God generally conform to the picture of God built up in the background system, the ways in which many different people independently discover through their experience the same reality—for example, the love of God—and the ways in which the belief system provides illuminating explanations of many facts of our life, both "spiritual" and otherwise. In fact, "significant self-support" ranges over much of what has gone under the heading of "coherence". In this section I am merely exhibiting some particular impressive forms of the phenomenon.

At this point it might help to bring in another doxastic practice—interpersonal perception, our awareness of other persons as persons. There is controversy over whether to regard this as an autonomous practice or simply as a department of sense perceptual practice; I shall adopt the former view. That is, I shall suppose that we have a practice of objectifying certain ranges of our experience in terms of the presence, conditions, characteristics, and activities of other persons, and that this practice can no more be justified from the outside than any of the others we have been considering. This practice is, in a way, intermediate between SP and CMP. In particular, and this is the point I want to stress here, its self-support is not so purely in terms of predictive efficacy as is SP. To be sure, by perceiving what we do of other persons we are thereby enabled to anticipate their behavior to some extent, and this is of practical value. But persons are notoriously less predictable than things, and the value of this practice for our lives is not restricted to a predictive payoff. To compensate for this relative unpredictability, there is the possibility of entering into communication and fellowship with others. And, most basically, that is what this practice enables us to do; it enables us to enter into social relations with other persons. We might, analogously, rephrase the above statement about the function of CMP by saying that it enables us to enter into communication with God and thereby to become what God intends us to become.

I will try to be a bit more explicit as to how we should think of these fruits as providing self-support for CMP. CMP, including the associated Christian scheme that has been built up over the centuries, generates, among much else, the belief that God has made certain promises of the destiny that awaits us if we follow the way of life enjoined on us by Christ. We are told that if we will turn from our sinful ways, reorder our priorities, take a break from preoccupation with our self-centered aims long enough to open ourselves to the sanctifying work of the Holy Spirit, then we will experience a transformation into the kind of nonpossessive, nondefensive, loving, caring, and serene persons God has destined us to become—not immediately and not without many ups and downs, but eventually, so long as we stick to the regimen. Moreover, even though the fulfillment of this promise is compatible with an indefinite number of setbacks along the way, one can expect definite signs that the process of sanctification is proceeding. Assuming that we get such indications in many of those cases in which the person is satisfying, to a significant extent, the conditions laid down as necessary for the promised transformation, this constitutes a fulfillment of the divine promises, and hence a fulfillment of the *predictions* that are based on these promises. And in so far forth this provides support for the epistemic claims of the practice to be putting us in effective cognitive contact with God, the source of those promises.

Please note that I am not suggesting that we can justify particular Christian beliefs by pointing out that one will become a better person if he accepts them, or anything of the sort. That kind of pragmatic defense of religious belief is very far from my position. Particular beliefs are justified by virtue of what they are based on within the doxastic practice in question. My suggestion is rather that the *practice* can receive a degree of self-support by the way in which spiritual development constitutes a fulfillment of promises that, in the practice, we come to believe are made by God.

It may seem that no epistemic circularity is involved in discerning these fulfillments of promises, and hence that this is stronger than *self*-support. But that would be an illusion. I don't want to cite in this connection the fact that we need CMP to determine what the promises are. That merely gives us the candidates for testing; the crucial question is as to whether we can assess those candidates without relying on the practice under examination. The reason we cannot do so is that progress in spirituality cannot be spotted without reliance on CMP and its background system of belief. Such data as can be obtained from purely secular doxastic practices will inevitably be ambiguous. Is S a more truly humble person, or is she just beaten down by the struggles of her life? Is S truly unconcerned about success, or has she just substituted one form of success for another? And so on. It requires a special sort of "spiritual discernment" that is itself one of the fruits of spiritual development to discriminate between true progress in sanctification and its many counterfeits. The ability to discern forms of true spirituality in oneself and others is itself one of the perceptual skills and perceptual belief forming capacities that are involved in CMP, though one that has not been in the picture up to now. We have been focusing so exclusively on the perceptual awareness of God that we have neglected the important fact that CMP, in its fuller development, also involves the capacity to perceive things in one's physical and social environment to which one would otherwise be blind.[28] The spiritual condition of oneself and others is among those things. Since one cannot ascertain that the spiritual fruits in question are forthcoming without utilizing CMP, the support in question does fall under the rubric of *self-support*.[29]

But does CMP support itself in the way I have been discussing? It does if people who respond in the right way to God's call to us undergo the right sort

[28]This implies that our portrayal of CMP has been incomplete. I am afraid that a comprehensive treatment is beyond the scope of this book.

[29]Likewise, the support given SP by its success in generating accurate predictions is not rendered epistemically circular by the fact that the predictions are generated by the practice, but by the fact that we have to use the practice itself to determine whether they are accurate. Note the following difference between the two situations. In SP the determination of predictive success involves just the same sort of use of the practice as does the generation of the predictions. It is not quite like that with CMP. We get the promises from God's messages to us; but we don't have to ask God whether a given individual is developing spiritually. At least that is not our only resource, though it may be that one gets frequent reassurances from God that one is moving in the right direction. But even when the person in question or his fellows can "see for themselves" that that person is growing spiritually, it is not as if one can "see" this without any reliance on CMP and the Christian scheme.

of spiritual development. But is this the case? It follows from what I have been saying that this is a question that cannot be decided except from inside the practice, though outsiders can find out something about this from hearing what insiders say, seeing what they do, and reading what they write. At this point I must make explicit a hitherto suppressed difference between CMP and SP. It is inappropriate to equate the situation of the ordinary Christian believer, even the serious, devout, and committed Christian believer, vis-à-vis CMP with the situation of the normal adult human being vis-à-vis SP. For we are all masters of the latter practice. We emerged from our apprenticeship in early childhood, long before we reached the stage of philosophical reflection. But though we may have been initiated into CMP at an early age, we are, almost all of us, still at the stage of early infancy in this practice, just beginning to learn to distinguish the other reality from ourselves, just beginning to recognize the major outlines of the landscape and, one should add, just beginning to learn to respond to them appropriately. There are, to be sure, wide differences in the population in certain areas of SP; we have had occasion to mention some of them—for example, wine tasting and the aural analysis of complex musical performances. But over most of the range all normal, adult humans are on the same level. With CMP and other religious perceptual practices, on the other hand, there are sharp differences in expertise, with most participants at a low level. Hence authority plays a much larger role here, not just on theoretical matters, as in science, but even on the perceptual level. Most of us must look outside our own experience to the tiny minority that qualify as masters of the spiritual life, both for some intimation of what mastery of the practice is like and for an answer to the question of whether this enterprise proves itself by its fruits. Of course there is a remedy for that—to become masters ourselves. But that is an arduous and demanding task, one that few of us are prepared to undertake. Meanwhile, we must glean such hints as we can from the lives, works, and thoughts of those advanced in the spiritual life, both as to what it is to be more than a babe in the experience of God, and as to what it is to respond to this experience in the ways it indicates. The testimony of the experts is that CMP does prove itself by its spiritual fruits in the sanctification of the individual. This is abundantly brought out by the writings of the saints, officially so designated or not. It may be objected that I have loaded the dice here by restricting my witnesses to those from whom I can confidently expect a positive answer. But, in the nature of the case, what is the alternative?

CHAPTER 7

The Problem of Religious Diversity

i. Preview

I have saved the most difficult problem for my position—religious diversity—for a separate chapter. I believe that I have succeeded in drawing the fangs of the various objections considered up to now by the simple expedient of looking them in the face and challenging their basic assumptions. In doing so I have identified certain recurrent fallacies that underlie many of these objections—epistemic imperialism and the double standard. The objections in question are made from a naturalistic viewpoint. They involve unfavorable epistemic comparisons between mystical perception and sense perception; it is not difficult to show that they either condemn the former for features it shares with the latter (the double standard) or unwarrantedly require the former to exhibit features of the latter (imperialism). But the problem posed by religious pluralism, more specifically by the existence of a plurality of incompatible religious perceptual doxastic practices, cannot be handled in these ways. It deserves, and will receive, more serious consideration.

The first task is to set out the difficulty clearly. Just exactly what is it about religious pluralism that poses a difficulty for the claims I have made for CMP? I have just alluded to the difficulty as posed by "the existence of a plurality of incompatible religious perceptual practices"? But in what way are they incompatible? And given that they are incompatible in whatever way this turns out to be, just how or why does that cast doubt on the rationality of CMP? The intuitive idea here, no doubt, is that if the general enterprise of forming perceptual religious beliefs is carried on in different religions in such a way as to yield incompatible results, no such practice can be considered to be reliable, and so none is rationally engaged in. But it will take much honing and sharpening to get this idea into acceptable shape.

ii. How Different Forms of MP Are Incompatible

Let's begin, then, by tackling the first of the two issues I just distinguished: the precise way in which perceptual doxastic practices in different religions are incompatible. And we may as well begin by setting aside an idea that might be suggested by the formulation I just gave of the objection. That formulation spoke of "the general enterprise of forming perceptual religious beliefs". That suggests that if perceptual beliefs formed in Christianity are incompatible, at certain points, with those formed in Islam and Buddhism, we are confronted with a form of internal contradiction, contradictions in the output of a single doxastic practice. But that can't be the right way to look at it, for there is no single practice of forming religious perceptual beliefs. We have seen that doxastic practices are individuated by, inter alia, their associated overrider systems, and these, as noted in Chapter 5, differ markedly between religions. Hence such incompatibilities as we discover involve *inter*-practice rather than *intra*-practice contradictions. But in just what way(s) is a Hindu mystical perceptual doxastic practice, for example, incompatible with CMP? The most obvious suggestion would be that the outputs of the practices contradict each other, not just here and there but in a massive fashion, so as to make it impossible that both are reliable modes of belief formation. Let's explore this possibility.

To simplify matters, let's suppose that the doxastic outputs are all of the singular subject-predicate form, and that they all attribute to a perceived subject some putatively perceivable property or putatively perceivable activity—'God is merciful', 'God is comforting me'. Now the most obvious ways in which a pair of such beliefs can be incompatible is that they attribute incompatible properties to the same subject. Is that what is going on here? This divides into two questions. Is the subject the same? Are the predicates incompatible? Let's consider them in turn.

Sometimes we do have reason to judge that adherents of different religions are perceiving, and forming beliefs about, the same being, as where the religions share common roots, as with Judaism and Christianity and, to a lesser extent, Islam. Adherents of all these religions take themselves to be in contact with the God of Abraham, Isaac, and Jacob, with the God Who led the Israelites out of Egypt under the leadership of Moses, and Who spoke through the prophets. Therefore, it is not implausible to suppose that if their adherents are perceiving anything like what they take themselves to be perceiving, it is the same being. But we do not have this kind of reason when dealing with traditions that developed independently. And if the characterizations of the deity differ widely, as in the comparison of Christianity with various forms of Hinduism and Buddhism, that counts against a commonality of referent. To be sure, it is possible that a Christian and a Hindu are perceiving the same God, even though their conceptions of God differ markedly. It is a general point about perception that *what* it is that I am perceiving is not determined by my beliefs concerning it. I can take what I see to be a cow, while you, at a different distance and from a different angle, take it to be a boulder, even though we are seeing the same thing (an automobile). And there may be theological reasons for supposing that people in all religious traditions are aware of the one God, even though He appears to them in different guises and they form divergent beliefs about Him.[1]

Thus even if the predicates attributed to the perceived object of worship are frequently incompatible across different religions, that would not show that the beliefs are incompatible until we find sufficient reason for supposing that those perceived objects are the same. There is no incompatibility in A saying that *his* house is red and B saying that *his* house is white. There is also the point that this approach seems to assume that in each case there is a genuine, objectively real and transcendent object of perception to which the predicate in question is attached; the only question being as to whether it is the same object across religious boundaries. And, needless to say, this may be questioned. When I present an alternative approach I will show how to avoid this assumption. For now, though, I want to take a brief look at the predicate side and consider the extent to which the predicates of religious perceptual beliefs across traditions could not be true of the same subject. This issue will obviously be affected by how we construe the beliefs in question, a matter that will be briefly discussed below. For now I only wish to point out that it is easy to overestimate the degree of conflict. Much of the controversy between religions comes not from incompatibility in positive assertions, but in the fact that each implicitly denies what is said by the others. If Vedanta or Yoga mystics report that they are aware of an undifferentiated unity, that attribution in itself is not incompatible with characterizing that same being as a personal agent, unless a denial of the latter is read into the former. Aquinas and many other theologians take the two to be compatible. Again, attributing to God the message that Jesus is His Son is not, so far as positive content is concerned, incompatible with attributing to God the message that Mohammed is His prophet, unless the former message also contains the stipulation that the life and work of Jesus Christ is the only way to salvation. And the more common reports of God as loving or powerful, comforting or sustaining, are mostly quite compatible with perceived features of the deity in other religions. A thoroughgoing treatment of this topic would be an enormous undertaking, one that I must forego here. I would only urge the reader to exercise caution in supposing that, even granting commonality of subject, what is said of God in Hindu perceptual reports contradicts what is said of God in Christian perceptual reports.

What we have seen thus far is that it is unpromising to look for massive interreligion incompatibilities in perceptual attributions of incompatible predi-

[1]I will not attempt to argue for this claim. So far as I can see, it would require theological premises, and that is outside the limits of this book

cates to the same subject. Let's try another approach by raising a question that should have been posed at the outset, namely, how do we identify those doxastic practices in other religions that are to be compared with CMP? Remember that we explained CMP as a form of the practice of forming perceptual beliefs on the basis of what we have been calling "mystical perception". And mystical perception was marked out in terms of the perceiver supposing herself to be directly experientially aware of *God*. 'God' was explained in standard theistic terms. But then how do we locate "mystical perception" in nontheistic religions? How do we determine what counts as a practice of forming beliefs on the basis of mystical perception in Buddhism or nontheistic forms of Hinduism? To do so we must enlarge our conception of mystical perception as follows. In the major religions of the contemporary world, those to which we are restricting our attention here, the religious responses of devotion, commitment, faith, hope, prayer, worship, adoration, and thanksgiving are directed to what is taken to be Ultimate, the ultimate determiner of one's existence, condition, salvation, destiny, or whatever. This Ultimate is conceived of differently in different religions. It may or may not transcend the world of nature, may or may not be personal, may or may not exhibit a tight unity. Thus as a wider conception of mystical perception I suggest the following. It is what is taken by the subject to be a direct experiential awareness of the Ultimate.

This provides the basis for exhibiting a massive incompatibility of the output of mystical perceptual practices. As just noted, one's conception of the Ultimate will differ in different religions. Even where the broad outlines of the conception is the same, as it is among the various theistic religions, the details will differ. After all, a religiously very important feature of the Christian, Jewish, and Moslem conceptions of the Ultimate has to do with God's purposes for mankind and His work in history; and the account of this varies drastically from one of these traditions to another.[2] And all these will diverge sharply from the conception of the Ultimate in Buddhism and certain forms of Hinduism, where the Ultimate is not thought of as a personal agent. Let's further note that one's conception of God (the Ultimate) enters, to a greater or lesser degree, into a particular subject's identification of the perceived object as God (Brahman . . .). When I take *God* to be present to me I will, if I am a Christian, but not if I am Moslem or a Hindu, most likely take it that *He who became man in the person of Jesus Christ to save us from our sins* is present to me. Indeed, it is generally true we make use of what we believe about perceived objects when we perceptually identify them. When I take the person I see across the room to be Joe Walker, I thereby take him to be the person

[2]It is, I take it, obvious that I do not restrict a *conception* of the Ultimate to the most basic beliefs concerning its nature, in which case all theistic religions would share the same conception, but think of it as embracing all the beliefs about the Ultimate that play a major role in the religion.

with whom I went to college, who lives two blocks from me, and so on. Because of this leakage of the background belief system into perceptual beliefs, the latter will be incompatible with each other across religious traditions, *even if the predicates attributed in these perceptual beliefs are as compatible with each other as you like*. I take myself to be aware of God sustaining me in being by pouring out His creative love into me. The predicate of this perceptual belief may not be strictly incompatible with anything centrally believed about the Ultimate in Judaism, Islam, or Hinduism, though love may be stressed more in Christianity. Nevertheless, I take my conception of who it is I am aware of here, as pouring out creative love into me, from the Christian tradition. To be sure, I don't have all the details of that tradition actively before my mind at the moment of the experience, but it is there in the background, and even if I don't rehearse it in my mind, still part of what I am committed to in forming my perceptual belief is that He Who raised Jesus Christ from the dead is pouring out His creative love into me. And in taking this to be true of the Ultimate ("raised Jesus Christ from the dead", etc.), I am committing myself to something incompatible with the beliefs of other religions that recognize no divine action. Even if the Christian's attribution of love to God is perfectly compatible with the Moslem's attribution of justice, still the background conception of what God is like, what He has done, what His plans and requirements are, and so on, that enter into the identification of the subject of attribution, will be incompatible with each other; and so the total content of the perceptual beliefs will be incompatible just because of that.

Since a great deal hangs on this point, I will have to go into the matter more carefully.[3] Just how the central beliefs of the tradition enter into the identification of a perceived object of mystical perception will differ, depending on the propositional content of the perceptual belief about this object. The most natural reading of the last paragraph is in terms of a "descriptivist" account of reference. Since the issues I will be discussing here have been much more extensively explored for the speech acts of reference and assertion than for propositional attitudes like belief, I shall conduct the discussion in terms of the former, taking the application to the latter to be obvious. To continue, it is clear that if when I assert "God was present to me" I am using 'God' as shorthand for a "definite description", such as "The creator of the universe, He Who became incarnate in Jesus Christ to save us for our sins"—or perhaps, less explicitly, "the Being of Whom the main doctrines of the Christian religion are true"—then it follows in the most direct way possible that in making that assertion I am asserting, in part, that He Who became incarnate in Jesus Christ to save us from our sins was present to me". If that is the right way to think about reference to God in perceptual beliefs and their linguistic expression, then, provided the descriptions involved are rich enough

[3]Here I am indebted to Alvin Plantinga.

to be incompatible with the way the Ultimate is referred to in other religions, we will unquestionably get incompatibilities across religions between the perceptual beliefs themselves.

However, it may well be doubted that this is the way the name 'God' works that way in these contexts. One reason that is often given is the following. If 'God' is an abbreviation for some conjunction of descriptions like those just mentioned, then if we attribute one of those descriptions to God, by saying, for example, "God created the universe", then what we say is "analytically" true, true just by the meaning of the words; but that doesn't seem right. But this objection may be countered by supposing the descriptive meaning of 'God' to vary with context in such a way that the predicate ascribed to God never figures in the set of descriptions for which 'God' is shorthand in that context. Be all that as it may, there are reasons for supposing that 'God', along with other proper names, typically function simply as *labels* for something perceived, described, or taken from the talk of others.[4] These labels do not have as part of their meaning that certain things are true of the item labelled; in using a name to pick out something it is no part of what I mean that the thing in question has certain properties or has performed certain actions. Let's call this "direct reference". In this case when I say "God was present to me" it is no part of what I explicitly assert that He Who became incarnate in Jesus Christ was present to me. Although I may be said to be committed to this, that is not only because of the content of the perceptual belief expressed in that report, but because of that, *together with* the fact that I also believe that God became incarnate in Jesus Christ. Thus, if this is the way reference to God is carried out in perceptual beliefs and reports, the perceptual beliefs do not themselves conflict with each other across religions because of conflicts in the central doctrines of those religions. It is only some wider systems of belief that are incompatible with each other.

Still, even if we make direct reference to God and my M-beliefs are not themselves incompatible with those of the Moslem or Hindu, I believe it can be shown that just by virtue of engaging in CMP I am involved in conflict with analogous practices in other religions, and just because of the conflicts between the basic belief systems of the religions. To get at this, I will, for the moment, go back to the idea that our reference to God in M-beliefs is of a descriptivist sort, and the descriptions are such as to bring central features of the religious belief system into the content of M-beliefs. In the face of this situation, the strategy suggests itself of avoiding the difficulties of religious pluralism by taking only what is based on the experience in question as prima facie justified by the experience, rather than taking the whole package (including the identification of the object in terms of the background system) as so justified. Here we can profitably borrow some terminology introduced by Fred Dretske in 1969 (chap. 3). There he speaks of the "incremental infor-

[4]See my "Referring to God" in 1989a.

mation" provided by a given perception that is added to the "background information" that is brought to the perception. Thus, to use one of his examples, if I look at the kettle and say "The water is boiling", I can't really tell from that look that the liquid that is boiling is water rather than some other clear liquid—for example, gin. I take it that it is water; this is something I know, or assume, in advance of taking the look. What the look tells me is that that liquid, whatever it is, is boiling. In this case, as in those in which we are interested, it is the subject of the perceptual report that carries the information or assumption brought to the perception, and the predicate that embodies what one takes oneself to have learned about the object from the experience itself. Gary Gutting (in 1982, chap. 5) employs this approach to the epistemic assessment of religious perceptual beliefs. He holds that the "core" of belief that is justified by religious experience does not include "any substantive account of the details of God's nature and his relations with us (such as those offered by the creeds and theologies of religions), but only to the reality of a superhuman power and love in our lives, as this has been revealed by religious experiences of the presence of God" (p. 175). We need not take Gutting's proposal to be narrowly restricted to power and love but to range also over other features and activities that are directly presented in mystical experience.

To be sure, one difficulty with this approach is that we seem to be left without a subject to which to attach the predicates. We are justified in believing that *who* or *what* is very powerful and loving? However this can be handled by a switch from the subject-predicate form to the existentially quantified form. Instead of 'God is permeating me with His power and love', we have 'There is a very powerful and loving being present to me'. Admittedly, this is not the way in which our subjects typically report their experiences,[5] but the point would be that the claims have to be stripped down in this way if they are to avoid running afoul of the conflict between different religions over the background systems.[6]

However, this way out is blocked by the fact that the background system ineluctably intrudes in another way, by providing an overrider system. We have had more than one occasion to note that (a) the contradictions among reports of divine appearances even in the same religion, especially reports of divine communications, will force us, even in the absence of other reasons,[7]

[5]But remember that some of our lay subjects did not explicitly mention God, but were much more cautious in speaking of "Someone" (10), and "a Presence" (14).

[6]Actually, of course, the ways in which the Ultimate perceptually appear to one do differ markedly in different religions, and if we were not going to abandon this approach for a reason to be made explicit in the next paragraph, we would have to go into this aspect of the matter much more carefully.

[7]There are other reasons. For one thing, there is the general point that an appearance of X as ϕ does not guarantee that X is ϕ, where we can think of this either as a logical point that there is no entailment between, e.g., *X looks* ϕ and *X is* ϕ, or as the empirical point that we have ample evidence, from sense perception, that things are sometimes not what they experientially appear to be.

to recognize that an apparent experiential presentation of God as ϕ will provide only *prima facie* justification of the belief that God is ϕ, justification that is, in principle, subject to being overridden by sufficient reasons to suppose that God is not ϕ or that this experience does not carry the indication that God is ϕ that one might expect it to. But the concept of prima facie justification has application only where there is a system of knowledge or justified belief about the relevant subject matter, against which a particular prima facie justified belief can be checked for correctness and this particular experiential justification checked for efficacy. Hence we can justifiably attribute prima facie justification to M-beliefs only if the practice of forming M-beliefs carries with it such a background system, namely, the very one we have been talking of as utilized in identifying what is perceived as God.[8] If we try to cut the perceptual doxastic practice loose from dependence on that background system, we will be at the mercy of objections like those of Martin 1959 (see above, Chapter 5, section iiiE) to the effect that since there is no "society of checks and testing procedures", CMP cannot be credited with genuine truth claims concerning objective reality (or, in our revision of the criticism, cannot make justified objective truth claims). If there is no way of subjecting M-beliefs to further tests, where that is indicated, we will either have to give up the idea that M-beliefs draw epistemic justification from their experiential provenance, or we will have to accord equal credit to beliefs that contradict each other—equal credit to the alleged revelations of Julian of Norwich and of James Jones (of the Jonestown massacre)—so that the practice issues in a chaos instead of a coherent system.

There is, then, no alternative to construing each of our religious perceptual doxastic practices as including within it at least the main lines of the body of beliefs of the religion within which it flourishes. And hence, even if we typically make direct reference to God and M-beliefs themselves do not themselves come into any sort of conflict with each other across religious boundaries, the *practices* of forming such beliefs would still be subject to serious conflict by virtue of the associated belief systems, provided the latter come into serious conflict. To that topic we must now turn.

iii. Are the Major World Religions Compatible?

Prima facie the belief systems of the major world religions are, as wholes, seriously incompatible with each other. Let's be clear that we are concerned

[8]If one should ask "Why must the system of Christian doctrine be the system from which potential overriders of prima facie justification of M-beliefs are drawn?" the answer is given by the discussion of the individuation of religious doxastic practices in Chapter 5. The *Christian* perceptual doxastic practice is precisely the one that takes its conceptual scheme and overrider system form the body of Christian doctrine. If the overrider system came from elsewhere it would be a different practice.

with logical conflicts between beliefs, or, if you prefer, between the propositions believed, conflicts that consist in the impossibility of both propositions being true. We are not concerned here with practical conflicts: pairs of injunctions such that it is impossible for the same person to carry out both—incompatible disciplines, ways of life, or patterns of behavior. There are many such practical conflicts between world religions. One cannot be totally detached from things of the world including human society, as is enjoined by certain forms of Buddhism, and also actively engaged in loving behavior toward one's fellows, as is enjoined by Christianity. But we are concerned with such practical incompatibilities only to the extent that they reflect doxastic incompatibilities, and then only with the doxastic incompatibilities reflected. And it does look for all the world as if the belief systems of the major world religions are in serious conflict at certain points. To be sure, there is significant overlap. They are united, as against naturalism, in recognizing a reality that transcends the natural word and is of supreme concern to us.[9] They inveigh against the self-centered greediness for the superficial and transient goods of this world that human beings fall into all too readily. And so on. But these areas of agreement are quite general and unspecific. Though a transcendent dimension of reality is recognized on all sides, that dimension is characterized very differently in theistic and non-theistic religions. And when it comes to specific ideas about what is radically unsatisfactory about the human condition, what God (the Ultimate) plans to do about it and/or wants (requires . . .) us to do about it, what God (the Ultimate) has laid down as constituting our supreme fulfillment, what, if anything, God has done and is doing in history to achieve His purposes—on all these points we get very different stories. A nontheistic religion, not recognizing the Ultimate to be a personal agent, is not going to represent the Ultimate as carrying out an overall purpose in history. And among the theistic religions, we get quite different accounts as to what God's master plan is and what he has been doing and will do to carry it out.

Nevertheless, a number of attempts have been made to construe the various bodies of doctrine as mutually compatible. The simplest way of doing this is to trim each system of its "exclusivist" claims, so that it presents only one possible way to salvation, only one part of the story as to what the Ultimate is like and how we are and should be related to it. This would leave each religious system compatible with further pieces of the picture. If we could delete Christian claims that faith in Christ is the only way to salvation ("No one comes to the Father except through Me"), so that the Christian message is simply that this is one way in which God has acted to provide salvation, Christian doctrine on this point would be compatible with a Moslem or Hindu

[9]One may doubt that this is true of certain forms of Buddhism, and there certainly are deviant forms of Christianity in these latter days that try to avoid this feature. But the statement in the text holds for the major trends in the major world religions.

formulation, similarly toned down where necessary, of what God (the Ultimate) has done to provide other creatures with a chance of salvation. Again, if we take Hindu and Buddhist impersonalist accounts of the Ultimate as giving us merely one aspect of the matter, with personalist accounts giving us other aspects, and if we delete any claims to be giving the "most fundamental" account, they will all be compatible, assuming that these various "aspects" can in principle be possessed by the same being. After all, persons have impersonal aspects. I am a person, but I have many things in common with nonpersons, such as weight and size. This kind of point has often been made. Thomas Aquinas, for example, in common with many other classical Christian theologians, has tried to show that God's being a personal agent (that's my term, not Thomas's) is quite compatible with God's being an absolute unity without any distinguishable components or parts.[10]

I will not try to decide whether all serious doxastic conflicts could be resolved by this device of abandoning exclusivist claims, though I very much doubt it. Instead I will confine myself to the following point. If I were to pursue this program, I would be *advocating* a quite substantial *revision* of each of the major world religions, in the *hope* that thereby the incompatibilities between their doctrines would be reduced or eliminated; I would not be analyzing or describing a situation that actually exists. In my chosen terms, there are no doxastic practices of a nonexclusivist sort that are actually engaged in by any significant community. Since in this book I am concerned with the epistemic evaluation of doxastic practices that are socially established and widely engaged in, this particular pipe dream falls outside my purview. However nice it might be for religions to abandon their exclusivist pretensions, I am concerned here to determine whether religious perceptual practices, as they are actually carried on, are sources of justification for M-beliefs. And the fact that a certain kind of revision of those practices would obviate certain problems has no direct bearing on that enterprise.

However, there are other suggestions that involve not proposals for detailed revisions of existing systems of religious belief, but rather a more global reconstrual of what they are up to. The most prominent such view on the current scene is that of John Hick. Hick, inspired by Kant, distinguishes between "the Real" (his latest preferred term for what we have been calling "the Ultimate") *an sich*, as it is in itself, and "the Real as variously experienced-and-thought by different human communities".[11] On the model of Kant's interpretation of our experience and thought of the physical world, Hick takes it that the accounts of the Real we have in various religious traditions constitute the Real as it *appears* within the conceptual and other cultural forms utilized by each tradition. Again on the model of Kant, Hick thinks that we cannot suppose that any of these characterizations are true of the Real as it is in

[10]Aquinas 1945, *Summa Theologiae* 1, Q. 3.
[11]1989, p. 236. This is the latest version of Hick's position.

itself. ". . . we cannot apply to the Real *an sich* the characteristics encountered in its *personae* and *impersonae*. Thus it cannot be said to be one or many, person or thing, substance or process, good or evil, purposive or nonpurposive. None of the concrete descriptions that apply within the realm of human experience can apply literally to the unexperienceable ground of that realm. For whereas the phenomenal world is structured by our own conceptual frameworks, its noumenal ground is not . . . the noumenal Real is such as to be authentically experienced as a range of both theistic and nontheistic phenomena . . . we cannot, as we have seen, say that the Real *an sich* has the characteristics displayed by its manifestations, such as (in the case of the heavenly Father) love and justice or (in the case of Brahman) consciousness and bliss. But it is nevertheless the noumenal ground of these characteristics" (pp. 246–47). But though the content of, for example, Christian doctrine is not strictly true of the noumenal Real, it serves, just as the phenomenal world does for Kant, quite well in articulating, structuring, and orienting our responses to the Real in our search for salvation. Other major world religions, with their differing portrayals of the Real, also serve adequately as soteriological guides.

Thus Hick leaves each system of belief as is, so far as its detailed content is concerned. Nevertheless, the logical relations between these systems is drastically altered by treating them as dealing with phenomena rather than noumena. A personalistic and an impersonalistic account of the Ultimate are, or can be, incompatible if each purports to be the basic account of what the Ultimate is like in itself. If, on the other hand, each is simply spelling out the way the Ultimate is encountered, experienced, and conceptualized from the standpoint of a given cultural tradition, there is no logical conflict between them. If the rules of melodic composition in Europe, in (traditional) India, and in (traditional) China are taken as competing attempts to lay bare the intrinsic structure of some objective entity called music or musical sound, they are logically incompatible. But if each set of rules is merely designed to make explicit the way in which "musical reality" is experienced and conceptualized in one or another cultural tradition, they can all be adequate to the task.

I think that Hick's position has much to be said for it as an attempt to come to grips with the persistent fact of religious pluralism, without giving up the idea that religious experience, thought, and activity involve a genuine contact with a transcendent reality. Nevertheless, from the standpoint of my concerns in this book, it will have to be viewed as a proposal for a reconception of religious doxastic practices, rather than as a description and evaluation of those practices as they are. It seems clear to me that most practitioners of one or another religion are pre-Kantian in their realist understanding of their beliefs. They think that these beliefs embody true accounts of the Ultimate as it really is in itself and in its relations to the Creation. Theistic religions hold that the basic truths of the religion were revealed to us by God. If so, why should God fail to give us propositions that are strictly true of Himself? Would it not be misleading at best, and deceptive at worst, if He were to provide us with accounts that are couched in terms of one of the many ways in which He could appear to us, rather than in terms of what He is and does? In nontheistic religions we don't have the same concept of revelation as central, but there too we find the general conviction that Buddha, for example, tells it like it is, and not just as it appears to people in his cultural milieu. Therefore, since I take my task to be the analysis and evaluation of real life religious doxastic practices, not the reform, or degradation, thereof, I will not avail myself of Hick's way out. I will continue to take the major systems of religious belief to be making (noumenal) truth claims that are logically incompatible with each other, and I will undertake to assess the implications this has for my position that CMP is a source of prima facie justification for M-beliefs.

In saying that religious believers think that their beliefs are true of the Ultimate as it really is, I do not mean to be neglecting the important role of analogy, symbol, metaphor, and the like in religious language. No doubt, many things said of God are not true, and are not taken to be true, on a literal interpretation. "The Lord is my shepherd", "He is the rock of my salvation." Indeed, it may even be, for all I am saying here, that, as Aquinas thought, no term is applied to God in exactly the same sense as that in which it applies to creatures.[12] But these points all have to do with the linguistic devices we use to make our truth claims, not the status we take those claims to have. It is on the latter point that I am distinguishing the usual religious realism from Hick's Kantianism.

iv. Religious Diversity as a Difficulty for the Claims of CMP

Having made explicit the way(s) in which mystical perceptual doxastic practices in different religions are incompatible with each other, we can turn to the question of why this should pose a difficulty for the rationality of engaging in CMP.[13] And the first point to make is that this difficulty is by no means just a matter of a lack of universal consensus on, or universal participation in,

[12]I believe that there is a "univocal core" to talk about God and about creatures (see Alston 1989a, chaps. 3, 4). But the realism I opposed to Hick is equally compatible with the Thomistic position. It is worthy of note that Hick (p. 247) takes Aquinas's doctrine of analogical predication as an alternative way of formulating his position, but it is clear to me that that is not the case.

[13]In addition to epistemic problems, there is, from within any particular religion, a theological problem. In a theistic religion this will take the form: Why does God allow such a diversity of incompatible systems of belief about Himself? This is allied to the more general question: Why doesn't He make at least the main outlines of the truth about these matters clear to everyone? And both are simply particular versions of the familiar problem of evil. As with other versions, there have been many attempts to deal with this one. Then there are social-psychological problems as to what factors lead to the particular forms taken by religious belief, organization, and practice in the various world religions. All this falls outside the purview of this book.

CMP. We have already drawn the fangs of that objection in pointing out that we lack sufficient reason for supposing that any reliable cognitive access to a sphere of reality will be enjoyed by all normal human beings.[14] Nor is the difficulty posed by the more specific point that CMP is not engaged in even by all those who take themselves to be experientially aware of Ultimate Reality. Here too the mere lack of universal participation cuts no ice.

A more serious attempt to uncover a difficulty here is this. The best explanation of religious pluralism will leave the claims of CMP, and of any other religious perceptual doxastic practice, discredited. We can distinguish a more and a less radical form of this argument. The more radical form takes a hard naturalist line and contends that the best explanation is that there is no objective reality with which the practitioners of such practices are in effective cognitive contact. The best explanation for the fact of the persisting incompatibility is that the whole thing is internally generated, generated by psychological needs and other pressures, structured by the distinctive conceptual resources and prevailing modes of thought of one or another culture. For if there were some objective reality with which the various contenders are in cognitive contact, there would not be such persistent disagreements as to what it is like and how we are related to it. *This* argument proceeds to the dismissal of CMP by way of denying that any such practice can lay claim to objectivity. But why should we suppose that this is the best explanation of the diversity? The assumption presumably is that if any person or group enjoys a certain kind of cognitive contact with a sphere of reality, then any other person or group that takes itself to cognize that reality in that way would come up with the same, or similar, results. Put more concisely, any genuine cognitive contact with reality will yield agreement, and we can measure its reliability by the extent of the agreement. But I see no reason to accept this principle. The rough agreement we find across cultural boundaries in the contemporary world with respect to the physical and social environment has seduced us into thinking that this must characterize any genuine mode of cognition. But a better reading of the situation is that the agreement in these areas is due to the fact that they are areas ideally suited to our cognitive powers, and that there is no reason to expect such agreement in areas not so amenable to human cognition even if we do achieve veridical cognition there. Why shouldn't there be realms, modes, or dimensions of reality that are so difficult for us to discern that widespread agreement is extremely difficult or impossible to attain, even if *some* veridical cognition of that realm is achieved. It is a familiar fact that the more difficult the task, the more widely dispersed the attempts to carry it out. This holds in areas as diverse as mathematical exercises and target practice. Why should it be surprising that attempts to discern the Ultimate Source of all being should vary so much, even if some of those attempts get it straight?

[14]See Chapter 5, pp. 197–99.

I have just suggested an explanation of persistent disagreement in terms of the difficulty of the subject matter. But that is not the only way of reconciling persistent disagreement with genuine cognition. There can also be noncognitive bars to getting things right. It may be that God makes basic truths about Himself readily available to all persons, regardless of race, creed, or color, but that many of us are too preoccupied with other matters to take sufficient notice. This angle on the matter has been stressed in the Christian tradition under the rubric of "original sin", and it provides another alternative to supposing that persistent disagreement can best be explained by a total lack of genuine cognition. Thus I would suggest that the facts of religious diversity are at least as well explained by the hypothesis that there is a transcendent reality with which some or all religions are in touch, though of course they cannot all have it exactly straight.

A more modest way of rejecting the epistemic claims of all forms of MP, a way that does not involve denying that there is any objective reality of which one is aware in mystical experience, is to suggest that the diversity is best explained by supposing that none of the competing practices is a reliable way of determining what that reality is like. For if one of the practices were reliable, that would show itself to us in such a way as to distinguish it from the rest. But no such distinguishing marks are evident. Therefore the best explanation of the diversity is that they all miss the mark to such a degree that none of them can be considered sufficiently reliable for rational acceptance.

But why should we suppose that any reliable doxastic practice will bear external marks of its reliability for all, participants and nonparticipants alike, to see? That is not the case, as I argued at length in Chapter 3, with respect to familiar, universal, noncontroversial practices like SP. The marks of reliability displayed by SP, the ways in which it exhibits itself as a (by and large) veridical access to the physical environment, are displayed only from within the practice. One has to be a participant in order to ascertain those marks and see how they betoken reliability. Why should we suppose it to be otherwise with respect to religious practices? Even if CMP is a by and large reliable cognitive access to God, why suppose that its reliability could be exhibited apart from reliance on the outputs of that practice? And from *within* CMP, just as from *within* SP, there are abundant indications of reliability. For example, God is experienced within CMP as telling us that He will be present to us. Once more the explanatory claim lacks force by reason of being based on an unwarranted assumption.

But surely the existence of a plurality of mutually incompatible forms of MP poses some difficulty for the claim of any one of them to be a source of justified belief about Ultimate Reality. Yes, I think it does. Let's see if we can do better by way of saying just how. Since each form of MP is, to a considerable extent, incompatible with all the others, not more than one such form can be (sufficiently) reliable as a way of forming beliefs about the Ultimate. For if one is reliable, then most of the beliefs that issue from it are true;

and hence, because of the incompatibility, a large proportion of the beliefs issuing from each of the others will be false; and so none of those others is a reliable practice. Now why should I suppose that CMP is the one that is reliable (if any are)? No doubt, *within* CMP there are weighty reasons for supposing it to be much more reliable than its rivals; in the practice of CMP we find God telling people things that imply this. It is claimed from within the Christian tradition that God has assured us that His Holy Spirit will guide the church in its decisions, will keep it from error, will provide a "testimony" to the accuracy of the words of Christ, and so on. But, of course, each of the competing traditions can also produce conclusive internal reasons in support of its claims. Hence, if it is to be rational for me to take CMP to be reliable, I will have to have sufficient *independent* reasons for supposing that CMP is reliable, or more reliable or more likely to be reliable, than its alternatives. But no such reasons are forthcoming. Hence, it cannot be rational to engage in CMP; and by the same reasoning it cannot be rational to engage in any other particular form of MP.

Note the differences between this argument and the previous arguments that I have rejected. This last argument does not aspire to show that no form of MP is reliable. It allows the possibility that one such practice is, thus avoiding the naturalistic orientation shown by the earlier arguments. It is directed rather to the need for some reason to take a particular practice as more likely to be reliable than its competitors if one is to be rational in taking it, rather than them, as a source of beliefs about the Ultimate. The strength of the argument lies in its insistence that, *even if some form of MP is reliable*, we have no non-question-begging grounds for determining which one that is; and hence it cannot be rational for a person to suppose any particular form to be reliable. Thus it strikes directly at the claim of CMP (and of any of its rivals) to rationality. How can it be rational for me to form beliefs in a certain way if I have strong reasons for doubting that this way is reliable?

Note too that we have added to the ways mentioned in Chapter 4 of overriding the prima facie rationality of socially established doxastic practices. There we mentioned reasons for supposing the practice to be unreliable, and we distinguished these into (1) internal and (2) external, where (1) consists of massive internal contradictions in output or in associated belief system and (2) consists in massive contradictions between the output or associated belief system and corresponding elements of more firmly established practices. The religious-pluralism difficulty conforms to neither model. Not (1) because the incompatibilities are interpractice rather than intrapractice. Not (2) because none of the competitors (at least among the major world religions) are more firmly socially established than any of the others. Thus the fact that Christianity comes into fundamental conflict with Buddhism, for example, does not show that either party to the dispute is unreliable, just because neither party has stronger prima facie credibility on grounds of social entrenchment. Where we have a serious conflict between equally established practices, the outcome is not a victory for either side, but the engendering of a doubt, in each case, that the practice is sufficiently reliable for rational acceptance. We can put it this way. Each of our rival practices is confronted with a plurality of uneliminated alternatives. Thus, in the absence of some sufficient independent reason, no one is justified in supposing her own practice to be superior in epistemic status to those with which it is in competition. And hence, in this situation no one is being rational in proceeding to employ that practice to form beliefs and to regard beliefs so formed as ipso facto justified.

Now this line of argument assumes that there are no independent reasons for *epistemically* preferring one form of MP to the others. And this may well be challenged. The Christian may have recourse to natural theology to provide metaphysical reasons for the truth of a theism as a general world-view; and then, within the field of theistic religions, he may argue that historical evidence gives much stronger support to the claims of Christianity than to those of its theistic rivals—Judaism and Islam. To proceed in this way would be to argue directly for the truth of Christian beliefs from starting points that do not depend on prior acceptance of the Christian faith. One may also attempt to argue that Christian ways of arriving at beliefs are epistemically superior to those of other religions; I have no idea of how this argument would go, and so I will not pursue it. But I believe that the attempt to argue from neutral starting points for the truth of Christian beliefs deserves much more serious consideration than is commonly accorded it today in philosophical and (liberal) theological circles. I believe that much can be done to support a theistic metaphysics, and that something can be done by way of recommending the "evidences of Christianity". But all that is a very long story, and I will not embark on it in this book. Instead I shall adopt a "worst case scenario" and consider the prospects for the rationality of CMP on the assumption that there are no significant independent reasons for epistemically preferring it to its rivals. I shall seek to show that even on those assumptions, the justificatory efficacy of CMP is by no means dissipated, though it may be significantly weakened.

v. A Response to the Difficulty

To form a just assessment of the extent to which the argument under consideration diminishes the rationality of engaging in CMP, it will be useful to consider various analogues of the situation of religious diversity, analogues where we seem better able to find our way around. Consider first the familiar sort of case in which different people give conflicting sense perceptual reports of an automobile accident, and in which there is no neutral ground on which it can be determined which account is most likely to be correct or which witness was in the best position to determine what happened. A particular one of these witnesses, X, lacks sufficient reason, aside from the question begging reason drawn from her own account and her own self-confidence, to regard herself as in a better position to make accurate observations of the accident. Therefore the fact that she is confronted by several accounts that diverge from hers should drastically reduce her confidence in her own. Here it seems clear that the existence of these uneliminated conflicting alternatives nullifies whatever justification she otherwise would have had for believing that the accident was as she takes it to be.

There are two important differences between this kind of case and the diversity of conflicting religious doxastic practices. First, the former has to do with the epistemic status of particular beliefs, while the latter has to do with the status of entire practices. We could find a closer analogue in this respect by switching to competitions between methods. Consider ways of predicting the weather: various "scientific" meterorological approaches, going by the state of rheumatism in one's joints, and observing groundhogs. Again, if one employs one of these methods but has no non-question-begging reason for supposing that method to be more reliable than the others, then one has no sufficient rational basis for reposing confidence in its outputs.

But whether the examples concern particular beliefs or belief forming procedures, there remains a crucial difference between these cases, where it is clear that uneliminated alternatives reduce or eliminate one's basis for one's own belief or practice, and the religious situation. That difference can be stated very simply. In the clear cases the competitors confront each other within the same doxastic practice, and hence it is clear what would constitute non-circular grounds for supposing one of the contestants to be superior to the others, even if we do not have such grounds. We know the sorts of factors that would disqualify an observer of the accident (inattention, emotional involvement, visual defects, a poor angle of observation), and we know what would decisively show that one account is the correct one (e.g., agreement with a number of new witnesses). In the weather prediction case it is, in principle, a simple matter to run a statistical test on the predictive success of the various methods and choose between them on that basis. It is just because of this that in the absence of sufficient reasons for supposing himself to be in a superior position, one of the contestants, X, is not justified in reposing complete confidence in his alternative. It is because the absence of such reasons is the absence of something there is a live possibility of one's having, and that one knows how to go about getting, that this lack so clearly has negative epistemic consequences. But precisely this condition is lacking in the religious diversity case. Since, as we are assuming, each of the major world religions involves (at least one) distinct perceptual doxastic practice, with its own way of going from experiential input to beliefs formulated in terms of that scheme, and its own system of overriders, the competitors lack the kind of common procedure for setting disputes that is available to the participants in a shared practice. Here, in contrast to the intrapractice cases, my religious adversary and I do not lack something that we know perfectly well how to get. Hence the sting is taken out of the inability of each of us to show that he is in an epistemically superior position. The lack does not have the deleterious consequences found in the intra-practice cases. Or, at the very least, it is not clear that it has those consequences. To put the point most sharply, we have no idea what noncircular proof of the reliability of CMP would look like, *even if it is as reliable as you please*. Hence why should we take the absence of such a proof to nullify, or even sharply diminish, the justification I have for my Christian M-beliefs?

To further nail down this point it will be useful to consider a criticism, by William Hasker, of an earlier version of my defense of CMP. He puts forward the following analogue of religious diversity.

> Suppose you are playing a game of hide-and-seek, and Johnny, who is "it", has taken refuge somewhere in the second story of the house you are playing in. As you reach the top of the stairs you realize that there are four rooms that offer good hiding places and that you don't have any particular reason for supposing Johnny to be in one of them rather than another. If you pick the right room to search, you will find him, but you can't search all of them, because the other players in the game are right behind you and will search the rooms you don't choose. So we can say that in choosing a room to search, you are choosing a "method" of finding Johnny. Now, are you *justified* . . . in making the choice you do make? . . . whichever room you choose, the fact remains that there are three other rooms, each of which is, on the available evidence, just as likely to be the right one as the one you have chosen. So it is more likely than not that the room you have chosen is the wrong one and that your "method" is unreliable. (1986, pp. 139–40)

> . . . the application is obvious: If there are several conceptual schemes for interpreting religious experience which are alternative to, and incompatible with, Christianity, and if there are no decisive reasons for thinking those schemes to be incorrect, then there is a good reason to think the Christian practice unreliable. (P. 141)

But again the evaluation of these methods, prior to their being tried, takes place *within* a doxastic practice that provides effective procedures for testing the efficacy of methods, so that once again the lack of any reason to think method A superior to its alternatives is the lack of something we know how to go about getting. And in this respect the situation is quite different from the diversity of incompatible forms of MP.

This conclusion, that the lack of a common ground alters drastically the epistemic bearings of an unresolved incompatibility, can be illustrated by secular examples. Consider the methodological opposition between psychoanalysts and behaviorists concerning the diagnosis and treatment of neurosis and, more generally, concerning human motivation. Psychoanalytic formulations are based heavily on clinical "insight" and "interpretation". Behaviorists typically reject these as data and restrict themselves to "harder" data, the observation of which can be easily replicated under controlled conditions. Since psychoanalysts do not reject the legitimacy of the behavioral data, but hold only that they are insufficient for dealing with the problems with which they are concerned, the issue is over the status of the analysts' "data". Let's say that there is no common ground on which the dispute can be resolved.[15] Here we are not so ready, or should not be so ready, to judge that it is irrational for the psychoanalyst to continue to form clinical beliefs in the way he does without having noncircular reasons for supposing that his method of forming clinical diagnoses is a reliable one. Since we are at a loss to specify what such noncircular reasons would look like even if the method is reliable, we should not regard the practitioner as irrational for lacking such reasons.[16]

Next let's consider a counter-factual analogue. Suppose that there were a diversity of sense perceptual doxastic practices as diverse as forms of MP are in fact. Suppose that in certain cultures there were a well established "Cartesian" practice of seeing what is visually perceived as an indefinitely extended medium that is more or less concentrated at various points, rather than, as in our "Aristotelian" practice, as made up of more or less discrete objects scattered about in space. In other cultures we find a "Whiteheadian" SP to be equally socially established; here the visual field is seen as made up of momentary events growing out of each other in a continuous process.[17] Let's further suppose that each of these practices serves its practitioners equally well in their dealings with the environment. We may even suppose that each group has developed physical science, in its own terms, to about as high a pitch as the others. But suppose further that, in this imagined situation, we are

[15]One might think that there is a predictive test in terms of the success of the therapies based on the respective methodologies. But, alas, parallel methodological controversy will break out over the assessment of therapeutic success. I am also assuming that psychoanalytic theories do not have implications that have been disconfirmed by ordinary empirical investigation; or if there have been such, the theories have been modified to take account of them without losing their distinctive thrust.

[16]There are many other examples. With ethical and other normative disagreements, at least of a fundamental sort, there will be no neutral procedure for settling the matter. Does that show that no one can rationally engage in a certain way of arriving at ethical positions where there are radically different ways of doing so, and no neutral standpoint for adjudicating the differences? Philosophy generally is a rich source of analogues. (Alvin Plantinga is constantly reminding me of this.) It is most striking that epistemologists so pervasively ignore the epistemology of their own discipline. (Perhaps this is not surprising; it is quite depressing to think about.) In philosophy we notoriously lack neutral ways of determining which party to fundamental debates over free will, over materialism, or over knowledge (!) is in the right, is more likely to be right, or is in a better epistemic position to get the truth. Does it follow that no one is rational in forming views on these matters in the way they do? If so, we philosophers had better pack our bags and move to an activity in which we can more honestly engage.

[17]Note that as we are envisaging the situation, it is not that the world *looks* the same to people in all these different cultures and they only apply different higher-level theories as to the real nature of what they are seeing. No, the world *looks* different to them in the ways I have been specifying. What is seen *presents* itself, phenomenologically, as a continuous medium to the Cartesians and as a flux of momentary events to the Whiteheadians. Thus my imagined situation is on all fours with the situation of religious diversity as it bears on the perception of the Ultimate and the formation of perceptual beliefs therefrom.

as firmly wedded to our "Aristotelian" form of SP as we are in fact. The Cartesian and Whiteheadian *ausländer* seem utterly outlandish to us, and we find it difficult to take seriously the idea that they may be telling it like it is. Nevertheless, we can find no neutral grounds on which to argue effectively for the greater accuracy of our way of doing it. In such a situation would it be clear that it is irrational for us to continue to form perceptual beliefs in our "Aristotelian" way, given that the practice is proving itself by its fruits? It seems to me that quite the opposite is clear. In the absence of any external reason for supposing that one of the competing practices is more accurate than my own, the only rational course for me is to sit tight with the practice of which I am a master and which serves me so well in guiding my activity in the world. But our actual situation with regard to CP is precisely parallel to the one we have been imagining. Hence, by parity of reasoning, the rational thing for a practitioner of CP to do is to continue to form Christian M-beliefs, and, more generally, to continue to accept, and operate in accordance with, the system of Christian belief.

I have been suggesting that if there actually were a diversity of sense perceptual practices we would be faced with an epistemological problem there exactly parallel to the one we actually face with respect to CP. But why shouldn't we say that the mere *possibility* of an SP diversity gives rise to the same problem? If it is so much as possible that human beings should construe what is presented in visual perception in radically different ways, and so much as possible that the practice so constituted should be as internally viable as our actual SP, then doesn't that *possibility* raise the question of why we should suppose that it is rational to form beliefs in the SP way, given that we have no reason to suppose it to be more reliable than these other possibilities? And if it is rational to engage in SP, despite the lack of any noncircular reason for regarding our Aristotelian SP as more reliable than its *possible* alternatives, that conclusion should carry over to the CP problem.

Yet it is difficult to work ourselves up into worrying about these possibilities, and even difficult to convince ourselves that it is our intellectual duty to do so. Insofar as this has a respectable basis, it is that it is not really clear that the alleged possibilities are indeed possible. At least they may not be real possibilities for us, given our actual constitution and the lawful structure of the world. It may be that we are innately programmed to perceive the environment in Aristotelian terms, and that this program does not allow for social reprogramming into a "Cartesian" or a "Whiteheadian" mode. Nevertheless, it seems clear to me that *if* these alternatives really are possible, then they give rise to difficulties for the rationality of engaging in SP that are quite parallel to those arising from the actual diversity of religions for the rationality of engaging in CP. And so, in that case, if it is rational to engage in SP despite these difficulties, the same conclusion follows for CP.

It goes without saying, I hope, that the conclusions I have been drawing concerning the epistemic situation of practitioners of CMP hold, *pari passu*, for practitioners of other internally validated forms of MP. In each case the person who is in the kind of position I have been describing will be able to rationally engage in his/her own religious doxastic practice despite the inability to show that it is epistemically superior to the competition. It may seem strange that such incompatible positions could be justified for different people, but this is just a special case of the general point that incompatible propositions can each be justified for different people if what they have to go on is suitably different.

vi. Genuine Epistemic Consequences of Religious Diversity

I have been arguing that the existence of a plurality of uneliminated interpractice competitors does not damage the credibility of any one of them to nearly the same extent as a plurality of uneliminated intrapractice competitors. Nevertheless, I do not wish to deny that the situation does have significant adverse consequences for the epistemic status of CMP and other forms of MP. It can hardly be denied that if we were not faced with such persistent incompatibilities the participants in CMP (at least those who reflect seriously on the facts of religious diversity) would feel much more confident in CMP and would be justified in so feeling. Even if it is true, as suggested above, that the mere possibility of this kind of diversity poses problems for the epistemic status of a particular practice, it still remains true that whether or not the possibility is realized is significant for the issue. This is so, if for no other reason, because an actual plurality of incompatible perceptual practices shows that the possibility in question is genuine, that the reality in question does admit of being perceived in incompatible fashions; and this forces on us the question of which, if any, of these ways can best lay claim to represent that reality as it is. Thus it can hardly be denied that the fact of religious diversity reduces the rationality of engaging in CMP (for one who is aware of the diversity) below what it would be if this problem did not exist. Just how much it is reduced I cannot say. We do not have the conceptual resources to quantify degrees of rationality or justification in this area (and perhaps in any area). I have just been giving reasons for denying that the reduction is of such a magnitude as to render it irrational to engage in CMP, and such as to force the conclusion that perceptual beliefs that issue from CMP are not thereby prima facie justified. Can anything further be done to provide at least a rough indication of the epistemic status of CMP in the face of religious diversity?

Look at the matter this way. Suppose that our sole basis[18] for a positive epistemic evaluation of CMP were the fact that it is a socially established doxastic practice that has not been shown to be unreliable. In that case I am

[18]That is, our sole respectable basis. This excludes trivial self-support that is illustrated by the practice of taking each output twice, once as tester and once as testee.

afraid that religious pluralism would reduce the epistemic status to an alarming degree. For given the equal social establishment of a number of mutually incompatible practices, each with its built-in system of belief, it is at least arguable that the most reasonable view, even for a hitherto committed participant of one of the practices, would be that the social establishment in each case reflects a culturally generated way of reinforcing socially desirable attitudes and practices, reinforcing these by inculcating a sense of the presence of a Supreme Reality and a way of thinking about it.[19] That would imply that the justificatory efficacy of any of these practices has been dissipated altogether. But, as pointed out in Chapters 4 and 6, that is not the whole story. For both secular and religious practices, though in different ways, there are also significant forms of self-support that rightfully shore up the participants' confidence that the practice gives them at least a good approximation to the truth. In the case of CMP we saw in Chapter 6, section vi, that this significant self-support amounts to ways in which the promises God is represented by the practice as making are fulfilled when the stipulated conditions are met, fulfilled in growth in sanctity, in serenity, peace, joy, fortitude, love, and other "fruits of the spirit". This, I submit, markedly changes the picture. In the face of this self-support it is no longer the case that the most reasonable hypothesis is that none of the competing practices provide an effective cognitive access to the Ultimate. It is by no means guaranteed that a social establishment of a religious system for the sake of desirable social goals will bring in its train a fulfillment of putative divine promises in the spiritual life of the devotees; the fact that this happens is a significant point in favor of the epistemic claims of the practice. Given the "payoffs" of the Christian life of the sort just mentioned, one may quite reasonably continue to hold that CMP does serve as a genuine cognitive access to Ultimate Reality, and as a trustworthy guide to that Reality's relations to ourselves, even if one can't see how to solve the problem of religious pluralism, even if one can't show from a neutral standpoint that Christianity is right and the others are wrong on those points on which they disagree.[20]

Another consideration bears on the status of Christian belief in the face of religious pluralism. Thus far in this book nothing has been said about faith, a

[19]In saying this I have not forgotten the point emphasized in Chapter 4 that the most basic way in which social establishment renders it rational to participate in a doxastic practice is that to abandon it would be a disruption of established modes of social life, and hence that this should not be done unless there is a sufficient reason to do so. The reverse side of this coin is that the support does not come primarily from the fact that the social establishment is best explained by supposing the practice to be (reasonably) reliable. Nevertheless, and consistent with this, questions of how the social establishment is to be explained can come into the issue of whether the prima facie rationality that a socially established practice enjoys is overridden. The statement in the text should be construed as having to do with overridding.

[20]Again, I am not putting this forward as a point about CMP rather than about its rivals. Assuming that comparable modes of self-support are enjoyed by other forms of MP (and I don't want to assume that they are all equal in this respect), the same point applies to them.

term that normally bulks large in discussions of religious belief. My avoidance of the term may have given the impression that I take religious belief to be subject to exactly the same epistemology as beliefs of other sorts, and that I see no room for "believing on faith" or "taking it on faith". But such is not the case. In this book I have undertaken to articulate and defend one kind or experiential basis for religious belief, and that basis, I have been arguing, works in basically the same way as direct experiential bases for other sorts of belief. But this is only part of the total picture, albeit a crucial part. In Chapter 8 I will seek to place the perception of God in the larger context of grounds of religious belief. For the moment, the point I wish to make is that even when we have marshalled all the sorts of grounds we possess for supposing a particular system of religious belief to be true, that will still fall short of the degree of support we enjoy with respect to beliefs of many other sorts, including sense perceptual beliefs, memory beliefs, and beliefs in generalizations about the physical world. There is still need for faith, for trusting whatever we do have to go on as providing us with a picture of the situation that is close enough to the truth to be a reliable guide to our ultimate destiny.[21] Since it is an essential part of the religious package that we hold beliefs that go beyond what is conclusively established by such objective indications as are available to us (or alternatively, holds beliefs more firmly than the available objective evidence warrants), it should be the reverse of surprising that religious diversity should render us less than fully epistemically justified in the beliefs of a particular religion. This is an additional reason for denying that the appropriate response to the lowering of the degree of epistemic justification that is consequent on religious diversity is the abandonment of beliefs that would otherwise be held with confidence.

It is also relevant to put our problem into historical perspective. When religious diversity is used as a basis for downgrading the epistemic status of religious belief, this is against the background of a contrast with scientific unanimity. A sensible treatment will not, of course, deny that disagreements do occur in science, even disagreements between large organized bodies of investigators (different schools of quantum physics, for example), as well as disagreements between individual scientists. Nevertheless, there is an impressive degree of convergence in science, at least in the more highly developed physical sciences. This stands in sharp contrast with the persistent disagreements between the major world religions. But if we take this to be a timeless contrast between religion and science, our historical memory does not stretch back as far as 400 years, when there was as little consensus in science as in religion. At that time, opposing schools in physics and astronomy—Aris-

[21]There is, of course, also need for trusting the supreme being in whom we believe to deliver us from whatever it is we need saving from and to guide us into an ultimate fulfillment. This is the practical side of faith, which is of fundamental importance in religion, but it falls outside the special concern of this book. Here we are concerned with faith on its doxastic side, faith as a belief that is more firmly held than the objective evidence strictly indicates.

totelian, Galilean, and Cartesian—were each pursuing their own tacks and seeking to discredit the alternatives. Thus the degree of unanimity in a given area of thought can change radically in the course of history. And so it may be in religion. We may be in as early a stage of religious development as physicists were in the high Middle Ages. The system of Christian belief has undergone a great deal of change in its history, and we cannot be sure that it will not continue to do so; the same holds for other major religions. Future development in the major world religions might be in the direction of greater consensus. I am not going so far as to predict that we were on the threshold of a single world religion. This may never occur, until the end of the age. It may be that our intellects are not suited to attain the definitive truth about God until God reveals Himself more unmistakably to all and sundry, and who can say what God's timetable is for that? Be that as it may, reflection on religious diversity should be carried on in the light of a sensitivity to historical changes in situations of that sort.

It should be clear from the above that even though I hold that a Christian is epistemically justified (at least prima facie) on the basis of mystical perception in holding certain Christian beliefs about God, I do *not* take this to imply that the proper procedure for the Christian, or the member of any religious community, is to shut herself up within the boundaries of her own community and ignore the rest of the world. On the contrary. The knowledgeable and reflective Christian should be concerned about the situation, both theologically and epistemically. As for the latter, the implication of the foregoing discussion is that she should do whatever seems feasible to search for common ground on which to adjudicate the crucial differences between the world religions, seeking a way to show in a non-circular way which of the contenders is correct. What success will attend these efforts I do not presume to predict. Perhaps it is only in God's good time that a more thorough insight into the truth behind these divergent perspectives will be revealed to us.

vii. Summary of the Case for CMP

I have now completed my case for the rationality of CMP—the rationality of engaging in it and the rationality of taking it to be sufficiently reliable to be a source of prima facie justification for the beliefs it engenders. Let me briefly recapitulate the main elements of that case. CMP is a socially established doxastic practice, and as such, according to the approach to epistemology set forth in Chapter 4, it can be rationally engaged in, and rationally taken to be reliable and a source of justification, provided it is not disqualified by reasons to the contrary, particularly reasons for supposing it to be unreliable. That status will be strengthened if the practice generates significant self-support for its claims. As for this last point, we saw in section vi of Chapter 6 that significant self-support of CMP is indeed forthcoming. As for possible disqualifiers, in Chapter 5 I examined a number of reasons for denying that CMP is a full-fledged, respectable doxastic practice, possessing all the rights and privileges pertaining thereto. The objections we took most seriously were (a) in CMP there is no generally employed system of checks and tests for the criticism of particular perceptual beliefs, and (b) such tests as it does possess lack some crucial features of the tests involved in SP. I argued that these considerations fail to show that CMP is ruled out as a source of epistemic justification. In Chapter 6, I considered some reasons for supposing CMP to be insufficiently reliable to serve as a source of justification, leaving the most serious such reason for Chapter 7. The main reasons discussed in Chapter 6 were (1) the claim that mystical experience can be explained in purely naturalistic terms, (2) inconsistencies in the output of CMP, and (3) contradictions between the output of CMP and that of various secular practices, particularly science, history, and metaphysics. Again it was concluded that none of these considerations are fatal to the epistemic claims we have made for CMP. Finally, in this chapter we have considered the argument against the reliability of CMP, and of any other particular religious perceptual doxastic practice, from the fact of radical religious diversity. I concluded that although this diversity reduces somewhat the maximal degree of epistemic justification derivable from CMP, it leaves the practitioner sufficiently prima facie justified in M-beliefs that it is rational for her to hold those beliefs, in the absence of specific overriders. The upshot of all this is that CMP does provide prima facie justification for M-beliefs, and can thus make a contribution to the total range of support for Christian belief, interacting with other supports in ways we will explore in the final chapter.

viii. First- and Third-person Perceptual Justification

Before concluding this chapter, I wish to touch on two further issues. The first of these concerns the relation of first- and third-person justification. What I have explicitly argued for, up to this point, is that one to whom God is apparently presenting Himself as ϕ is thereby prima facie justified in believing God to be ϕ. But that claim is restricted to the experiencer himself. How about others? Can this justification be "transferred", perhaps in a weaker form, through testimony, as is the case with sense-perceptual beliefs, memory reports, and scientific results? This is a thorny issue that has generated much controversy. Much of the twentieth-century discussion has centered on William James' famous pronouncements in *The Varieties of Religious Experience* (1902).

> (1) Mystical states, when well developed, usually are, and have the right to be, absolutely authoritative over the individuals to whom they come.

(2) No authority emanates from them which should make it a duty for those who stand outside of them to accept their revelations uncritically. (P. 414)

Let's strike the last word, for it can be plausibly argued that I have no duty to accept anything uncritically. And so as not to get hung up in difficulties over voluntary control of belief, let's replace talk of duty and authority with talk of justification. This will give us the following reformulation.

(1A) Beliefs formed directly on the basis of mystical states by the subjects of those states, are thereby justified.

(2A) One is not justified in believing that p just because a subject who has become justified in believing that p in the way indicated by (1) has testified that p.

I will first consider what is to be said for and against this position, and then I will indicate what position on the matter is indicated by the results of this book.

First, let's remind ourselves that the role of testimony in secular matters would seem to indicate that there is something seriously wrong with James's position. Much of what a particular individual knows (justifiably believes) about the world is acquired from testimony. If I had to rely on my own experience and reasoning alone, I would know little of history, geography, science, and the arts, to say nothing of what is going on in the world currently. We generally suppose that justification is transferred via testimony from someone who has learned something from perception, memory, reasoning, or some combination thereof, to society at large. Why should it be different in the religious sphere? Why should it be impossible for me to learn that p (become justified in believing that p) from someone who has herself learned that p from perception? Do we have another double standard at work?

To be sure, it has been contended that it is not sufficient for my believing that p justifiably that (1) X is justified in believing that p and (2) X tells me that p. In addition I have to have sufficient reasons for trusting X. I have to have sufficient reasons for regarding X as sufficiently competent, reliable, or authoritative. This could be neatly summed up as the further condition: (3) I am justified in supposing that X is justified in believing that p. The necessity for this additional condition could be questioned. It may be contended that if X is in fact a reliable source of information on such matters, then I can receive a justified belief by trusting this source, whatever reasons I may or may not have for supposing the source to be reliable; just as I will acquire justified perceptual beliefs provided my sense experience is a reliable source of information about the external environment, whether or not I have reasons for regarding my experience as reliable. I will not try to settle this issue. Let's accept the additional condition, and let's agree that it is frequently satisfied in the case of secular testimony. But then why shouldn't it also be satisfied in the religious case? I have presented reasons for supposing that CMP endows its products with prima facie justification. Assuming that my reasoning has been sound, why shouldn't a third party have good reasons for supposing a mystical perceiver to be prima facie justified in her perceptual beliefs? And if condition (3) is to be read as making the stronger requirement that the receiver of the testimony be justified in supposing the testifier to be justified, all things considered, in believing that p, then we can accommodate that as well. I have also presented reasons for supposing that mystical perceivers can be justified, all things considered, in their perceptual beliefs; and so, again, if my contentions are sound, a recipient of testimony could have those reasons for supposing that the stronger requirement is satisfied. So if these conditions are sufficient for the generation of justification by testimony in secular cases, why not in the religious case?

No doubt, the person, Y, who believes that p on testimony of X, is in a *different* epistemic position from X, assuming that X believes that p on first hand experience. Y's basis is the testimony of another, plus whatever reason he has for crediting that testimony, while X's basis is his experience of the matters in question. Thus the bases of their beliefs are quite different, and different kinds of questions can be raised about them. Y's claim to justification can be challenged by questioning whether he is entitled to credit X's testimony, whether he has understood X correctly, and so on. Nothing like that is at all relevant to X's situation. It is solely a matter of whether his experience constitutes a sufficient basis for the belief.[22] But even though their epistemic situations are different, we ordinarily suppose that in secular matters the receiver of the testimony can acquire justified beliefs in this way. So again we are faced with the question "Why suppose that the religious case works with a different set of rules, rules that prevent this transfer of justification?" Such a supposition is warranted only if we can point out some difference between the cases that warrants a different treatment. But what could that be?

James himself is not very helpful here. He seems to take it that an outsider would have to have evidence available to him, while remaining an outsider, for the reliability of mystical experience. "What comes must be sifted and tested, and run the gauntlet of confrontation with the total context of experience, just like what comes from the outer world of sense. Its value must be ascertained by empirical methods, so long as we are not mystics ourselves" (pp. 417–18). But this is our double standard again. Sense-perceptually supported beliefs are allowed to generate testimonial justification without receiving any validation external to sense perceptual practice. Why, then, is external proof of reliability required for mystical experience? James also invokes

[22]As noted in Chapter 2, many epistemologists will add other requirements for experiential justification, e.g., that X be justified in supposing that the experience is a sufficient indication of the truth of the belief, but even if we add this it leaves a strong contrast between X's and Y's positions.

the diversity of belief systems that are supported by mystical experience. "The fact is that the mystical feeling of enlargement, union, and emancipation has no specific intellectual content whatever of its own. It is capable of forming matrimonial alliances with material furnished by the most diverse philosophies and theologies, provided only they can find a place in their framework for its peculiar emotional mood. We have no right, therefore, to invoke its prestige as distinctively in favor of any special belief" (pp. 416–17). Here I need only refer the reader to the body of this chapter for my answer to this charge. We may also note that if these considerations are fatal to transfer of justification by testimony, they should be equally fatal to first person justification. In fact, I have been considering religious diversity precisely as a problem for first person justification. If CMP must prove itself empirically (on the basic of sense perception) before one is justified in accepting its outputs on the testimony of another, why shouldn't this also be required for the experiencer herself to be justified in forming the belief on the basis of experience? Put another way, if I can be justified in believing that God is present to me on the basis of my experience of God, without validating the reliability of this mode of experience by empirical (sense-perceptual) investigation, then if another is justified in supposing that I am so justified, what could possibly prevent the latter from also being justified in the same belief? We are still without a sufficient basis for discrimination. And, as just pointed out, I take myself to have shown in this book that these problems do not prevent M-beliefs from being justified on the basis of first hand mystical experience.

In defense of treating mystical perception differently, appeal is sometimes made to the "private" character of mystical experience. But in what way is mystical experience more "private" than sense experience? Here are the points we have long since admitted: (1) mystical experience is not universally shared, and (2) we lack tight conditions for intersubjective testing of mystical reports. But why should they prevent the transfer of justification by testimony *in those cases in which the recipient is justified in believing that the testifier is justified*? These differences have been thought to prevent first-person justification, but I have responded to that charge in Chapter 5. So once again, if my argument in this book has been sound and if the recipient can appreciate it, that would suffice for him to be justified (often) in supposing the testifier to be justified.

Thus we are left without any sound reason for denying that justification of M-beliefs can be transferred via testimony. And, indeed, if there is a body of justified belief in a religious community, it must be possible for testimony to work here as it does with sense perception. For religious communities are built up on the basis of testimony of certain people (the recipients of revelation) to what they have learned about God, His nature, purposes, activities through their experience of Him.[23] And if those not blessed with first hand

[23]As will be pointed out in Chapter 8, there are other possible forms of revelation.

experience of God cannot become justified in their beliefs about God from the testimony of those who are so blessed, then we are of all men the most miserable. I don't suppose that this paragraph constitutes an argument for a testimonial source of justification in the religious sphere; but it does remind us that the assumption of this is deeply rooted in religious communities.

Nevertheless, we are left with a nagging feeling that the religious case is different, that believing that God is loving on the say-so of one who reports experiencing God as loving is more problematic than believing that your house burned down on the say-so of someone who saw it burn down. Perhaps this discrimination could be fully explained by the fact, repeatedly noted in this book, that CMP and other forms of MP are less firmly established, can lay claim to a weaker degree of epistemic status, give rise to more critical questions, and are subject to more doubt, than, for example, SP. If that is the whole story, then the differentiation of the two spheres does not attach to the *transition* from firsthand to secondhand experience, pace James. It is rather that the firsthand experiential beliefs are weaker epistemically, and hence that this is inherited by their testimonial progeny. But, in fact, I believe that there is more to the story, and that the more does concern the testimonial process specifically. That process, or, better, its evaluation, is more complex in the religious case. At least it is more complex when the recipient of the testimony stands outside the perceptual practice in question; and that is the case people generally have in mind when they consider this issue. There the recipient not only has the task of determining whether the testifier is justified in his belief according to the standards of the practice that generated the belief, but also the task of determining whether that practice is reliable or rational. In SP and other secular cases we can take it for granted that both parties to the transaction participate in the practice in question, as we can when information is transmitted from one practitioner of CMP to another. But when practice boundaries are crossed in the exchange things become stickier. Now a question arises for the recipient as to whether the practice in question is an acceptable one, and that introduces additional possibilities for doubt, error and lack of justification. So just as the additional requirements for testimonial belief within the same practice implies some weakening of justification in the transfer, so the additional requirements for cross practice testimony (the recipient being justified in supposing the foreign practice to be reliable, rational, or whatever) will imply some further weakening. That is not to say that this additional requirement cannot be satisfied. I believe that it can; I believe that my arguments in this book provide anyone, participant in CMP or not, with sufficient reasons for taking CMP to be rationally engaged in. Nevertheless, I have identified an additional source of our sense that testimony is a more problematic source of belief in religious than in secular cases.[24] But within the

[24]This constitutes another way in which the cross-practice epistemic situation differs from the intrapractice situation, over and above the point noted earlier in the chapter, that the epistemology

religious community, we have, so I claim, an exact parallel to secular cases of testimony, though, no doubt, at a lower epistemic level all around.

ix. Knowledge of God

The second issue concerns the bearing of the central thesis of this book on the question of whether we have *knowledge* of God, and if so, where and how much. As advertised at the outset, I have restricted myself to issues of justification, reliability, and rationality, and avoided any discussion of knowledge. To tackle the latter I would have to go into the question of how to think about knowledge generally, as well as issues concerning whether necessary conditions for knowledge are ever satisfied in religion and if so where. That would inflate the book beyond its already generous bounds. However, I will conclude this chapter with a brief indication of where I stand on the matter, including a word on how the issue of knowledge is related to the issue of justification.[25]

To begin with the latter, if I were to follow most contemporary English-speaking epistemologists in holding that justification is a necessary condition for a belief's counting as knowledge, I could build on the results of this book in a straightforward way to carry out an investigation of knowledge of God. Having established that we have some justified beliefs about God, I could than proceed to consider whether in these cases additional requirements for knowledge are satisfied. Since one of these requirements is truth, many would think there are insuperable obstacles to assuring ourselves of its satisfaction but I believe this is the case only if we impose unrealistically stringent conditions on such assurance, such as knowing with absolute certainty that the condition is satisfied. On a more sensible approach, we could claim that if one is justified in believing that p, that fact in itself *justifies* one in believing that it is true that p (since it is true that p if and only if p); and so really nothing beyond justification is needed to receive reasonable assurance that the truth condition is satisfied (though obviously more is needed for the condition to *be* satisfied). Anti-Gettier conditions will, of course, pose problems of their own. However I hold the problem to be more complex than this, since, though I agree that true justified belief, together with appropriate safeguards against Gettier problems, is sufficient for knowledge, justification is by no means necessary. This, of course, depends on what justification is as well as on what knowledge is. As the course of this book has indicated, I take the justification of belief to require that the belief be based on an adequate ground, where the grounds of our beliefs are the sorts of things of which the

---

of conflicts between practices is very different from the epistemology of conflicts within a practice.

[25]For a more extended treatment of the former see Alston 1991b. For the latter see my "Justification and Knowledge" in 1989b.

subject can become aware on reflection; this paradigmatically includes beliefs and experiences. I have been arguing in this book that the experiential grounds of religious beliefs are sometimes sufficient to confer justification. But I do not hold that justified belief is necessary for knowledge. Provided a true belief is generated by a sufficiently reliable belief forming process (and Gettier problems are foreclosed), the belief counts as knowledge, whether or not the belief is based on an adequate ground of one of the above sorts. Though I believe that the bulk of human knowledge does involve belief that is based on such grounds, the contrary possibility is, I believe, sometimes realized. The strongest candidate for this within religion would be those cases in which a person simply finds herself believing the doctrines of some religion, she knows not why and whence, and where the believer has in fact been moved to this belief by the grace of God, a highly reliable belief forming process, even though she is not conscious of this influence. The question of how we can tell that a particular case satisfies this description is a theological question and falls outside the scope of this book.

Be this as it may, the specific bearing of this book on the topic of religious knowledge concerns the more normal case in which a justified belief counts as knowledge. And here I have just one more point to make. It is worth noting that even if I cannot show that my ground for believing that God is speaking to me at time t, or that God has promised salvation to those who repent and follow the way of the cross, is an adequate ground, is sufficiently indicative of the truth of the belief, it may *be* adequate nonetheless, and if it is, and if the other conditions for knowledge are satisfied, I will know that God is speaking to me at time t, or whatever, even though I may not know that I know this or be able to show that I know it. We must always be alive to the point that just as I may be resentful or witty without realizing that I am or being able to show that I am, so I may know that p without knowing that I do or being able to show that I do. At least, that is true on the relatively externalist approach to knowledge I am adopting, where the satisfaction of the conditions for knowledge does not depend on the subject's knowing or being able to show that they are satisfied, an approach I am prepared to defend, though I cannot take the space to do that here. And so it is quite possible that knowledge of God extends more widely than many of us suspect.

CHAPTER 8

The Place of Experience in the Grounds of Religious Belief

i. Prologue

This book has been devoted to exploring and defending the credentials of one particular ground of belief about God, namely, direct experience of God, what we have been calling the "perception of God" or "mystical perception". At more than one place I have hinted that this is not the whole story of the epistemic support of religious belief and that in a comprehensive treatment, mystical perception would be integrated into a larger picture. I cannot attempt a complete theory in this book, but in this final chapter I will provide some indications as to how mystical perception is related to other grounds of religious belief.

In formulating my task in this way I am, of course, assuming that there are other grounds, not just psychologically but epistemically as well. I assume not only that people base religious beliefs on other grounds, but that at least some of these grounds do lend support to those beliefs, do provide some indication of the truth of those beliefs. I do not suppose that any is sufficient by itself to render religious belief rationally acceptable, but I take it that each can carry part of the load. I will not attempt to argue for this assumption at the tag end of this book.[1]

ii. Types of Experiential Support

In canvassing the variety of grounds, I first want to mention a different way in which experience can support religious beliefs, different from the way in which mystical perception does so. Some experiences that do not count as perceptions of God can be *explained* by divine activity. Thus if one experi-

[1]For an epistemological treatment of one of these grounds, revelation, see Mavrodes 1988.

ences a different kind of relationship to others after a conversion or a renewal of one's faith, if one finds oneself able to love other people in a new way, one may explain this (complex) experience-cum-attitude-cum-activity by the hypothesis that the Holy Spirit is active in one in a new way. If this explanation has the proper credentials, that goes toward justifying the belief that the Holy Spirit is at work here. This is mediate justification, since the belief about the holy Spirit is justified, proximately, by being based on the belief that it constitutes a good (or the best) explanation of the personality changes cited. Again, if one prays for greater serenity in the face of the ups and downs of daily life and then finds oneself getting much less upset by vicissitudes, one may explain this as a result of God's response to prayer, as due to God's having acted to lower one's emotional lability and enable one to remain calmer. And again, depending on the plausibility of this explanation, one may thereby be justified in the belief that God has so acted. More globally, the total experience of leading the Christian life, with all that it involves—cognitively, emotionally, practically, devotionally, spiritually—may be such that one feels the need to suppose that God is taking an active hand in the matter in order to fully explain what is going on.

The difference between this explanatory support and the kind provided by mystical perception is analogous to the difference between the support for the belief that there is a mouse under the straw in the barn provided by one's seeing the straw moving around in such a way as to be explainable by the hypothesis that a mouse is under there, and the support provided by actually seeing a mouse in the straw. In the second case but not the first, a mouse is occupying a place in one's visual field. Something that presents itself to one's experience can be identified as a mouse. And similarly in our religious cases. The new feelings and attitudes toward others may well be due to the activity of the Holy Spirit and may be so explainable. But one didn't actually "see" or otherwise perceive the Holy Spirit; the Holy Spirit cannot be identified with anything that occupies a portion of one's "experiential field", sensory or otherwise. Where mystical perception, by contrast, supports a belief about God, the individual is experientially aware of something s(he) identifies as God. God, so she supposes, appears in person to her awareness; God presents *Himself*, not some effect of His activity. Note how Angela of Foligno in excerpt (3) of Chapter 1 makes this very distinction. In the first of her three experiences "the soul believes this comes from God, and delights therein. But she does not yet know, or see, that He dwells in her; she perceives His grace. . . ." This is our first sort of case in which the effects of God's activity, rather than God Himself, is what is directly perceived. But then, skipping over the intermediate case, "the soul receives the gift of seeing God. She sees him more clearly than one man sees another." God Himself directly presents Himself to the consciousness of the subject.

The "explanatory" sort of experiential support I have just introduced contrasts not only with direct perception of God, on which we have been concentrating in this book, but on indirect perception of God as well. In order for something to count as indirect perception of God, as that notion was explained in Chapter 1, God must still be presenting Himself to one's awareness, though via one's perception of something else. So long as that condition is satisfied, so long as one is genuinely experientially aware of God Himself in perceiving the beauties of nature or in hearing another human being speak—rather than simply taking these natural phenomena as due to God—then beliefs formed on the basis of that experience will typically be justified, if at all, by these beliefs constituting a "reading off" what is presented in the experience, rather than by way of any supposition that the experience is best explained by some activity of God.[2] This distinction is philosophically controversial both for sense perception and for mystical perception. Many philosophers hold that any perception provides support for beliefs about what is perceived only by way of such reasons as we have for supposing that facts about those perceived objects provide the best explanation of the perceptual experience involved.[3] In Chapters 1 and 2, I have already defended the contrasting direct-realist position I take on this issue. Even if there are beliefs involved in the total ground for a perceptual belief about what is perceived (whether a tree or God), the perceptual experience itself functions as a ground simply by the fact that in that experience the object presents itself to the subject as so-and-so. From this standpoint the support given by a perceptual experience of X as ϕ to the belief that X is ϕ stands in sharp contrast to the support provided by explanatory considerations.

Note that experience of any sort could conceivably provide support of the explanatory sort for beliefs about God. The limits to this are only the limits to what can be best explained in terms of divine activity. As with other such issues, we have no a priori insight into what those limits are; we have to discover this by experience, or by being informed of them by God. This is why my distinction in this section is not between different kinds of experience but between different kind of experiential support. Even perceptions of God can be supposed, perhaps rightly, to provide support of the explanatory sort. They are so thought of by people who talk about "the argument from religious experience". My quarrel with such people is not that the putative support they are discussing is nonexistent or insignificant, but rather that they ignore the possibility of direct perceptual support.

[2]In terms of the taxonomy introduced in Chapter 1, this means that when experience functions in a ground of religious belief as explanandum, it is more like "perceptual identification" of God than *perception* of God. These cases don't exactly conform to our account of perceptual identification in Chapter 1 because the experience (of loving others in a new way, e.g.,) is not itself a perception of anything. Nevertheless, it contrasts with perception of God in basically the same way, for it is a matter of being experientially presented with something that one takes to be due to, and hence best explained by, God.

[3]See, e.g., Moser 1989, chap. 2.

iii. Other Grounds of Religious Belief

Although it is by no means uncontroversial what grounds, or even what putative grounds, there are for religious belief, certain candidates have traditionally been stressed. These include revelation, tradition, and natural theology. Let me explain how I am thinking of each, taking them in reverse order.

Natural theology is the enterprise of providing support for religious beliefs by starting from premises that neither are nor presuppose any religious beliefs. We begin from the mere existence of the world, or the teleological order of the world, or the concept of God, and we try to show that when we think through the implications of our starting point we are led to recognize the existence of a being that possesses attributes sufficient to identify Him as God. Once we get that foothold we may seek to show that a being could not have the initial attributes without also possessing certain others; in this manner we try to go as far as we can in building up a picture of God without relying on any supposed experience of God or communication from God, or on any religious authority. The credentials of this enterprise have often been challenged in the modern era. Hume and Kant are prominent among the challengers. Its death has repeatedly been reported, but like the phoenix it keeps rising from its ashes in ever new guises. One of the latest is the Bayesian probabilistic version of the traditional arguments developed by Richard Swinburne.[4] As for myself, though I have no tendency to suppose that the existence of God can be demonstratively proved from extrareligious premises, I find certain of the arguments to be not wholly lacking in cogency. In particular, I think that there is much to be said for the ontological, cosmological, and moral arguments, in certain of their forms. However I will have no time to argue that here.

This characterization of natural theology sticks closely to the classically recognized "arguments for the existence of God", but it need not be construed that narrowly. It also includes attempts to show that we can attain the best understanding of this or that area of our experience or sphere of concern—morality, human life, society, human wickedness, science, art, mathematics, or whatever—if we look at it from the standpoint of a theistic, or more specifically Christian . . ., metaphysics. This wider approach is exemplified by an issue of *Faith and Philosophy*, entitled "Philosophy from a Christian Perspective",[5] which includes theistic treatments of natural laws, probability, mathematics, and knowledge.

Tradition. From the standpoint of the community, *tradition* (as far as doctrine is concerned) constitutes a set of beliefs the grounds for which we need to explore, rather than constituting a type of ground. But from the standpoint

[4]See Swinburne 1979.
[5]Vol. 4, no. 4 (October 1987).

of the individual, a standpoint we are occupying here, tradition is one source of belief and a possible supporting ground thereof. Let's think of tradition as constituted by the teaching activity of the church, its role of transmitting to each successive generation the beliefs about God and His relations to us that have become central in the life of the church and have been made normative for believers.

Revelation. This is the most complex of our categories. Without pretending to go fully into the matter, let's distinguish three forms that God's revelation to us can take.

(1) *Messages* delivered to His people at large through selected messengers. The messenger supposes himself to have been addressed by God (whether in audible words, auditory imagery, or by some more interior intellectual route) and entrusted with a message that he is enjoined to deliver. This is the pattern classically illustrated by the Hebrew prophets, the book of Revelation and, indeed, by Jesus himself. Some have thought of all or most of the books of the Bible as having been written in order to communicate divine messages construed in this way (the "dictation" theory), but this is, at best, highly controversial.

(2) *Divine inspiration* of writings or oral communications, where the human agent does not consciously receive a specific communication. If one takes the Pauline epistles to be divine revelation, this is the way to do so. Paul, one must suppose, did not think of himself as taking down dictation from God when he dashed off his letters to churches. This construal would seem to fit many other portions of the Bible as well.

(3) *Divine action in history.* It has traditionally been supposed that God reveals Himself, His purposes and His requirements for us, by what He does as well as by what He says and what He inspires us to say. By bringing the Israelites safely out of Egypt and installing them in Palestine, by using the Assyrians and the Babylonians to chastise Israel for its apostasy, and, most centrally, by becoming man in Jesus of Nazareth—living the kind of life and dying the kind of death He did and rising again from the dead—God shows us much about what He is like, what His purposes are, and what He would have us do and be. To be sure, these divine activities have been accompanied with commentaries and explanations that fall under categories A. and B., but it is not as if the messages do the whole job. It was important for God's self-revelation, as well as for the divine scheme of salvation, that He actually did these things.

iv. Basic Categories of Grounds of Religious Belief

So there we have it, a plurality of sources of Christian belief and, we are assuming, a corresponding plurality of justifying grounds of those beliefs.

Now I want to look into how these are interrelated and how they fit together into a cumulative case.

Let's begin by considering whether these items might not be reduced to a few basic categories. First, *tradition*. The derivative status of this source was brought out above when I pointed out that tradition is, on its doctrinal side, a system of beliefs that has become generally accepted in the community and/or received explicit endorsement. That implies that these beliefs originally had some other basis; otherwise the building up of the tradition would require that the tradition already exist. Thus we can omit *tradition* from the list of basic grounds.

Looking now at the three forms of revelation, it is clear that the first, *messages*, depends on a particular form of mystical perception. The human bearer of the message from God must have been aware of God as communicating that message to him. If he were simply inspired by God to utter certain sentences without his being experientially aware of God's doing so, this would fall under our second type of revelation.

Thus this kind of revelation counts as a perceptual ground for the messenger's belief, but how about those who receive the message from him? At this point I must make it explicit that when I speak of perception as a ground of certain religious beliefs of a person, S, I take this to include not only S's perceptions of God, but also the reports of others' perceptions of God that S has received. This is in line with the way we speak of perception as a ground of belief about the physical world. If my knowledge of the world were confined to my own experience it would be miserably impoverished. By virtue of belonging to a community I am able to draw on the experience of countless others; and this is equally true of religious communities. As brought out in Chapter 7, section vi, the acceptance of perceptual testimony poses more complex epistemological problems than the formation of belief on the basis of first hand experience, but these problems are not insoluble. I will take it that for both sense perception and mystical perception there are criteria for the credibility of witnesses, and that they can be used to acquire justified beliefs from perceptual reports.

The other two types of revelation are, epistemologically, forms of an inference to the best explanation. In supposing that certain writings or oral utterances that do not record direct experiences of God are shaped by God in order to send us messages, we are taking it that certain features of the writings, their authors, and/or the process of their composition are best explained by that supposition. These "features" can include the sanctity of the authors, miracles they wrought, the effects of their writings on the lives of others, general acceptance of the writings by the community as having a certain status, and the fulfillment of prophecies. As for the third type of revelation, in accepting certain events in the world as brought about by God for certain purposes we are obviously supposing that those events are best explained in this way. We can also use messages from God (the first type of revelation) to support such explanations.

Most of the traditional philosophical arguments for the existence and nature of God boil down to explanatory claims also. A supreme being with certain attributes is invoked by the cosmological argument as the best explanation for the existence of the universe,[6] by the teleological argument as the best explanation for the (apparent) design in the universe, by the moral argument as the best explanation for moral obligation, the distinction between right and wrong, or moral value. The only major argument that does not fit this pattern is the ontological argument, which proceeds by analyzing the concept of God.[7]

Finally, the "explanatory" type of experiential ground explicitly functions as an explanandum that, it is claimed, can best be explained by the action of God. The changed life one leads when one accepts Jesus Christ as one's savior is, one claims, best explained by supposing these changes to be due to the work of the Holy Spirit.

v. How Different Grounds Interact in the Total Picture

Apart from the purely a priori, then, the grounds of Christian belief can be reduced to forms of the perception of God and explanatory claims. How do these relate to each other in the total case for Christian belief?

The most obvious relation is an additive one. Such grounds as have some individual merit can be combined so that the total basis will be greater than any of its individual parts; just as the various bits of evidence that support a scientific or diagnostic hypothesis add up to a support that is greater than that contributed by any one piece of evidence alone. Thus the belief that God is supremely loving will be supported by the many perceptions of God as loving, by God's self revelation in the New Testament, and, perhaps, by natural theology.[8] But there is more than one reason why this simple additive relationship is not the whole story. For example, in this book we have run into more than one way in which CMP is dependent for its operation on a background system of belief that is based, at least in part, on grounds of other sorts. Hence we can't suppose that CMP simply adds a completely independent quantum of justification to that provided by the other grounds. The situation is more complicated than that. The ensuing discussion will bring out some dimensions of this complexity.

[6]This does not appear on the surface of most traditional forms of the argument (as contrasted with a newfangled version like that of Swinburne 1979). However, scratch any version of the cosmological argument and one finds claims to a best explanation (or even stronger, the only possible explanation). For support for this claim see Rowe 1975.

[7]In the ensuing discussion I will leave aside the ontological argument and any other purely a priori grounds of religious belief there may be.

[8]As for the latter, Aquinas supposed himself to have supported this claim from his metaphysics of infinite being, being itself. See, I, Q. 20, art. 1 (1945, Vol. I, p. 215).

Perhaps the simplest of these further modes of interaction involves the way in which different grounds will support different propositions, will shore up different parts of the structure. Speaking most generally, mediate and immediate justification have complementary strengths and weaknesses. There is something of a "percepts without concepts are blind, concepts without percepts are empty" situation here. Perception generates beliefs full of force and conviction. "Seeing is believing." "There's no substitute for being there." But often the content is very limited, and it doesn't give us by itself a full theoretical characterization. We have repeatedly pointed out the limits of what God experientially presents Himself to us *as*. With rare exceptions one doesn't suppose that God presents Himself as creator, three Persons in one Substance, the actor in salvation history, or even omnipotent, omniscient, and a se.[9] To get all that we have to go to revelation and natural theology. To be sure, I have already claimed that the *message* form of revelation involves perceiving God as "saying" something; and no limit can be put on what God could *tell* a human being, other than limits set by our capacities for understanding. But for present purposes let's set the content of divine messages to one side and confine mystical perception to what God presents Himself as being and doing. Here we have an area in which revelation and natural theology can give us what perception cannot.

On the other side, we have to recognize that perception has its own contribution to make by way of propositional content as well as by way of force and vividness. In mystical perception one can learn what God is doing vis-à-vis oneself at the moment, reproving, forgiving, instructing, guiding, comforting, just being present; and one can learn what God's will is for oneself in particular. We can't get any of this out of natural theology and general revelation. Thus each type of source has its own distinctive propositional contribution to make to the total system of belief. A given part of the structure will depend on some grounds and not on others—even though some parts will gain support from more than one source, as when the doctrine of creation is supported by divine messages, by other modes of revelation, and by natural theology.

Nor is this differential support a matter of mere aggregation. The relationship is often more intimate than that. The doxastic output from one source can fill out what is gleaned from another. Here I think particularly of the point, discussed in some detail in Chapter 2, that frequently what is explicitly presented in putative experience of God fails to uniquely identify the object as God. One is aware of God's being *very* loving and powerful but not infinitely loving and powerful. One is aware of something sustaining one in being, but not aware of it as the creator of all. Christians regularly fill out these fragmen-

[9]See St. Teresa 1957, chaps. 39, 40, for an example of claims by mystics to have experienced such things. I call these rare exceptions, even though they are not rare among the classic mystics, because these giants of the mystical world constitute an elite that is only a tiny percentage of those who take themselves to have perceived God.

tary epiphanies with what they have garnered from their tradition, taking what they perceive to go beyond what is revealed in experience in ways spelled out in the Christian tradition. This is often made a reproach to mystical perception; since the perceiver is reading his tradition into what he perceives, the perception has no epistemic significance. But the alleged weakness is really a strength. It is precisely what happens in sense perception where we construe what we are seeing, feeling, or hearing in terms of what we take ourselves to know about the object from elsewhere. If we weren't able to do that we would learn much less from perception. To be sure, the value of this procedure depends on the credentials of this independent information. But given such credentials, it is of the first importance to be able to fill out the perceived situation in this way.

The filling out can go in the other direction as well; perception can fill out what we get from public revelation and natural theology. The latter may tell us what God is like and the broad outlines of what He has done, is doing, and will do in the world to carry out His plans, but they will not tell me what God has to say to me at this moment or what God's will for me is at this stage of my life, or how God is interacting with me at this moment. These details can be filled in by mystical perception. The other sources can give us the master plan; perception provides the application of that plan to the immediate situation.

Thus far the discussion in this section has concerned purely *additive* relationships in the sense of relations between contributions that are made by each source independently of any dependence on the others. We now move to more intimate relationships in which a given source is involved in the *operation* of another source, so that the support lent to religious belief by the latter is not wholly independent of the former.

To begin, let's remind ourselves of the ways in which we have already seen mystical perception to be beholden to other grounds. In justifiably forming beliefs about God on the basis of mystical perception we depend on a background system of belief at more than one point. First, we use that system to determine whether what we are aware of is God. As just noted, God does not uniquely identify Himself just by the way He appears to us. Even if He says that He is God, there is the problem of distinguishing the real thing from imposters. And apart from self-identification, though God may appear to one as good, powerful, and loving, He typically does not appear as *infinitely* good, powerful, or loving, or as possessing any other characteristics that are peculiar to God Himself. Hence we depend on the background theology and other aspects of the tradition for principles that lay down conditions under which what we are aware of is God.[10]

[10]This is subtly, but significantly, different from a similar point made three paragraphs back. There the point was that other sources fill out what we learn from perception. Here the point is that we draw on those sources to formulate what we learn from the perception. The difference is

It may also be that MP is dependent on other grounds for the principles linking phenomenal content with objective properties, for example, a principle that when one has an experience of such-and-such a phenomenal sort one is justified in taking what is appearing to one to be God pouring out His spirit.[11] Such principles have to be true if objective attributions are to be justified by being based on appearances; and the subject must be justified in accepting such principles if he is to use them in reflective criticism of perceptual beliefs. Do we need some input from other sources of information about God to determine what appearances reliably indicate what features of what objects? I don't feel confident about any answer to this question. On the one hand, it is plausible to accept a blanket principle that licenses going from how something seems experientially to what it is, in the absence of sufficient reasons against this in a specific case. That would make mystical perception independent of other sources on this point. On the other hand what we are justified in believing about God and our relations to Him from other sources may well be required for justifiably accepting such principles. I won't try to decide this issue here.

Finally, putative perceptions of God are not "self-authenticating", but instead are in principle subject to being shown to be incorrect, or inadequately based, by relevant considerations, that is, "overriden". But this is possible only if we have a stock of knowledge or justified belief concerning the matters in question, in this case concerning God, His nature, purposes, and activities. Thus mystical perception can function as a source of justification for M-beliefs only against the background of a system of epistemically justified beliefs concerning the matters just mentioned. Such a system is built up at least partly on the basis of mystical perception itself. But apart from worries as to how we could ever get started building up the system on the basis of MP if each utilization of MP (including the earliest ones) required that we already have such a system,[12] we have seen that MP is limited in the range of beliefs that it can effectively support. Except for the matters on which God has communicated messages in a direct perceptual manner, MP will not by itself give us the word on the essential nature of God, His purposes, and the course of salvation history. Even where God has putatively conveyed messages on such matters, we need to distinguish genuine divine communications from counterfeits, and it is dubious that we could do that without relying on what we have learned about God from other sources. The upshot is that we can't have the

---

between "I learned from perception that there is a very good, powerful and loving being; and from other sources I gather that this being is *infinitely* good, powerful, and loving and hence is God" and "I learned from perception, with the help of background beliefs garnered, in part, from other sources, that *God* was present to me".

[11]See Chapter 1, for an indication of why we have to use the lame, unspecific locution 'such and such'.

[12]This worry was addressed in Chapter 2, section ivC.

kind of background system we need for overriding without relying on other sources of information. Hence MP depends on other grounds of religious belief for its viability as a source of epistemic justification.

What about the other grounds? Does each of them depend on other sources for its epistemic credentials? Well, consider the proposition that no one ground suffices by itself for building up the background system for overriders for beliefs based on that ground. And though I won't produce a full dress argument for that proposition, it seems very plausible on the basis of considerations we have already adduced. We have seen that each of the grounds in question is fitted to provide some parts of the total background system and not others.[13] Hence, at least as far as the overrider system is concerned, each of the other grounds is also dependent on others for its effective operation.[14]

Another way in which one ground depends on others has to do with the resolution of doubts. Doubts can be raised about the genuineness or the strength of any one of these grounds. These doubts can be, to some extent, assuaged by appeal to other grounds or their output. Although none of the grounds is immune from such worries, the fact that the output of each supports the claims made for the others rightfully increases our confidence in all of them, and thus increases the total support given to Christian belief by their combination. Let me elaborate.

In the course of this book, particularly in Chapters 5–7, we have seen many reasons for being dubious about claims to directly perceive God in a way that provides genuine information about God. Such perceptions are far from universally distributed in the population. Even for most people who enjoy them, they are infrequent, fleeting, indistinct, and obscure. Putative experiences of divine communications frequently yield mutually contradictory claims as to what God is like, what His purposes and plans are, and what He requires of us. It is not implausible to suppose that such experiences can all be explained naturalistically. How the Supreme Reality presents Itself to our experience varies greatly across religious traditions. And so on. I believe that all these doubts, and others, have been resolved in Chapters 5–7 in ways that leave putative direct perceptions of God with a significant quantum of justificatory force. But it would be rash to claim that my defense establishes the epistemic credentials of mystical perception beyond the shadow of a doubt. It obviously makes a difference to our judgment on this whether we have other reasons for supposing that there exists a being of the sort one seems to be perceiving in these experiences. In the same way the credibility of alleged perceptions of flying saucers or extra-terrestrial visitors will get a substantial

[13]Above, pp. 293–94.

[14]Natural theology would not seem to exhibit any mode of dependence that is closely analogous to the way MP depends on a background system, built up at least in part from other sources, for the identification of what is perceived as God. But revelation, even of the nonperceptual sort, may well exhibit a similar dependence. We certainly draw on what we take ourselves to have learned about God from whatever source in identifying the revealer as God.

boost if we have more indirect, explanatory reasons for supposing that such things exist, or may well exist. Such reasons will not, of course, entail that any particular alleged perception of a flying saucer is veridical, or even that some of them are veridical. But if we have other reasons for believing in the existence of flying saucers and the perceivability thereof, a claim to perceive one is, ceteris paribus, more plausible than if we lacked such reasons. In like fashion, if postulating a being like the Christian God carries substantial explanatory advantages, that will boost the credibility of claims to perceive such a being.

The converse also holds. The explanatory arguments we have been considering are equally subject to criticism. Why suppose that my changed life could not be adequately explained in terms of psychosocial factors like my new relationships with people in the church, my sense of release from guilt that comes from confession, or more recondite factors of a psychodynamic sort? The evaluation of explanations is a tricky affair at best. Even in empirical science where predictive efficacy can be factored into the equation it is difficult to show that one competing explanation is superior to all its competitors, not to mention the fact that we usually cannot be sure that we have identified all the (serious) competitors. Standard criteria of explanation like simplicity, economy, scope, systematicity, and explanatory power can be appealed to, but such appeals are far from providing us with effective decision procedures. If the explananda are complex patterns of experience, feeling, thought, and behavior—where there is no possibility of a precise predictive test, where the explanations are not embedded in any rich theoretical matrix, and where the competing explanations have not been developed to the point at which it is clear just what consequences can be derived from them—we are in a much worse position to support any particular explanatory claim. All this cuts both ways, of course. We are in no better position to definitively award the verdict to purely psychosocial explanations of "the new life of the spirit" than we are to find in favor of the theistic explanation.[15] But the fact remains that because of the considerations just mentioned one is not in a position to repose unqualified confidence in Christian explanations of the Christian life.

Similar points can be made concerning the Christian explanation of the composition of biblical writings and of the major events in salvation history. Here we are in an even worse position to nail down explanatory claims. In dealing with patterns of the Christian life, we at least have repeatable phenomena that can be subjected to observation and analysis in situ. But with events in ancient history, including literary composition, we have only highly indirect access to the explananda themselves, and so are in a correspondingly

[15]I have not forgotten that in Chapter 6 I argued that a naturalistic explanation of mystical experience, even one that is completely adequate by the usual scientific standards, is quite compatible with a theistic explanation, since both have to do with different levels of explanation. For purposes of this discussion let's take the naturalistic explanation to carry with it the claim that nothing beyong natural factors is involved. That will generate an incompatibility.

weaker position to determine how they are best explained. At this point I am thinking of attempts to explain the phenomena apart from divine messages concerning them. To bring in the latter is to exploit a way in which mystical perception can strengthen explanatory claims, a point to which I will turn shortly.

To be sure, it is frequently claimed that the life, death, and resurrection of Jesus is such as to cry out for explanation in terms of divine activity and to be palpably inexplicable otherwise; similar claims are made for events in Old Testament history. Here we must be careful to separate historical narration from theological explanation in the biblical texts themselves. I'm afraid that in saying this I will become embroiled in debates over whether there is any such thing as history without interpretation—a bare record of what happened, devoid of any suggestions as to what is responsible for it. Let this be as it may; I am not concerned here to take any position on the nature of history. The present point is simply this. If we want to support Christian beliefs by showing that the truth of some of them is required to explain certain facts that can be recognized to obtain without making any Christian suppositions in doing so, that enterprise will require that the facts in question do not come with a Christian reading attached. And so the facts about Jesus that we claim to be best explained in a Christian way will have to be unvarnished facts with no Christian overlay: not that the Holy Spirit descended on Jesus at his baptism, but that Jesus changed water into wine or that he appeared to his disciples in bodily form after having been medically dead. And without properly going into the enormously complex issues involved, I venture to suggest that there is considerable room for doubt as to whether such unvarnished facts are best explained in the Christian way.

Finally, enough doubts have been raised about the traditional arguments for the existence of God to fill a sizable library. I certainly won't go into all that. Suffice it to say that for each argument there is a variety of not wholly implausible alternatives, each of which needs to be excluded. At least it needs to be argued, in the case of each, that theism is explanatorily superior. For example, with respect to the cosmological argument there are the alternatives of no explanation at all (the spatiotemporal universe is just a brute fact), production by a physical or at least nonintelligent cause, and production by a nonabsolute spiritual being that itself depends for its existence on something else. For my money the theistic explanation is superior to all the competition, but I am not prepared to condemn someone as irrational for failing to agree with me on this.

We can respond to these doubts, to some extent, by appealing to the (alleged) direct awareness of God. That will not establish, or even directly support, the adequacy of any of the explanations we have been discussing. Even if there is a God of the Christian sort, it does not follow that He is active in history and in the lives of Christians in the ways supposed in Christianity. Nevertheless, assuming that mystical perception does provide significant support for supposing that there does exist a God of the Christian sort, it thereby provides a significant degree of support for the proposition that there exists a being that might well act in ways in which Christian explanations portray Him as acting. By familiar principles, that would constitute some support for those explanations. It is generally true of explanatory claims that where we have independent reason for supposing that entities of sorts invoked by the explanation do exist, our explanatory claims are in a stronger position, ceteris paribus, than where entities of those sorts are simply postulated in order to make the explanation go. To take a familiar example, the planet Neptune was originally postulated just to explain deviations in the antecedently predicted orbits of recognized planets. When Neptune was telescopically sighted, that properly and justifiably shored up scientists' belief in its existence.

Let's be more explicit about the structure of this mutual support. We have been speaking loosely of one "source" or "ground" supporting another, but a more accurate portrayal would be this. In the dependence of a source of justification on a "background system of belief", as well as in the appeal to other sources to allay doubts, what happens is that the other source(s) themselves provide support for certain beliefs, which are then called upon to do service for the source in question. This is obvious in the first kind of case, where it is a system of belief (supported in large part by other sources) that provides the overriders or the principles of identification or the principles of phenomenal-objective correlation. But it equally holds in the second kind of case too; for the source in question is shored up against doubts by appealing to beliefs that have been supported by the other sources (God really does exist, or God is Lord of all); it is not that doubts are allayed by the other source of belief *directly*, whatever that would mean.[16]

I hope it is not necessary at this time of day to defend the thesis that one belief, or source of belief, may provide support for another, even though the former is not incorrigible or indubitable and can itself be strengthened by support from other quarters, including the ones for which it is providing support. The strong foundationalist assumptions that any genuine knowledge (justified belief) must rest on foundations each of which is certain in a strong sense (incapable of being mistaken), quite apart from any support it might gain from other quarters, is not the only model of knowledge with some considerable plausibility. Nor is the only alternative an extreme coherence theory that regards no belief as possessing any positive epistemic status apart

[16]There are also, of course, relations of mutual support among the beliefs that make up a religious, or other, belief system. The general picture of God in the community is supported by reports of perceiving Him as being that way, and vice versa. Beliefs in the mighty acts of God in salvation history are supported by the general picture of what God is like and vice versa; both are supported by what is learned about God in mystical experience. This is a familiar story in theology and elsewhere; it has to do with the way in which propositions fit together into a system that is coherent, at least in part because it involves relations of mutual support. What we are discussing here is analogous to this but also different. It has to do not with the way in which beliefs support one another, but with the way in which the operations or credibility of one source of a belief depends on the output of other sources.

from its involvement in a total system. Indeed, the strong foundationalism just mentioned is not even the only plausible type of foundationalism. There is also the modest foundationalism I favor, according to which there are fallible and corrigible foundations, beliefs that possess prima facie justification from experience, but where this justification is subject to being overridden by sufficient indications to the contrary. Note that this modest foundationalism is committed to the possibility, and the reality, of mutual epistemic support. Since some perceptual beliefs count as foundations that are prima facie justified by experience, they can provide support for beliefs that rest solely on other beliefs. But since these perceptual beliefs are only prima facie justified by experience, they can be overridden by sufficient evidence in support of their contraries. And, again, since they are only prima facie justified by experience, there are room for their epistemic status being improved by support from other justified beliefs. It is just this kind of view that is presupposed in the previous discussion.

The reciprocal support we have been discussing, though historically most emphasized by coherence theory, is by now a feature of almost any developed epistemology. And once we recognize that a belief can receive a significant amount of justification from a certain source but still profit from justificatory additions from other sources, the way is clear for recognizing the possibility and desirability of *reciprocal* support. Belief B gets some, but not enough support from source S. Belief C gets some but not enough support from source T. This being the case, there is no reason in principle why C could not get additional support from B, and B get additional support from C. Each of the beliefs prior to their interaction has enough independent support to serve as a source of justification for other beliefs, but not so much that it cannot profit from further strengthening. This is a way of construing reciprocal support that saves us from the paradoxes of extreme coherentism.

vi. Can Any of the Sources Make a Distinctive Contribution?

We have been exploring ways in which the capacity of one source of belief to confer justification is dependent on the same capacity of other sources. It may seem, at first glance, that this prevents any of the sources from making any contribution to the sum total of support for religious belief. Let's spell out the reasons for this gloomy assessment in the case of mystical perception, where the dependence on other sources is more obvious than in other cases, though, as I have indicated, I believe that the other sources are really in the same boat.

With mystical perception we have seen that a background system of beliefs is drawn on for the support of the identification of the perceived object as God and for the provision of an overrider system, as well as for allaying doubts about the epistemic credentials of MP. Hence, mystical perception depends for its justificatory efficacy on the justificatory efficacy of whatever other grounds provide bases for the background system and so on. Therefore, mystical perception can contribute to the pot only if the other grounds do so. Hence it is not pulling any weight on its own. It makes no independent contribution to the sum total of support. Its contribution cannot be counted separately.

This last conclusion does not follow from the premises. From the dependence of MP on other grounds of religious belief in the ways specified, it does not follow that MP makes no contribution to the total case for religious belief. It is, for the reasons given, true to say that it makes no (wholly) independent contribution; its epistemic value is not independent of the epistemic value of other grounds. But that does not imply that it is making no contribution of its own. There are two points to be made here.

First there is the level distinction invoked in Chapter 2 in response to the puzzle about how "adequacy principles" for the perceptual attribution of objective properties could be empirically justified. There the point was that one can *be* justified in particular perceptual beliefs provided the relevant adequacy principle is *true*. It is not also necessary that one be justified in supposing it to be true. Thus one can pile up a lot of inductive evidence for a particular adequacy principle in the form of particular justified perceptual beliefs without having been justified earlier in accepting the adequacy principle.[17] The analogous point here is that one can be justified in forming M-beliefs on the basis of mystical perception provided one is in fact justified in accepting the background system (on the basis of other grounds or whatever). One doesn't also have to be justified in the higher level judgment that the system is justified. Hence even if the other grounds must in fact have justificatory efficacy in order for MP to do so, the user of MP need not know, or be justified in supposing, that they do, in order that his MP based beliefs be thereby justified. Hence the acquisition of justified beliefs from MP does not require that the subject himself know anything about epistemic status of other grounds, or, indeed, of MP itself. This, as I will go on to point out next, does not in itself resolve the problem, but it does save us from a mistaken way of posing the problem. That is, in thinking that MP depends on the epistemic status of other grounds for its status, one may be thinking that one must have determined that the other grounds have that status in order to become justified in forming M-beliefs on the basis of MP; and one may not be able to do that without having beliefs that are justified by MP. The above considerations are designed to save us from that line of thought.

However, as just intimated, that does not in itself resolve the problem. It is still the case that MP can contribute something to the total support of religious belief only if various other grounds can do so likewise. Doesn't that prevent it from adding to the sum total of support? Isn't it just riding piggyback on the

[17]See Chapter 2, section ivC.

others? NO. An affirmative answer would be based on a false picture of the situation, according to which whenever the efficacy of one putative source of justification presupposes the efficacy of others, this involves a simple transfer of justification from the latter to the former. The former is functioning, so to say, as a channel that lets the justification provided by the latter to make contact with the target beliefs. But that's not the kind of setup we have here. It is, rather, that the other sources of justification contribute to a background system that allows MP to do its distinctive thing effectively. Since the other sources really do provide support for that background system, it is possible for MP to provide a kind of support for kinds of beliefs that cannot be provided by the other sources. Thus, as we have pointed out, natural theology and the "public" body of divine revelation will not suffice to tell me what God is doing vis-à-vis me at this moment. And even if they could, it would not provide the kind of justification (reading off what is presented to experience) that MP provides. Hence even though MP does not make a wholly independent contribution,[18] it still makes its weight felt by providing a kind of justification not otherwise available, and, often, by providing it for a kind of belief that is susceptible of no other sort of justification.

vii. The Importance of Experiential Grounds

For some time now I have been stressing the ways in which mystical perception depends on other grounds for its operation. This may give the impression that I take mystical perception to have a wholly subsidiary, derivative, and peripheral role, so far as the justification of religious belief is concerned. But that is not my view. A close reading of the last two sections will disclose an insistence that mystical perception makes its own contribution to the total system of Christian belief. (1) It is the only source for particular beliefs about what God is doing vis-à-vis one at the moment and about God's will for one's own life. (2) It gives the human bearer of revelation access to the divine communicator. (3) It is an important source of our assurance that the source of general revelation, the chief actor in the drama of salvation, and the creator of the universe, really does exist. Let me go into this last point once more in a slightly different way.

Earlier I stressed the point that many doubts can reasonably be raised concerning the credentials of Christian explanatory claims. The same goes for claims of revelation through the Bible and the Church. If one is confined to what we might call these external sources of belief (external to the experience of a contemporary person), a reflective intelligent individual, alive to various critical questions that have been aired concerning the Christian tradition and its traditional supports, may well feel, at best, uncertain about its credentials.

[18]By the same argument, none of the other sources do so either.

Suppose that, in this situation of doubt, she takes herself to be directly aware of God not just once but repeatedly, and aware in such a way as to be in line with the picture of God and His purposes that is embodied in the Christian tradition. Will that not change the epistemic situation? "I knew of thee then only by report but now I see thee with my own eyes" (Job 42:4). Instead of relying exclusively on questionable inferences from questionable data, one can now advert to an actual encounter, a "personal appearance" of the being Himself. This gives one a new kind of assurance, one not subject to doubts about the cogency of explanatory and other inferences. One now has the *kind* of assurance one normally has of the existence and character of the things and people in one's physical environment. Thus mystical perception makes a distinctive and valuable contribution to the total epistemic situation of the believer. Note that I am restricting this discussion to the *epistemic* role of the perception of God, but that is, of course, only a small part of its importance for the Christian life. The experience of God greatly enlivens one's religious life, it makes an enormous difference to the quality and intensity of one's devotional life, it greatly stimulates one's aspirations to virtue and holiness, and most important, it makes possible the loving communion with God for which we were created. All this is undoubtedly far more important than the epistemic contribution of mystical perception. But it is the latter with which I am concerned in this book.

A good way to appreciate the importance of one source among others, of epistemic justification or of anything else, is to imagine oneself without it and compare that situation with the actual one. We have seen in the foregoing that if we were bereft of all the "indirect" grounds of religious belief we would be in a much worse position epistemically. Not only would we be left with nothing but mystical perception on which to depend for knowledge of God; that source itself would not provide justification to nearly the same extent as it does in fact. We would not have the same degree of support for the background system on which MP depends, nor would we have the defense against doubts about MP provided by the output of other sources. And, as we have also seen, the same story can be told in the opposite direction; the indirect sources would be similarly hampered in their operation were it not for the contributions made by MP. But that is not all. Think of how different our relation to Christian doctrine would be if we were unable to *perceive* God. That body of doctrine would have the status of an explanatory theory. We would be related to it in a purely theoretical fashion. God—His nature, purposes, and doings—would be for us a speculative hypothesis.[19] Moreover, this would have profound implications as to the character of our interrelations with God. Just think of the differences between the ways we can relate to someone we know by face to face contact, and the ways we can relate to someone we have only heard about or have only hypothesized. It is only in

[19]This is not to imply that it could not be used as a guide to action.

the former case that the distinctively "personal" relationships of love, friendship, mutual sharing, resentment, delight in each other's company, and self-revelation are possible. Likewise it is only if we can perceive God that such modes of human-divine interaction are possible. This is not itself, perhaps, a strictly epistemic point; but it is a consequence of differences in mode of epistemic access. And these consequences are of the utmost importance for the religious life.

My discussion of the place of experience has concerned the perception of God almost exclusively. Other aspects of Christian experience have figured only as providing explananda for Christian explanation. Now I want to bring out a hitherto suppressed piece of the picture, one that in a way is the capstone of the entire edifice. I have so far, in effect, been presenting the Christian believer as a passive spectator, at least so far as epistemic assessment is concerned. I have thought of him as leading the Christian life, but I have thought of that as feeding into his epistemic assessment of Christian belief only as providing one more set of data for Christian explanation. To put it another way, I have thought of the Christian, insofar as his epistemic situation depends on reasoning, as engaged only in post hoc explanation of religious and nonreligious facts. I have put nothing into the picture analogous to the active, interventionist, experimental attitude of modern science. But such a feature can be found there. The final test of the Christian scheme comes from trying it out in one's life, testing the promises the scheme tells us God has made, following the way enjoined on us by the Church and seeing whether it leads to the new life of the Spirit.[20] Admittedly, it is not always clear exactly what this involves; it is not always clear whether we are satisfying the conditions laid down for entering into the kingdom; it is not always clear where we are at a given moment in our pilgrimage, whether, for example, an apparent setback or regression is part of the master plan or a failure on our part. And then there is the inconvenient fact that not all members of the body of Christ agree as to just what is required and just how the payoff is to be construed. But with all this looseness and open texture, the fact remains that over the centuries countless Christians who have set out to follow the way have found in their lives that the promises of God have been fulfilled, that their lives have been different, not 100 percent of the time and not as quickly and as dramatically as they may have wished, but unmistakably and in the direction the tradition predicts. From this standpoint the perception of God, and the personal communion with God that requires such perception, is a central aspect of the total fabric of Christian experience that makes up the new life promised to those who would open themselves up to the Holy Spirit and cooperate with His transforming activity. When all is said and done, this fulfillment in the total experience of leading the Christian life is perhaps the most fundamental contribution made by experience to the grounds of Christian belief.

[20]See Chapter 6, section vi, for another allusion to this point.

viii. Summary: A Case of Christian Belief

I will conclude by trying as briefly as possible to put all the foregoing together into a composite portrait of the epistemic structure of a typical case of Christian belief. In this connection, we should not ignore the differences between the grounds that different people have for one and the same set of beliefs, whether in religion or elsewhere. Different people will have had different experiences; they will have been exposed to different batches of information; because of differences in their training they will have acquired somewhat different doxastic tendencies; they will differ in reasoning capacities and in their appreciation for one or another relevant consideration. This makes it difficult to make general points by scrutinizing particular cases. But something can be done along this line if the cases are carefully chosen. I will endeavor to portray a sincere contemporary Christian of good education who is thoroughly into leading the Christian life. She takes herself to be directly aware of God in her life from time to time, though she is not Teresa of Avila. She knows the Bible and the teachings of her church, and she has a passing acquaintance with natural theology. Let's call her Denise. Not your average person in the pew perhaps, but her background is rich enough to illustrate the complexities in the grounds of Christian belief.

Denise grew up in a reasonably devout Christian family and imbibed the Christian faith from early childhood. She received more Christian instruction than is, I fear, typical in many churches today. By the time she reached the age of reflection she found herself in fairly firm possession of a richly articulated Christian faith, one that she worked at living out in her life, with lapses that are endemic to the human condition. Being an intelligent, well-educated person, alive to the temper of the times, she came eventually to question her faith. She realized that she had just taken it on trust from her parents, her teachers and, more generally, from her church. And she learned from her study of philosophy to ask why she should suppose that these witnesses knew what they were talking about. Becoming aware of the diversity of high religions on the contemporary scene, she asked why she should suppose that Christianity had it straight rather than one of its competitors. And, more radically, she asked what reason she or anyone else has to suppose that any religion is purveying truth rather than wish fulfillments and elaborately decked-out fantasies. She is aware of traditional Christian apologetics, involving appeal to miracles, the fulfillment of prophecies, the growth of the church, and so on. But in reflecting on these she is led to ask whether she has sufficient reason to suppose that the biblical record is accurate, and the search for such reasons leads her back to the witness of the Church, which she was questioning in the first place. She studies the traditional arguments for the existence of God, but though they seem to her not wholly without merit, they do not appear sufficiently strong to hold up the entire edifice. These skeptical doubts are not so corrosive as to eat away her faith completely, but they do leave her upset, disturbed, and inhibited from entering wholeheartedly into the life of prayer, worship, and Christian love.

At some point in this process she is led to reflect on her own experience of the Christian life: her sense of communion with God in worship and prayer, her sense of renewal when she confesses her sins and receives absolution, her sense of inner support and strength when she quits trying to manage everything herself and opens herself up to the work of the Holy Spirit. And on occasion the sense of the presence of God that she frequently experiences in a mild form blossoms into a more distinct awareness of God as pouring out His creative love, sustaining her in being and working to transform her into the kind of person He would have her to be. She asks herself whether this personal acquaintance with God, displaying Himself to be the kind of being and to be doing the kinds of things that the Christian tradition would lead one to expect, is not the crucial evidence she has been looking for to support her initially blind and uncritical acceptance of the faith. But she also becomes aware of the doubts that can be raised about the epistemic force of these experiences. She falls into despair and feels that her last refuge has crumbled about her.

But then, perhaps inspired by contemporary work in epistemology, she has a new idea. Perhaps it is a mistake to look for a foundation of one's faith that stands infallible, indubitable, and incorrigible, in no need of support from any other source. Perhaps no system of belief can be grounded in that way. Perhaps a more reasonable aspiration for the human condition is to have multiple sources of support such that although each can be questioned and none renders any of one's beliefs absolutely certain, they lend support to each other as well as to the beliefs they are invoked to support; so that in the way the whole assemblage fits together we have sufficient reason to take the beliefs to be true. Thus in order to answer the claim that one's putative experience of God is this-worldly only, one can appeal to the witness of others who are more advanced in the Christian life, to the revelation of God in His historical acts, and to general philosophical reasons for believing that God as construed in Christianity does exist and rules His creation. Though each of these considerations can itself be doubted and though no single strand is sufficient to keep the faith secure, when combined into a rope they all together have enough strength to do the job. The sources just mentioned combine to provide reasons to suppose that there is a being of the sort she takes herself to be aware of in her Christian life, a being that could be expected to do the things she is aware of this being as doing. Conversely, when these more indirect (at least more indirect from her perspective) sources seem dubious, seem to provide at best a tenuous and shaky indication of the reality in question, she can fall back on her immediate, intimate sense of the presence and activity of God in her life to (rightfully) assure herself that it is not all the work of human imagination.

Thus I take the "cumulative case" and "mutual support" perspective on the grounds of Christian belief to be clearly superior to any story according to which the whole thing rests on some particular basis, a basis that will inevitably be subject to serious doubts that it cannot satisfactorily resolve with its own resources alone. This book has been devoted almost entirely to arguing the merits of one particular ground, mystical experience. In this chapter I have been concerned to adumbrate the larger picture of the bases of Christian belief into which the results of this book should be integrated.

Bibliography

Alston, William P. 1981. "The Christian Language-Game". In *The Autonomy of Religious Belief*, ed. F. J. Crosson. Notre Dame, Ind. University of Notre Dame Press.

——1982. "Religious Experience and Religious Belief". *Nous*, 16:3–12.

——1983. "Christian Experience and Christian Belief". In *Faith and Rationality*, ed. A. Plantinga & N. Wolterstorff. Notre Dame, Ind.: University of Notre Dame Press, 103–34.

——1985. "Plantinga's Religious Epistemology". In *Alvin Plantinga*, ed. J.E. Tomberlin and P. Van Inwagen. Dordrecht: Reidel, 287–309.

——1986a. "Religious Experience as a Ground of Religious Belief". In *Religious Experience and Religious Belief*, ed. J. Runzo and C.K. Ihara. Lanham, Md.: University Press of America.

——1986b. "Is Religious Belief Rational?". In *The Life of Religion*, ed. S.M. Harrison and R.C. Taylor. Lanham, Md.: University Press of America.

——1986c. "Perceiving God". *Journal of Philosophy*, 83: 655–65.

——1988a. "Religious Diversity and the Perceptual Knowledge of God". *Faith and Philosophy*, 5: 433–88.

——1988b. "The Perception of God". *Philosophical Topics*, 16: 23–52.

——1989a. *Divine Nature and Human Language*. Ithaca, N.Y.: Cornell University Press.

——1989b. *Epistemic Justification*. Ithaca, N.Y.: Cornell University Press.

——1989c. "A 'Doxastic Practice' Approach to Epistemology". In *Knowledge and Skepticism*, ed. M. Clay and K. Lehrer. Boulder, Colo. Westview Press.

——1990. "Externalist Theories of Perception". *Philosophy and Phenomenological Research*, 51.

——1991a. "Higher Level Requirements for Epistemic Justification". In *The Opened Curtain*, ed. K. Lehrer and E. Sosa. Boulder, Colo.: Westview Press.

——1991b. "Knowledge of God". In *Faith, Reason, and Skepticism,* ed. M. Hester. Philadelphia: Temple University Press.

Aquinas, St. Thomas. 1945. *The Basic Writings of St. Thomas Aquinas*, ed. A. C. Pegis. 2 vols. New York: Random House.

Armstrong, David M. 1961. *Perception and the Physical World*. London: Routledge & Kegan Paul.

——1968. *A Materialist Theory of the Mind*. London: Routledge & Kegan Paul.

Audi, Robert M. 1978. "Psychological Foundationalism". *The Monist*, 62: 592–610.

Aune, Bruce. 1967. *Knowledge, Mind, and Nature*. New York: Random House.

Ayer, A.J. 1959. "Privacy". *The Proceedings of the British Academy*, 45: 43–65.

——1976. *The Central Questions of Philosophy*. London: Penguin Books.

Ayer, A.J., ed. 1959. *Logical Positivism*. New York: The Free Press.

Baillie, John. 1939. *Our Knowledge of God*. London: Oxford University Press.

——1962. *The Sense of the Presence of God*. New York: Scribner's.

Beardsworth, Timothy. 1977. *A Sense of Presence*. Oxford: Religious Experience Research Unit.

Bennett, Jonathan. 1966. *Kant's Analytic*. Cambridge: Cambridge University Press.

——1979. "Analytic Transcendental Arguments". In *Transcendental Arguments and Science*, ed. P. Bieri, R.P. Horstmann, and L. Krüger. Dordrecht: Reidel.

Blanshard, Brand. 1939. *The Nature of Thought*. 2 vols. London: Allen & Unwin.

Bonjour, Laurence. 1985. *The Structure of Empirical Knowledge*. Cambridge, Mass.: Harvard University Press.

Bosanquet, Bernard. 1911. *Logic or the Morphology of Knowledge*. London: Oxford University Press.

Bouwsma, O.K. 1965. *Philosophical Essays*. Lincoln: University of Nebraska Press.

Bradley, F.H. 1914. *Essays on Truth and Reality*. Oxford: Clarendon Press.

——1922. *The Principles of Logic*. 2d ed. London: Oxford University Press.

Browne, Henry. 1925. *Darkness or Light: An Essay in the Theory of Divine Contemplation*. St. Louis and London: Herder.

Carnap, Rudolf. 1950. "Empiricism, Semantics, and Ontology". *Revue Internationale de Philosophie*, 11.

Carroll, Lewis. 1895. "What Achilles Said to the Tortoise". *Mind* 4: 278–80.

Chihara, C., and J.A. Fodor. 1965. "Operationalism and Ordinary Language: A Critique of Wittgenstein". *American Philosophical Quarterly*, 2: 281–95.

Clark, R.W. 1984. "The Evidential Value of Religious Experience". *International Journal for the Philosophy of Religion,* 16.

Daniels, Charles B. 1989. "Experiencing God". *Philosophy and Phenomenological Research*, 49: 487–99.

Davis, Caroline Franks. 1989. *The Evidential Force of Religious Experience*. Oxford: Clarendon Press.

de Guibert, Joseph, S.J. 1953. *The Theology of the Spiritual Life*. New York: Sheed & Ward.

Dewey, John. 1938. *Logic: The Theory of Inquiry*. New York: Henry Holt.

Dretske, Fred. 1969. *Seeing and Knowing*. London: Routledge & Kegan Paul.

——1970. "Epistemic Operators". *Journal of Philosophy*, 67: 1007–23.

Edwards, Denis. 1983. *Human Experience of God*. New York: Paulist Press.

Edwards, Jonathan. 1959. *A Treatise Concerning Religious Affections*, ed. J.E. Smith. New Haven, Conn.: Yale University Press.

Farges, Albert. 1926. *Mystical Phenomena*, trans. S.P. Jacques. London: Burnes, Oates.

Farmer, H.H. 1943. *Toward Belief in God*. New York: Macmillan.

Flew, Antony. 1966. *God and Philosophy*. London: Hutchinson.

Flew, A., and A. MacIntyre, eds. 1955. *New Essays in Philosophical Theology*. London: SCM Press.

Foley, Richard. 1987. *The Theory of Epistemic Rationality*. Cambridge, Mass.: Harvard University Press.

Gale, Richard. 1991. *On the Nature and Existence of God*. New York: Cambridge University Press.

Garrigou-Lagrange, Père Réginald. 1937. *Christian Perfection and Contemplation*, trans. M.T. Doyle. St. Louis: Herder.

Gaskin, J.C.A. 1984. *The Quest for Eternity*. New York: Penguin Books.

Goldman, Alan. 1988. *Empirical Knowledge*. Berkeley and Los Angeles: University of California Press.

Goldman, Alvin I. 1977. "Perceptual Objects". *Synthese*, 35: 257–84.

——1979. "What Is Justified Belief?" In *Justification and Knowledge*, ed. G.S. Pappas. Dordrecht: Reidel.

——1986. *Epistemology and Cognition*. Cambridge, Mass. Harvard University Press.

Grayling, A.C. 1985. *The Refutation of Scepticism*. (Peru, Ill.: Open Court.

Gutting, Gary. 1982. *Religious Belief and Religious Skepticism*. (Notre Dame, Ind.: University of Notre Dame Press.

Hasker, William. 1986. "On Justifying the Christian Practice". *The New Scholasticism*, 60. 139–40.

Hick, John. 1966. *Faith and Knowledge*. 2d ed. Ithaca, N.Y.: Cornell University Press.

——1989. *The Interpretation of Religion*. New Haven, Conn.: Yale University Press.

Hilton, Walter. 1957. *The Ladder of Perfection*, trans. Leo Sherley-Price. London: Penguin Books.

Hocking, William Ernest. 1912. *The Meaning of God in Human Experience*. New Haven, Conn.: Yale University Press.

Hume, David. 1988. *A Treatise of Human Nature*, ed. L.A. Selby-Bigge. Oxford: Clarendon Press.

James, William. 1902. *The Varieties of Religious Experience*. New York: The Modern Library.

Kant, Immanuel. 1929. *Critique of Pure Reason*, trans. Norman Kemp Smith. New York; St Martin's Press.

Katz, Steven T., ed. 1978. *Mysticism and Philosophical Analysis*. New York: Oxford University Press.

Kripke, Saul. 1972. "Naming and Necessity". In *Semantics of Natural Language*, ed. D. Davidson and G. Harman. Dordrecht: Reidel.

Lehrer, Keith. 1974. *Knowledge*. New York: Oxford University Press.

Lewis, C.I. 1946. *An Analysis of Knowledge and Valuation*. La Salle, Ill.: Open Court.

Locke, John. 1975. *An Essay Concerning Human Understanding*, ed. P. Niddich. Oxford: Clarendon Press.

Losin, Peter. 1987. "Experience of God and the Principle of Credulity: A Reply to Rowe". *Faith and Philosophy*, 4: 59–70.

Mackie, John. 1982. *The Miracle of Theism*. Oxford: Clarendon Press.

Macquarrie, John. 1977. *Principles of Christian Theology*. New York: Charles Scribner's.

Maritain, Jacques. 1938. *The Degrees of Knowledge*. London: Geoffrey Bles.

Martin, C.B. 1959. *Religious Belief*. Ithaca, N.Y.: Cornell University Press.

Mavrodes, George I. 1988. *Revelation in Religious Belief*. Philadelphia: Temple University Press.

Moore, G.E. 1953 *Some Main Problems of Philosophy*. London: Allen & Unwin.
——1959. *Philosophical Papers*. London: Allen & Unwin.
Moser, Paul. 1989. *Knowledge and Evidence*. New York: Cambridge University Press.
Müller, Max, trans. 1884. *The Upanishads*. Oxford: Clarendon Press.
The New English Bible with Apocrypha. 1976. New York: Oxford University Press.
Nozick, Robert. 1981. *Philosophical Explanations*. Cambridge, Mass.: Harvard University Press.
Oakes, Robert. 1979. "Religious Experience, Self-Authentication, and Modality De Re: A Prolegomenon". *American Philosophical Quarterly*, 16: 217–24.
——1985. "Mysticism, Veridicality, and Modality". *Faith and Philosophy*, 2: 217–35.
O'Hear, Anthony. 1984. *Experience, Explanation, and Faith*. London: Routledge & Kegan Paul.
Oldenquist, Andrew. 1971. "Wittgenstein on Phenomenalism, Skepticism, and Criteria". In *Essays on Wittgenstein*, ed. E.D. Klemke. Urbana: University of Illinois Press.
Origen. 1957. *The Song of Songs: Commentary and Homilies*, trans. R. P. Lawson. Westminster-London.
Otto, Rudolf. 1932. *Mysticism East and West*. New York: Macmillan.
Parente, Pascal P. 1945. *The Ascetical Life*. St Louis: Herder.
Peirce, Charles Sanders. 1934. "Questions Concerning Certain Faculties Claimed for Man". In *Collected Papers*, ed. C. Hartshorne and P. Weiss. Vol. 4. Cambridge, Mass.: Harvard University Press.
Penelhum, Terence. 1971. *Religion and Rationality*. New York: Random House.
Plantinga, Alvin. 1979. "Is Belief in God Rational?". In *Rationality and Religious Belief*, ed. C. Delaney. Notre Dame, Ind.: University of Notre Dame Press.
——1981. "Is Belief in God Properly Basic?". *Nous*, 15: 41–51.
——1983. "Reason and Belief in God". In *Faith and Rationality*, ed. A. Plantinga and N. Wolterstorff. Notre Dame, Ind.: University of Notre Dame Press.
Plotinus. 1964. *Enneads*, VI, 9, trans. Elmer O'Brien, S.J. In *Varieties of Mystic Experience*. New York: Holt, Rinehart, and Winston.
Pollock, John. 1974. *Knowledge and Justification*. Princeton, N.J.: Princeton University Press.
——1986. *Contemporary Theories of Knowledge*. Totowa, N.J.: Rowman & Littlefield.
Poulain, Anton. 1950. *The Graces of Interior Prayer*, trans. Leonora Yorke Smith and Jean Vincent Bainvel. London: Routledge & Kegan Paul.
Proudfoot, Wayne. 1985. *Religious Experience*. Berkeley and Los Angeles: University of California Press.
Putnam, Hilary. 1981. *Reason, Truth, and History*. Cambridge: Cambridge University Press.
Quine, Willard van Orman. 1969. *Ontological Relativity and Other Essays*. New York: Columbia University Press.
Rahner, Karl. 1978. *Foundations of Christian Faith*. New York: Seabury Press.
Reid, Thomas. 1969. *Essays on the Intellectual Powers of Man*. Cambridge, Mass.: MIT Press.
——1970. *An Inquiry into the Human Mind*, ed. T. Duggan. Chicago: University of Chicago Press.

Rowe, William L. 1975. *The Cosmological Argument*. Princeton, N.J.: Princeton University Press.

——1982. "Religious Experience and the Principle of Credulity". *International Journal for Philosophy of Religion*, 13: 85–92.

Runzo, Joseph. 1977. "The Propositional Structure of Perception". *American Philosophical Quarterly*, 14: 211–20.

——1982. "The Radical Conceptualization of Perceptual Experience". *American Philosophical Quarterly*, 19: 205–17.

Russell, Bertrand. 1910–11. "Knowledge by Acquaintance and Knowledge by Description". *Proceedings of the Aristotelian Society*, 11.

——1935. *Religion and Science*. London: Oxford University Press.

Saudreau, Auguste. 1924. *The Mystical State, Its Nature and Phases*, trans. D.M.B. London: Burns, Oates, & Washbourne.

Shoemaker, Sydney. 1963. *Self-Knowledge and Self-Identity*. Ithaca, N.Y.: Cornell University Press.

Smart, Ninian. 1965. "Interpretation and Mystical Experience". *Religious Studies*, 1: 75–87.

Stace, W.T. 1952. *Time and Eternity*. Princeton, N.J.: Princeton University Press.

——1960. *Mysticism and Philosophy*. Los Angeles: Jeremy P. Tarcher.

Stark, Rodney, and Charles Y. Glock. 1968. *American Piety: The Nature of Religious Commitment*. Berkeley and Los Angeles: University of California Press.

Strawson, P.F. 1959. *Individuals*. London: Methuen.

——1966. *The Bounds of Sense: An Essay on Kant's Critique of Pure Reason*. London: Methuen.

Stump, Eleonore, and Norman Kretzmann. 1981. "Eternity". *Journal of Philosophy*, 78: 429–58.

Swinburne, Richard. 1979. *The Existence of God*. Oxford: Clarendon Press.

Teresa, St., of Avila. 1957. *The Life of St. Teresa of Avila by Herself*, trans. J.M. Cohen. London: Penguin Books.

Tillich, Paul. 1953. *Systematic Theology*. Vol. 1. London: Nisbet.

Tracy, David. 1978. *Blessed Rage for Order*. New York: Seabury Press.

Underhill, Evelyn. 1955. *Mysticism*. New York: World.

Unger, Johannes. 1976. *On Religious Experience: A Psychological Study*. Uppsala: Acta Universatatis Upsaliensis.

Wainwright, William. 1981. *Mysticism*. Brighton, U.K.: Harvester Press.

——1990. "Jonathan Edwards and the Sense of the Heart". *Faith and Philosophy*, 7: 43–62.

Wittgenstein, Ludwig. 1953. *Philosophical Investigations*, trans. G.E. M. Anscombe. Oxford: Basil Blackwell.

—— 1969. *On Certainty*, trans. D. Paul and G.E.M. Anscombe. Oxford: Basil Blackwell.

Wolterstorff, Nicholas. 1983. "Thomas Reid on Rationality". In *Rationality in the Calvinian Tradition*, ed. H. Hart, J. Van der Hoeven, and N. Wolterstorff. Lanham, Md.: University Press of America.

Zaehner, R.C. 1961. *Mysticism Sacred and Profane*. New York: Oxford University Press.

Index

Library of Congress Cataloging-in-Publication Data

Alston, William P.
Perceiving God : the epistemology of religious experience / William P. Alston.
p. cm.
Includes bibliographical references and index.
ISBN 0-8014-2597-2 (hard : alk. paper)
1. God—Knowableness. 2. Experience (Religion) 3. Knowledge, Theory of (Religion) I. Title.
BT102.A46 1991
248.2'01—dc20 91-55068